Praise for *How I Learned*

How I Learned To Speak Israel is ъ
rare works as Walt and Mearshimer's *The Israel Lobby and U.S. Foreign Policy* in its display of courage to speak the truth about the unspeakable, it delves even deeper into explicating the strange, unwise, and increasingly dangerous trance most American leaders are under when it comes to Israel — and the book does so in almost every way and area important and imaginable. The explanations are so powerful they explode the trance, if only the reader will listen and learn.

—LAWRENCE WILKERSON
Former chief of staff to Secretary of State Colin Powell

The Israel-Palestine dilemma has been a source of confusion for many people for many decades, so it is refreshing that Alex McDonald's new book dispels the confusion with common sense, simple logic, and integrity. *How I Learned to Speak Israel* offers readers a path to clarity and understanding, and freedom from one-sided beliefs that influence our perception of the world and induce us to lose our humanity. In conjunction with that approach, McDonald's analyses rely on both objective research and firsthand observation from his time in Israel and the occupied territories. If you want to broaden your knowledge and develop a solid and rational understanding of one of the world's most intractable dilemmas, read this book!

—RICHARD FORER
Author of *Wake Up and Reclaim Your Humanity:
Essays on the Tragedy of Israel-Palestine* and
*Breakthrough: Transforming Fear into Compassion —
A New Perspective on the Israel-Palestine Conflict*

Americans need to read *How I Learned to Speak Israel* because it covers some of the history I have not seen covered elsewhere. The book does an excellent job of tying together American involvement, historically and today, and the price Americans pay financially, politically, and morally every day for our position on Israel. This book covers what we as Americans don't learn in World History class nor in our media; it shows how we are hurting both Palestinians and Jews.

—SETH MORRISON
Activist, Jewish Voice for Peace

How I learned to Speak Israel is a must read for any American. Learning to Speak "Israel" is a crucial part of any American's political awakening. Alex McDonald's book is an important contribution to the education of Americans wishing to understand how a wealthy apartheid state, Israel, manages to receive the largest foreign aid package and total diplomatic immunity from the US, more so than any other country in the world.

—MIKO PELED
Author and activist
Author of *The General's Son: Journey of an Israeli in Palestine* and
Injustice: the Story of the Holy Land Foundation Five

How I Learned to Speak Israel is an easy-reading, conversational history of Palestine and Palestinian-Israeli relations. It's a book that helps us talk to others who may have a different view of the history of the region and who may use words and phrases that take on new meanings in this dialogue. Author McDonald calls these word choices the "Israel" language and the book is about his day-to-day efforts within his family and community to figure out the language. A few examples include the phrases "security fence/wall," "defensive," and "terrorism," which he points out all have different connotations depending on whom is using them and their experience. McDonald has written a very cogent description of the challenge these words bring to communicating the important issues for Palestinians, Israelis and the rest of us who are interested in learning more. He compellingly demonstrates how miscommunication about the conflict is a major hindrance to peace and democracy in Israel/Palestine and how it directly affects the US.

—ANN WRIGHT
Retired US Army colonel and former US diplomat
Author of *Dissent: Voices of Conscience*

When one finds a key that helps to open us to understand, even heal memories that break the heart, it is time to rejoice. Rarely does one discover a book whose author ranks with the important current prophetic spokespersons of the Jewish, Muslim and Christian communities. Alex McDonald stands with people who challenge courageously the heretical religious and political cult figures of our era. *How I Learned to Speak Israel* must have a place on my desk next to the Bible, dictionary, and scholarly commentaries. It is a carefully researched encyclopedic source of knowledge which provides direction about what helps bring about a brighter future.

If it had been available for reference when I was working in the occupied Palestinian territories and the UN in Geneva it would have made my advocacy more effective. McDonald's book emboldens seekers with enlightenment and relief. A modern-day oppressive colonial empire can be transformed into the dream of a "holy land" by all the cousins understanding one another as "chosen" Children of Abraham. Now there is an aide for all those of varied backgrounds who continue the journey for peace with justice even when it seems naïve.

There surely are people of all religions who pursue faith ideals and ethical principles who want the clouds of misunderstanding, mythic history, ethnic division and racial persecution addressed in Israel as well as America. Alex McDonald's understanding of the basics of the "Israel language" is beyond the notional and leads to ways of dealing with the present "hopeless" anger and fear. He reminds me of Psalm 27's promise that there can be witness to the "Goodness of the Lord in the land of the living".

—TOM GETMAN
Former Senate staffer, Israel/Palestine NGO director,
and a Geneva UN Representative for non-profits

Alex McDonald's *How I Learned to Speak Israel: An American's Guide to a Foreign Policy Language* provides an invaluable perspective to the most fraught political issue of our time. Comprehensive in scope, the book interrogates all the arguments commonly cited to justify the disproportionate economic, military, and diplomatic support the US accords Israel. McDonald earns readers' trust by sharing with them what first led him to question these arguments and how further research made him change his views. In the process, he teaches readers how to discern hidden manipulation in the news media. McDonald's most original contribution is his analysis of "Israel" as an Orwellian language in which "words like *security, equality, defensive, peace, authority, rights, voluntary,* and *illegal,*" as well as *democracy, terrorism,* and *retaliation,* do not mean what they seem to, but must be translated into "plain English" before readers can exercise independent judgment.

—**CAROLYN L. KARCHER**

Editor of *Reclaiming Judaism from Zionism:*
Stories of Personal Transformation

Alex McDonald's book *How I Learned to Speak Israel* attracts our attention to the importance of words in the struggle for justice in Palestine. This attention to discourses and narratives is quite often underrated. This book exposes methodically how texts and images help to produce and perpetuate the perceptions and framing of Israel and Palestine within the American public. And although there has been a dramatic shift in certain sections of civil society in support of the Palestinians, the continued twisted perceptions still dominate, unchallenged, and provide a crucial layer in Israel's shield of immunity.

—**ILAN PAPPÉ**

Professor of History
Director of the European Centre for Palestine Studies
University of Exeter
Author of: *Ten Myths About Israel,*
A History of Modern Palestine: One Land, Two Peoples,
The Forgotten Palestinians: A History of the Palestinians in Israel,
The Ethnic Cleansing of Palestine, The Biggest Prison on Earth, among others.

HOW I LEARNED TO
SPEAK ISRAEL

HOW I LEARNED TO SPEAK ISRAEL

*An American's Guide
to a Foreign Policy Language*

ALEX MCDONALD

Great Tree Publishing, LLC
Houston, Texas

Editor: Allan Edmands
Cover photography: Mohammed Fawzi Ghanayem

Published by Great Tree Publishing, LLC, Houston, TX
GreatTreePublishing.com

ISBN: 978-1-954221-04-8 (Paperback)
ISBN: 978-1-954221-05-5 (ePub)

Library of Congress Control Number: 2021908698

*To my dad, who taught me
that I am responsible for my beliefs*

Listen with curiosity.
Speak with honesty.
Act with integrity.

—Roy T. Bennett,
The Light in the Heart

Reality is easy.
It's deception that's the hard work.

—Lauryn Hill

Contents

Introduction

I grew up learning about Israel/Palestine* in school, church, and at home. I would occasionally read about Israel in magazines my parents had in the family room. As an adult I learned about Israel from the news. Growing up, I never thought about there even being different perspectives on this subject. I thought there was only one truth. The "truth" I knew was a combination of what I have come to call the "Israeli narrative" and the "American narrative."

The Israeli Narrative

Jews have a long history of being the victims of discrimination and persecution. From biblical times to today, examples abound from repeated pogroms to the mass killing of Jews during the Holocaust.

Therefore, it seems to many Jews that the only way to be safe is to have their own country. For that reason, many Jews will never let Israel become a state with a Jewish minority; political control is a necessity. To lose control would be to put their lives into the hands of others, to again risk persecution and even genocide. This fear of being discriminated against—or worse, getting wiped out—is rooted deep within Jewish culture. Numerous holidays remind Jews of this discrimination; Passover, Hanukkah, and Purim are but a few

---

* The term *Israel/Palestine* describes a piece of land for which there is currently no universally accepted name; it also applies to the people residing on that land. The term *Israel* is inadequate, because the state of Israel, which has never defined its borders, claims and controls land that the international community calls "the occupied Palestinian territories" while it denies the population it controls in those territories Israeli citizenship and rights under its civilian legal system. The term *Palestine* is also inadequate to describe the land covered in this book, because although most of the countries of the world recognize the state of Palestine, that state does not include all the land this book is about—historic Palestine under the British mandate (1923–1948).

examples. This existential threat to security is confirmed every time rockets fly from Gaza or a Jew is killed in a hate crime.

There are a number of justifications for a Jewish state. Some believe that Jews have a right to Israel because of the UN Partition Plan of 1947, which divided Palestine into a Jewish state and an Arab state. Some believe that Jews have a right to that land because God gave it to them. Others claim that the Balfour Declaration or League of Nations documents entitle Jews to all of Mandatory Palestine. Many Jews have considered historical Palestine as the perfect Jewish homeland; it has Jewish historical and religious significance and was "a land without a people for a people without a land."[1] Finally, Jews have made Israel flourish economically and culturally; as the "only democracy in the Middle East," Israel is the regional example of Western civilization.

The Jewish need for safety is reinforced by the continual conflicts that Israel faces. The state has been defensive since its inception, having to protect itself from both domestic and foreign aggression. Jews are regularly attacked by Palestinians within Israel and from nearby countries in the Middle East. Arab armies invaded on May 15, 1948, only one day after Israel declared its independence. After the armistice agreements in 1949, Arab countries expelled over 700,000 Jews from their countries.

Israel's much larger neighbors attacked again during the 1967 Six-Day War and the 1973 Yom Kippur War. The Yom Kippur War was so devastating that the US had to come to Israel's aid. Some considered it a miracle that Israel won these wars; it was as if it were a blessing from God for God's Chosen People in their Promised Land.

Israel has participated in numerous efforts to reach peace with its neighbors and the Palestinians; yet in 2005, the Iranian president declared his will to "wipe Israel off the map."[2] While Israel successfully reached peace agreements with Jordan and with Egypt, the country has never had a reasonable Palestinian negotiating partner for attaining peace. Despite Israel reaching out and wanting peace, the Palestinians have rejected offers that many Israelis considered generous. Israel even pulled out of Gaza in 2005 and left it to the Palestinians. The terrorist organization Hamas has controlled Gaza since then, showering rockets into Israel.[3] In the eyes of Israeli Jews, the Palestinians "never miss an opportunity to miss an opportunity" for peace.[4, *]

Many Jews believe that people who oppose a Jewish state are anti-Semitic—that is, they are racist against Jews. By extension, some even believe that those who oppose Israel as a Jewish state want the destruction of the Jewish people. In contrast, Israel has treated its Arab citizens equally; they are even represented in the Knesset (the Israeli parliament). In fact, Israel treats its Palestinians better than either the Palestinian Authority or the Arab countries treat their Palestinians.

Israel's supporters claim that the Palestinian demand for their "Right of Return" is a ruse for destroying the Jewish state, since a return of Palestinian refugees would make Jews a minority in their own land. Some Jewish Israelis believe that children of Palestinian refugees should not be considered refugees themselves because that would give Palestinians special privileges over other refugees.

Finally, many Jews say that non-Jews need to be pragmatic in bringing peace to the region. The reality is that Jews want peace, but many will never give up Israel as a Jewish state.

The American Narrative

In many ways, Americans relate to Israel as "like us" because of our common belief in democracy and Western, Judeo-Christian values. The Israeli narrative is often promoted in American schools and in our news coverage.

Americans have also been accused of complicity in the Holocaust by having delayed efforts to free Jews from the Nazi concentration camps. Some Americans feel guilty because the United States

---

* "The Arabs never miss an opportunity to miss an opportunity" is often attributed to Israeli politician Abba Eban.

restricted Jewish immigration when Jews were being persecuted; we turned our backs when Jews needed safety and refuge. It is true that the US has a history of discrimination against Jews. Americans try to make up for that history by protecting Jews and Israel by passing laws against anti-Semitism. Our government includes criticism of Israel in its definition of anti-Semitism.

Americans have been the mediators, trying to bring peace between two peoples who have clashed since the Jews were slaves in Egypt, even since Sarah demanded that Abraham send Hagar into the desert.* As a result of our efforts, we helped make great progress toward peace through agreements such as the Camp David Accords.

Palestinians have repeatedly rejected Israeli offers for peace. Israel disengaged from Gaza in 2005, giving it to the Palestinians. What was the result? Palestinians elected the terrorist organization Hamas to lead their legislature in 2006. There would be peace if the Palestinians had only accepted Israel's offers.

We Americans have been good mediators by insisting that no solution would be acceptable unless derived through negotiations by both parties. Consequently, we have defunded United Nations organizations that have accepted Palestine as a state without Israel's approval. The Trump administration increased pressure on the Palestinians to return to the negotiating table; unfortunately, the Palestinians declined meetings with Trump administration officials.

The large Muslim world has been dedicated to eliminating the Jewish state. We Americans have had to defend the only democracy in the Middle East, and with it the people who are the foundation to Christianity, the people who have been persecuted and who suffered the Holocaust. It is our duty to protect our greatest ally— especially in the hostile Middle East, where domestic and regional terrorism abound.

---

* According to the tradition (from both Genesis and the Qur'an), Jews (Hebrews, the "Children of Israel") are descendants of Isaac, Abraham's second son, through his wife, Sarah. Arabs ("Ishmaelites") are descended from Ishmael, Abraham's eldest son, through Hagar, Sarah's handmaiden. Sarah insisted that Ishmael would not share in Isaac's inheritance and that Abraham should cast Hagar and Ishmael out into the wilderness of Beersheba.

By supporting Israel, we support our own values. As Americans, we want peace, as any good person does, and therefore we are proud of our efforts to bring peace to the region. We value loyalty, so we are proud of our loyalty to our allies. We value compassion for the downtrodden and persecuted, so we are proud to have been the first country to recognize the Jewish state and to have stood by it strongly ever since. Finally, many Christians believe that we have followed and continue to follow God's will by helping Jews return to their ancestral land.

~~~~~~~~~~~~~~~~

I believed these two narratives and thought they made sense until I heard news about the wall being built in the West Bank, news that conflicted with these two narratives. And that discrepancy piqued my curiosity and started me on a journey. This is the story of my journey to learn what parts of what I had been taught were true and what parts were mythology. This book is about how I learned the history, learned about the current situation, and learned the language and messaging that had been blocking my view. Welcome to *How I Learned to Speak Israel*.

1

Israel Is Also a Language

srael is a people and a country. Unbeknownst to most, it is also
a language. It is a language used to describe the state of Israel, its
history, and its conflicts. It is a language that sounds like English,
but its words have different meanings.

Because the Israel language uses English words, we don't question
them; we let them through our filters. We think of words like
security, *equality*, *defensive*, *peace*, *authority*, *rights*, *voluntary*, and
illegal as normal English words, even though these words carry very
different meanings in the language of Israel.*

Learning how to speak Israel requires knowing some history; it also
requires knowing about what is happening today. How can we evaluate
a description of an action as "defensive" or as a "retaliation" if we don't
know who initiated the attack? How can we evaluate "equality"**,5 or

---

* The term *Israel* is used in this book to mean a language, the country, its
government, its citizenry, and a people, depending on the context of the
sentence.

** The term *equality* is predominantly defined in this book as the state of having
equal rights. Quoting James Wilson, a signer of the Declaration of Independence
and an original justice of the United States Supreme Court:
> When we say, that all men are equal; we mean not to apply this equality
> to their virtues, their talents, their dispositions, or their acquirements. ...
> There is still one aspect, in which all men in society, previous to civil
> government, are equal. With regard to all, there is an equality in rights
> and in obligations; there is that "jus aequum," that equal law, in which the
> Romans placed true freedom. The natural rights and duties of man belong
> equally to all.

7

"apartheid"*,6 if we don't know the context? The only way to know that the "Palestinian National Authority" is neither national nor has any real authority is by knowing some history. The only way to know that "voluntary transfer" is hardly voluntary is through familiarity with the situation on the ground.

This book provides foundational Israeli history, a review of the current situation in Israel/Palestine, and an analysis of language and messaging. Throughout this book I take messaging from politicians and articles from the press, analyze them, and translate them from this Israel phraseology into plain English. This exercise will help you recognize these phrases when you hear or see them in the news.

I wrote this book from an American perspective. As an Eagle Scout, I grew up proud of my country, and I believe that it is my duty to make sure my country's actions reflect my values. I consider American values, and by extension my own, to be based on the United States Declaration of Independence, which states, "We hold these truths to be self-evident, that all men are created equal," that all have unalienable rights, including "Life, Liberty and the pursuit of Happiness." It further states that people have a right to replace governments that do not honor those rights. We as a country deviated from these ideals with slavery, Jim Crow laws, and the ill treatment of Native Americans—just to name a few examples. Nonetheless, we must measure ourselves relative to these ideals if we are to claim that we are a moral and civilized society.

I wrote this book because I learned by accident that a lot of what I had been taught by people I respected was not true. I learned that what I had been taught about Israel/Palestine actually didn't make sense; I had just never connected the dots. The truth was particularly well hidden because of the Israel language, which I had not even

---

* The term *apartheid* is based on the International Convention on the Suppression and Punishment of the Crime of Apartheid, which defines the crime as "policies and practices of racial segregation and discrimination" and "inhuman acts committed for the purpose of establishing and maintaining domination by one racial group of persons over any other racial group of persons and systematically oppressing them." For more information, see the Glossary.

known existed. My kids, who were between four and six at the time of my realization, helped me see that what I believed was untrue.

Since that realization and after much research, I have learned that the United States is deeply involved in the Israel/Palestine situation and in how it is described to us. The United States was instrumental in the creation of the state of Israel and is a significant influencer of its current cultural and political status. For Americans to decide what role we should play in the future, it is helpful to understand the involvement that our government has had, and continues to have, in this region. We also need to understand the repercussions of our government's actions on Israel/Palestine, including how those actions affect daily life in the United States.

With limited facts of the situation, we are vulnerable to distorted messaging. With a distorted view of the situation, we are dangerous to ourselves and to others. Even worse, with a distorted view, we think we are choosing our destiny when, in fact, we are merely following the messaging's lead. We have the real freedom to choose our future role only after we have the knowledge of the history, of the current situation, and of America's involvement.

The situation in Israel/Palestine is continually changing. When I started writing this book in 2016, Hebrew and Arabic were the official languages of the state of Israel. Since the Knesset's passage of the Basic Law: Israel as the Nation-State of the Jewish People on July 19, 2018, Hebrew is now the only official language. The history will evolve, and details on the ground will change. What matters, however, are the underlying values that are represented by the situation in Israel/Palestine and our position relative to that situation. Hopefully, this book will equip you to decide whether our actions as Americans represent your values and whether they dignify or dishonor the soul of our great nation.

This book is about looking ourselves in the mirror and prioritizing our values. When we look in the mirror, we see our faults as well as our strengths. But honestly evaluating the situation and our role in it brings clarity and personal freedom. It has for me, and for that I am grateful.

How to Use This Book

Distinguishing between correlation and causation is important. I am reminded of an example showing the danger of confusing the two: If someone discovers a strange statistic that the average academic grades of children of Volvo drivers happen to be higher than that of Chevrolet drivers, then they may erroneously buy a Volvo so that their kids would get better grades. Is terrorism down because of a "Security Fence," as we are told? Is Gaza blockaded and bombed because of rockets fired from Gaza? These actions and events are correlated; use the history and information about the current situation to decide for yourself what is correlational versus causational.

Many chapters of this book highlight language that is misleading. I have already pointed out that "the Palestinian National Authority" has very little authority and that "voluntary transfer" is hardly voluntary. To highlight and clarify terms, words and terms are defined throughout this book. Three types of definitions are provided:

- A **dictionary definition**, as its name implies, would be found in a source, such as a dictionary. Since dictionaries such as Merriam-Webster are dictionaries of the English language, both the term and its definition are in English.

- A **usage definition** is based on what the word means in common usage. For example, a usage definition of *put to sleep* has nothing to do with going to bed or sleeping; instead, it is a euphemism. Its usage definition is "to kill" or "to euthanize." Usage definitions in this book are English definitions of Israel terms, also known as Israelspeak.

- An **aspirational definition** is what one might want the word or phrase to mean, what it would mean if we came from a position of integrity and good will and without hypocrisy. An aspirational definition of *public service* would be "actions that help the people" in contrast with a usage definition, such as "a government job."

To distinguish between English dictionary definitions and Israel usage definitions, I am rendering the terms that have usage definitions in BOLD SMALL CAPS when they are being defined (for example, ILLEGAL) so as not to confuse them with terms having English dictionary and aspirational definitions, which are **regular boldface** (for example, **blockade**). A glossary of some words that I define for clarity (for example, *Palestinian* and *Zionist*) and abbreviations has been included at the end of this book. A separate Israel-English dictionary is also included at the end of the book, repeating the translations provided in the different chapters; this dictionary includes the Israel usage definitions.

Welcome to this journey of discovery of different peoples, their dreams, and their actions. Welcome to this journey of introspection and self-assessment. Welcome to this Israel language course.

Bias and Balance on Israel/Palestine

In this book I share the history I learned so that you have the context of the Israel language. I also look at how the history and current situation are covered in different media, further highlighting the importance and use of language. Finally, I compare the facts and coverage through the lens of what I consider to be the American values of equality, freedom, and self-determination, values that are shared by such international organizations as the United Nations and promoted in such international documents as the Universal Declaration of Human Rights and the Geneva Conventions. This is the bias that I bring to this book.

A number of readers have told me that this book is not balanced. It is far more critical of Israeli policies and actions than of Palestinian ones. This is true. And that criticism deserves a response.

First, we need to define *balance*. Does balance entail equal time for each perspective, equal weight for each person affected, or is a greater weight afforded for voices of authority on a subject? Each of us may have a different definition.

If your definition of *balance* denotes equal time for the two major perspectives, then this book will not appear to be balanced. I have chosen not to give equal coverage to both sides because Israel/Palestine is not a balanced situation. We clearly want to be open to other perspectives, but can one really discuss the world being flat versus it being spherical in such a "balanced" way? Would we give equal time to both sides of that argument? Is it appropriate to give both sides equal time to talk about slavery, or about such massacres against civilians as the Holocaust, the Armenian Genocide, and the Darfur massacre? Is it appropriate to give equal time to those who committed those atrocities? We do need to understand the other side, but if giving equal time or emphasis to both sides discounts the atrocities committed, then we become complicit in supporting such crimes. Such "balance" in describing one-sided situations is not appropriate, nor is it truly balanced.

If your definition of a "balanced" perspective is one where each violation of human rights—where each person persecuted or life lost—is given equal weight, then you are more likely to find this to be a balanced book.

However, there is another factor we need to consider when evaluating "balance." We need to look at not only how balanced the book is but also how balanced we are. We each look at the world through a personal lens and filter. This lens and filter has been molded by the messaging we have received over the years. We do not expect nor demand a "balanced" book on whether the world is flat or spherical. We do not expect nor demand half of a slavery museum be dedicated to the perspective that such an inhumane act is justified. Why is it that some crimes against humanity pass through our filters whereas others do not? Why do we ask for balance to criticism of Israel or the US but not the same when we hear criticism of Iran, Egypt, Saudi Arabia, or South Africa under apartheid?

We need to be conscious of how our lenses and filters affect even our perception of balance. When evaluating the content of this book and the Israel/Palestine issue in general, I recommend that you step back and ask yourself if your definition of balance would change if the Israeli and Palestinian roles were reversed. If you have asked for balance whenever someone criticized Israel, will you ask for balance whenever someone criticizes Palestinians? We know we are balanced when we are willing to accept or denounce actions based on the actions themselves, independent of who did them and whom they were done to. Only when you are willing to evaluate the actions committed by each side, rather than who performed them, can you be balanced.

My experience is that our balance is what is most important. It is because of my previous filters, and my associated imbalance, that I was unable to see and evaluate what was going on in Israel/ Palestine. My imbalance controlled me; my imbalanced filters chose my views for me. Only by becoming conscious of my imbalance and by opening myself to look at the facts in a balanced way was I free enough to evaluate for myself.

Once I was able to shed my lens and filters, I saw that the Israel/ Palestine situation is different from other issues facing Americans. I now see it as a significant force that is corrupting American society, debasing both Palestinians* and Jews, and bullying and penalizing people who stand for equality, liberty, democracy, free speech, and human rights. This corrupting force uses language as its tool to distort our worldview and blind us from the atrocities committed on our behalf. Only by stepping back, understanding our situation, and selecting another path, a path closer to balance, can we reverse our perilous trajectory.

I hope you find your personal journey into the language of Israel illuminating, thought-provoking, and empowering. I hope this book helps you, as the journey has helped me, clarify which values

---

* The term *Palestinian* is defined for this book to mean someone whose ancestors came from Palestine. This generally means Arabs (Muslim, Christian, and Jewish) whose ancestors lived in or were from Palestine prior to 1948. This book defines *Palestinian* to exclude Zionists, partly to distinguish Zionists from Palestinians but also because Zionists who had Palestinian passports prior to the creation of the state of Israel do not consider themselves Palestinians.

are important to you individually and to us as Americans. I hope this book will help you along your faith journey, whether you are Jewish, Christian, Muslim, or of another or no faith. And finally, I hope this book will provide food for thought about what it means to be American and a human being.

2

The "Security Fence" /Barrier/Wall

The separation fence will remain in place and will not be dismantled. I hear they are saying today that because it's quiet, it's possible to take down the fence. My friends, the opposite is true. It's quiet because a fence exists.

—*Prime Minister Benjamin Netanyahu[7]*
at a session of the Knesset, July 22, 2009

Because I had learned about Israel in school, church, and from the news, I considered myself somewhat knowledgeable on the subject. But sometimes we mistake beliefs for knowledge. And beliefs can be worse than ignorance. Beliefs can cause us to filter out information that is counter to those beliefs. We all have filters; it's human nature. Luckily, one piece of information slipped through my filter.

In the early 2000s, Israel was building a barrier—in parts a wall and in other parts a fence.* It was described in the American press as separating the West Bank from Israel. As Prime Minister Netanyahu said in this chapter's epigraph, Israel was building it

---

* In this book I refer to the barrier as the *wall*, or *security fence*, or *separation fence*, or *fence*, or *barrier*, depending on the context.

to stop the terrorists from coming from the West Bank. Based on what I had been taught about Israel, this made logical sense to me; I believed in the "Israeli narrative" and the "American narrative" (described in the Introduction).

There had been the Palestinian Intifada (the Arabic term *intifāḍa*, انتفاضة, means "uprising"). Suicide bombers had self-detonated on buses in Israel. Other Palestinians had blown themselves up and killed many others in cafés.[8] I totally understood people needing to protect themselves from terrorism and hatred.

Then I heard something on the radio that caught my attention: The reporter mentioned that the wall was being built *inside* the West Bank. I was surprised to hear that because I had expected any fence or wall to be built on the Green Line, the internationally recognized border between the West Bank and Israel.

Based on the Israeli narrative, I believed that the object of the barrier was to provide safety for Israelis. If Israel was concerned about protecting Jews from Palestinians, then why would Israel build a fence or wall only to leave Palestinians on both sides of it? If Palestinians are the threat, then logically the barrier needed to be built in such a way that the Jews would be on one side and the Palestinians on the other. Maybe I had misheard the report, or the reporter had been sloppy in his language.

After doing some research, I found out that the barrier did in fact weave throughout the West Bank. It took the form of a wall as it encircled East Jerusalem, thus placing East Jerusalem on the Israeli side of the wall. East Jerusalem, which historically has been the center of Palestinian life, is east of the Green Line, as established by the 1949 Armistice Agreements. Figure 1 shows a map from the United Nations Office for the Coordination of Humanitarian Affairs,[9] which I have marked up to show where the Green Line is relative to Israel's fence or wall.

I realized then that there was a flaw in my "Israeli narrative" understanding of the situation; something was not adding up. Having a fence or wall on someone else's land made me suspicious. The Israeli narrative of always being defensive seemed to conflict

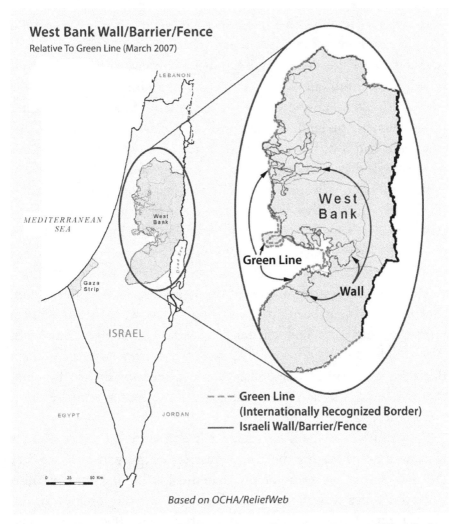

West Bank Wall/Barrier/Fence
Relative To Green Line (March 2007)

Based on OCHA/ReliefWeb

Figure 1. The encroaching wall. The map shows the wall/barrier/fence encroaching deep into the West Bank rather than being on the Armistice "Green Line." [*Source: Based on OCHA/ReliefWeb*]

with putting one's wall on other people's land, especially when it wasn't near the border. Why would Israel build a combination of fence and wall throughout the Palestinians' land? How can it really be protecting Israel from Palestinians if Palestinians are on both sides of the barrier? I began wondering if I was being overly critical of where the barrier was being built. I wanted a reality check.

At that time, my boys were between four and six years old. I wanted to find out if they thought I was being overly critical. It is said that we learn our foundational knowledge in kindergarten, so why not find out what kindergartners think? One day while I was with them in the car, I asked them to imagine a situation. I told them to pretend that we had a big, scary dog and that our neighbors had a very young child. I told them that our neighbors were scared that our dog would hurt their toddler. I asked them if they thought it would be OK if the neighbors put up a fence. They said, "Sure." Then I told them that when the neighbors built that fence, it was not on the property line but instead went into our yard. They immediately yelled out: "No way!" I had learned that Israel's barrier had in fact surrounded a large settlement called Ariel, which sat on top of one of the largest aquifers in the region. My plan had then been to tell the boys that when the neighbors built the barrier, it had encircled a swimming pool in our yard. We would no longer be able to get to our own swimming pool! But with their spirited response to the neighbors' merely building the barrier on our side of the property line, there was no sense in taking the example further.

Sometimes courts and laws seem fair and ethical. Other times, as with South African apartheid and American slavery, the laws reflect the will of the powerful rather than justice. Taking into account where the fence or wall was being built, the advisory opinion of the International Court of Justice (ICJ) of July 9, 2004, seemed just when it unequivocally concluded with a vote of 14 to 1 that the "construction of the wall being built by Israel, the occupying Power, in the occupied Palestinian territory, including in and around East Jerusalem, and its associated regime, are contrary to international law." The ICJ reemphasized the prohibition and illegality of acquisition of any territory by force and "the principle of self-determination of peoples."[10] The ICJ also stated:

As regards international humanitarian law, the Court refers to the provisions of the Hague Regulation of 1907, which have become part of customary law, as well as the Fourth Geneva Convention relative to the Protection of Civilian Persons in Time of War of 1949, applicable in those Palestinian territories which before the armed conflict of 1967 lay to the east of the 1949 Armistice demarcation line (or "Green Line") and were occupied by Israel during that conflict.[11]

Having discovered where the barrier was being built, and where it had already been built, I now realized that Israel is a language, not just a country. I learned that I had previously totally misunderstood the meaning of the word *security* when I learned about Israel's "security fence."

Supporters of the barrier point to a reduction in terrorism after its construction. And the bombings certainly did decrease; the timing of those two facts did correlate. But correlation is not causation, and there were other factors that might have caused the reduction in terrorism.

One of the factors was the creation and buildup of the Palestinian National Security Forces (NSF). As part of the Oslo Accords (the 1993 peace accords between Palestinians and Israel), the Palestinian Authority (PA) was allowed to set up armed police forces with Israeli approval and coordination. A January 2011 article in the British newspaper *The Guardian** stated: "the CIA played the central role in building up PA security forces from the late 1990s, in close co-operation with the Israeli military and intelligence, detailed in ... leaked documents."[12] The United States was directly involved in training the newly armed Palestinian security forces, whose job was to be proxies for the Israeli authorities.

Fatah (the Palestinian National Liberation Movement), the political party that is the largest faction in the Palestine Liberation Organization (PLO), took advantage of its weaponized police force

---

* I have tried to cite American news sources throughout this book. However, one of the lessons that I learned about Israel is that much is left out of the American media on this subject. I therefore highlight quotes that are from foreign sources to give you an idea of what we are missing in the United States—what we are not told.

under the protection of the Israelis, Americans, British, and others in order to go after its political rivals. The British intelligence service MI6 even had a plan that recommended

> degrading the capabilities of the rejectionists [including Hamas and others] ... through the disruption of their leaderships' communications and command and control capabilities; the detention of key middle-ranking officers; and the confiscation of their arsenals and financial resources.[13]

These Palestinian security forces were brutal to the point of raising concerns by their British sponsors and supporters. The British suggested that they could "explore the temporary internment of leading Hamas ... figures, making sure they are well-treated, with [European Union] funding"[14]—thereby reflecting a concern to distance the intelligence agency from the PA security forces' established reputation for prisoner abuse.

General Keith Dayton, US security coordinator for Israel and the Palestinian territories, was responsible with his British deputies for building up the Palestinian security forces. He even complained about the PA intelligence service's use of torture on fellow Palestinians and how the CIA had trained them on torture techniques. Leaked notes from a meeting General Dayton had with chief PLO negotiator Saeb Erekat in June 2009 tell us a lot:

> "The intelligence guys are good. The Israelis like them," Dayton says. "But they are causing some problems for international donors because they are torturing people," adding: "I've only started working on this very recently. I don't need to tell you who was working with them before"—in an apparent reference to the CIA.[15]

In other words, at the time the barrier was being built, so was the Palestinian security apparatus. Fatah was disempowering its Palestinian rivals and clamping down on Palestinian dissent while being trained by and working with Israel, Britain, and the United States. The

United States was actively training the Palestinian intelligence service in torture techniques, and the concern General Dayton shared with his Palestinian counterpart was not that Palestinians were being tortured but that the torture was hampering fundraising.

Maybe the aggressive campaigns against Fatah rivals were a factor in reducing suicide bombers. Maybe there was a reduction of suicide bombings because the Palestinian security forces were supervised by the Israelis, Americans, and British. But a more significant factor may have been a change in Palestinian strategy. Suicide bombings were not helping the Palestinian cause; the Palestinians' plight was worsening, and they were losing the public relations battle:

> There is no doubt that the Palestinians have recognized the devastating toll on their society and political goals caused by the violence witnessed in the second Intifada [Palestinian uprising] from 2000 into 2005. Suicide bombings and attacks on Israeli civilians led to the Israeli army recapturing the West Bank in an iron-fisted crackdown that left more than 4,000 dead and more than 5,000 prisoners in Israeli jails along with colossal economic losses, territorial fragmentation and incalculable social suffering.
>
> Now, nearly a decade later, the Palestinians have slowly regained a hold on their cities, but their fight for statehood and the end of Israeli control has taken a more passive turn as they remain wary of another uprising. A poll done by the Palestinian Center for Public Opinion found that 25.9 percent of Palestinians favored holding huge demonstrations to overrun barriers and Israeli settlements; 15.2% supported violent actions; and a silent majority of 53.4% were in favor of peaceful negotiations. (5.5% answered, "I don't know.")[16]

Palestinians had felt the repercussions of violent uprisings and were ready for an alternative strategy, a more peaceful approach.[17] So when Benjamin Netanyahu said, "It's quiet because a fence exists," he was projecting a narrative of causation that may have merely been correlation; their seeing the poor results of violence may actually have been the cause for the Palestinian change of tactics.

Although it is rarely covered in the American press, Palestinians participate in extensive peaceful resistance. After seeing how horribly Palestinians are treated by the Israeli military and settlers, after seeing how their homes are demolished and their land is confiscated, after hearing how their children are taken by the Israeli military from their beds in the night and imprisoned under Israeli military courts, I now recognize that one of the clearest forms of peaceful resistance is simply to stay put. Palestinians staying on their land rather than emigrating—while enduring all this hardship, abuse, and humiliation—is a remarkable and steadfast form of peaceful resistance.

It was at this point that I realized that the term *security fence*, promoted by politicians and the press, was not what I had understood it to be. I had thought "security fence" meant a fence that protected innocent victims from thieves and aggressors. I now realized that the opposite was true. In this case, the "security fence" protected those taking the land by force from the innocent victims.

Even worse, this "security fence" further strangled the innocent civilians by limiting their economic opportunities, taking their property from them, and limiting their freedom of movement. I came up with my own usage definition based on what I had learned and ultimately experienced there:

> SECURITY FENCE. *n.* A barrier, typically in the form of a metal fence or concrete wall, that protects the party taking land from civilians by force rather than protecting the victims from the aggressor. The metal fence is electrified in segments and/or contains razor-wire sections. The concrete wall can exceed 26 feet in height and has occasional observation towers (by contrast, the Berlin Wall was less than 12 feet tall). The "security fence," or wall, cuts off and impedes Palestinians from reaching their agricultural lands, schools, and markets. It creates ghettos. It limits movement and trade, thereby crippling the Palestinian economy. It limits freedom of movement in the West Bank and to East Jerusalem, including to the Christian and Muslim religious sites. The "security fence" then enables the newly conscripted land to be developed for Jewish-only colonial settlements without impediments from its displaced Palestinian owners.

My becoming consciously aware of the usage definition of *security fence* affected my perception of the Israel/Palestine situation. Historically, I had vouched for Israel and was proud to defend the state from critics. Yet here was the Israeli government taking land by force from people who had no military or other means to protect themselves. In fact, under the Geneva Conventions, the military that was forcing Palestinians off their lands was the same

Figure 2. The wall cutting through Bethlehem, approximately one mile from the Green Line. [*Source: the author*]

Figure 3. The wall as a tool for land theft. It separates Palestinians from their agricultural land, cutting off their livelihoods and creating ghettos. Land is then given to Jewish-only communities. [*Source: the author*]

military that by international law was supposed to be protecting them. Israeli leadership, my media, and American politicians had misled me into believing the Israelis were the victims when in fact they were taking Palestinian land.

I am used to hype, such as beer commercials that depict pool parties with pretty girls in bikinis to encourage me to drink their beer. I know that every time I have a beer, there's not an instant party with beautiful people. How is a beer commercial different from the official story about Israel's "security fence"? I have never been asked to go to bat for a beer company. I have never been asked to defend the beer company from supposed unfair, discriminatory aggressors. No beer company ever said that it needed protection from MADD (Mothers Against Drunk Driving). No beer company claimed that MADD members were unfair or discriminatory. Yet Israeli and American leaders regularly insist on the need to go to bat for Israel. The United States has vetoed numerous UN Security Council resolutions, including on the subject of the barrier, claiming the resolutions are unfair. Numerous groups claim that criticism of Israeli policies and actions are discriminatory. It is not unfair or discriminatory to condemn those who enable drunk driving, and it is even less unfair or discriminatory to condemn those who commit human rights violations.

So maybe Israel had been a little greedy with its so-called "security fence." Maybe it had taken advantage of being the powerful one on the block. Maybe the placement of the barrier was just a symptom of the corruption of power—the placement a result of the overwhelming power Israel has over its occupied population. My awakening to the misleading nature of the term *security fence* heightened my sensitivity to the messaging in the news and to what was really happening. I researched more and listened more carefully to what was being said.

As I researched, I found examples and consequences of Israel's land grab. One example was Sur Bahir in the East Jerusalem area. When Israel built the barrier around East Jerusalem, it encircled land so far into the West Bank that it included land from Areas A and B (the parts of the West Bank that even Israel acknowledged in the Oslo Accords as being under Palestinian administration). Because Israel's barrier blocks access to some of the town's land, the Palestinian Authority cannot provide services to their own territory. In addition, Israel has issued demolition orders for houses in Sur Bahir, claiming that they were built too close to the barrier, even though the houses were built with valid permits and are supposedly under the jurisdiction of the PA rather than Israel.[18]

While visiting the West Bank, I heard about the complicated permitting process required just to visit one's father or sister who has always lived on the other side of the barrier. I learned about the different-colored license plates; Israeli yellow license plates are everywhere in Israel and throughout the West Bank, but I never saw a single green and white Palestinian license plate in Israel. The United States has problems with discrimination, but imagine how much worse it would be if Latinos or African Americans had to have different-colored license plates from Whites and could travel only on designated roads at certain times.[19] Imagine how much worse it would be if Latinos and African Americans were subject to a set of laws different from that of Whites.

Figure 4. The segregated road system. [*Source: Based on Visualizing Palestine*]

I also paid more attention to what I was seeing on the ground. Inside the West Bank (not on the border between Israel and the West Bank), I encountered Israeli military checkpoint after checkpoint. It was obvious that the purpose of these checkpoints was to impede the freedom of movement within the West Bank itself. They make the Palestinian population feel unwelcome in their own homeland. The soldiers' abusive treatment of Palestinians at the checkpoints make the population feel inferior and without dignity. Like the barrier itself, the checkpoints were clearly not for security purposes; they were designed for harassment, and they make everyday Palestinian life unnecessarily burdensome.

The Barrier and Arab Israeli Citizens

The next piece of information that caught me by surprise was that 20 percent of Israeli citizens are Arab. I was confused when I heard that statistic because I had thought Israel was a Jewish state. I did the math and calculated that of about 8 million citizens of Israel, 1.6 million were Palestinian. If the security problem was Palestinians attacking Jews, then I expected the barrier to separate the Palestinians from the Jews. So what were 1.6 million of the so-called enemy doing on the Israeli side of the internationally recognized Green Line border? And that would be undercounting, since the barrier weaves into the West Bank instead of staying on the border, meaning that even more Palestinians were on the Israeli side of the fence.

How could Prime Minister Netanyahu's claim "It's quiet because a fence exists" be true if there were more than 1.6 million Palestinians on the Israeli side of the fence?

What was the difference between the Palestinians in Israel and those on the other side of the barrier in the West Bank? Why would Palestinians on the other side of the barrier be more violent than those on the Israeli side?

Because Palestinians in the West Bank and Gaza are denied basic rights, including citizenship. This lack of citizenship for most

---

* Human Rights Watch has documented Israel's exclusion of Palestinians from its official population registry as well as the restrictions the state of Israel imposes on Palestinians who are registered:

> The population of the West Bank (including East Jerusalem) and Gaza, as recorded by the 1967 census, was 954,898. Following the census, Israel issued identification documents (ID cards) to Palestinians registered in the population registry. Under Israeli military orders, bearers of these ID cards were not granted Israeli citizenship but were allowed to reside, work, and own and inherit property in the occupied territory.

Palestinians under Israeli control has profound implications. It is the pretext that the Israeli government uses to deny Palestinians freedom of movement. It is the excuse used to justify a barrier that separates Palestinians from their relatives and their land. That barrier is a tool to limit commerce, the flow of products and services, thereby crippling the Palestinian economy. The lack of citizenship also puts Palestinians under arbitrary military law rather than under civilian rule with due process.

The repercussions of the denial of Palestinian citizenship and the continuing occupation are significant. The occupation is expensive. Israeli troops need to enforce and control Palestinians on a daily basis with an elaborate infrastructure of permits, checkpoints, and a military court system. The racist treatment against Palestinians only leads to violence, both to enforce the oppression and to rebel from and defend against it. All this cost to lives, to Israeli and Palestinian humanity, and to everyone's well-being is artificial and unnecessary. We know that this cost is unnecessary because Jews and Palestinians have lived peacefully together for more than seventy years on the Israeli side of the Green Line.

The simple solution to all these problems, including the Palestinian grievances, is to grant equal rights, including citizenship, to Palestinians who live in the occupied territories. It would be a win-win: Palestinians would no longer need to fight for equality and against oppression, and Jews would have the security that they have had since Israel's creation with the Palestinians inside Israel.

That one step of granting citizenship to Palestinians under Israeli control in the West Bank, Gaza, and East Jerusalem would have significant implications. It would mean that the non-Jewish citizenry of Israel would suddenly go from today's 20 percent to about 50 percent. Unfortunately, those in power in Israel today clearly prefer an overwhelming Jewish majority, even at the great societal and personal cost of being a society that denies basic human rights to people based solely on their ethnicity.

The second potential option for having a peaceful resolution is for Israel to return land it captured so that Palestinians could have self-determination without Israeli occupation and dominance. If all the Jews returned from their illegal settlements in the West Bank, the concentration of Jews in the smaller Israel would make it both democratic and Jewish by majority. However, that option would entail Israel returning land, such as the West Bank and East Jerusalem, that its leadership desperately wants to keep.

There is a third option, the one that Israel appears to be choosing: *Israel can keep all the land and make life so miserable for Palestinians that they leave. This option requires laws that discriminate against Palestinians. It requires that Israel violate Palestinians' human rights. The barrier is a tool for making Palestinian life miserable and for violating their human rights.*

3

Home Demolitions

Concluding observations on the fourth periodic report of Israel

The State party [Israel] should

(a) Immediately put an end to conducting punitive demolitions given their incompatibility with the State party's obligations under the Covenant and provide effective remedies to victims of destruction of property, forced eviction and forcible transfer;

(b) Refrain from implementing evictions and demolition orders based on discriminatory planning policies, laws and practices affecting Palestinians, including Bedouins, in the West Bank, including the East Jerusalem periphery; remove discriminatory provisions from relevant planning and zoning legislation; provide for procedural protection and due process guarantees against forced evictions and demolitions; ensure the participation of Palestinians in the planning and zoning process and withdraw the so-called "Bedouin Regulation" plan;

(c) Desist from any actions that may facilitate or result in forcible transfer and forced evictions, particularly of the Bedouin communities in the central West Bank, including the eastern Jerusalem periphery, and forced displacement and dispossession of Bedouins residing in the Negev. ...

International Covenant on Civil and Political Rights
United Nations Human Rights Committee
November 21, 2014[20]

Not only had I heard that the barrier had been built to protect Israel from terrorism, I had also heard that Israel had a policy of demolishing terrorists' houses. I thought that was a strange policy because the terrorists overwhelmingly died during their attacks. It's not as if a suicide bomber is going to know that his home was demolished; he's already dead.

Home demolitions are a form of collective punishment because it is the family of the terrorist, not the dead terrorist himself, who is left homeless. Even though I strongly disagreed with such a policy, I thought I understood the logic of punishing the family members of a terrorist by destroying their most valuable asset: their home. It was a way to discourage people from committing terrorism; one would know that one's own family would be hurt. Collective punishment is illegal under international law, but I understand why it is done as a deterrent to suicide bombers and other terrorists.

Then I heard in the news about a lot of home demolitions, even though I had not heard about any recent terror attacks. Suddenly terrorist actions and demolitions no longer seemed connected. After looking into it, I found that terrorist home demolitions applied only to Palestinians who kill Jews but not Jews who kill Palestinians.

More surprisingly, I found out that Palestinian home demolitions were rarely related to Palestinian terrorism. Instead, the demolitions were regular and systematic.

One of the systematic approaches for demolishing Palestinian communities is to never recognize them. If the villages and towns "don't exist," then any building in that location is illegal and should be demolished. I visited a Bedouin village in southern Israel that is "unrecognized" and has been subjected to demolition orders.

Human Rights Watch reported in March 2008 that close to 85,000 Israeli Bedouins are directly affected by their villages and towns being "unrecognized":

> Today the Bedouin of the 39 unrecognized villages possess no security of tenure and face the constant threat of having their homes destroyed. According to government figures, there are 45,000 illegal structures in the Negev today. Not all have demolition orders against them, but all are candidates for demolition.[21]

After personally seeing demolished homes, I became extremely impressed with the peaceful, resolute tenacity and dignity exhibited by those who are literally abused and terrorized daily. What we don't hear in the US media is that there are millions of peaceful Palestinian activists who just refuse to leave their homes and communities despite the violence and oppression that the state of Israel and its military, settlers, and civilians are putting them through.

Despite this tactic of demolitions, the Palestinian form of peaceful protest is to stand their ground by standing on their ground. They even have a word for their standing for their rights and their ground: **samoud.** *It translates to "steadfastness" in English.* Peaceful Palestinian protests occur weekly in the occupied Palestinian territories, yet I do not hear about them in the US media or from US politicians.

I visited one of the dozens of unrecognized Bedouin villages and towns in Israel itself. The peaceful steadfast approach from these Palestinian citizens of Israel was awe-inspiring. Again, because Israel does not recognize them, the communities receive no electricity, no schools, and no roads. Most importantly in the Negev desert, they get no water. And as a slap in the face, the villages and towns, which predated the state of Israel, are absent on official maps.[22] Yet these people stay put on their land.

And their resourcefulness is impressive. They have been early adopters of solar power. They do water capture from rooftops. They use gray water (drained from sinks and showers) for watering their plants. They showed us how they set up the Internet through a wireless connection to the cellular network. But as if that struggle is not enough, because their communities are unrecognized, their homes are always under threat of being demolished. On one house in the village I visited, I saw a demolition order.

Before my trip I had not heard about the Bedouin plight in Israel. After my return to the US, I wanted to learn more, so I did some research. I found out that there was one village, Al-Araqeeb, that had particularly resilient residents. I found an article in the *Middle East Monitor* that reported how on October 3, 2017, *"Israeli bulldozers, accompanied by police forces, raided the Arab Bedouin village of Al-Araqeeb in the Negev region this morning and demolished it for the 119th time."*[23] I later learned that Israeli policy goes beyond demolishing Palestinian Bedouin homes and villages:

> Not only has Israel destroyed Al-Araqeeb numerous times in violation of international law, it actually delivers a bill to the homeless residents expecting them to cover the cost of the very ruins wrought by the Israeli state.

> According to latest estimates, the families that live in makeshift huts and rely on rudimentary means to survive, are expected to pay up a bill of 2 million shekels, around $600,000.[24]

Israel starts the process with a demolition order. Then the Palestinian family has a couple of choices: Either they can wait until that fateful day when the state's bulldozers come to demolish their home, or they can demolish their home themselves. In the language of Israel, these are called "self-demolitions," and they are reaching record levels. The UN Office for the Coordination of Humanitarian Affairs (OCHA) reported that

> owners are forced to demolish their properties to avoid heavy fines, following the issuance of demolition orders by the Israeli authorities. Since the beginning of 2019, a third of demolished [East Jerusalem] structures (36 of 111) were self-demolitions. A total of 260 structures were demolished by their owners in East Jerusalem since January 2009, half of them residential homes.[25]

House and school demolitions are what slow ethnic cleansing looks like. This is also terrorism; it is a form of violence against civilians for political and economic purposes. It is just a form of terrorism I had never been taught about in school nor by the US media.*

In the village I visited, the residents had challenged the demolition orders up to the Israeli Supreme Court. During my trip, I heard time and again about such issues as building permits, pump installation permits, and demolition orders going to the Supreme Court. The administrative and legal costs for taking something like a pump permit all the way to the Supreme Court are extremely high, especially for the financially poor Palestinians.

Why are there such inhumane and racist policies and procedures? *It is a systematic effort to eliminate hope.* It is a way to tear apart a civilized society one family at a time.

Demolishing a home often also demolishes a family. After having their home demolished, children will wet their beds; any feeling of safety vaporizes. As women in a traditional society no longer have the base from which they build their lives—their home—couples become estranged. Since men no longer have their home, are faced with an invoice to pay for their home's demolition, and cannot get permits to rebuild, they develop severe depression and hopelessness. These militarily enforced administrative policies create a feeling of powerlessness and inferiority.

---

* See chapter 12. This book defines *terrorism* as "the threat or use of violence against civilians for economic or political purposes."

Seeing the costs of military personnel everywhere and the bureaucracy that has been created to manage all these restrictions, and taking into account that Israel is the largest recipient of US foreign aid, I realized the important role that Americans play in funding this oppression, this effort to lead a population to give up hope.

This slow psychological torture and ethnic cleansing is hidden under a bureaucratic cover. Imagine the psychological torture of living under the threat of your home being demolished and not knowing when it will happen. It took thirteen years for one Bedouin village in Israel to get its final ruling in the Israeli Supreme Court on May 5, 2015:

> The 2–1 decision sets a very dangerous precedent by confirming that the state is now legally authorized to demolish the village and forcibly displace its residents, despite the fact that they hold full Israeli citizenship, and for the sole purpose of building a new Jewish town called "Hiran" on its ruins, and grazing area. In its ruling, the SCT [Israeli Supreme Court] acknowledged the state's intention to demolish the Bedouin village in order to build a town "with a Jewish majority."[26]

The situations faced by this village and Al-Araqeeb, both in Israel, are not unique. In February 2017, OCHA (the United Nations Office for the Coordination of Humanitarian Affairs) posted some statistics about demolitions in the West Bank:

> During January 2017, OCHA recorded the demolition of 140 structures by the Israeli authorities, displacing around 240 Palestinians and affecting another 4,000. The number of structures demolished during the first month of the year was over 50 per cent higher than the monthly average of structures targeted in 2016 (91). All of these demolitions were carried out in Area C*,[27]

---

* "Over 60 per cent of the West Bank is considered Area C, where Israel retains near exclusive control, including over law enforcement, planning and construction. Most of Area C has been allocated for the benefit of Israeli settlements or the Israeli military, at the expense of Palestinian communities."

and East Jerusalem on the grounds of lack of building permits, although these are nearly impossible to obtain for Palestinians.[28]

When the United Nations report compares home demolitions from one month to the next and one year relative to another, then it becomes clear that these home demolitions are not unique. They are part of a systematic ethnic cleansing and land theft; they are part of a larger plan.

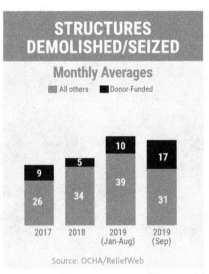

Figure 5. West Bank demolitions and displacement. This OCHA demolitions report shows a 42-percent increase in demolitions for the first nine months of 2019 over those in 2018. The top portion of each bar represents the number of donor-country-funded structures demolished or seized. According to the report, "seventeen of the structures demolished this month had been provided as humanitarian assistance, including 13 by the EU and its member states. A total of 97 donor-funded structures have been targeted so far this year, a three-fold increase compared to the equivalent period of 2018 (32)."[29] [*Source: OCHA Based on OCHA/ReliefWeb*]

In southern Israel, even a one-hundred-year-old woman and her sixty-year-old daughter could not escape their home being demolished. A relative interviewed by the Ma'an News Agency described how both women had health issues and could not walk. On February 8, 2017, Israeli bulldozers, escorted by Israeli police, demolished their home. The relative went on to say that "the family had renovated the home in accordance with their doctor's suggestions due to their health conditions" and that "Ghaytha and her daughter now were homeless following the demolition."[30] *Not only is this one-hundred-year-old lady not a suicide bomber or someone who climbed over the wall; she is supposedly an "equal" Israeli citizen.*

Donor funded residential structure demolished in Khallet Athaba' (Hebron), 11 September 2019.

Photo by OCHA.

Figure 6. Donor-funded home demolished by Israel. The residential structure was demolished in Khallet Athaba (Hebron) on September 11, 2019.[31] [*Source: UN Office for the Coordination of Humanitarian Affairs (OCHA)*]

Not only does Israel target homes, they demolish schools as well, thereby destroying the hope for a future across generations. A story that did make CNN was of a brand-new school that Israel demolished hours before classes started in August 2017 in the town of Jub El-Thib, east of Bethlehem:

> The brand-new building, paid for by the European Union, was constructed just three weeks ago. Now, little more than the concrete floor and an outhouse remain. ... [The students—] 64 children from the first to the fourth grade—had only been back

in class for three days when Israeli forces arrived to demolish the school, which Israel says was built illegally. Now they've been left with only a tent to shelter from the searing heat of the August sun—and no tables to sit and study at.

"Just when they were due to return to the classroom, Palestinian children are discovering that their schools are being destroyed," said Hanibal Abiy Worku, a director of the Norwegian Refugee Council (NRC). "What threat do these schools pose to the Israeli authorities? What are they planning to achieve by denying thousands of children their fundamental right to education?"[32]

The CNN article described how in the preceding two weeks, three educational facilities for Palestinian children had been damaged or destroyed in the West Bank by Israeli authorities. The Israeli administrative department for those parts of the West Bank, COGAT (Coordinator of Government Activities in the Territories), reported that the buildings were all illegal and that it had followed Israeli law in demolishing them. Note that this was Israeli law in Palestinian territories. The article continued:

A kindergarten for the Bedouin community of Jabal Al Baba was torn down, and a primary school in Abu Nuwar had its solar panels—the only source of power at the school—dismantled and taken away. ...

The European Union says about 100 structures—homes, shelters, water networks, as well as schools—in the West Bank and East Jerusalem, for which the EU or EU member states have provided funding, have been demolished or seized over the past year.[33]

Construction in Area C of the West Bank requires Israeli building permits, but Israel rarely provides them to Palestinians. Consequently, the Palestinians and the international agencies helping Palestinians, are forced to build homes, schools, and other amenities on Palestinian land without permits.

As with the unrecognized Bedouin villages in Israel, these schools and homes in the West Bank do not have power, because Israel controls the utilities and does not hook up Palestinian communities it does not recognize. Israel also does not "recognize" what it calls illegal Jewish outposts in the West Bank. Nonetheless, Israel provides those outposts with paved roads and utilities and rarely demolishes them.

What I learned from this and other articles was that these demolition practices were racist, based not even on citizenship but on the ethnicity of the victim. I also realized that Israel has perfected the historical Chinese water torture and "death by a thousand cuts." Like with the water torture, Palestinians don't know when the next drop will fall; their home or school could be demolished tomorrow or next year. Like with the death by a thousand cuts, where someone is cut as many times as possible while being kept alive so that they feel the increasing pain, Palestinian families are picked off one at a time, increasing their homelessness and desperation. Finally, I learned that Israel feels immune from prosecution in committing these inhumane acts. Israeli actions demonstrate not only the lack of concern for a Palestinian response but also for an international response.

The passage cited demonstrates the impunity Israel feels it has in destroying humanitarian projects sponsored by even our European allies. Not only does Israel regularly destroy humanitarian aid to Palestinians, it thereby also discourages future donations because donors will think that their contributions will be wasted.

Despite all these physical, economic, and mental burdens, Palestinians persist. The CNN article quoted Sami Mruwwah, the Palestinian director of education:

> We will stay here and resist against the occupation. ... We will rebuild the school soon, what happened against the school and its students violates human rights and childhood in particular. ... It is inconceivable for this world to remain silent in the face of the crimes of occupiers against education in Palestine.[34]

Palestinians know they cannot change their situation alone; they are powerless under the occupation of one of the world's most sophisticated and mighty militaries. They depend on the outside world to stand for human rights, and they assume that our humanity will finally call us into action.

This situation reminds me of another vocabulary word I learned in Israel. That word is *illegal*. "Illegal" has multiple usage definitions, depending on the party making the accusation, but here is one:

ILLEGAL. *adj.*
1. *As used by Israel:* Against Israeli law.
2. *As used by Palestinians (and most of the world):* Against international law, such as the Geneva Conventions and international humanitarian law.

Example: Construction in Area C of the West Bank, in the occupied Palestinian territories under Israeli administrative and military control, is illegal (under Israeli law) without Israeli permits. Permits to build on this Palestinian land are granted overwhelmingly to settlements that are illegal under international law. These same building permits are not granted to the local indigenous population, who are there legally by international and Israeli law, many of whose families have been there for hundreds, if not thousands, of years. As a result, Israel is demolishing Palestinian buildings against international law but in accordance with Israeli law in the Palestinian territories.

Imagine the psychological impact on a child who sees his or her brand-new school destroyed by these bulldozers, next to a brand-new town of Jewish-Israeli invaders, or colonists. Imagine the psychological impact on a soldier whose job it is to demolish this brand-new school for elementary school kids.

I mentioned earlier the resilience, steadfastness, and dignity I found with Palestinians while I was there. That same spirit apparently showed itself in response to the Jub El-Thib school demolition. The community reaction was not murder—not stabbing, as we tend to hear in our press. In this case, however, CNN followed up a month later, reporting that "activists reconstructed one of the buildings [there were three originally] under the cover of darkness." A local resident, Al Wahsh, was reported to have said, "They were throwing stun grenades, and tear gas to prevent [us] from building [the school], but in the end we made it." [35] The community renamed the school "al-Taḥadī," which means "Challenge" in Arabic.

I found yet another school mentioned in an article by B'Tselem (the Israeli Information Center for Human Rights in the Occupied Territories):

> On 10 Sept 2020, four days after the beginning of the school year, in the early morning hours before students arrived, Civil Administration personnel came with a military and Border Police escort and a crane truck to the Palestinian community of Ras al-Tin, east of Ramallah [West Bank]. The forces confiscated tin panels from the school's roof, 30 chairs and 12 classroom tables.[36]

This was not the first action against this school. A week earlier, the "Civil Administration" confiscated ten tin roof panels, four pallets of concrete blocks, and another thirty classroom chairs and a dozen tables. Students were left to study outside in the sun, sitting on the ground.

It is sad that the oppression does not end even after one's home or school is demolished; for many Palestinians that is just another day. I pity the poor folks whose nose gets further rubbed in this abuse when the only way they can support their families is to be in a construction trade, building homes for settlers. They are helping these same settlers who will violate Palestinian rights and terrorize Palestinians while taking more land. Some Palestinians even have to do this work near or where their house once stood.

4

It's Not Just about Israel; It's about Us

As I learned more about the situation in Israel, I began to see how it was affecting the United States. The more I researched, the more I learned that this was not merely a conflict far from home; it was significantly affecting American politics, our media, our freedoms and rights, and our reputation. This issue was not just about them; it was about us.

I. The United States–Israel Relationship

Americans have a lot at stake with Israel. The United States has historically been Israel's "greatest ally." Israel has been the largest recipient of American foreign aid since right after World War II. Israel is typically the largest annual aid recipient, with the possible exception of countries we have heavily bombed and/or where we now put our bases—if you want to call that "aid." We have committed a minimum of $38 billion over ten years to Israel.

Much of that foreign aid is weaponry. Through the QME (qualitative military edge), enacted in our Naval Vessel Transfer Act of 2008,[37] the United States government guarantees Israel military superiority over its regional neighbors. This guarantee is not just superiority over individual countries but superiority over all its neighbors combined. It's because of this guaranteed military superiority that Israel can feel confident when it attacks countries throughout the Middle East, from Lebanon to Syria and even Iran.

Besides guaranteeing Israel regional military superiority through the QME, the United States government has also guaranteed oil for Israel above our own needs through the Israel–United States Memoranda of Agreement of 1975, which states that if Israel and the United States are both under embargo, "the United States Government will promptly make oil available for purchase by Israel."*,[38] It would seem treasonous that American lawmakers would pass legislation that puts a foreign country's defense ahead of our own, yet this official agreement has been in effect for decades.

In addition, the United States has vetoed for the benefit of Israel more UN Security Council resolutions in the past thirty years than for all other subjects combined.[39] Congress enacted public laws 101-246 (1990) and 103-236 (1994) that prohibit the funding of any United Nations organization that grants full membership to Palestine as a state.[40] After UNESCO (United Nations Educational, Scientific and Cultural Organization) member states voted 107–14** to admit Palestine in October 2011, the US stopped funding it. UNESCO was created to advance "the objectives of international peace and of the common welfare of mankind."[41] Prior to October 2011, we had been contributing 22 percent of the UNESCO overall budget.[42]

---

* The Memoranda of Agreement between the Governments of Israel and The United States specifies the following:

    3. (b) If the oil Israel needs to meet all of its normal requirements for domestic consumption is unavailable for purchase in circumstances where quantitative restrictions through embargo or otherwise also prevent the United States from procuring oil to meet its normal requirements, the United States Government will promptly make oil available for purchase by Israel in accordance with the International Energy Agency conservation and allocation formula as applied by the United States Government, in order to meet Israel's essential requirements. If Israel is unable to secure the necessary means to transport such oil to Israel, the United States Government will make every effort to help Israel secure the necessary means of transport.

** The vote also included 52 abstentions.

We stand so strongly with Israel and against Palestine that we are willing to cut ties with international organizations, including ironically an organization dedicated to international peace. Our positions that so favor Israel and limit Palestinian self-determination make a mockery of any US claim that it is a balanced mediator of peace talks and that it supports a two-state solution.

The fact that we are kidding ourselves about being ethical or balanced is evidenced by votes in the United Nations General Assembly. Only the United States, Israel, Australia, Canada, the Marshall Islands, Federated States of Micronesia, Palau, and Tuvalu voted against allowing the state of Palestine to fly its flag at the United Nations Headquarters in September 2015. By contrast, 119 countries supported the resolution.[43] The United States is showing either brave leadership or rogue positioning against the world.

Not only have we protected Israel from answering for its human rights and other violations of international law with our UN vetoes, we have hidden Israel's activity on the ground with the Kyl-Bingaman Amendment (KBA).[44] Since 1997, the United States has approved an amendment to each annual National Defense Authorization Act (NDAA) that restricts availability of high-resolution satellite imagery of Israel and the occupied territories. This law in effect makes it difficult to track international law violations, including settlement growth, house demolitions, and such humanitarian issues as casualties of protests. We do this for no other country, including our own. The United States shields Israeli crimes against the Palestinian people.

To further protect Israel from accountability, the US Department of State associates certain criticisms of the state of Israel in their definition of anti-Semitism.*,[45] The US government also monitors what it calls anti-Semitism in countries throughout the world

---

* Examples of anti-Semitism cited include
  - Accusing Jewish citizens of being more loyal to Israel, or to the alleged priorities of Jews worldwide, than to the interests of their own nations
  - Denying the Jewish people their right to self-determination—e.g., by claiming that the existence of a state of Israel is a racist endeavor
  - Drawing comparisons of contemporary Israeli policy to that of the Nazis

through our 2004 Global Anti-Semitism Review Act, which asserts that "anti-Semitism has at times taken the form of vilification of Zionism,"[*][46] the Jewish national movement, and incitement against Israel."[47] By conflating anti-Zionism and incitement against Israel with anti-Semitism, our government is dangerously silencing free speech and legal opposition to racism.[**]

By not being able to criticize Israeli policies in American schools or boycott Israel because of their human rights abuses, Americans are losing free speech and an understanding of the world we live in. Legislation limiting criticism of Israel affects children; it subjects them to a deceptive reality. Kenneth Marcus, the assistant secretary of education for civil rights, reopened a case against Rutgers University in 2018 based on a definition of anti-Semitism that includes criticism of the state of Israel.[48] In February 2019, Tennessee introduced H.B. 600 and S.B. 1250, which included such a definition of anti-Semitism.[49] Florida passed a similar law, H.B. 741,[50] on May 31, 2019. These state laws affect what schools can teach. President Donald Trump signed an executive order on December 11, 2019, that threatens to withhold public funding from colleges that allow debate or certain criticism about Israel.[51]

In addition to the US government's financial, political, and military support of our ally, many of our state governments have passed laws that place penalties on American individuals or companies that boycott or divest from companies participating in the Israeli occupation. The US government boycotts—and requires Americans and American companies to boycott—Cuba, North Korea, and Iran. Yet there is no other country that the United States criminalizes Americans for boycotting. An American can boycott the United States in protest of

---

* Merriam-Webster defines *Zionism* as "an international movement originally for the establishment of a Jewish national or religious community in Palestine and later for the support of modern Israel." More information on the different forms of Zionism are in the Glossary.

** Racism is defined in this book as "the preferential treatment of one group over another based on national or ethnic origin or descent." For more information, see the Glossary. There is a chapter on racism in this book's sequel, *Speak Equality: Revealing the Root of the Israel/Palestine Struggle*.

our own policies without violating any law, yet we cannot do the same against only one foreign country: Israel.

On December 15, 2016, President Trump chose David Friedman as the US ambassador to Israel. Friedman has been a strong supporter of Jewish-only settlements in the West Bank, even though these settlements are violations of international law.[52]

On December 6, 2017, against international law, President Trump recognized Jerusalem as Israel's capital and said that the United States would move its embassy from Tel Aviv to Jerusalem.[53] Two weeks later, the UN General Assembly convened a rare emergency meeting and released the following statement:

> The Assembly declared "null and void" any actions intended to alter Jerusalem's character, status or demographic composition, by the terms of the draft resolution "Status of Jerusalem," adopted by a recorded vote of 128 in favour to 9 against (Guatemala, Honduras, Israel, Marshall Islands, Federated States of Micronesia, Nauru, Palau, Togo, United States), with 35 abstentions.[54]

The UN press release further stated:

> Calling on all States to refrain from establishing embassies in the Holy City, the Assembly also demanded that they comply with all relevant Security Council resolutions and work to reverse the "negative trends" imperiling a two-State solution to the conflict between Israel and the State of Palestine, both of which call Jerusalem/Al-Quds Al-Sharif their capital.[55]

The General Assembly had met a few weeks prior (on November 29 and 30), when it had adopted six related resolutions, stating that

> any actions by Israel to impose its laws, jurisdiction and administration in the Holy City were illegal and therefore "null and void." Convening on the seventieth anniversary of the United Nations resolution that had partitioned Palestine with the aim of

creating two separate States, the Assembly heard expressions of concern that Israel's occupation of Palestinian land continued to thwart that goal.[56]

US actions are demonstrating our disregard for international law. Furthermore, our support for Israel's violations of Palestinian human rights also undermines the credibility and efficacy of the United Nations. In 1948 Eleanor Roosevelt chaired the creation of the Universal Declaration of Human Rights. We helped found the United Nations after World War II, and we rigged it to give ourselves special powers. But despite these values and advantages, we still undermine these institutions, human rights, and international law in order to benefit one foreign country: Israel.

As Americans, we are isolating ourselves from the rest of the world when the only countries that vote with us are primarily those that depend on us for aid: Guatemala, Honduras, Israel, Marshall Islands, Federated States of Micronesia, Nauru, Palau, and Togo. Our government's lack of international support for these UN resolutions shows that, instead of considering the United States a leader, most countries oppose the United States. Our violating resolutions we had previously approved makes us hypocrites.

Having most of the people of the world view the United States government as a hypocritical bully only helps to recruit anti-American terrorists. In these days of concern over international terrorism, it is important to understand what our government is doing abroad. Its actions affect our safety, our pocket books, and our reputation. To translate what our government and the media are telling us, we need to know the facts and understand the Israel language.

II. The American Jewish–Israel Relationship

Since this book is about language, it is important to clearly define words. The word *Jew* in this book primarily refers to someone who is of Jewish descent—although in some situations, I may be referring to someone of the Jewish faith. Occasionally, I use the term *ethnic Jews* to more clearly distinguish people of Jewish descent from religious Jews. The term should not be confused with the many different ethnicities of Jews. These are not the only definitions for these terms, and therefore for clarity, it is important to share which definition(s) of these terms I am using throughout this book.

Similarly, the term *Zionist* is defined for this book as a supporter of Israel as a country where Jews have rights that others do not, such as the ability to easily gain citizenship. Zionists can be Jewish, but they can also be Christian. Jews may or may not be Zionist. One is typically born Jewish, but one is Zionist by choice.

Israel is central in many Jews' upbringing. The Israeli flag is on display in synagogues. Israeli holidays are celebrated by Jews in countries other than Israel. Many Jews receive calls asking for financial support for Israeli causes. Jewish schools teach about Israel being the safe place for Jews after all the horrors of the Holocaust and the long history of persecution. Jewish camps prominently include the subject of Israel as part of the Jewish experience. The Jewish Agency for Israel describes their organized effort to build that Jewish-Israel connection in young American Jews:

> The North American Summer Camp Shlichim (emissaries) are Israelis who participate in, and are integrated into, all aspects of programming in their assigned Jewish camp settings. ... They reached more than 10,000 American-Jewish camp counselors and tens of thousands of campers.[57]

Jewish young adults are encouraged to go on free "birthright" trips to Israel in order to make them feel connected to the country.

Many Jews do feel a close connection to Israel: 62 percent of American Jews agree "strongly" or "somewhat" that caring about Israel is a "very important part of my being a Jew"; 72 percent "think that a thriving State of Israel is vital for the long-term future of the Jewish people."[58]

Israel calls itself "the Jewish state." And this association has caused controversy in the United States. On April 6, 2019, President Trump referred to Benjamin Netanyahu as "your prime minister" when talking to the American Republican Jewish Coalition.[59] On August 21, Trump ratcheted up the old trope of Jews being loyal to a foreign country by saying, "If you vote for a Democrat, you're being disloyal to Jewish people and you're being very disloyal to Israel."[60]

The language and association around Jews and Israel has become tenuous; a double standard is also evident. The US Department of State and US states such as Tennessee and Florida have defined anti-Semitism to include "accusing Jewish citizens of being more loyal to Israel, or to the alleged priorities of Jews worldwide, than to the interests of their own nations."[61] On the other hand, here the president of the United States was accusing some Jews of not being loyal enough to Israel.

Whether or not an American Jew is "loyal" or not to Israel, there is a strong association between Jews and Israel. It is therefore important for Jews to understand what Israel is doing in their name, how Israel is perceived by others, and how Israel's actions affect Jews. An important step to reaching that understanding is to learn the Israel language and recognize when it is used.

III. Israel: The Terrorism Excuse

Americans are constantly reminded of terrorism throughout the world. We therefore need to be looking at ways to effectively combat it. Maybe because the US has the strongest military in the world, our government's strategy for fighting terrorism appears to be focused on border security and military action abroad. Unfortunately, Afghanistan has been the scene of our longest-running war in American history, and terrorists—ISIS (also known as Isil, IS, and Daesh) and others—are now stronger than the original Al-Qaeda was when they attacked us on September 11, 2001. It is evident that our strategy does not appear to be working. In fact, our Middle East foreign policy, with Israel as its cornerstone, appears to *feed* terrorism.

On March 16, 2010, General David Petraeus, commander of US Central Command (CENTCOM), testified before the Senate Armed Services Committee that

> the [Israeli-Palestinian] conflict foments anti-American sentiment, due to a perception of U.S. favoritism for Israel. Arab anger over the Palestinian question limits the strength and depth of U.S. partnerships with governments and peoples in the AOR [the CENTCOM area of responsibility] and weakens the legitimacy of moderate regimes in the Arab world.[62]

Meanwhile, Al-Qaeda and other militant groups exploit that anger to mobilize support. A letter believed to have been written by Osama bin Laden, which was translated and published in English in November 2002, supports General Petraeus's assessment. Bin Laden's "Letter to the American people" includes reasons for the 9/11 attacks:

> As for the first question: Why are we fighting and opposing you? The answer is very simple:
> (1) Because you attacked us and continue to attack us.
>   a) You attacked us in Palestine:
>   (i) Palestine, which has sunk under military occupation for more than 80 years. The British handed over Palestine, with your help and your support, to the Jews, who have occupied it for more than 50 years; years overflowing with oppression, tyranny, crimes, killing, expulsion, destruction and devastation.[63]

When I found that letter and read it, I was surprised by its contents. I barely remember its being mentioned in the US mainstream media. The letter was consistent with an interview bin Laden did with Al-Jazeera shortly after 9/11, in which he responded to the accusation that Al-Qaeda operatives were terrorists:

They [the Americans] describe those brave guys [the 9/11 hijackers] who took the battle to the heart of America and destroyed its most famous economic and military landmarks [the World Trade Center and the Pentagon].

They [the hijackers] did this, as we understand it, and this is something we have agitated for before, as a matter of self-defense, in defense of our brothers and sons in Palestine, and to liberate our sacred religious sites/things. If inciting people to do that is terrorism, and if killing those who kill our sons is terrorism, then let history be witness that we are terrorists.[64]

As recently as February 8, 2017, *CBS News* published an article quoting a letter dated January 2015 by Khalid Sheikh Mohammed, the person described as the 9/11 mastermind. In his letter to President Obama he wrote, "The war crimes perpetrated in Palestine since 1948, and those taking place in Gaza today, are the clearest indication of why 9/11 happened, and why it may happen again in the future."[65]

We can't fight terrorism without resolving its underlying causes. If we really want to fight terrorism, we need to change world public opinion about the United States. We need people around the world to regard the United States as the good guys. Unfortunately, when we support the human rights violations referred to in Osama bin Laden's statement and Khalid Sheikh Mohammed's letter, we become the best salespeople for terrorist recruiting.

When Secretary of State Michael Pompeo was in Jordan on April 30, 2018, Jordanian Foreign Minister Ayman Safadi said that the Palestinian-Israeli conflict is "the main cause of instability in the region, and its resolution is the key to achieving the lasting and comprehensive peace that we want."[66]

With a large Palestinian refugee population, only 14 percent of Jordanians view the United States favorably, despite the Jordanian government receiving $600 million annually in US foreign aid. Similarly, only 16 percent of Palestinians view the United States favorably, despite the US having provided $500 million in annual aid.[67]

Justice cannot be purchased. Even our money cannot overcome public sentiment against the suppression of freedom and human rights. Fighting terrorism requires justice, not military oppression or money.

This sentiment goes beyond Palestinians and extends to others who are sympathetic. A 2013 Pew Research Center poll showed that the populations of other countries to whom the United States gives large amounts of foreign aid also do not like us. The report points to Pakistan (11 percent favorable) and Egypt (16 percent), whose governments have supported US policies against the will of their people—Egyptian government policies being overwhelmingly anti-Palestinian.[68]

As Americans, we need to understand Israel and the Palestinian situation as a matter of our personal security as well as theirs.

IV. Israeli Policies: Dividing Israel Supporters from Other Americans

The topic of Israel/Palestine seems to be getting more and more heated in the United States. Israel, and the US as its primary defender, seem to be under attack politically and economically by critics. In order to respond to these critics, Americans need to be able to understand Israel (the language, the country's history, and the current situation).

And these attacks are intensifying. More groups are taking a position against actions by the state of Israel, with some voices even in support of Palestinians. Examples include the following:

- **Evangelical Christians** used to overwhelmingly support Israel, and although that support is still very strong, it is being challenged. David Brog, executive director of Christians United for Israel (CUFI), wrote the following in 2014:

  How quickly things change. The days of taking evangelical support for Israel for granted are over. As they are increasingly confronted with an evangelical-friendly, anti-Israel narrative, more and more of these Christians are turning against the Jewish state.[69]

51

- **Black Lives Matter** criticized aid to Israel in their 2016 platform: The platform, published Monday by a coalition of more than 50 groups called the Movement for Black Lives, encompasses a broad set of economic and social policy goals aimed at eliminating racism, mass incarceration and police violence. It includes a section criticizing United States aid to Israel, accuses Israel of practicing apartheid and says Israel is committing "genocide" against the Palestinians.[70]

- **American professional athletes** have taken a public stand against Israeli treatment of Palestinians. In 2017 eleven NFL stars were offered an all-expense-paid trip to Israel. Six declined in an embarrassing public relations blow to Israel. Seattle Seahawks defensive end Michael Bennett said, "I want to be a voice for the voiceless, and I cannot do that by going on this kind of trip to Israel."[71]

- **Some Jewish groups** are publicly speaking out against Israeli policies. More and more Jews and Jewish organizations are critical of Israel's occupation, blockade, and inequality; they are openly forcing the American public to question the Jewish relationship with Israel, and especially Israel as a representative of Jews. Such questioning is opening conversations about criticism of Israel being anti-Semitic. Historically outspoken Jews, including Norman Finkelstein and Noam Chomsky, have criticized Israeli policies and actions over the years, but they have more recently been joined by more visible Jews, including such popular public figures as ex–*Comedy Central* host Jon Stewart and Senator Bernie Sanders. Leading Jewish columnist Peter Beinart sent shock waves through the Jewish community in July 2020, when he changed his position from supporting a Jewish state to supporting a Jewish homeland in a democratically equal state. He called support for the two-state solution a "fig leaf for this status quo, which is morally indefensible."[72] Jewish organizations from J Street to Jewish Voice for Peace openly criticize Israel's occupation and settlement building among other policies. On campuses, organizations for Jewish students whose members no longer feel aligned with Israel are growing. In 2013 the pro-Israel Anti-Defamation League (ADL) identified the top ten anti-Israel groups, and at least three of those organizations have significant Jewish leadership.[73]

- **Many other Americans**, including a small number of congresspeople, are being critical of Israel. Some are going as far as supporting the Palestinian-led BDS (Boycott, Divestment, Sanctions) movement.[74] BDS is a worldwide economic movement that is working to affect Israel's economy and reputation; its goals are to encourage Israel to change its policies. Similar to the South African boycott that led to the end of apartheid there, BDS targets products made in Israel and the occupied territories as well as companies that have supported the occupation, such as Airbnb, Hewlett-Packard, and Caterpillar. The BDS movement discourages the purchase of goods from, and the investment in, companies making those products or providing those occupation-enabling services.

Politically, Americans are becoming more divided on the subject of Israel. Republicans have become more sympathetic toward Israel, whereas younger Democrats are now favoring Palestinians. According to a July 2014 Pew Research Center poll, Republican "sympathy for Israel" increased significantly from 1978 to 2014:[75]

Sympathy for Israel	1978	2014
Republican	49%	73%
Democrat	44%	44%

However, in 2016 for the first time, liberal Democrats favored the Palestinians over Israel:[76]

2016	Favor Israel	Favor Palestinians
Liberal Democrats	33%	40%
Millennials	43%	27%
Generation X	54%	17%
Baby boomers	61%	14%
Silents (born 1928–1945)	65%	15%

Although most Americans still sympathize more with Israel, younger, left-leaning Americans are becoming more sympathetic to Palestinians. Younger generations are important to watch because they often portend future public opinion.

As groups are speaking out against Israeli policies and actions, Israel supporters* are not only defending Israel; they are also on the offensive. They are speaking out in favor of Israel and are punishing those who speak out against this foreign country. To punish speech is to chill speech. Israel has thereby become an issue that chips away at our First Amendment to the Constitution by penalizing freedom of expression and ultimately undermining our democracy.

- Israel supporters have gone to the trouble of working across the United States with state legislatures to pass anti-BDS legislation. Anti-BDS laws require individuals and companies to pledge not to boycott Israel before they can do business with a state government entity. The cases that have gone to trial include teachers in Kansas and Texas and student debate judges in Texas, among others.** To get paid for their work, all were required to sign a pledge not to boycott Israel. In 2015 South Carolina was the first state to pass such anti-BDS legislation.[77] By 2017 half the states of the Union had already passed such laws.[78] As of late 2017, two anti-BDS laws in support of Israel and limiting Americans' freedoms, H.R. 1697 and S. 720, were being considered at the federal level. Also at the federal level was S. 170, the "Combating BDS Act of

---

* This book defines *Israel supporters* as people who support a state with a Jewish-majority citizenship and therefore a Jewish control over the country, often described as a "Jewish state." Supporters are either unaware of, or accept, the consequences of that choice: racist policies. Such policies include unequal rights to citizenship and the violation of human rights on the land that Israel currently controls. This book defines *anti-Israel* and *Israel opponents* as those who place a higher value on equality, freedom, and human rights—even if the consequence is a multiethnic (rather than a Jewish) state in the land that Israel controls. Although anti-racists clearly oppose Israel as a state that gives preferential rights to one ethnic group at the expense of another, there are also people who are antagonistic toward Israel for racist reasons—because they choose to be racist against Jews—however, this book does not represent their views, and they are not who this book refers to as "Israel opponents."

** Judges have ruled against the anti-BDS laws when they have been challenged in Kansas, Arizona, Texas, and Arkansas.

2017," which enabled state and local governments to pass laws prohibiting the state from contracting with entities that boycott Israel. These laws are aggressive or desperate, depending on one's point of view, because in 1982 the Supreme Court ruled that economic boycotts are constitutionally protected free speech in *NAACP v. Claiborne Hardware Co.*[79]

- Israel denied access to two United States congresswomen, Rashida Tlaib and Ilhan Omar, on August 15, 2019. They had been scheduled to be part of a congressional delegation to Israel. Both are critics of Israeli policies and supporters of the BDS movement.[80] The Israeli government reversed its blocking of Tlaib so that she could visit her ninety-plus-year-old grandmother, who lives in the occupied West Bank, on condition that she be "committed to accept all the demands of Israel to respect the restrictions imposed on her in the visit, and she also promised not to advance boycotts against Israel during her visit." Tlaib responded in a tweet: "I have decided that visiting my grandmother under these oppressive conditions stands against everything I believe in—fighting against racism, oppression & injustice."[81] Our largest recipient of foreign aid shows boldness or desperation by denying access and limiting free speech to members of the US Congress. Israel's action not only creates division between our representatives; the restrictions on speech undermine democracy.

- Israel supporters are particularly concerned about the younger generations and the messaging they get on college campuses. Professors have been penalized for their criticism of Israeli policies, resulting in punishment as severe as loss of tenured positions to being deported from the United States:

  - Sami Al-Arian, a tenured Palestinian computer science professor at the University of South Florida, was arrested in 2003[82] and finally deported in 2015 after never having been convicted. He was accused of supporting terrorism based on his criticism of Israeli policies and support for Palestinian human rights. As he left the US, he told a reporter: "I came to the United States for freedom, but four decades later, I am leaving to gain my freedom."[83]

- Norman Finkelstein, a Jewish professor at DePaul University and a vocal critic of Israeli policies and practices, especially related to Gaza, was denied tenure in 2007 despite his Political Science Department voting 9–3 and the College of Liberal Arts and Sciences Personnel Committee 5–0 in his support. This was after aggressive criticism—some might say defamation—of Professor Finkelstein by the Anti-Defamation League (ADL) and lawyer and Israel supporter Alan Dershowitz. In 2008 Professor Finkelstein was denied entry into Israel for ten years.[84]

- Steven Salaita, a Palestinian American professor, had his offer for a tenured teaching position at the University of Illinois withdrawn after he tweeted critically of Israel's 2014 bombing of Gaza. According to the Center for Constitutional Rights,

  documents obtained through FOIA [Freedom of Information Act] requests reveal pressure from donors who threatened to withdraw financial support from the university if it did not fire Salaita. ... More than 5,000 academics from around the country pledged to boycott the institution, resulting in the cancellation of more than three dozen scheduled talks and conferences at the school. Sixteen academic departments of the university voted no confidence in the university administration.[85]

  Salaita settled his lawsuit claims with the university and university officials for $875,000.[86] As of February 2019, Steven Salaita was driving a school bus in the Washington, DC, area to support his family.[87]

Not only have Israel supporters attacked professors, they also try to limit criticism of Israel by targeting students:

- Casino magnate and Israel supporter Sheldon Adelson led a massive campaign campaign called the Maccabee Task Force, which purports to fight organizations critical of the Israeli government. He also funded other campus efforts, including a campaign by the David Horowitz Freedom Center in Los Angeles. That center promoted posters saying, "Stop the Jew Hatred on Campus," and accusing the Muslim Students Association (MSA) and Students for Justice in Palestine (SJP) of "being murderers and terrorists." Horowitz then listed individual names of students and faculty. These actions in return were criticized by the administration.[88]

Israel supporters have created a McCarthy-like list of students, professors, and others who oppose Israel. Lists are broadcast on such sites as CanaryMission.org.

These are examples of individuals and groups taking an active role on the Israel issue in the US. Tensions are also mounting between the United States and other countries on the subject of Israel. Other countries in the UN have voted against Israeli actions for a number of years despite US lobbying for Israel. Despite that lobbying, Palestinians appear to be getting more support:

> The United Nations voted overwhelmingly Thursday to recognize a Palestinian state, a long-sought victory for the Palestinians but an embarrassing diplomatic defeat for the United States.[89]

The only countries who voted against the recognition of a Palestinian state were Canada, Czech Republic, Israel, Marshall Islands, Federated States of Micronesia, Nauru, Panama, Palau, and the United States.

The heightening tensions in the United States and throughout the world are primarily between two increasingly combative positions: one supporting Israel's Zionist policies for a state preferential to Jews versus one supporting Palestinian equality and human rights. This tension from incompatible visions has led to, and will continue to lead to, conflict. The US government's predominant support for the Israeli Zionist project over Palestinian equality has led to greater American isolation from the world community.

Seeing how the Israel/Palestine issue was dividing my country and alienating us from the world, how there was much more to the West Bank barrier and house demolitions than I had been told in the news, I wanted to better understand Israel's history and current situation. I wanted to know what my country, and therefore I, was supporting.

5

Zionism and the "Jewish State"

Palestine is a country without a people; the Jews are a people without a country.

—*Israel Zangwill, 1903*[90]
using Christian Zionist terminology from the late nineteenth century

The first time I remember hearing the term *Zionist* was at a bar mitzvah. I guess I was the only non-Jew at a long table of probably a dozen men. They were talking about Israel, and then they were talking about Zionists. I asked what a Zionist was. That was the end of that conversation. I gathered from the immediate change of subject and the unwillingness to even explain the term that the topic was not meant for me. That experience left me curious about Zionism.

Long before the British took control of Palestine in the aftermath of World War I, a Jewish movement had been growing in Europe. This movement advocated a Jewish national homeland. It had grown out of a long history of persecution against Jews in Europe. At different times and in different parts of Europe during the Middle Ages, and especially during the Crusades, Jews had faced restrictions from positions of authority, extra taxation, lack of citizenship, dispossession, forced baptism, and even slaughter. In the eighteenth century, Jews could not enter certain countries, they could not buy land, and they were sometimes forced to live in restricted ghettos. In some places they did not have freedom of movement and were restricted from jobs other than trading and money lending.[91]

The Age of Enlightenment brought positive changes during the eighteenth century, after centuries of restrictions and laws discriminating against Jews. France became the first Western European country to emancipate its Jews in 1791, two years into the French Revolution. Jews were thereupon granted full legal equality. Other European countries followed France's example, emancipating their own Jews during the nineteenth century.

Treatment of Jews had been rough. Russia was especially notorious for its violence against Jews; *pogrom* was a Yiddish word derived from Russian, describing organized massacres.[92] Around the turn of the twentieth century, a number of pogroms occurred in the Russian Empire, including multiple ones in Odessa and others in Warsaw, Kishinev, Kiev, and Białystok.

But the racism against Jews was not limited to Eastern Europe. In spite of their emancipation, Jews still faced discrimination in France, the Austro-Hungarian Empire, and Germany as well. In 1894 French artillery captain Alfred Dreyfus, a Jew, was wrongfully found guilty of treason and convicted for sharing military secrets with Germany. He was sent to Devil's Island off of French Guiana with a life sentence.[93] The French Third Republic was in a tenuous political situation, and the Dreyfus Affair, as it became known, was the scandal that triggered French society to the streets. The government was on the defensive, trying to maintain power both with its population and relative to its neighbors. After evidence came to light that another soldier had committed the offense, the army tried to avoid reopening the Dreyfus case. It fabricated evidence against Dreyfus, arrested whistle-blowers, and claimed that "calls for *révision* [a new trial] were a Jewish plot to undermine the army and France."[94] Newspapers wrote extensively on both sides of the affair. Army supporters spread anti-Jewish messaging. Riots against Jews swept France and French-controlled Algeria in early 1898.*,95

France was not the only government that was facing turmoil. In the 1890s an emergent movement of nationalist democracy was threatening the Austro-Hungarian Empire. Racist, populist candidates were running for office. Karl Lueger of the *Christlichsoziale Partei* (Christian Social Party) won a post in the Vienna municipal elections and charged Jews for controlling the economy and press.96 This time also saw the rise of the German *völkische Bewegung* (people's movement), a German ethnic and nationalist campaign that envisioned a hierarchy of ethnicities where Aryans were superior.97

Writer and playwright Theodor Herzl moved in 1891 from Vienna to Paris, where he became the correspondent for the Viennese newspaper *Neue Freie Presse*. He was exposed to both what was happening in Vienna as well as the tumultuous situation in Paris triggered by the Dreyfus Affair. These unsafe environments for Jews affected his belief in the need for a Jewish state.98 Earlier Jewish Zionists had been religious—for example, Orthodox Jews had often mentioned the return to Zion. But Herzl argued that it was not a religious or social need; it was a secular, political need. He thereby founded political Zionism, which he described in his 1896 pamphlet *Der Judenstaat* (*The Jewish State*), which argued that anti-Semitism would never be eliminated and that the only hope for Jews was to possess a state of their own.99

The open anti-Jewish sentiment across Europe was fertile soil for Herzl's Zionist movement to take hold. Unlike most nationalist movements, which are based on heroic and glorious efforts, Zionism became a national movement based on vulnerability and rejection, with the goal of safety and self-determination.

The Zionist vision of taking over Palestine, a land already inhabited by an indigenous population, was consistent with

---

* The "Dreyfusards," politicians who supported Dreyfus, formed a center-left government in 1899, and senior army officers involved in the Dreyfus Affair were reassigned or retired. On July 12, 1906, the French Supreme Court of Appeal overturned Dreyfus's case. Eight days later Dreyfus was promoted to commandant and made a knight of the Legion of Honor.

the culture in which the new Zionists lived; Europe accepted colonialism as normal. In fact, part of the colonial mentality was the concept of Europeans being superior to indigenous peoples. It was not just the Germans who had a supposed hierarchy of ethnic groups; many European countries possessed colonies throughout the world. (Even the United States had only recently declared its people of African descent as free, even though Whites still treated them as inferior.) With this European mentality, it is understandable that a European Jewry felt righteous and empowered to pursue colonization of Arab Palestine.

Through Herzl's leadership and vision, the Zionist movement grew. Herzl organized the First Zionist Congress in Basel, Switzerland, in August 1897, which was attended by religious and atheist Jews. After the meeting Herzl wrote in his diary:

> If I had to sum up the Basel Congress in one word—which I shall not do openly—it would be this: At Basel I founded the Jewish state. If I were to say this today, I would be greeted by universal laughter. In five years, perhaps, and certainly in 50, everyone will see it.[100]

Theodor Herzl died on July 3, 1904, but his dream lived on.

Herzl had known that Palestine was populated, but I had not. As I mentioned in chapter 2, it was only while researching the barrier that I discovered that Palestinians were also on its Israeli side. I was surprised to learn that approximately 20 percent of Israeli citizens were Arab, that Israel had 1.6 million Palestinian citizens. I started wondering why there were so many non-Jews in a Jewish state. Did these non-Jewish people come with the Jews to the land without a people? Or were they already there? I started wondering about the veracity of the oft-repeated phrase "a land without a people for a people without a land."

The answers came as I researched the history of that land. Israel/Palestine's history is rich and is documented for thousands of years. It is a land that changed hands regularly through the ages, but it did have periods of stability. Most recently, the Ottoman Turks had ruled the region for four hundred years—from 1517 until the closing months of World War I.

I learned a few other things that surprised me. For one thing, it was not the Holocaust and the United Nations that laid the foundation for the state of Israel; instead, it had been the British and their Balfour Declaration more than two decades before the Holocaust. I learned that the Balfour Declaration had planted the seed of the Israel/Palestine conflict, the seed that one people could have another people's land. The expectation implicit in the Balfour Declaration made it difficult for the British to rule Palestine for the quarter century after World War I.[101]

The Balfour Declaration

During World War I, the British suffered a shortage of munitions, leading to what became known as the 1915 Shell Crisis. In response, Parliament passed the Munitions of War Act 1915, which put a priority on the munitions industry. Private munitions companies became "controlled establishments." Employees in that industry were not allowed to resign without approval by the company; munitions tribunals were set up for offenders.[102]

Dr. Chaim (Charles) Weizmann, one of the most prominent British Jewish Zionists in the years preceding and during the war, was also an accomplished biochemist. In 1915 he industrialized the acetone–butanol–ethanol (ABE) fermentation process to make cordite, a slow-burning, smokeless propellant used in munitions from rifle cartridges to tank and naval gun shells. Development of this industrial-scale "Weizmann process" was supported by First Lord of the Admiralty Winston Churchill and Minister of Munitions David Lloyd George (both of whom would become prime minister). Lloyd George built the largest British cordite factory, HM Factory, Gretna; production started in 1916; and Dr. Weizmann became director of the British Admiralty laboratories.[103]

Foreign Secretary Arthur Balfour asked Weizmann what he wanted in return for his help in the war effort, to which Dr.

Weizmann replied, "There is only one thing I want: a national home for my people."[104] (In 1949 he would become the first president of Israel.) In 1917, still during the war but before there were British troops in Palestine, the foreign secretary included in his letter to Lord Rothschild, a prominent Jew, what became known as the Balfour Declaration, which promised British support for creating a "national home for the Jewish people" in Palestine.[105]

The Balfour Declaration was made without consulting the majority Christian and Muslim population on the ground in Palestine. Even worse, it was made a couple of years after Britain had promised Arabs independence in exchange for their help in beating the Ottoman Empire. Just as Weizmann had helped the British, so had the Arabs. Sir Henry McMahon, the British high commissioner in Egypt, had corresponded over an eight-month period with Sherif Hussein of Mecca and had executed an agreement on October 24, 1915:

> Subject to the above modifications, Great Britain is prepared to recognize and support the independence of the Arabs in all the regions within the limits demanded by the Sherif of Mecca.[106]

The boundaries promised in the McMahon-Hussein Correspondence included Palestine.[107] The Arabs then did fight the Ottomans for the British and lost twenty thousand men, ultimately handing the region to Britain. Then Lord Balfour sent Lord Rothschild the Balfour Declaration.

To summarize: Britain promised the land of Palestine to two peoples who helped it during the war. However, they broke their promise with the land's inhabitants, people who lost their lives for Britain and who had lived on the land for centuries.

Lord Edwin Montagu, the only Jewish minister in the British government at the time, submitted a memorandum to the British cabinet shortly after Lord Balfour's letter to Lord Rothschild, in which he shared his concerns with the Balfour Declaration. He presciently predicted the ethnic cleansing to ensue in Palestine and elsewhere:

When the Jews are told that Palestine is their national home, every country will immediately desire to get rid of its Jewish citizens, and you will find a population in Palestine [Zionist Jews] driving out its present inhabitants [Palestinians].[108]

Lord Montagu also highlighted the Zionists' selective view of history, stating that

a religious test of citizenship seems to me to be only admitted by those who take a bigoted and narrow view of one particular epoch of the history of Palestine, and claim for the Jews a position to which they are not entitled.[109]

Lord Montagu obviously knew that many conquerors had preceded and followed the Israelites in Palestine.

Thirty years later, the War of Independence would erupt in Palestine, in which, as Lord Montagu had predicted, Palestinians would be—as they continue to be to this day—removed from their land by Zionist military forces. He also predicted a drive to push Jews out of other countries, as happened in Arab countries after Palestinians were exiled. Lord Montagu made these predictions based on a simple declaration that the British government had made.

The Mandate of Palestine

After World War I the League of Nations was formed "in order to promote international co-operation and to achieve international peace and security."[110] The permanent members of the executive council of the League of Nations were the United States, Britain, France, Italy, and Japan.[111] The assembly elected another four countries to serve temporary positions in the council. This structure clearly allowed the primary five "Allied Powers," if united, to rule the League. As is the case with the United Nations today, the

League was a way for the great powers to maintain control while creating a perception of diplomatic democracy.

Under Article 22 of the Covenant of the League of Nations, "Class A" mandates were created out of the "territories formerly controlled by the Ottoman Empire."[112] The mandate system was a remnant of hegemonic colonialism. Article 22 defines these mandates as "inhabited by peoples not yet able to stand by themselves under the strenuous conditions of the modern world." The "well-being and development of such peoples [and their] tutelage ... should be entrusted to advanced nations who by reason of their resources, their experience or their geographical position can best undertake this responsibility." The mandate language reflected the arrogance of the "advanced" powers, with the presumption that these powers knew better than the people in the mandated territories what was best. In the case of Palestine, the mandate was a tool to undermine rather than support democracy and self-determination.[113]

The Mandate of Palestine was drafted on July 24, 1922, and became effective on September 29, 1923. It included language from the Balfour Declaration and stated the following:

> Whereas the Principal Allied Powers have also agreed that the Mandatory should be responsible for putting into effect the declaration originally made on November 2nd, 1917, by the Government of His Britannic Majesty, and adopted by the said Powers, in favour of the establishment in Palestine of a national home for the Jewish people, it being clearly understood that nothing should be done which might prejudice the civil and religious rights of existing non-Jewish communities in Palestine, or the rights and political status enjoyed by Jews in any other country; and

> Whereas recognition has thereby been given to the historical connection of the Jewish people with Palestine and to the grounds for reconstituting their national home in that country.

Article 2 stated:

The Mandatory shall be responsible for placing the country under such political, administrative and economic conditions as will secure the establishment of the Jewish national home, as laid down in the preamble, and the development of self-governing institutions, and also for safeguarding the civil and religious rights of all the inhabitants of Palestine, irrespective of race and religion.

Article 6 stated:

The Administration of Palestine, while ensuring that the rights and position of other sections of the population are not prejudiced, shall facilitate Jewish immigration under suitable conditions and shall encourage, in co-operation with the Jewish agency referred to in Article 4, close settlement by Jews on the land, including State lands and waste lands not required for public purposes.

Article 7 stated:

The Administration of Palestine shall be responsible for enacting a nationality law. There shall be included in this law provisions framed so as to facilitate the acquisition of Palestinian citizenship by Jews who take up their permanent residence in Palestine.

Article 9:

The Mandatory shall be responsible for seeing that the judicial system established in Palestine shall assure to foreigners, as well as to natives, a complete guarantee of their rights. Respect for the personal status of the various peoples and communities and for their religious interests shall be fully guaranteed.[114]

After much research, I learned that the language of this mandate was crucial. The nuances of the language are used to justify even the abrogation of rights of Palestinians. For example, the mandate removes the rights of the majority of the population to control its immigration. Some even say that "safeguarding the civil and religious rights of all the inhabitants of Palestine" (Article 2) means that Palestinians maintained certain rights but lost their political rights.

After Lord Balfour made a promise to create a Jewish homeland in another people's land, Britain chose to support that declaration by being its implementer. This turned out to be a difficult task. It is difficult to support the mass immigration of a population against the wishes of the majority indigenous population. It is especially difficult to get the indigenous population to agree to giving equal rights to this large number of immigrants, believing that these immigrants will eliminate the possibility for Palestinian self-determination, something the indigenous population had negotiated and fought for.

Those minority immigrants, moreover, were given more than just equal rights. They were given a special say in the administration of the land, including the use of state property, since such administration was to be done, "in co-operation with the Jewish agency" (Article 6). By contrast, there was no such language for the local population's benefit.

This highlights the primary issue: The creation of a Jewish homeland in Palestine was done not only without the co-operation of the majority population (Palestinians) but against their objection.

Under this British mandate, Jewish Zionists flooded into Palestine. In the 1922 British census, Jews represented 12.5 percent of the population of Palestine, overtaking the indigenous Palestinian Christian population of 10.6 percent.[115] A third of the Jewish population had arrived in the preceding four years—that is, only since the Balfour Declaration.[116] By the end of 1947, twenty-five years later, Jews represented close to 32 percent; the Jewish population had increased from 84,000 in 1922 to approximately 600,000 (Christians still represented close to 10 percent at that time).[117]

The assimilation of so many European Jewish citizens was difficult. Rather than integrate with the local customs, the Jewish immigrants created their own communities. They adopted Hebrew as their language rather than Arabic. As Europeans coming from colonizing societies, their actions reflected the European prejudicial views; they looked down on Middle Eastern and African people. Unfortunately, a rapidly growing immigrant population that considers the natives to be inferior is not a good recipe for equality, peace, and justice. Americans are well aware of such a mindset, considering how White settlers had attacked Native Americans and expelled them from their lands.

With this combination of conditions, the British had a difficult time maintaining the peace between the immigrants and the indigenous population, who fought back in the Palestine Arab Revolt of 1936–1939. It started as a strike but then became a violent revolt against the British administration. Britain was punitive: Starting on June 16, 1936, the British army blew up over two hundred multifamily homes in Jaffa, leaving close to six thousand Palestinians homeless.[118]

From a language perspective, it is interesting to distinguish a "revolt" from a "war of independence." Would the American "Revolutionary War" be called a war of independence had the British army won? Maybe 1776 could have been the year of the "Colonial Uprising" or "Colonial Revolt." It is worth noting the language used in naming the "Palestine Arab Revolt of 1936–1939" because the Arabs were in fact fighting for independence: independence from the British colonial power. The Palestinians were fighting against Britain imposing mass immigration on the local population. Palestinians were fighting the British colonial ruler, who was empowering the settler population, who was funding and ultimately training those settlers to fight against the indigenous people.[119]

The Palestine Royal Commission, headed by Lord Robert Peel, was formed to investigate the causes of the unrest. Its July 7, 1937, report stated that the British mandate of Palestine was unworkable and that Palestine should be partitioned.[120] The Jewish Agency for

Palestine attacked the recommendation as a breach of the Balfour Declaration, which they claimed had promised a Jewish homeland in all of Palestine. The Arab leaders also opposed partition and repeated their demands for independence from the British, as had been promised in the McMahon-Hussein Correspondence. Both the Jewish leaders and the Palestinian leaders wanted independence from British rule, but their definitions of "independence" were different.

The British imposed "statutory" (partial) martial law in the fall of 1937. The report recommending partition led to the revolt reaching its peak in 1938, when the British lost control of major towns. An additional twenty-five thousand British troops were sent to Palestine, and they came down hard on the rebellion, using torture and committing atrocities. The Palestinian village of al-Bassa was burned to the ground, and at least twenty villagers were put on a bus and forced to drive over a British mine.[121] The statutory martial law included the death penalty for Arabs found carrying a weapon or ammunition. The British imposed strict censorship of the Palestinian Arabic-language press, which was unable to criticize British military actions after 1936. The Zionist press ended up providing more coverage of Britain's repression of the revolt than did Arab media.[122]

To help fight the revolt, Captain Orde Wingate established in 1938 the Special Night Squads, a joint British-Jewish counterinsurgency unit. Captain Wingate also worked with commandos from the Haganah, a Jewish paramilitary organization that would ultimately become an important core to the Israeli forces. Wingate trained the Jewish fighters on mobile ambushes. British soldiers would also train Jewish fighters during World War II for commando night raids.[123]

On May 17, 1939, the British government published its "1939 White Paper," which included a plan to create a government for an independent Palestine within ten years. During the first five years, Palestinian Arabs would replace British officials at the head of government departments. The new policy also established a limit on the amount of Jewish immigration, and it put restrictions on Jewish land purchases. Jews defied these restrictions by committing "acts of terrorism" and organizing for the "unauthorized entry of a large number of [Jewish] immigrants."[124]

On June 9, 1942, during World War II, the Holocaust, and the British Mandate of Palestine, Deputy Resident Minister of State Lord Moyne spoke to the British Parliament in a House of Lords sitting:*

> Lord Wedgwood's proposal that Arabs should be subjugated by force to a Jewish régime is inconsistent with the Atlantic Charter,** and that ought to be told to America. The second principle of that Charter lays down that the United States and ourselves desire to see no territorial changes that do not accord with the freely expressed wishes of the peoples concerned; and the third principle lays down that they respect the right of all peoples to choose the form of Government under which they will live.
>
> Surely it is time for the Zionists to abandon this appeal to force, and to seek a settlement with the Arabs by consent.[125]

This view that democracy should prevail, and that all, including the Arabs, should have a say in their government in Palestine, was counter to the Zionist plan. Two years later, on November 6, 1944, members of the Zionist Lehi militia*** assassinated Lord Moyne, then the British minister-resident for the Middle East, and his driver in Cairo. On October 26, 1993, former Israeli Prime Minister Yitzhak Shamir had this to say about the assassination of Lord Moyne:

---

* The British Parliament has a House of Commons and a House of Lords. Meetings of the House of Lords are known as sittings.

** The Atlantic Charter was developed by President Franklin Roosevelt and Prime Minister Winston Churchill and was issued on August 14, 1941. Twenty-six governments pledged their support for it on January 1, 1942. The principles set out by the Atlantic Charter included the opposition to territorial gains from war and any territorial changes made against the wishes of the people concerned. The Atlantic Charter supported people having the right to choose their own form of government.

*** A Zionist paramilitary group in Mandatory Palestine.

Certainly, we had known about his hostile attitude towards Zionism, towards the idea of ingathering of the Jewish people here [in Israel]. He was against any Jewish aliyah,*,126 any Jewish immigration. He didn't believe that there exists such a thing like a Jewish nation, or a Jewish people ... and therefore, we decided to make this operation.[127]

A British Lord who was for equality and self-determination as per the Atlantic Charter, which the United States and Britain had signed, was deemed by Zionists worthy of being assassinated. In 1975 the corpses of Eliahu Bet-Zuri and Eliahu Hakim, Lord Moyne's two assassins, were exchanged for twenty Arab prisoners. Israel then reburied them in "hero's graves on Mount Herzl."[128]

By early 1946 the Arab leaders in Palestine demanded that the 1939 White Paper be implemented with the rapid granting of independence to the Arab-dominated Palestine. By then Jews, fueled by repression in Europe and Zionist recruitment efforts, were illegally immigrating to Palestine, and they strengthened their own military organizations, including the Haganah and its offshoot, the Irgun. By the early 1940s, Jewish armed groups were committing terrorism in Palestine and abroad. Tensions were high between Zionists, Palestinian Arabs, and the British. Zionist groups detonated cars filled with explosives near Arab markets, and they set off bombs and grenades in those markets. They also threw a grenade in front of a mosque as worshipers were coming out.[129]

There were also Zionist bombings of government buildings and the famous July 22, 1946, bombing of the King David Hotel in Jerusalem, where the British had offices. Future Israeli Prime Minister Menachem Begin was a member of the Irgun, which conducted that bombing. The hostile environment had become pervasive; Jewish boys and girls were being trained in combat.

One can understand how Jews from Europe, escaping the violence of World War II and the horrors of the Holocaust, wanted a safe place to move to. The new arrivals wanted to defend themselves

* **aliyah** (עליה). *n.* The immigration of Jews to Israel.

from further violence and were eager to train for such defense in their new home.

Unfortunately, the Arab population of Palestine was getting very anxious by this huge immigration of people who disrespected the Arab sovereignty of the land. Furthermore, land being bought by Jewish organizations was designated only for Jewish use, which further antagonized the Arab communities. Despite the aggressive drive to buy land through such organizations as the Jewish National Fund (JNF), Jews still owned less than 6 percent of the land of Palestine in 1943.[130]

Arabs were also being treated as second-class citizens, even though they were the natives and still constituted the majority. Many probably wanted to get rid of both the immigrant invaders and the British enablers and enforcers. What they saw happening was unjust and dangerous; if this was how "advanced nations" acted, they did not want what the mandate called "tutelage."

The Palestinian Arabs probably looked at their situation then as some Americans look at immigration in the United States today. As a comparison, the United States has seen a quadrupling of the Hispanic population in the past twenty-five years (even though two-thirds of Hispanics in the US were born here).[131] By contrast, Jewish population in Palestine multiplied by seven times over the same amount of time during the mandate.

With roughly half the immigrant population growth that Palestinians witnessed, the United States government endured its longest-ever shutdown in 2019 because of disagreement over building a border wall between the US and Mexico. Like many Americans in 2019, Palestinian Arabs under the mandate wanted to curb immigration. Now imagine how today's anti-immigration Americans would feel if someone had promised these immigrating Hispanics that they would rule this country over the majority population. Then imagine those Americans' feelings if the Hispanic immigrants were arming themselves and training their population to fight to take our land. This was the situation that the Palestinians faced as they saw these waves of Jewish immigrants arrive. This is probably how Native Americans felt as they saw colonists arming themselves, taking over their lands, and pushing them out.

By the onset of World War II, the League of Nations was collapsing, and its demise wrought changes in the Middle East. In 1940, Denmark, Norway, Luxembourg, the Netherlands, Belgium, and France fell to Hitler. Switzerland wanted to maintain its neutral position in the war, but hosting the League in Geneva would make Switzerland appear as though it were taking sides with the Allies. At that point the League started to dismantle operations. Most of its "Class A" mandatory territories, those that used to be under the Ottoman Empire, were officially granted full independence, becoming the states of Iraq, Syria, Lebanon, and Jordan. There was only one Class A mandatory that was not granted independence: Palestine.

The British had promised a homeland to the Zionist Jews, and those Zionists wanted safety and would not accept anything less than sovereignty over the land. On the other side were the Palestinian Arabs, who were the majority and did not think it fair for a minority to control them or for their self-determination to erode because of the British requirement of allowing substantial Jewish immigration. The British foreign secretary shared the following with the House of Commons on November 13, 1945:

> The whole story of Palestine since the mandate was created has been one of continued friction between the two races culminating at intervals in serious disturbances. The fact has to be faced that since the introduction of the mandate it has been impossible to find common grounds between the Arabs and the Jews.[132]

The British Balfour Declaration and Mandate of Palestine had created a major problem in Palestine.

Believing the Israelspeak expression "A land without a people for a people without a land" had lured the British into a quagmire. It turned out there were people on the land, and those people did not want to give the land or their sovereignty away.

74

It was obvious to the British that this impasse was difficult. Their representative to the United Nations, Sir Alexander Cadogan, stated,

> We have tried for years to solve the problem of Palestine. Having failed so far, we now bring it to the United Nations, in the hope that it can succeed where we have not.[133]

Giving away someone else's land is easy. Dealing with the blowback is hard.

The United Nations Partition Plan

The United Nations officially came into existence with the ratification of its charter on October 24, 1945, shortly after the end of World War II. On April 2, 1947, the United Kingdom delegation to the UN requested that the General Assembly make recommendations concerning the future government of Palestine, and the request was placed on the agenda for April 28. Five member states (Egypt, Iraq, Lebanon, Saudi Arabia, and Syria) requested that the following also be placed on the agenda: "The termination of the Mandate over Palestine and the declaration of its independence."[134] That request, for merely placing on the agenda the possibility of terminating the mandate, was denied.

The United Nations Special Committee on Palestine (UNSCOP) was formed and generated a report that it submitted to the General Assembly on September 3, 1947. The report included the following table:

Estimated population of Palestine in 1960

	Muslims	Jews	Christians	Other	Total
1946 (actual)	1,076,783	608,225	145,063	15,481	1,845,559
1960 (estimated)	1,533,000	664,000	176,000	21,000	2,394,000

This sentence followed the report: "Thus, according to this estimate, the population of Palestine would increase 30 per cent in fourteen years, assuming no immigration took place, and the Jewish population would decline from about 31 per cent of the total to 28 per cent."[135] The Arabs had higher birth rates, and that hampered the Zionists' objectives of becoming a majority. A Jewish-majority state in Palestine was achievable only by using one or more of the following means:

- Cutting up Palestine so that Jews were a higher percentage in one of the Palestine pieces
- Significantly increasing the Jewish immigration to Palestine
- In the words of the previously quoted Lord Montagu, "driving out" Palestinian Arabs[136]

The UNSCOP report made it clear that everyone, including the Zionists, was aware of the math. The committee acknowledged that

the Jewish case frankly recognizes the difficulty involved in creating at the present time a Jewish State in all of Palestine in which Jews would, in fact, be only a minority, or in part of Palestine in which, at best, they could immediately have only a slight preponderance.

The report stated that "in the Jewish case, the issues of the Jewish State and unrestricted immigration are inextricably interwoven."[137]

The report also pointed out the following, emphasizing the importance of language:

Few phrases in history have provoked such lasting contention as "Jewish National Home." Twenty years after the issuance of the Balfour Declaration, the Royal Commission devoted a chapter of its report to a careful appraisal of the relevant texts and historical antecedents in order to clarify the meaning of the phrase.[138]

The British understood the importance of the language in defining "Jewish Home." The reason we still have a conflict today is because different parties are trying to implement different definitions of a "Jewish Home."

The British position was nuanced and dangerous. On the one hand, in 1922 then Secretary of State for the Colonies Winston Churchill stated that Britain regarded a wholly Jewish Palestine as "impracticable and [that it has] no such aim in view," and further, that there were no plans—as would later be feared by the Arab delegation—of "the disappearance or the subordination of the Arabic population, language or culture in Palestine."[39]

On the other hand, in 1937 the findings of the Palestine Royal Commission (the Peel Commission) included the following statement: "There is nothing in it to prohibit the ultimate establishment of a Jewish State," and "it would depend mainly on the zeal and enterprise of the Jews, whether the Home would grow big enough to become a State."[140]

The UNSCOP report also recommended a three-way partition of Palestine into a Jewish-majority state, an Arab-majority state, and a separate city of Jerusalem. Here are the 1946 estimated populations of these three areas:

	Jews	Arabs and Others	Total
Jewish-majority state	498,000	407,000	905,000
Arab-majority state	10,000	725,000	735,000
City of Jerusalem	100,000	105,000	205,000

The table is followed by this sentence: "In addition there will be in the Jewish State about 90,000 Bedouins, cultivators, and stock owners who seek grazing further afield in dry seasons."[141] If one included the Bedouins, the proposed Jewish state would have 1,000 more Jews than Palestinian Arabs yet be a Jewish-controlled state. By contrast, the proposed Arab state had a much smaller land area and had 715,000 more Palestinian Arabs than Jews. This division of land and population was clear gerrymandering to put the maximum amount of land under the authority of the minority population.

After the presentation by UNSCOP, the General Assembly formed the Ad Hoc Committee on the Palestine Question, which enjoined two subsequent subcommittees to draw up a detailed plan. The second subcommittee criticized UNSCOP for inaccurate population figures; it found that the Bedouins had actually been undercounted, leading to a total in the Jewish-majority state of 509,780 Arabs and 499,020 Jews. The maps had been so gerrymandered to the advantage of the Jewish state that the slight miscount of Palestinian Arabs had caused both states to have Arab majorities and Jewish minorities.

The map had been cut up so that the two states looked like a jigsaw puzzle, each having sections that were connected by one point. The Jewish-majority state had three sections, only one of which was majority Jewish. The report of the second subcommittee highlights the behind-the-scenes frustrations of its members in cramming so much Arab land into the Jewish state:

> It is surprising that the majority of an international committee such as the Special Committee should have recommended the transfer of a completely Arab territory [the most southern section, known as the Beersheba area] and population to the control of the Jews, who form less than 1 per cent of the population, against the wishes and interests of the Arabs, who form 99 per cent of the population. Similarly, in the northern section of the proposed Jewish State—eastern Galilee—the Arab population is three times as great as the Jewish population.[142]

The one section that did have a Jewish majority was even gerrymandered. The report pointed out that the Jewish-majority section included a lot of land that had an Arab majority:

> Even in this region, the majority is more apparent than real because almost half the Jewish population is located in the Jewish towns of Tel Aviv and Petah Tiqva.[143]

In other words, even the subcommittee responsible for ensuring that the numbers would ensure that there was a Jewish majority in one state were complaining that the maps had been so gerrymandered that overwhelmingly Arab lands and communities were being put under Jewish control.

The Ad Hoc Committee changed some boundaries so that the Jewish state would have a Jewish majority. However, instead of adjusting the borders to re-create a Jewish majority by allocating one of the large, overwhelmingly Arab sections to be part of the Arab state, the Ad Hoc Committee had cut out Arab population centers of the Jewish state while leaving the majority of the land to the Jewish state. One of those changes was to make the city of Jaffa, adjacent to Tel Aviv, part of the Arab state, even though it was completely surrounded by the Jewish state and was therefore in no way connected to the Arab state.

The Partition Plan divided Palestine into two countries: the larger country, where the Jewish population was 55 percent and the Arab population 45 percent, and the smaller country, having a 98-percent Arab population.*,[144],[145] Based on the

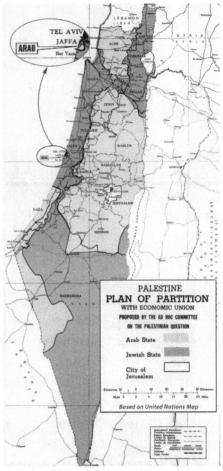

Figure 7. Map of the UN Partition Plan modified to highlight Jaffa as part of the Arab-majority state. [*Source: Based on United Nations Map*]

---

* A report submitted by a United Nations subcommittee on November 11, 1947, as part of the UN's decision-making process on Palestine, estimated the population of the territory to be assigned to the Jewish-majority state as having 498,000 Jews, 407,000 Arabs other than Bedouin, and 105,000 of the nomadic Bedouin. The final changes to the boundaries called for in the Partition Plan reduced the Arab population of the Jewish state by some 80,000, leaving a total of 332,000.

slight Jewish majority in the Jewish state and the larger Arab birth rates, it was estimated that the Jewish state would have a Jewish majority for only a little over a decade without Jewish immigration.[146]

Jewish immigration and/or Arab expulsion were the only ways to maintain a Jewish majority.

On November 29, 1947, the UN General Assembly adopted Resolution 181 (II), accepting the plan for the partition of Palestine, by a vote of thirty-three to thirteen. Britain and nine other countries abstained. The six Arab state members of the General Assembly walked out in protest. Resolution 181 was hypocritical. On the one hand, it stated the following in item B:10 (d):

> Guaranteeing to all persons equal and non-discriminatory rights in civil, political, economic and religious matters and the enjoyment of human rights and fundamental freedoms[147]

On the other hand, this same resolution denied equal and nondiscriminatory rights by being passed against the wishes of the majority of the population.

The United States played a crucial role in passing this resolution. The Democrats had lost congressional seats in the 1946 midterm election partly because of a defection of the "Jewish vote." President Harry Truman wrote to a US senator: "I received about thirty-five thousand pieces of mail and propaganda from the Jews in this country while this matter was pending."[148]

A number of countries were coerced to change their votes in favor of the Partition Plan, including France. The French delegate was told that its United States aid was contingent on its voting to support the resolution. The US delegation threatened other countries as well with cuts to their aid, aid that was important to countries rebuilding after World War II. Liberia, the Philippines, and Haiti, all recipients of US aid, were asked to change their votes to support the resolution. The pressure was so pervasive that even members of the US Congress were calling on United Nations foreign delegations. And the pressure was so public that a State Department policy group was concerned about the United Nations' reputation; if the UN were just a body where the US bullied other countries, then it would no longer be perceived as truly representative.[149]

The intense United States lobbying, and its threats to countries opposing the Partition Plan, effectively transferred the ownership of the Palestine problem from Britain to the United States. Britain finally could see an end to its involvement in Palestine: It could now rid itself of the problem it had created with the Balfour Declaration and then its mandate, and it was happy to pass the buck to the country whose president had a sign on his desk stating: "The Buck Stops Here."

With this history as context, I moved on to study Israel's War of Independence and the related language of Israel.

6

Israel's "War of Independence" and "Defensive Wars"

Israel's War of Independence is the first war between the State of Israel and the neighboring Arab countries. It started on the eve of the establishment of the state (May 14, 1948) and continued until January 1949. The war broke out following the rejection of the United Nation's Partition Plan, Resolution 181 of the General Assembly (November 29, 1947), by the Arab states and the Arab Higher Committee. The representatives of the Arab states threatened to use force in order to prevent the implementation of the resolution.

—About the War of Independence
The Israeli Knesset (Parliament) website [150]

Growing up, I had heard that Israel always had to defend itself against its aggressive neighbors. It had been attacked, as the Knesset website proclaims, by Arab countries that rejected the UN's Partition Plan. It had been a miracle that a country in existence for just a single day had been able to fend off the great neighboring armies! I understood why people believed that in

1948 it was as if God had reproduced little David beating the giant Goliath.

But then I heard that Jordan had told Zionist representatives that it would not challenge the UN decision and would allow the Zionists to have the Partition Plan's Jewish-majority state. I wanted to know if Israel had really been defending itself from all these aggressive armies or if the arrangement between Jordan and Israel was the reason that Israel had gotten its territory and Jordan had gotten the West Bank. This question led me to research Israel's War of Independence.

I found that shortly before the passage of Resolution 181 and the UN Partition Plan, Golda Meir, head of the political department of the Jewish Agency in Jerusalem (and later prime minister of Israel), had secretly met with King Abdullah I of Jordan. She asked for assurances from the king that if the Partition Plan passed in the United Nations, he would not attack the Zionist Jews. During the meeting the king is reported to have provided such assurances, but he made it clear that he intended to take over the West Bank portion of the Partition Plan's Arab-majority state.[151]

"Stages 1 and 2"

The hostilities of December 1947 to March 1948 triggered the start of the exodus of Palestine's Arabs.

—*Israeli historian Benny Morris* [152]

The Knesset website defines "Stage 1" of Israel's War of Independence as spanning November 29, 1947, through March 31, 1948, and "Stage 2" as April 1, 1948, through May 14, 1948. But the war during the first two stages did not involve any Arab states. Almost six months after the beginning of the war, a few days before Israel declared independence, Meir returned to see King Abdullah. There she learned from him that war with Jordan was imminent.

The war was about control of the land. The Jewish minority population was to control a majority of the land. The Palestinian and Arab world leadership had repeatedly requested independence from Britain, something that would have been possible had the Zionists agreed. However, the Zionists insisted on control in Palestine despite being a minority of the population.

David Ben-Gurion, who would be known as Israel's founder and would become its first prime minister, expressed how Zionists insisted on controlling Palestine: "We as a nation, want this country to be ours; the Arabs as a nation, want this country to be theirs."[153] He made that statement in 1919, when Jews represented around 12.5 percent of the population.*,[154] Here is how Palestinian nationalist leader 'Awni 'Abd al-Hadi described the situation: "The goal of the Jews was to rule the country, and the aim of the Arabs was to fight against this rule."[155]

The distinction between these two perspectives is that the Arabs wanted self-determination, whereas the Zionists wanted self-determination only for the Jews.

The only way for a minority population to control a majority is through supremacy. Ben-Gurion and other Zionist leaders may have made statements promoting the virtues of equality, but we cannot ignore that a Jewish-controlled state in an overwhelmingly Arab land cannot be based on equality.

Control by an ethnic minority can be achieved through legal preferential treatment, as with the immigration laws and citizenship rights provided to Jews under the British mandate. Control can also be achieved through military supremacy, as during Israel's War of Independence. And control can be achieved both ways, as is the case in Israel today. We cannot lose sight of the fact that ethnic supremacy is the opposite of equality—and that supremacy and discrimination are the foundations for tension anywhere.

---

* The Jewish population was measured as 12.5 percent in a 1922 British census. Note that this was three years after David Ben-Gurion's statement.

Martin Luther King Jr. said, "Black supremacy is as dangerous as White supremacy." He added, "God is interested in the freedom of the whole human race, the creation of a society where all men will live together as brothers."[156] That was not the Zionist objective, however; they insisted on Jewish supremacy despite being the minority. Israeli leaders, public opinion, and policies continue to insist on Jewish supremacy today.

The Knesset website states the following about what it calls "Stage 1":

> There were still 100,000 British troops stationed in Palestine, which were much stronger than both Arab and Israeli forces. Nevertheless, the British policy was not to intervene in the warfare between the two sides, except in order to safeguard the security of British forces and facilities.[157]

By January 1948 the Palestinian villages of Monsurat al-Kheit* (in the Upper Galilee) and Lifta (in the Jerusalem corridor) were emptied of Arabs by Zionist militia assaults.[158] The town Lifta was not even located within the proposed Jewish state; it was deep into the proposed Arab state, near the border of the internationally administered zone portion of the Partition Plan. In other words, barely over a month after the Partition Plan was approved by the UN General Assembly, and months before any Arab army had crossed into Palestine, Zionist militias had already depopulated villages and towns deep into the Arab state.

On April 9, 1948—more than one month before Israel declared itself a state and Arab armies moved into Palestine—under the approval and cooperation of the Haganah, Zionist troops attacked the Palestinian village of Deir Yassin. Israeli historian Benny Morris, who specializes in this period, describes the civilian massacre by Zionist troops:

---

* The name of the town is transliterated as either "Monsurat al-Kheit" or "Mansurat al-Khayt."

Whole families were riddled with bullets and grenade fragments and buried when houses were blown up on top of them; men, women, and children were mowed down as they emerged from houses; individuals were taken aside and shot. ... The adult males were taken to town in trucks and paraded in the city streets, then taken back to the site and killed with rifle and machine-gun fire. Before they were put on the trucks, the IZL and LHI men [Irgun and Lehi Zionist troops] searched the women, men, and children [and] took from them all the jewelry and stole their money. ...

During the next three days a variety of outsiders ... visited the village to investigate. All saw bullet-riddled, sometimes charred bodies of men, women, and children.[159]

This massacre was not some story fabricated by the Palestinians; it was documented by the Zionists and outsiders. Benny Morris further describes how Israeli intelligence determined that Deir Yassin was "a decisive accelerating factor" in the Palestinian population's exodus. Terror and barbarism had successfully caused the civilians to flee for safety.

Palestinian civilians tried to return to their villages and towns after the fighting and occasionally were successful. The British on occasion even helped the returning Palestinians by removing Haganah roadblocks. Arab leaders broadcast calls for the Palestinians to return. However, the Haganah forcefully stopped such attempts. In fact, a lobby of Zionists worked to make the blocking of return official.

Yosef Weitz was a leader in this effort; he had promoted the exodus of Palestinians since the late 1930s. Ezra Danin and Eliahu Sasson, who had accompanied Golda Meir to visit King Abdullah of Jordan, would join Weitz to form the Transfer Committee in order to make the exodus of Palestinians a permanent reality. It would have its first official working session on May 30, 1948, two weeks after Israel had declared itself a state.[160] Using Jewish National

Fund (JNF)*,161 resources, they went about razing villages to further prevent the return of Palestinians. (Weitz was JNF director of land and forestry from 1932 to 1972.[162] Today the JNF owns approximately 13 percent of the land of Israel.[163])

From the end of 1947 through May 14, 1948, when the British high commissioner left Palestine, it was clear that Zionists and Palestinians were both offensive and defensive. As with most wars, it was messy; there were atrocities and casualties on both sides. Cities and towns that had mixed populations became segregated, resulting in the expulsion of one group or the other. Armed attacks and terrorism drove out populations.

The results, however, were very one-sided. The Zionist immigrants were the best organized, armed, and financed.[164] Per Israeli historian Benny Morris: "The Israelis conquered 400 Arab villages and towns in the course of the [1948] war, and the Arabs conquered almost no inhabited Israeli villages in the course of the war."**,165

As a result of the fighting, about 400,000 Palestinians were displaced from their homes, lands, and a couple of hundred villages before Zionists declared Israel a state on May 14, 1948, and before any Arab army attacked.***,166 By July up to 500,000 Palestinians

---

* Here is a description of the Jewish National Fund from its website:
JNF is the single largest provider of Zionist programs in the U.S. Its work is divided into seven program areas: Forestry & Green Innovations, Water Solutions, Community Building, Zionist Education & Advocacy, Research & Development, Heritage Sites, and Disabilities & Special Needs.
Since 1901, JNF has:
  • Planted more than 250 million trees
  • Built over 250 reservoirs and dams
  • Developed over 250,000 acres of land
  • Created more than 2,000 parks
  • Provided the infrastructure for over 1,000 communities
  • Connected thousands of children and young adults to Israel and their heritage

** Professor Benny Morris was answering questions after a lecture at the House of Literature in Oslo, Norway, on September 27, 2014. The event was sponsored by the Norwegian organization Med Israel for Fred (MIFF) "With Israel for Peace," the largest nonreligious pro-Israel membership group in Europe.

*** Al Jazeera referred to 220 villages. According to Benny Morris, at least 150 villages and towns were captured by May 15, 1948.

but fewer than 5,000 Jews are estimated to have become forcefully displaced.[167] What may have been claimed to be an implementation of the UN Partition Plan had become a massive ethnic cleansing process and land grab deep into the designated Arab state, months before Arab armies moved in. The process continued after Israel declared itself a state.

The Knesset website pointed out that before May 14, 1948, the major military power in Palestine was British, not Palestinian and not Zionist. However, although Britain was partially involved, its forces did not maintain order; they were unsuccessful in the conflicting environment they had created.[168]

The British were betraying the Arabs yet again. They had promised the Arabs self-determination in exchange for Arab cooperation in fighting the Ottoman Empire in World War I. But the British then undermined their agreement documented in the McMahon-Hussein Correspondence, when they made the Balfour Declaration. They had developed the 1939 White Paper, and the Arabs had asked for its rapid implementation with the granting of independence to the Arab-dominated Palestine. Again, the British did not oblige. All of Palestine's mandate neighbors (Lebanon, Syria, Iraq, Jordan) attained independence, but the British held back Palestine's independence. Then the UN Partition Plan was developed, awarding most of the land to the Jewish state and leaving a smaller Arab state; Britain was again complicit. And now that the subsequent internal war was on, the British were not protecting the civilians from the immigrant, colonial militias.

The only way that the UN Partition Plan, created by the Allied Powers, might have had a chance of being peaceful rather than resulting in terror, massacres, and expulsions, would have been for Britain to manage its implementation. Britain would have had to enforce the Partition Plan and in the process to guarantee equality of all peoples.

Unfortunately, instead of maintaining order and investing in the future, as the United States did in Germany and Japan after World War II, Britain let the massacres and expulsions occur and rushed for the exit as Israel declared statehood. Granted, Britain's job was harder than ours with Germany and Japan; we had not granted control of Germany or Japan to a minority, significantly immigrant population. As an analogy, it is a lot easier to tell children that you will make sure that everyone plays nicely with their toys; it's completely different if you take most of Bill's toys and give them to Joe.

After five and a half months of fighting between Zionist and Palestinian militias, Israel declared itself a state on May 14, 1948. The next day, Egypt, Iraq, Jordan, Lebanon, Saudi Arabia, and Syria declared war on Israel. Had I not researched and learned this history about the War of Independence, I would easily have believed the Knesset website passage quoted at the beginning of this chapter: "It started on the eve of the establishment of the state (May 14, 1948)."[169] Now I know better; the War of Independence had already been going on for almost six months.

"Stages 3 Plus"

By the very day that the Zionists declared Israel an independent, sovereign, Jewish state, they had already taken land that even the Partition Plan had set aside for the Arab state. Deir Yassin was one example of that; the village was deep into the Arab partition, close to Jerusalem. That massacre had occurred on April 9, 1948, five weeks before Israel became a state and before the first Arab army came to help the Palestinians.

Once those Arab armies attacked, the war continued into 1949. Ultimately, armistice agreements were signed with the neighboring Arab countries: Egypt on February 24, 1949, Lebanon on March 23, Jordan on April 3, and Syria on July 20.

During the war, some 10,000 Jews had fled, were expelled, or were killed from communities in the West Bank.[170] A total of 4,000 Israeli soldiers and 2,000 Israeli civilians died during the war.

For the Palestinians, this war is called the Nakba (Arabic النكبة, al-Nakbah, "the Catastrophe"). They suffered over seventy massacres. The Zionists destroyed—or renamed and repopulated—hundreds of villages and towns, resulting in about 750,000 Palestinian refugees and 15,000 killed Palestinians.[171] The Zochrot NGO (nongovernmental organization), which has been working since 2002 to promote acknowledgment and accountability for the ongoing injustices of the Nakba, has a map showing the more than 500 depopulated towns and villages.[172] The armies from the neighboring Arab states also had their casualties. But the Israeli army did not just fight the Arab armies; they continued the expulsion of Palestinians:

> On 12 July [1948], before the shooting in Lydda had completely died down, Lt. Col. Yitzhak Rabin [future prime minister of Israel], the operation's officer of Operation Dani, issued the following order: "1. The inhabitants of Lydda must be expelled quickly without attention to age." ... A similar order was issued at the same time to the Kiryati Brigade concerning the inhabitants of the neighboring Arab town of Ramle.

> On 12 and 13 July, the Yiftah and Kiryati brigades carried out their orders, expelling the fifty to sixty thousand inhabitants of the two towns, which lie about ten miles southeast of Tel Aviv.[173]

These expulsions of Palestinians from Lydda and Ramle were not anomalies; they were part of a master plan. On March 10, 1948, more than two months before Israel declared itself a state, the final touches of an ethnic cleansing plan known as Plan D (Dalet in Hebrew) were made. Israeli historian Ilan Pappé described this moment:

> That same evening, military orders were dispatched to the units on the ground to prepare for the systematic expulsion of the Palestinians from vast areas of the country. The orders came with a detailed description of the methods to be employed to forcibly evict the people: large-scale intimidation; laying siege to and bombarding villages and population centres; setting fire to homes, properties and goods; expulsion; demolition; and, finally planting mines among the rubble to prevent any of the expelled inhabitants

from returning. Each unit was issued with its own list of villages and neighbourhoods as the targets of this master plan. ...

Once the decision was taken, it took six months to complete the mission.[174]

Many Palestinians have told me that the Nakba is still ongoing. Palestinians are still being killed and expelled from their homes and land even today, over seventy years later.

Israel's Primary Opponent

Israel had a number of opponents during what it calls its "War of Independence." One might say that the British were an opponent because they had restricted both the Palestinians and the Jews from originally having access to arms. The British had also put restrictions on Jewish immigration.

But calling Britain the Zionists' opponent in its War of Independence does not make sense, since a war was not needed to convince the British to leave. The Partition Plan had defined a timetable for the British handoff, and the British did leave in mid-May 1948, when the Knesset website asserts that the war "started."[175] Naming the British as the opponent in that war would also be strange, since it had been the British Balfour Declaration that promised a Jewish "homeland." Had it not been for the British, there would not have been the British mandate of Palestine, the massive Jewish immigration, and ultimately the Partition Plan that followed.

Many claim that the Arab armies were Israel's opponents. But those armies were not involved until almost six months into the war, not until after May 14, 1948. Those armies did not attack until after Israel had declared itself a state, after Israel had conquered land in the Partition Plan's "Arab-majority state," and after hundreds of thousands of Palestinians had already been purged from the land. Jordan had also been an ally of the Zionists. In Golda Meir's first visit with the king of Jordan, she learned that he wanted the West Bank, a piece of what the Partition Plan had designated as the Arab state. We can only speculate, but it seems plausible that there would not have been much of a fight between Jordan and Israel, if any, had the Zionists not first invaded the Arab-partition West Bank, and had the Zionists not caused a mass exodus of Palestinians.

Israel's other opponents included those who had worked toward a solution that gave Arabs more rights or land than the Zionists wanted them to have. Yitzhak Shamir, who would become Israeli prime minister, plotted the assassinations of both previously mentioned Lord Moyne, the British minister for Middle East affairs, and Count Folke Bernadotte.[176]

Count Bernadotte was appointed United Nations mediator in Palestine per UN Resolution 186 on May 14, 1948. He led the mediation for a temporary cease-fire in the War of Independence. In his progress report dated September 16, 1948, he described the challenge, sharing how the Palestinians and the Arab states recognized "the right of many Jews now in Palestine to be there and to remain there as citizens of a Palestinian State," but "they bitterly reject Jewish nationalistic aspirations for a separate State." He wrote that the Arabs "have consistently advocated a unitary Arab State in Palestine, with full rights and guarantees for the Jewish minority, as the acceptable solution," but he asserted that "in the light of developments during recent months the Arab position is unrealistic."[177]

Bernadotte acknowledged the impasse:

The combination of Jewish strength and international intervention has decided the issue of the Jewish State.

But he was also empathetic to the Arab perspective, saying that

the Arabs look upon the nationalistic Jews of Palestine as interlopers and aggressors. They point to the fact that the Arab population is the preponderant population of the country and that it has been an Arab country for many centuries.[178]

Bernadotte also shared that the Arabs

harbour grave fears that a Jewish State in Palestine will not stay within its defined boundaries, and through population pressure resulting from unlimited immigration, encouragement and support from world Jewry, and burgeoning nationalism, a threat will be posed not only to Palestine but to the entire Arab Near East.[179]

Finally, Bernadotte mentioned in his report the problem of more than 300,000 Palestinian refugees:

It is, however, undeniable that no settlement can be just and complete if recognition is not accorded to the right of the Arab refugee to return to the home from which he has been dislodged by the hazards and strategy of the armed conflict between Arabs and Jews in Palestine. The majority of these refugees have come from territory which, under the Assembly resolution of 29 November, was to be included in the Jewish State. The exodus of Palestinian Arabs resulted from panic created by fighting in their communities, by rumours concerning real or alleged acts of terrorism, or expulsion. It would be an offence against the principles of elemental justice if these innocent victims of the conflict were denied the right to return to their homes while Jewish immigrants flow into Palestine, and, indeed, at least offer the threat of permanent replacement of the Arab refugees who have been rooted in the land for centuries.[180]

Two days later, on September 18, 1948, Count Bernadotte was assassinated in Jerusalem. General Aage Lundstrom, Bernadotte's chief of staff, gave his eyewitness account:

In the Katamon quarter, we were held up by a Jewish Army type jeep placed in a road block and filled with men in Jewish Army uniforms. At the same moment, I saw an armed man coming from this jeep. I took little notice of this because I merely thought it was another checkpoint. However, he put a Tommy gun through the open window on my side of the car, and fired point blank at Count Bernadotte and Colonel [Andre] Serot. I also heard shots fired from other points, and there was considerable confusion. The Jewish liaison officer came running to our car and told Mr. Begley, who was at that time outside the car, to drive away as quickly as possible. In the meantime, the man was still firing.[181]

Clearly, the Zionists saw certain members of the British government, the United Nations, and the Arab armies as adversaries. However, the Zionists' and Israel's real adversary in Israel's War of Independence was the local Palestinian population. The Zionists wanted the land without the Palestinian population on it. Having the local indigenous population as the adversary for a war of independence is interesting from a language perspective.

Usually, wars of independence involve civilians fighting against their colonial power or ruler. That was what had happened ten years earlier in what is called the Palestine Arab Revolt of 1936–1939. Israel and the United States both had the same colonial power before their formation: Britain. So, if one were to fight a war of independence, would it not be against the colonial power?

But Israel's meaning of "War of Independence" is different from the meaning in the United States. In the United States, we call the war against Britain our War of Independence (also known as the American Revolutionary War). Our wars against the indigenous people are called the American Indian Wars.

Independence for the Americans was freedom from our oppressor, or ruling power. Independence for Israel was freedom from the indigenous Palestinian population. Unlike for the United States, independence for Israel today is still dependent on freedom from its indigenous population.

The "Defensive" "War of Independence"

Israelis and their supporters have traditionally referred to the conflict as the War of Independence, seeing it as a defensive war to prevent the destruction of the fledgling Jewish state in the face of overwhelming Arab aggression.

—*Matt Plen*[182]

As with any war, each side wants to describe the situation to its advantage. Greek tragedian Aeschylus (525–456 BCE), who lived through the Persian Wars, said, "In war, truth is the first casualty."[183] Language plays a large part in the framing of war, especially when it comes to blame.

Zionists call their War of Independence "defensive." But can the party causing the majority of the indigenous population to no longer be in their homes and villages make that claim? I have used a number of words, including the term *expulsion*, as a way to describe Palestinians who fled their homes before or during the Zionist conquest of their villages and towns. Other descriptions could include *banishment, deportation,* and *expatriation.* This book uses the term *expulsion* not to distinguish the exact conditions under which Palestinians fled or were forced to leave but because they were not allowed to return. Expelled people are forced to move, whether they are driven away at gunpoint or prevented from returning at gunpoint. Expulsion is forcing people who had no intention of living elsewhere to move against their will. If a man comes home to changed locks on the door, his wife has "kicked him out" even if no foot was involved.

The bottom line is that civilian expulsion, banishment, and expatriation are all offensive tactics. Preventing people from returning to their homes is only defensive in that it defends the ethnic cleansing of the land.

When Did the War of Independence Start?

The earlier quote from the Knesset website stated that the Israeli War of Independence started "on the eve of the establishment of the state (May 14, 1948)." It also stated that "the war broke out following the [Palestinian] rejection of the United Nations' Partition Plan, Resolution 181 of the General Assembly (November 29, 1947)."[184] So, which is it? Did the war start in mid-May 1948 or five and a half months earlier, in late November 1947?

Language is important in describing war. By defining the start of the war as May 1948, Zionists can frame the conflict as a defensive war, protecting Israel from invading Arab armies. If the war start date is set as November 1947, however, then the conflict was an offensive war of settler colonialists ethnically cleansing the land of its indigenous people. The Knesset describes it this way: The start was in May 14, 1948, but "Stage 1" was in November 1947.

Based on the hundreds of villages depopulated and the hundreds of thousands of refugees before mid-May 1948, we know the Knesset's use of the word *start* is Israelspeak rather than English. Therefore, here is the usage definition of the Israel word *start*:

START. *n.* A continuation.

START. *v.* To continue.
Example: The War of Independence *started* in mid-May 1948, more than five months after the beginning of the conflict.

Israel makes the claim that it was being defensive.[185] By starting the clock of its independence war after it had taken by force and ethnically purged most of Palestine, Israel could leave those non-defensive details out of its history and description of the war. Claiming that the war started at that point in time reminds me of the expression "It all started when he hit me back."

Britain had set the foundation for a Jewish homeland in Palestine in 1917. The United States in 1947 had coerced the passage of the UN Partition Plan, which allocated 56 percent of Palestine to a "Jewish state" with only a slight Jewish majority.[186] In fact, the Zionists, who (per records) had owned less than 6 percent of the land of Palestine

U.N. PARTITION PLAN VERSUS GREEN LINE

▢ U.N. Partition Plan Jewish majority state

▢ Additional Land Conquered by Israel 1948-9

▢ Land Bordered by the Green Line Conquered by Israel in 1967

Based on map by AnonMoos

Figure 8. Land taken by force in 1948 and 1967. [*Source: Based on map by AnonMoos*]

just five years earlier, ended up taking 77 percent of Palestine and expelling a majority of the indigenous population.[187]

One can argue that all parties were both aggressive and defensive. However, just as a thief might claim he punched the elderly lady in self-defense because she was hitting him with her cane, one cannot disregard the fact that the thief was trying to run away with her purse when she hit him. Similarly, one cannot disregard the fact that the Zionists have taken, and continue to take, the land from Palestinians by force and against the wishes of the majority population.

To translate WAR OF INDEPENDENCE from Israel into English, we would need to call it "Israel's War of Colonization, Ethnic Cleansing,*,[188] and Conquest."

US Language in the War

The United States government has historically assumed the role of intermediary in Israeli-Palestinian "peace" talks. Given such a role, I was hoping that the intermediary might take a factual, accurate, and balanced position. With that role as context, I wanted to see how the United States government documents this time in history.

Rather than call it the Israeli War of Independence, the United States Department of State describes it as the Arab-Israeli War of 1948.

---

* **ethnic cleansing.** *n.* According to Dictionary.com, "the elimination of an unwanted ethnic group or groups from a society, as by genocide or forced emigration."

According to our State Department, "the Arab-Israeli War of 1948 broke out when five Arab nations invaded territory in the former Palestinian mandate immediately following the announcement of the independence of the state of Israel on May 14, 1948."[189] Our government's historical account of the creation of Israel[190] leaves out the killing of Palestinians,[191] the expulsion of about 750,000 Palestinians,[192] and Israel's taking more land than the UN Partition Plan offered. It does not mention that for the five and a half months prior to May 14, 1948, Zionist militias had depopulated hundreds of Palestinian villages and towns and had invaded territory that even the UN had not allocated to a new Jewish-majority state. This State Department description of the formation of Israel would be similar to the Japanese describing American aggression toward Japan in World War II while never mentioning their attack on Pearl Harbor.

Unfortunately, the United States government is complicit in the misleading messages and description of history. The US government is fluent in Israel.

"Population Transfer"

There is no room for both peoples together in this country. We shall not achieve our goal of being an independent people with the Arabs in this small country.... And there is no other way but to transfer the Arabs from here to the neighboring countries, to transfer all of them; not one village, not one tribe should be left.[193]

The uprooting of the Arabs should be seen as a solution to the Arab question.[194]

—*Yosef Weitz*
Jewish National Fund director of land and forestry *

---

* The Jewish National Fund (JNF) was founded in 1901 to buy and develop land for Jewish settlement. It is responsible for planting hundreds of millions of trees and creating parks, many on top of demolished Arab villages that had been depopulated in 1948.

When Yosef Weitz referred to "transfer" in the foregoing epigraph, he was referring to the forcing out of a people. The term TRANSFER is a euphemism for "force out" or "expel." The first Weitz quote is from an entry in his diary made on December 20, 1940, seven years before the UN partition of Palestine and seven and a half years before the creation of Israel. He made that diary entry when Jews represented only about one-third of the population of Palestine.[195]

The concept of forcing out Palestinians from their homeland was not unanimous nor omnipresent. Nonetheless, it was a necessary requirement for changing the demographics from one that was overwhelmingly Arab to one with a Jewish majority. As more Zionists bought into the idea of Palestine becoming a Jewish state as opposed to it merely being a Jewish homeland, views on "population transfer" crystallized. Benny Morris describes the Zionist view of expulsion as follows:

> For many Zionists, beginning with Herzl, the only realistic solution lay in transfer. From 1880 to 1920, [however,] some entertained the prospect of Jews and Arabs coexisting in peace.

> Following the outbreak of 1936, no mainstream [Zionist] leader was able to conceive of future coexistence and peace without a clear physical separation between the two peoples—achievable only by way of transfer and expulsion. Publicly they all continued to speak of coexistence and to attribute the violence to a small minority of zealots and agitators. But this was merely a public pose, designed to calm the worried inhabitants and the troubled British: To speak out loud of inevitable bloodshed and expulsion could only have undermined both internal self-confidence and external support for their cause.[196]

Population transfers were not new in 1947/48. What was new was the world's condemnation of such action. On August 8, 1945, the United States, France, the United Kingdom, and the Union of Soviet

Socialist Republics (USSR) signed the Charter of the International Military Tribunal, also known as the London Agreement. This established the Nuremberg Tribunal "for the just and prompt trial and punishment of the major war criminals of the European Axis [Germany and Italy]."[197] This charter included everything from the constitution, jurisdiction, and general principles to the rules of judgment and sentencing. Twenty-two Germans were put on trial. The defendants were charged under Article 6 of the International Military Tribunal:

(a) **Crimes against peace:** namely, planning, preparation, initiation or waging of a war of aggression, or a war in violation of international treaties, agreements or assurances, or participation in a common plan or conspiracy for the accomplishment of any of the foregoing;

(b) **War crimes:** namely, violations of the laws or customs of war. Such violations shall include, but not be limited to, murder, ill-treatment or deportation to slave labor or for any other purpose of civilian population of or in occupied territory, murder or ill-treatment of prisoners of war or persons on the seas, killing of hostages, plunder of public or private property, wanton destruction of cities, towns or villages, or devastation not justified by military necessity;

(c) **Crimes against humanity:** namely, murder, extermination, enslavement, deportation, and other inhumane acts committed against any civilian population, before or during the war; or persecution on political, racial or religious grounds in execution of or in connection with any crime within the jurisdiction of the Tribunal, whether or not in violation of domestic law of the country where perpetrated.[198]

Twelve of the twenty-two tried were sentenced to death. Three were sentenced to life in prison, and four received prison terms from ten to twenty years. Three were acquitted.[199]

In mid-August 1947, India and Pakistan won their independence from Great Britain. The partition of the two states led to 10 million people migrating, which many consider the largest migration in history:

> As many as one million civilians died in the accompanying riots and local-level fighting, particularly in the western region of Punjab which was cut in two by the border."[200]

On November 21, 1947, the United Nations General Assembly adopted Resolution 177 (II) at its second session "in which it entrusted the formulation of the principles of international law recognized in the Charter of the Nürnberg* Tribunal and in the judgment of the Tribunal to the International Law Commission."[201]

The laws that had been used against the Nazis now applied to the world. They defined population transfer—or, as it is called in the charter, "deportation"—as both a war crime and a crime against humanity:

> *War crimes:* ... include ... deportation ... of civilian population of or in occupied territory, ... plunder of public or private property, wanton destruction of cities, towns or villages, or devastation not justified by military necessity.[202]

> *Crimes against humanity:* ... deportation, and other inhumane acts committed against any civilian population, before or during the war.[203]

The illegality of deportation and other abuse over a civilian population would later also be reflected in many forms, including Article 49 of the Fourth Geneva Convention and Articles 7 and 8 of the Rome Statute of the International Criminal Court.[204]

---

* Note that Nürnberg is spelled in different ways in this book. Some quoted sources use a German spelling (Nürnberg or Nuernberg), while others use an English spelling (Nuremberg).

Despite deportations being criminal, and history having shown the large number of casualties resulting from deportations (such as with India and Pakistan), many people have recommended, and continue to recommend, deportations for offensive and defensive reasons. Ethnic separation feeds racism rather than fights it; it creates an "us versus them" mentality. Forcing people to leave their homes does not achieve peace.

Eight days after the UN General Assembly passed Resolution 177 (II), defining these crimes, they passed Resolution 181: Palestine's Partition Plan. Theoretically, these two resolutions should not have been conflicting, because, as mentioned previously, Resolution 181 guaranteed "to all persons equal and non-discriminatory rights in civil, political, economic and religious matters and the enjoyment of human rights and fundamental freedoms,"[205] and Resolution 177 condemned crimes against humanity, including deportation. Learning this history of UN resolutions, I was not surprised to see the UN respond one year later, when the world faced the result of the "population transfer": refugees.

The Palestinian Refugee Problem

We must prevent at all costs their return. ... I will be for them not returning also after the war.

—David Ben-Gurion,
first Israeli prime minister,
Israeli cabinet meeting, June 16, 1948[206]

Refugees don't leave their homeland for greener pastures. Emigrants do. Refugees are forced to leave their land by terror, persecution and inhuman injustice.

—Brian Kelly [207]

The language of Israel also applies to the word *refugee*. On a number of occasions, I have heard people say that descendants of refugees are not refugees. I have also heard said that Palestinians are given preferential treatment by having their descendants considered as refugees. These narratives are promoted by Zionists in Israel and the United States. An August 4, 2018, *Times of Israel* article asserted the following:

> Uniquely, UNRWA grants refugee status to all descendants of Palestinians who left or fled Israel with the establishment of the state in 1948, swelling the number to an estimated five million at present, when the number of actual refugees from that conflict is estimated to be in the low tens of thousands. In peace talks, the Palestinian leadership has always demanded a "right of return" to Israel for these millions—an influx that, if accepted by Israel, would spell the end of Israel as a majority Jewish state.[208]

Whether or not children of refugees are also considered refugees is pivotal. As the article points out, that difference in definition significantly affects the number of people who have a right to return. However, the claim by Zionists that children of refugees are not refugees is curious and hypocritical. If children of so-called refugees are themselves not refugees, then how can Jews claim a right to return to Israel? The Jews wanting to "return" were not alive thousands of years ago.

The United Nations is clear on this subject, and it highlights the Israelspeak that we are told:

> Under international law and the principle of family unity, the children of refugees and their descendants are also considered refugees until a durable solution is found. Both UNRWA [the United Nations Relief and Works Agency for Palestine Refugees in the Near East, formed in 1949] and UNHCR [the United Nations High Commissioner for Refugees, the UN agency for other refugees, formed in 1950] recognize descendants as refugees on this

basis, a practice that has been widely accepted by the international community, including both donors and refugee hosting countries.

Palestine refugees are not distinct from other protracted refugee situations such as those from Afghanistan or Somalia, where there are multiple generations of refugees, considered by UNHCR as refugees and supported as such. Protracted refugee situations are the result of the failure to find political solutions to their underlying political crises.[209]

The number of Palestinian refugees from the Zionists' expulsion was so high that as of 2014, the original refugees and their descendants still represented the largest number of refugees worldwide.[210] As of 2019, only the Syrian civil war has led to a higher number of refugees.[211] There are over 5 million Palestinian refugees today; the longest-lasting unresolved refugee situation since the UN's inception.

Some claim that expulsion was not official Israeli policy. Others claim that Israel's founders did not anticipate nor plan for the mass exodus of Palestinians. Although there were Israelis who disagreed with the expulsion policy, Israel continues to block the return of the Palestinian refugees. This blockage and violation of the Palestinian Right of Return makes Israel responsible for the refugee problem. Israel cannot blame any rogue Zionist militias for expelling Palestinians; it also cannot claim that Palestinians voluntarily abandoned their land, since it is Israel that has been restricting the refugees' return for more than seventy years.

According to a common myth, the Palestinians were told to leave their homes via radio broadcasts by Arab leaders. These supposed broadcasts told Palestinians that the Arab armies would wipe out the Zionists, and then Palestinians could return home. Zionists claim that people voluntarily following those guidelines should not be considered refugees. This concept of Palestinian land renunciation is Israelspeak for two fundamental reasons:

First, the logic is faulty. Since when is someone who is leaving his or her home—whether to go to work or to the grocery store, or to flee in response to a natural disaster or even war—giving away property to any party coming to take it?

Some claim that the property was abandoned. One could make that argument if those who left had the freedom to return to their property but chose not to. However, that argument is invalid because refugees have been trying to return since before Israel declared itself a state. The land was taken by force.

Merriam-Webster defines "to steal" as follows:

> **steal.** *v.* To take the property of another wrongfully and especially as a habitual or regular practice.[212]

It is hard to describe Israel's taking of Palestinian land by force, blocking the refugees from returning, followed by confiscating their homes other than as Merriam-Webster describes the verb "to steal."

The United States is arguing with Russia because of its 2014 annexation of Crimea. How can we claim that Russia is committing a crime of taking the Ukrainian peninsula by force when we are OK with Israel having done much worse. Besides, Russia may now rule the land of Crimea, but it has not expelled a majority of the Crimean population.

There is a second reason that the radio broadcasts telling Palestinians to leave is Israelspeak. The story of those broadcasts is a generalized, misleading myth. Here is how Israeli historian Benny Morris answered a related question in 2014:

> There is no basis for the allegation that there were radio broadcasts calling on the Arabs to leave Palestine—not by their own leaders and not by the Arab leaders from outside. ... There simply were no such broadcasts. How do we know this? Because the Haganah intelligence service monitored on a daily basis the radio broadcasts from the Arab world and issued ... a circular saying what was broadcast in the Arab radio stations hour by hour, day by day. ... And you can go over these transcripts, the monitored transcripts, and you won't find anybody saying, "Leave"—no Arab leader and no local Arab leader. There were places inside Palestine—this has nothing to do with radio broadcasts—in which Arab leaders or military commanders

told Arabs to leave or advised them to leave. This happened in Haifa on the twenty-second of April. The local leadership remaining in the town said, "We are going to leave. We won't surrender." ...

What you do find in the Israeli intelligence material, the Haganah intelligence material, is contrary to what the Israeli propaganda leaders said, in the early days of May 1948, just before the pan-Arab invasion. You find Haganah intelligence reports saying that Arab radio stations were telling, or ordering, the Arabs in Palestine to stay put, or if they had already left to go back to their homes. And if they didn't, they would be punished, and their houses would be confiscated or blown up by the Arab armies once they arrived.

Abdullah, king of Jordan, made one of these broadcasts. ... Qawuqji—Fawzi al-Qawuqji, being head of the Arab volunteer army which helped the Palestinians before the Arab states armies invaded—and Abdullah, the king of Jordan, both issued statements "Stay in place, or go back to your places. Do not leave. You will be punished if you leave." So, it's completely contrary.[213]

But even if local officials had recommended that Palestinians leave to avoid being killed—as had been done in some communities, especially for women, children, and the elderly—why would that matter? Leaving one's property for safety does not imply or mean that one forgoes the rights to that property. It is interesting to observe how the radio myth has been used to create an illusion that leaving for safety reasons is equivalent to forfeiting one's land. The narrative created by the radio myth is used to justify the taking of land, or as Merriam-Webster defines it: *stealing*.

Jewish Expulsions from Arab Countries

Pro-Israel Zionists respond to the expulsion of Palestinians with the argument that Jews were also expelled from Arab countries.

The implied narrative is that those two expulsions are connected, that they are part of the same war. This narrative implies that any expulsion of Jews from other countries was a rationalization for the expulsion of the Palestinians. These Zionists acknowledge that— yes—around 750,000 Palestinians were forced off their lands, but they retort that so were around 700,000 Jews from Arab countries. That line of thinking has some flaws:

First, the overwhelming majority of the Jewish emigration from Arab countries was after Israel's Declaration of Independence and therefore cannot be claimed as a rationalization for the prior expulsion of hundreds of thousands of Palestinians. The Jewish Virtual Library reports that total immigration to Israel was as follows:[214]

Jewish Immigrants to Israel	From Africa	From Asia
1948 before independence	906	1,144
1948 after independence	8,192	4,739
1949 through 1951	85,759	232,613
Peak year and number of Jewish immigrants in that year	**1956**: 45,284	**1951**: 103,396

The peak Jewish immigration from Asia was in 1951, two years after the armistice agreements between Arab states and Israel, three years after Israel's formation. The peak immigration from Africa was in 1956, eight years after the creation of the state of Israel.*,[215] Rationalizing the expulsion of Palestinians before 1949 based on what Arab countries did years later is like a burglar justifying breaking into your house and stealing your TV because you were shooting at him as he ran away with your TV.

Second, this representation of an Arab world evicting Jews is not fully representative of the situation. To imply that the Arab countries were all hostile to Jews is inaccurate. Morocco, the country from which 300,000 of the 700,000 Jews are understood

---

* Here is a brief overview of the emigration of Jews from various Arab countries: Algeria (1961–1962), Egypt (1948–1967), Iraq (1950–1951), Morocco (1948– 1987), Syria (1948-1956), Tunisia (after 1956), and Yemen (1948–1949).

to have emigrated from,[*,216] was a country that during World War II protected Jews. King Mohammed V of Morocco, under French rule, denied the Nazi-controlled French Vichy government the internment of Moroccan Jews on the grounds that the entire Moroccan population was Jewish by solidarity and therefore that all Moroccans should be interned.[217] After its independence in 1956, Morocco imposed an anti-emigration law and blocked emigration from 1956 to 1961, preventing Jews from leaving Morocco.[218] According to the Jewish Virtual Library, "in 1963, emigration resumed, allowing more than 100,000 Moroccan Jews to reach Israel."[219] Note that this is fifteen years after Israel was created and Palestinians had been displaced.

An Al-Jazeera article explained what drove the Jewish exodus from Morocco:

> Mossad, the Israeli intelligence agency, played a key role in convincing thousands of Moroccan Jews that they were in danger and covertly facilitated their departure.

> According to Fanny Mergui, a political activist and Moroccan Jew returnee, the community felt "very threatened." She says "Zionist propaganda was very intense."[220]

The film *They Were Promised the Sea: Arab Jews between Homeland and Promised Land* by Jewish film director Kathy Wazana[221] is a documentary of the director's return to Morocco to interview remaining Jews; it includes visits with communities where Jews used to live and interviews with Moroccan Jews now in Israel. The people interviewed share the pressure exerted on their families by representatives of Israel, promising them homes and a better life to get them to move to Israel.

---

* The Jewish Virtual Library shows a total immigration to Israel between 1948 and 2015 from the following countries: Morocco, Algeria, and Tunisia: 361,339; Iraq: 131,013; Iran: 80,863; Yemen: 51,518; Egypt and Sudan: 37,953; Libya: 36,088; Syria: 10,239—for a total of 709,013 for the sixty-eight-year period.

The Jewish *Telegraphic Agency* described the situation:

> "All our Jewish subjects who want to leave the country, will be allowed to do so without any restrictions," the Moroccan ruler was reported to have told the Jewish delegation. However, an aide to Mohammed made it clear later to the delegation that "foreign" [Israeli] organizations would not be allowed to operate in Morocco either to assist the emigrants or to propagandize emigration.[222]

How can one claim that the Jewish emigration from these Arab countries was all expulsion when it was illegal to emigrate from Morocco for five years? How can one claim that the Moroccan emigration in the 1960s of another 100,000 Jews to Israel justified Zionist and Israeli actions in 1947–1949?

And Morocco was not the only example of Arab countries where Israel recruited Jews to come to Israel. Another example of Jews being recruited was Yemen. There had been attacks on Jewish communities in Aden after the UN Partition Plan. Israel organized for just under 50,000 Yemenite Jews to fly into Israel in 1949 as part of an Israeli initiative known as Operation Magic Carpet.[223]

The argument that Palestinians were expelled makes sense, based on the evidence: No country recruited Palestinians, and 15,000 Palestinians were killed in an environment of terror. Hundreds of villages were either destroyed or repopulated with Zionists. Israel passed multiple laws to prevent the return of Palestinians and to take their property. To this day, Israel blocks the overwhelming majority of Palestinians from living in their homeland.

When we review the argument that Jews were expelled as the Palestinians were, the evidence is less convincing. Yes, there were expulsions of Jews from Arab countries, but again, the largest single group of Jewish emigrants came from Morocco. And in the case of Morocco, I have yet to run across the documentation of systematic killing related to the emigration of the hundreds of thousands of Jews from Morocco. Furthermore, Morocco passed a law to do the opposite of the Israeli laws: a law to prevent, rather than promote, emigration, a law that was in force between 1956 and 1961. Also in the case of Morocco, some Jews did choose and were able to return to Morocco. That is why the Jewish emigrants are not considered refugees.

There is a third and much more important flaw with the rationalization of the expulsion of Palestinians based on the expulsion of Jews from Arab countries: The narrative implies that Palestinians were responsible for these Jewish migrations. Since when does a crime against one person, or people, justify a crime against another? This line of thinking makes the Palestinians victims of two crimes: (1) the expulsion from their land, and (2) blame for something they did not do.

Germany and Iraq committed immoral and racist acts against Jews. Therefore, Germany and Iraq ought to be the ones to take the blame and suffer the consequences—not the Palestinians, who were not involved. The Arab countries that did expel Jews made a mistake by doing so. Those expelled Jews, like expelled Palestinians, should pursue their own Right of Return to those countries if that is what they want. It is bad enough that people justify crimes based on revenge against the original perpetrator. But when victims of a crime (say, Jews in the German Holocaust) commit another crime against an unrelated party (Palestinians in the Nakba), then those original victims have themselves become criminals.

Finally, we need to face another unspoken narrative of the Jewish expulsions from Arab countries: the notion that Jews and Arabs can't get along and that Jews can't be safe in Arab countries. History has shown that Jewish populations have lived in peace in Arab countries for centuries. Jews lived with Christians and Muslims in Palestine for four hundred years under Ottoman rule—during the same centuries that Jewish populations in Christian Europe were being discriminated against, expelled, attacked, and ultimately annihilated. Jews have lived peacefully with Arab Israeli citizens for the past seventy-plus years.

The Palestinians were not expelled because Arab countries expelled Jews. On the contrary, Jews were unfortunately expelled by some Arab countries after, and because of, what Israel had done to the

Palestinians. Palestinians were not at fault for any Jewish exodus from Arab countries; Israel was. The exodus-of-Jews argument taught me how the Israel language frames situations completely backward; the victim is the aggressor, and the aggressor is the victim.

"Defensive Wars"

In June 1967 we again had a choice. The Egyptian army concentrations in the Sinai approaches do not prove that Nasser was really about to attack us. We must be honest with ourselves. We decided to attack him.

This was a war of self-defence in the noblest sense of the term. The government of national unity then established decided unanimously: We will take the initiative and attack the enemy, drive him back, and thus assure the security of Israel and the future of the nation.

We did not do this for lack of an alternative. We could have gone on waiting. We could have sent the army home. Who knows if there would have been an attack against us? There is no proof of it. There are several arguments to the contrary.

—Prime Minister Menachem Begin,
addressing the National Defense College, August 8, 1982[224]

Israel's history has been fraught with conflict since even before its founding, and Israel has been on the *defensive* throughout its history. So I had been taught. Israel's "War of Independence" by definition was *defensive* because "independence" entails defending oneself from oppression. Similarly, I had been taught that Israel had to defend itself against its Arab neighbors in 1967. The Israel Defense Forces spokesman stated the following on June 5, 1967:

From the early morning hours today, fierce battles are being fought on the southern front between Egyptian air and armored forces—which have moved toward Israel—and [Israeli] forces that went out to stop them.[225]

Then I heard Miko Peled speak. He is an Israeli author, writer, speaker, and human rights activist. I heard him share personal experiences and family stories of solidarity for Palestinian human rights. His sister is also a peace activist despite having lost a daughter to a Palestinian suicide bomber in 1997. Their father was Major General Matityahu "Matti" Peled, who fought as an officer in Israel's War of Independence in 1948 and was an Israeli general during the 1967 Six-Day War. Miko Peled mentioned that Israel was the aggressor rather than being on the defensive in that war; in fact, his father had insisted on initiating attack.[226]

Hearing this perspective, which was different from what I had learned, I researched some of Israel's major conflicts, primarily the 1967 Six-Day War and the recent wars with Gaza. I wanted to better understand if Israel and its Zionists were primarily the aggressor or the victim; I wanted to know if *defensive* was an English or an Israel word.

Defense denotes when the other side is on the *offense*. Yet Israel claims to have been on the "defense" in 1967 during the Six-Day War, even though it was the first to attack. Israel was on the "defense" as it destroyed more than 90 percent of the Egyptian air force's planes while they were on the ground. Israel, then in a "defensive" move, invaded and captured Egyptian territory. With no Egyptian air defense (note the word *defense*), Israel invaded and took control of Gaza and the Sinai. Egypt's casualties were more than 11,000. Jordan lost 6,000 and Syria 1,000. Israel suffered 700 casualties.[227] Israel more than doubled its land area in those six days.

There *were* wars where Israel was defensive. The 1973 Yom Kippur War (also called the October War) was such a war, in that Israel's neighbors were the first to attack. Even so, "defensiveness" may not be completely black and white. In the case of the Yom Kippur War, we need to keep in mind the context of the parties who attacked Israel that October; both Egypt and Syria, who initiated that war, had lost land to Israel six years earlier, in the 1967 Six-Day War.

We could argue that Egypt and Syria were defensive in their efforts to reclaim the land that had been taken from them, land that the United Nations had resolved as having been taken illegally by Israel. We could claim that they were defensive up to the point that they took more land than they had previously lost.

Israel has had a number of wars against Lebanon. But who were they really fighting against? In 1982 the main Israeli target was the Palestine Liberation Organization (PLO), composed of Palestinian refugees who had established themselves in refugee camps in southern Lebanon. Later wars with Lebanon were against Hezbollah, which had been founded in response to Israel's earlier invasion of Lebanon.

Often claims of being "defensive" are made, considering exclusively a single incident. Instead, we need to determine if a battle or war is defensive based on the context of that conflict: Most of the wars Israel has waged with its neighbors cannot be viewed out of the context of the creation of the state of Israel and the resulting Nakba. Had Palestinian refugees been allowed to return and been given equal citizenship, then there would not have been a PLO. Without the PLO there would not have been an invasion of Lebanon. Without an invasion of Lebanon, there would not have been Hezbollah.

"Defensive" Summary

Once I had an understanding of the history, I reevaluated the Zionist argument that their movement and Israel were acting defensively:

- Was convincing Britain in 1917 to make a Jewish homeland on an overwhelmingly Arab land, against the wishes of the population, defensive?

- Was the Zionist assassination of Lord Moyne, who stood for "the rights of all peoples to choose the form of Government under which they will live,"[228] and giving his assassins heroes' burials defensive?

- Was lobbying the world powers, including the United States and Britain, to cut the land into a jigsaw puzzle (the 1947 UN Partition Plan) to give the minority population maximum control of the land defensive?

- Was taking land by force against the will of the majority of the population defensive?

- Was taking land by force beyond the UN Partition Plan defensive?

- Were terrorism and massacres against civilian populations, causing them to flee, defensive tactics?

- Was the Zionist assassination of Count Bernadotte, the UN peace mediator, defensive?

- Was the demolition of Palestinian villages after they were emptied defensive?

- Was, and is, the violation of international law by blocking refugees' return to their land defensive?

- Was being the first to attack in the 1967 Six-Day War defensive?

- Was the more than doubling the land area from the Six-Day War defensive?

To summarize: In English, the taking of land by force and expelling a majority of the population is offensive, not defensive. Here again, the Israel language frames the situation in such a way as to create the illusion that the opposite of the situation is reality.

Here I find it useful to consider a couple of Israel usage definitions:

WAR OF INDEPENDENCE. *n.* An organized, financed, and armed offensive, primarily by relatively recent Jewish immigrants from foreign lands, against the indigenous population. The Zionist militias and Israeli forces purged the land of a majority of its non-Jewish inhabitants. Unlike the US, Israel's major opponent in its "War of Independence" was not its colonial power.

DEFENSIVE. *adj.* Descriptive of a comprehensive international campaign and lobbying effort to have world powers draw borders in such a way as to give a minority population the majority of the land. The campaign and effort is followed by an armed seizure of the land, the forcible expulsion of its civilian indigenous population, the destruction of their villages and towns, the confiscation of their property, and the blocking and killing of returning refugees—all in violation of international law. Racist local laws prevent the remaining indigenous majority population from ever becoming equal citizens or having proportionate political power.

The more that we hear a message, the more we believe the message to be true.[229] Therefore, if we don't question arguments, and we hear them repeated time and again, then we are likely to believe them. But once we think about them, shine a light on them, test them, and find that their logic fails, then they lose their strength over us. I hope this book on learning to speak Israel will help you more easily see which arguments are faulty and illogical, which terms are Orwellian and are used to promote hatred and theft.

It is worth stepping back and reviewing some of the Israel vocabulary and messaging we have learned. The fact that Palestinian refugees exist is a problem for the Israel language; it contradicts fundamental Israel mythology. If there are refugees, there once had to be people residing in the land that is now called Israel. The myth that there is no such thing as a Palestinian people is also debunked by the existence of Palestinian refugees. If there once were Palestinians on the land, then the myth of "a land without a people" also collapses.

The Israel language is a house of cards, which stands only when one does not see the reality of the situation. The real problems are described by such terms as *refugee*, *Right of Return*, and *occupation*. The Israel language cards cover those real cards, making them harder to see. But when we shine a light on and pull the real cards, such as the *refugee* card in this case, the Israel cards start toppling. Pulling the *refugee* card causes the *land without a people* card to topple.

The term *War of Independence* is exposed as misleading once we learn that the war was not against the colonial power but instead against the majority indigenous people. The fact that most of the indigenous population became refugees means that the term *War of Colonization, Ethnic Cleansing, and Conquest* would have been more accurate. If a majority of the indigenous population were ethnically cleansed from the land and are still refugees today, then the "defensive" myth fails, and with it the *defensive* card falls. The "equality" myth dissolves because Palestinians are not allowed to return, even though Jews are. More of the Israel-messaging house of cards collapses.

The United States Is Not Defensive

If Israel is an aggressive, ethnic-cleansing (and therefore racist) entity that stole and continues to steal land by force, then how does it get American popular support? Israel gets American support through propaganda written in a special language that looks like American English. It gets support with a language that hides reality. *Israel is the language that propagates these irrational myths of "offense" and "defense."*

The repercussions of Americans misunderstanding this situation are huge. This issue significantly affects our pocketbooks. The Israel/Palestine issue affects everything from US foreign aid to military spending for the "war on terror." It also affects American lives lost in combat, our reputation in the world, and the integrity of our core values. Our misunderstanding of this issue affects people throughout the world.

Concluding that the creation of the state of Israel and its War of Independence were offensive rather than defensive means that the United States has been supporting the aggressor. The people of the region know the US's role; they hear it in their press, and they see it on the ground. They lost their land, and they know that the US is behind the occupier. They see our vetoes in the UN Security Council when we are unwilling to condemn the West Bank barrier being built on their land. They experience the checkpoints daily, knowing that the US supports Israel militarily and with intelligence. They see American companies taking part in the oppression—from American computer systems that manage the permits they need to visit their

117

siblings to American bulldozers that are used to demolish their homes. Palestinians see when prominent nonviolent Palestinians are blocked from entering the United States, prevented from speaking here, and prevented from visiting their American children and grandchildren. One prominent Palestinian was even been blocked from attending his daughter's wedding in the United States.[230]

The problem is that Americans wonder why we are disliked and even attacked, as we were on 9/11. Americans think that our support for Israel is defensive, when in fact it is offensive. Our military, financial, and political support of Israel's occupation, blockade, and violations of human rights makes us accomplices to the offensive actions.

7

Stepping Back: Why Is Israel Different?

At this point in my Israel "coursework," I had become aware of the deceptive Israel language. And although all governments mislead and even lie, there are several ways the Israel deception and the way the deception is sustained are different:

Difference 1. **The deception is protected by accusing Israel critics of being racist.**

When I criticize my government's policies, I am not automatically accused of being racist. Israel supporters and even our Department of State now include criticism of Israel as part of their definition of anti-Semitism. Even peace and human rights organizations, such as Amnesty International[231] and the Quaker organization American Friends Service Committee (AFSC)[*,232] have been accused of being anti-Semitic.[233]

Israel is different because people and organizations that stand for equality are accused of racism (against Jews). With Israel, one is accused of racism because one takes a stand *against* racism.

---

* The AFSC was awarded the 1947 Nobel Peace Prize for helping feed starving children during and after the two world wars "without regard to nationality or race."

The accusation of being racist because one opposes racism is not the only unique aspect to Israel's racism accusation. I know of no other country for which one is accused of being racist by merely criticizing its policies. For example, I have never heard of anyone being accused of racism for criticizing Saudi Arabia, China, or the Palestinian Authority.

Difference 2. The deception is protected by aggressively bullying its whistleblowers, critics of Israel's policies and actions.

Although accusing someone of being racist is a form of bullying, the bullying against Israel critics is more aggressive than that of critics of other countries. This bullying has been aggressive to the point where critics have lost their jobs and careers, from politicians such as Paul Findley to professors such as Norman Finkelstein. Many, including American Jews who criticize Israeli policies, have been banned from entering the state of Israel.

Some bullying efforts have included death threats. Even worse, critics have been found dead, such as Alex Odeh, a Palestinian Christian anti-discrimination activist who was assassinated in his office in California.[234] And there is Riad Hamad, who was reported in 2008 to have committed suicide. He was found floating in Lady Bird Lake in Austin, Texas. According to the *Austin Chronicle*, "Hamad's eyes were covered in duct tape, his legs and his hands also bound."[235]

Why such brutal repercussions against someone who is merely speaking out against a foreign government's actions? When was the last time we heard about an American losing a job or getting killed in the United States for criticizing even one of the brutal regimes of the world? Many Americans criticize such countries as Iran, Cuba, Russia, North Korea, and Syria without suffering such fierce consequences. So why would supporters of a democratic ally of the United States partake in such actions? Isn't healthy debate what makes a democracy stronger?

Difference 3. We are deceived into believing that Jews, because they are Jews, support Israel—in effect, implying that all Jews support

ethnic discrimination. **Even stranger, this narrative comes to us from the people who claim to stand for them.**

The Israel deception misleads us into believing we are supporting Jews by supporting Israel when in fact taking that position merely debases Jews as inherently racist. How are we helping Jewish people by supporting tyranny in their name? The Jewish organization If Not Now highlights on their website how support for Israel is really anti-Jewish:

> The failed Jewish establishment has chosen the interest of the Israeli government over those of our own community. ... And, as we fight with others for an America for all of us, we know that ethos must extend abroad—with American Jews helping lead the fight. We must be able to look back and know that we were on the side of justice and freedom: not just for Americans but for all Israelis and Palestinians as well.[236]

Difference 4. **Israel deceptions are corrupting American values.**

We are led into compromising our values and honor when we support Israel because we, by default, are also supporting the discrimination that this ethnic country requires. We compromise, and therefore corrupt, our claims to the values of equality, freedom, and human rights. The Declaration of Independence states:

> We hold these truths to be self-evident, that all men [and women] are created equal, that they are endowed by their Creator with certain unalienable Rights, that among these are Life, Liberty and the pursuit of Happiness.[237]

Yet when we support a country that violates every truth listed in that declaration sentence, we are no longer who we claim to be.

If we want the United States to be a beacon of leadership and hope for the world, a moral example to others, then our actions need to reflect the values of justice, equality, democracy, and freedom. We would benefit by heeding the advice of the late Senator John McCain:

> I want to urge Americans for as long as I can to remember that this shared devotion to human rights is our truest heritage and our most important loyalty.[238]

If we allow our freedoms of speech, the press, and assembly to be compromised and do not stand for human rights, then what do we have to be proud of?

Difference 5. Israel supporters are corrupting our politicians.

I hear about Russia's attempts to affect our elections, but Russia doesn't have the lobbying organization that Israel has. Republican and Democratic presidential candidates do not make speeches and pledge support in front of the Russian lobby as they do in front of AIPAC (the American Israel Public Affairs Committee). American legislators across the country have passed anti-BDS bills that protect Israel by limiting Americans' freedom of speech. They are, in effect, supporting a foreign country rather than Americans.

Our politicians are happy to take campaign contributions from pro-Israel donors and repeat the Israeli deception. To Israel supporters' credit, Americans are going along, and we are letting ourselves be taken. We are falling for, and repeating, their lies. As a result, our support for this foreign country is bringing out our worst side: racism rather than equality, support for tyranny rather than for self-determination, corruption rather than transparency, and hypocrisy rather than integrity.

Difference 6. Israel supporters are eroding our constitutional rights.

The McCarthy era of the 1950s suppressed and punished speech about communism; today speech criticizing Israel's racist policies is suppressed and punished. The Center for Constitutional Rights and Palestine Legal issued a report in September 2015 documenting

> 300 incidents of [free speech] suppression; 85% of those incidents targeted students and professors, on a total of more than 65 US college campuses. This trend has significant implications for both the First Amendment and democratic principles like academic freedom, not to mention the mission of higher education to help develop critical thinking.[239]

Israel is different in that its supporters are using the deception to lobby for curbing our constitutional rights. I know of no other country or its supporters that have been able to pass legislation in a majority of our state legislatures to limit our freedom of speech.

***Difference 7.* The Israel deception is existential; its messaging is a house of cards.**

Unlike certain myths about the United States or other countries, where debunking a single myth does not cause the whole story of the country to come crashing down, that is the case with Israel. The more closely I examined and unpacked the messaging that was being promoted by the pro-Israel groups and media, the more I realized that the myths and deception are interrelated. The more I looked at the messaging closely, the more I noticed that the messages depended on one another to be believable—and therefore, if any one of them fell, then the whole deceptive story started to collapse.

If the "War of Independence" was not "defensive," then Jews were the aggressors rather than the "victims." If the land was not given to the Zionists, then they stole it. If Israel is a Jewish-majority state because it expelled the majority of its indigenous population, then how can we rightfully call it a "Jewish state" or "democratic"? If Israel depends on a violent occupation and blockade in order to keep it Jewish, then Israel is not really safe for Jews long term.

When the occupation, blockade, and requirement of human rights violations are needed to merely support Israel's identity, Israel's claim to want peace is pure deception.

Israel supporters try to stifle the public conversation because Israel's myths are so vulnerable.

I also realized that Israel's mythology and impunity depend on American support. If the United States condemned, rather than hid, Israel's occupation, blockade, racism, and other human rights violations, then the mirage of Israel being a Western, civilized, and progressive society would collapse. *Why else would Zionists go to such extremes to make criticism of Israeli actions painful? Why else would they accuse Israel critics of racism, even when those critics are standing for equality?* Israel cannot afford the truth to be openly visible; everyone would realize that the emperor (Israel) has no clothes and that Americans are being taken advantage of.

What about Palestinian Crimes?

This book places a majority of the responsibility for the Israel/Palestine conflict on Israeli policies. Zionist friends seem frustrated when I consistently focus on Israeli policies and actions rather than on Palestinian ones. I was asked recently whether I thought Palestinians had also made mistakes. Are they not to blame and should they not be held responsible for today's conflict as well? How about some balance?

Individual Palestinians and Palestinian groups such as Hamas have indeed committed crimes. But the core of the issue is not who committed the relatively small crimes, the issue is who is responsible for the inequality, the violation of human rights, and the perpetration of the overarching major crimes.

We can use the United States civil rights history as an analogy. Rosa Parks did violate the law by not giving up her seat on the bus; the real problem was that the law was racist. We can condemn African Americans who committed violent crimes against Whites during the first two hundred years of our country's history, but we cannot ignore the systematic injustice of our society. The injustices of slavery cannot be rationalized by a crime committed by a slave. Nothing can defend the abuse supported by Jim Crow laws in the trial of Emmett Till's murderers. No individual or group of African American crimes can justify the White racist legal system of the time. When reviewing the early history of the United States, we have to hold Whites as the group overwhelmingly responsible for the inequality of the times.

Similarly, condemnation of murders by Palestinians against Israeli civilians is warranted. But one cannot fall into the trap of justifying systematic racism as the justifiable response to crimes caused by that same systematic racism. ***We should condemn all racism rather than justify it.*** In reality, Palestinians don't have self-determination or authority, equality, or enjoyment of their human rights; therefore, they have a lot less accountability.

Finally, when evaluating Palestinian actions, we need to take context into account. ***Resisting and fighting an invading or occupying military is legitimate;*** it is also legal under international law. Was it legitimate for the French to resist German occupation, including derailing trains and killing German officers, during World War II? Was it legitimate for Tibetans to resist the Chinese invasion? Resisting occupation is standing for self-determination. If we did not believe in self-determination, then how can we justify the legitimacy of our Revolutionary War. We cannot change the rules just for Palestinians.

8

"The Only Democracy in the Middle East"

Our relationship with the only democracy in the Middle East is crucial to the security of both our nations and the president [President Donald Trump] looks forward to discussing continuous strategic, technological, military and intelligence cooperation with the prime minister.

—*White House Press Secretary Sean Spicer,*[240]
January 30, 2017

For years I have heard that Israel is the only democracy in the Middle East. Israel supporters repeat this messaging regularly, as do American politicians and news commentators. I didn't really think about this much until 2003, right after our invasion of Iraq. I was preparing a presentation for a breakfast meeting, and as part of that presentation, I put together a questionnaire, a tool for engaging the audience while bringing out regional facts. It covered a number of topics related to Iraq and our "war on terror," from the nationalities of the 9/11 hijackers to information about the largest oil-producing countries in the world.

Because President George W. Bush and his staff had told us that one reason we were going to invade Iraq was to spread democracy,[241]

I included a question about governments of the Middle East. While looking up the countries of the Middle East in the *CIA World Factbook*, I learned a lot about those governments.

Democracy versus Republic

I noticed that the *CIA World Factbook* described Israel as a "parliamentary democracy."[242] No big surprise. I then moved up the Mediterranean coast and looked up Lebanon's government: "parliamentary republic," with a constitution adopted on May 23, 1926.[243] That caught me by surprise. It was not that Lebanon was a republic that surprised me; it was that only then did I connect that our American government was a republic, not a democracy.

I looked up the United States in the *CIA World Factbook* and saw that it described our government as a "constitutional federal republic."[244] Then I looked up Turkey: a "presidential republic," with a constitution most recently ratified on November 9, 1982.[245] Even the much-criticized government of Iran calls itself an Islamic republic (the *CIA World Factbook* uses the term *theocratic republic*); it has an elected president and a parliament (a "consultative assembly").[246]

So, I then looked up the difference between a democracy and a republic:

> The key difference between a **democracy** and a **republic** lies in the limits placed on government by the law, which has implications for minority rights. Both forms of government tend to use a *representational system*—i.e., citizens vote to elect politicians to *represent* their interests and form the government. In a republic, a constitution or charter of rights protects certain inalienable rights that cannot be taken away by the government, even if it has been elected by a majority of voters. In a "pure democracy," the majority is not restrained in this way and can impose its will on the minority.[247]

It further states:

> A republic is similar to a representative democracy except it has a written constitution of basic rights that protect the minority from being completely unrepresented or abused by the majority.[248]

Note that by *republic*, we are referring to a form of government with a constitution as distinct from a political ideology.

As Americans, we greatly value our Constitution; we regularly refer to our freedom of speech, our freedom of religion, and our other rights. Those rights come from a constitution, not from a pure democracy. A republic or a constitutional democracy, unlike a pure democracy, is not about what the majority can do but instead about what it cannot do. In a republic the majority cannot violate the rights of the minority, rights protected in its constitution. Based on these distinctions, *a democracy is a worse form of government than a republic.*

People often say, "the only democracy in the Middle East" as if it were a good attribute. And although I suspect Americans would prefer a democracy over a kingdom or a dictatorship, we consider a democracy inferior to a representative government with a constitution. The Israel propaganda had worked on me: I had thought that being "the only democracy in the Middle East" was a good thing.

So, why do Americans and Israeli politicians put so much emphasis on Israel being the only democracy in the Middle East when a republic is better? Because it generates American sympathy toward Israel. If we consider ourselves ardent supporters of democracy and here is the poor lone country standing for democracy, then we should be there to support it.

Calling a government a "democracy" is a clever and sneaky way to make a government that is less like ours look more like ours. However, we really value our constitution, the amendments to it, and the rights that come with them. Israel does not have a constitution; it has only what it calls "Basic Laws," and some of those actually discriminate against its minority population.

I wanted to test my theory about the messaging of "the only democracy in the Middle East." I wanted to know if the narrative created by that expression was purely about democracy or if, in addition, it created an unspoken false narrative of Israel being the only country in the Middle East with a government like the one we have in the United States. To perform the test, I did not ask the breakfast meeting which state in the Middle East was the only democracy. Instead, I asked which country has a form of government that most closely resembles that of the US form of government. Everyone responded with the incorrect answer: Israel. Israelspeak had worked: The members of the group had subconsciously created the narrative that the United States was a democracy, even though they consciously knew it to be a republic.

The whole group had been bamboozled, as I had been. I thought back to a propaganda seminar I had attended and how the professor had distinguished between fact, context, and narrative and how we as human beings put the most emphasis on narrative. The *fact* in this case was true: Israel calls itself a democracy. The *context* was the Middle East, where there are kingdoms and totalitarian rulers. But the group had been swayed into creating the unspoken *narrative* that Israel is the only one like us.

No one ever specifically claimed that the Israeli government most resembles ours. No one hid that Lebanon, Turkey,* and Iran have representative governments. The narrative of Israel's government being most like ours had never been stated. It was a narrative that we each subconsciously created—and for that reason, it had more power over each of us. The phrase had worked. By stating that Israel was a democracy rather than a republic, the narrative had literally asserted that Israel was less like us than like some of its neighbors, yet we had thought Israel was more like us. That exercise reinforced to me the power of the Israel language.

So in reality, the statement "Israel is the only democracy in the Middle East" is a red herring, a diversion. It does not tell us much.

---

* Turkey's government in 2003, when I prepared my presentation at the breakfast meeting, was more representative than it is in 2021.

It does not tell us if there are republics like us in the region. It does not tell us if Israel is the most representative government that protects all who live there, including its minorities. It does not tell us if Israel is the one country in the region that ensures that all people under its jurisdiction have equal rights and self-determination.

Knowing that a republic, or constitutional democracy, was better than a democracy without a constitution, I still wanted to know if Israel was really a democracy. Was *democracy* an English or an Israel word?

Democracy: Available in Many Shades of Gray

Many governments have claimed to be democratic. Many countries have elections. However, in some countries one doesn't know if it is the voters who really count or the counters who really vote. The extreme example was the Iraqi election in 2002, where Saddam Hussein won 100 percent of the vote; all 11,445,638 eligible voters were reported to have picked the same candidate.[249]

I will go out on a limb and say that Iraq in 2002 was an example of a state calling itself democratic when in fact it was not. In China they have elections, but the Communist Party selects the candidates from which the public can choose. Don't tell my kids, but it reminds me of when they were growing up and I asked them, "Do you want to do the dishes or the laundry?"

In the US we have had criticism of our democratic process. In the 2012 election, House Democrats outdrew their Republican counterparts by 1.37 million votes,[250] yet Republicans ended up with thirty-three more House seats than Democrats.[251] Two out of our last three presidents lost the popular vote: George W. Bush lost the popular vote to Al Gore in 2000, and Donald Trump lost the popular vote to Hillary Clinton in 2016. These results are clearly not democratic.

So, it is worth reflecting not on whether something is democratic but instead on understanding the nuances and determining how democratic it is. To do that, we need to understand what makes a society more democratic and what makes it less so. Merriam-Webster's definition of *democracy* is:[252]

democracy. *n.*
   1. a: government by the people, *especially:* rule by the majority
      b: a government in which the supreme power is vested in the people and exercised by them directly or indirectly through a system of representation usually involving periodically held free elections
   2. a political unit that has a democratic government
   3. the absence of hereditary or arbitrary class distinctions or privileges

This definition makes sense because it states that a government by the people is meaningful only if all people are equal and have equal say ("the absence of hereditary or arbitrary class distinctions or privileges"). This is a first-level test of whether a government is democratic.

A second level of tests includes people's rights and government policies that support a healthy democracy. For example, we cannot have a healthy democracy without freedom of speech or freedom of the press. A healthy democracy also requires a strong public educational system. Without free speech, a free press, and a strong education, the public doesn't have the tools for thoughtful and informed discussion. Without thoughtful and informed discussions, the people can't make good decisions. As Thomas Jefferson wrote to William C. Jarvis from Monticello in 1820:

> I know no safe depositary of the ultimate powers of the society, but the people themselves; and if we think them not enlightened enough to exercise their controul with a wholesome discretion, the remedy is not to take it from them, but to inform their discretion by education. This is the true corrective of abuses of constitutional power.[253]

As a society obstructs accurate news and the open discussion of issues, the people's votes become influenced, and therefore manipulated, by those controlling the information. In such a society the people may think that they are part of a democracy, while in fact they are merely marionettes, and those who control the media and the public discourse are the ones who pull the puppets' strings.

How does one sell to the public a myth about being the victim when the opposite is true? Suppress access to historical documents. In January 2018, the Israeli chief archivist, Dr. Yaakov Lazovik, published a comprehensive report describing the state of publicly available material in the Israeli government archives. A 2018 *Haaretz* editorial described what Lazovik said:

> Israel isn't dealing with its archival material in a manner befitting a democracy. ... Most of the documents in the archives are inaccessible to the public for no reason, and unreasonable restrictions are imposed on studying the little material that is available.[254]

He added that the restrictions applied especially to

> documents that shed light on embarrassing incidents and events that aren't a source of pride to the country ... It's enough to cite two examples: Photos from the massacre at Deir Yassin (1948) and documents relating to the massacre at Kafr Qasem (1956) are both being kept closed to public scrutiny. ... Here and there, Israelis committed war crimes. ... If Israel commits acts that a court here or abroad would deem unacceptable, Israeli citizens should know about them and decide whether they agree. ... Disclosure of facts about conduct is a necessary condition for the existence of a democratic society, not a danger that must be avoided by withholding information.[255]

Lazovik warns that if we don't share the truth with the public by making the historical record openly available, then we have lost the foundation of democracy. A true democracy requires an informed public; otherwise, we have a manipulated public under the illusion of being part of a democracy.

Isn't it good that we, and our children, know about what the White settlers and soldiers did to the Native Americans? Isn't it good that our children are taught about our history of slavery in this country? I am more careful in criticizing other countries, including Israel, knowing US history and the racial problems we still have today. I am able to do so only because of freedom of speech, freedom of the press, and a good education.

Calling Israel a democracy is problematic because of 1b in the foregoing definition: "a government in which the supreme power is vested in the people and exercised by them directly or indirectly through a system of representation." That may be true for some people in the land controlled by Israel; unfortunately, it is false for a significant number of others. Hagai El-Ad, executive director of the Israeli peace organization B'Tselem, said it eloquently: "Democracy is the rule of the people, not the rule of one people over another."[256]

Approximately 5 million Palestinians in the West Bank and Gaza have no power or representation in the government that controls the most fundamental aspects of their lives: the Israeli government. Israel controls their freedom of movement. Israel controls what they can export or import. How much water Palestinians can get each month from aquifers under their land is under Israeli control. Israel determines where Palestinians may live in Israel and the occupied territories. Israel controls their lives yet denies most of them citizenship. Israel also denies Palestinians independent statehood.

As Israeli journalist and senior correspondent at *The American Prospect*, Gershom Gorenberg, wrote in 2017:

> The worst damage that the occupation does, though, may be to Israel's democracy. Across a border not marked on maps, our government rules over millions of people who cannot vote. With this mortal aberration accepted as normal, it was easier to pass an election law in 2014 that aimed (unsuccessfully) at keeping parties backed by Israel's Arab citizens out of parliament.[257]

The lack of voting rights of West Bank and Gaza Palestinians in Israeli elections undermines Israel's democratic claim. The denial of their right to vote also has a secondary effect: It reduces the voice of Palestinian citizens of Israel. Their cries for equal rights are denied because they are only a small minority. But those citizens' rights would be heard more loudly if there were Jewish-Palestinian parity, the result of letting those in the occupied territories vote. Gorenberg pointed out that not only is Israel not a democracy for Palestinians in the West Bank, Gaza, and Jerusalem; it is also not a democracy for Palestinian Israeli citizens because their community has been underrepresented.

As if not being able to vote for the government that controls your life is not enough, Palestinians have been held captive on the day that their oppressors go to the polls. Here is a description of a September 17, 2019, Israeli election day by Palestinian Canadian attorney and former spokesperson for the PLO Diana Buttu:

> What was interesting yesterday was that as Israelis were going to the polls, the checkpoints were completely shut down, so that while Israelis had freedom of movement, Palestinians were locked in their Bantustans,[*,258,259] in order to be able to make sure that Israel was able to vote. This is the essence of living under apartheid in a settler-colonial regime.[260]

Human rights attorney Noura Erakat tweeted on that election day, the day before appearing on *BBC World Service*:

> *The fact that about 5 million #Palestinians who will be governed by the Israeli Knesset cannot vote in todays #election should tell you all that you need to know about #Israel and the international community's normalization of its racist system. #Apartheid #SettlerColonialism[261]*

---

* **Bantustan.** *n.* Any of several all-black enclaves formerly in the Republic of South Africa that had a limited degree of self-government. The term *Bantustan* is used generically to mean a region created to be an ethnic enclave, often completely surrounded by, and at the mercy of, another country. An example of usage comes from the Office of the High Commissioner for Human Rights warning of consequences of Israeli annexation of the West Bank:

> These human rights violations would only intensify after annexation. What would be left of the West Bank would be a Palestinian Bantustan, islands of disconnected land completely surrounded by Israel and with no territorial connection to the outside world.

If Israel complied with humanitarian and other international law by letting refugees return and get citizenship, then those additional citizens' voices could really be heard. Until all the people of the land are allowed to vote, Israel is not a democracy.

An example of the impact of withholding citizenship and equal voting rights from Palestinians in the West Bank, Gaza, and refugee camps is that laws such as the "Basic Law: Jerusalem, Capital of Israel" could pass in the Knesset. An amendment to it that passed on the morning of January 2, 2018, leaving little time for the New Year festivities to wear off, states that "giving up Israeli sovereignty over any part of Jerusalem would require a majority of at least 80 MKs [Members of the Knesset], two-thirds of the Knesset."[262]

In other words, "the only democracy in the Middle East" has stacked the deck by letting only a small percentage of the Palestinians it controls vote, the ones to whom it chose to give citizenship. Then Israel has set up the rules and gerrymandering so that this same minority of Palestinians who have citizenship have an even more diminished representation in the Knesset: It is less than their percentage of the Israeli citizen population, further eroding the democratic claim. Finally, the Israeli Knesset then passes laws like the Jerusalem Basic Law, laws that change the rules: Instead of a majority being able to rescind the law, it now requires two-thirds of the Knesset, more than the 64–51 margin that initially passed it. Each of these steps turns the supposed Israeli democracy to a darker shade of democracy gray.

Vice President Mike Pence announced to the Israeli Knesset on January 22, 2018, that the US embassy would be moved to Jerusalem by the end of 2019. It was interesting to observe the "democratic" legislature of Israel in action during that announcement.[263] As Pence was speaking, the Arab members of the Knesset pulled out protest signs. They were immediately forced out of the chambers by security personnel. Benjamin Netanyahu smiled and most of the people in the room stood and applauded as the Arab members of the Knesset were being ejected. Stifling free speech of any legislative member compromises one fundamental pillar of democracy.

Democracy and Citizenship

The fundamental premise of a representative democracy is that voters choose who can lead; it is not a form of government where the leaders choose who can vote.

Zionists tell me that Palestinians in the West Bank and Gaza aren't citizens, so they should not be allowed to vote in Israeli elections. They also tell me that, of course, Palestinians living abroad don't deserve citizenship; they don't even live in Israel or the territories it occupies.

To Americans such arguments sound reasonable. They sound reasonable because we operate on the assumption that everyone has the same rights independent of their ethnicity. We know that everyone born in the United States is a citizen, independent of their ethnicity. As Americans, we know that our children are automatically American citizens no matter where they are born.

However, those rules do not apply to Palestinians. Palestinians who were born in Israel's claimed-capital, Jerusalem, who have always lived there, and whose ancestors have lived there since before Israel even existed are overwhelmingly not citizens. Even a child of a Palestinian with Israeli citizenship is not necessarily an Israeli citizen. Palestinians who were on vacation or on a business trip when Israel blocked their return in 1948 are not only not citizens, they and their descendants may not even be allowed to visit their homes.

By contrast, according to the Law of Return, a Jewish person whose relatives have never been to Israel can fly into Tel Aviv and become a citizen within forty-eight hours. They can then get subsidized housing.

In reality, Israel came as a foreigner to the land Palestinians owned and lived on. Although years after its founding, Israel finally gave citizenship to the Palestinians living inside the Green Line (in the land not including East Jerusalem, the West Bank, and Gaza), it has chosen to deny those same rights of citizenship to the Palestinians in the rest of the territory it occupies.

By calling itself a "Jewish state," Israel is denying the existence of its own non-Jewish people. How can one call Israel a democracy when it does not even acknowledge Palestinians as being part of its people. The circular argument around "Jewish state" rationalizes democracy through exclusion: A "Jewish state" is by definition for Jews, and therefore democracy there is defined to be for Jews. The language and framing of the term *Jewish state* is merely a tool to deny Palestinians, the people of the land, their rights.

These undemocratic policies are unilateral Israeli choices. Just as Israel chose to give certain Palestinians citizenship; it can give the others citizenship as well. It can choose to give Palestinians the same rights as Jews. No negotiation or agreement from any other party is needed. The choice is up to Israel and its voters as to whether they really want to be a democracy. True democracies give all their people citizenship, independent of ethnicity.

Citizenship based on ethnicity is a form of racism. Citizenship based on racism is not something to be proud of or defend. It is definitely not something that Americans should defend. We become complicit in the myth of Israeli democracy when we repeat the myth—when we support the racism by calling it "democracy."

In summary, Israel is not a real democracy, because it occupies the land of a large percentage of its population and denies the people there the right to vote for the government that controls them. Because rights and privileges are given based on heredity (ethnicity), Israel is instead more of an ethnocracy.

Does Israel Want to Be a Democracy?

On December 23, 2016, the United States abstained on Security Council Resolution 2334; all other fourteen members voted in favor. The abstention was a rare exception to the US using its veto power on a resolution condemning Israel. Resolution 2334 strongly condemned Israel's actions and stated that the Security Council:[264]

1. *Reaffirms* that the establishment by Israel of settlements in the Palestinian territory occupied since 1967, including East Jerusalem, has no legal validity and constitutes a flagrant violation under international law and a major obstacle to the achievement of the two-State solution and a just, lasting and comprehensive peace;

2. *Reiterates* its demand that Israel immediately and completely cease all settlement activities in the occupied Palestinian territory, including East Jerusalem, and that it fully respect all of its legal obligations in this regard;

3. *Underlines* that it will not recognize any changes to the 4 June 1967 lines, including with regard to Jerusalem, other than those agreed by the parties through negotiations;

4. *Stresses* that the cessation of all Israeli settlement activities is essential for salvaging the two-State solution, and calls for affirmative steps to be taken immediately to reverse the negative trends on the ground that are imperilling the two-State solution;

5. *Calls* upon all States, bearing in mind paragraph 1 of this resolution, to distinguish, in their relevant dealings, between the territory of the State of Israel and the territories occupied since 1967.

These five points are a last-ditch effort by the world community to salvage a two-state solution. The only way that a Jewish-majority state can exist in historic Palestine while honoring human rights would be for Israel to be a smaller state. Israel's moves to establish settlements in the West Bank and East Jerusalem and to reach beyond the 1967 borders add land that the international community views as Palestinian land with Palestinian people. Every move Israel makes to take more land means that it chooses to step further away from a democracy and human rights; the more Palestinian land Israel annexes, the more Palestinians it has to evict or permanently subjugate.

With the impending change of administration, Secretary of State John Kerry made a speech on December 27, 2016, a few days after the UN Security Council abstention:

If the choice is one state, Israel can either be Jewish or democratic, it cannot be both, and it won't ever really be at peace. ... Separate and unequal is what you would have, and nobody can explain how that works.[265]

The bottom line: Israel needs to choose whether it is to be a democracy or a Jewish state. If its supporters claim that it is already a democracy, then they need to understand that they are speaking in the Israel language, and in that language, the term *democracy* has a different definition. The following is an Israel usage definition of *democracy*:

DEMOCRACY. *n.* A form of government that
1. provides rights, including citizenship and the right to vote, primarily based on ethnicity;
2. is based on the expulsion of the majority of the indigenous population during its founding, causing the previous majority to become a minority;
3. is dependent on the violation of international law by obstructing the return of the indigenous refugees, thereby maintaining a majority of the minority; and
4. discriminates based on ethnicity, resulting in the further decrease in citizenship rights of certain ethnic group(s).

Haneen Zoabi, a former Palestinian member of the Israeli Knesset, said it best:

When I struggle for democracy, when I struggle for equality, when I struggle for justice, when I struggle to live in a normal state, within a normal life with the Jewish citizens, that state is described to me as a strategic threat. So, what is really threatening Israel is a democracy. Real democracy is a strategic threat for Israel.[266]

Real democracy is a strategic and existential threat to a Jewish state. Equality and justice cannot exist with a Jewish majority on the land that Israel controls. Israel therefore needs to promote the illusion of democracy while ensuring that it never occurs.

Another symptom of democracy being a strategic threat to Israel can be seen in how Israel penalizes free speech against it. A healthy democracy cannot exist without free speech, yet on January 7, 2018, Israel's Ministry of Strategic Affairs published a list of twenty organizations whose members will be banned entry into Israel because of their stated positions. A *Chicago Tribune* article reported the following:

> The list was created after Israel's parliament in March approved legislation that would deny entry visas to foreign nationals who publicly back or call for any kind of boycott—economic, cultural or academic—of Israel or its West Bank settlements.[267]

One of the named organizations, the American Friends Service Committee (AFSC), responded as follows:

> Throughout our history, we have stood with communities facing oppression and violence around the world. In 1947 we were awarded the Nobel Peace Prize in part for our support for Jewish refugees fleeing the Holocaust. We will continue our legacy of speaking truth to power and standing for peace and justice without exception in Israel, occupied Palestine, and around the world.

> All people, including Palestinians, have a right to live in safety and peace and have their human rights respected. For 51 years, Israel has denied Palestinians in the occupied territories their fundamental human rights, in defiance of international law. While Israeli Jews enjoy full civil and political rights, prosperity, and relative security, Palestinians under Israeli control enjoy few or none of those rights or privileges.[268]

Yara Hawari, a British Palestinian, summarized the validity of Israel's democratic claim in 2015 in the British newspaper *The Independent*:

> Israel is supposedly the only democracy in the Middle East, yet 4.5 million Palestinians under its control can't vote. A state that

ignores the rights of its indigenous non-Jewish people is not a democracy.[269]

In summary:

- Democracy is not black and white; it is gray. The Chinese can vote but only for preselected candidates. The United States has elected a number of presidents without a majority or even plurality of the popular vote. Governments have varying levels of democracy; it is for each of us to ascertain the real level of popular representation each government has.

- Because Israel restricts who can vote based on ethnicity, it is not a democracy. Democracy requires representation, and all the Palestinian population Israel controls are not represented. Israel is more of an ethnocracy.

- The United States is a republic, not a democracy. Americans value their constitution.

- A democracy without a constitution is inferior to a republic (or a constitutional democracy) because without a constitution minority rights can be trampled by the majority.

- There are republics in the Middle East. Israel is not the only elected government; it is just the one without a constitution.

- Therefore, Israel is not "the only democracy in the Middle East," because it is not really a democracy. And even if it were, its government would not be as good as that of a republic with a constitution.

If Americans and Jews across the world knew these points, they would refrain from promoting Israel as "the only democracy in the Middle East."

Since there are more Palestinians than there are Israeli Jews, here is the most succinct summary: "If Israel were a democracy, it would be called Palestine."[270]

9

"The Palestinian Authority"

The claim that Israel is "the only democracy in the Middle East" creates two unstated narratives:

- that governments are either democratic or they are not, and
- that in the Middle East the only government that is democratic is Israel.

As explained in the preceding chapter, there are levels of democracy, and whether one determines a country to be democratic or not depends on where in the continuum of democracy one draws the line. But even if we could determine that Israel's government meets the minimum threshold to qualify as a democracy, then what form of government is the Palestinian Authority?

The Oslo Accords between the Palestine Liberation Organization (PLO) and the state of Israel called for a "Palestinian Authority" to manage most of the populated areas in the occupied territories. This Palestinian Authority (PA) was formed in 1994 and included a legislative council as well as a president. In 2005, Mahmoud Abbas, a member of Fatah, was elected president for a four-year term.

In January 2006, Palestinians participated in the Palestinian Legislative Council elections, which were internationally monitored and supported, with the United States heavily involved. The following is from the 2006 final report of the National Democratic Institute:

At the invitation of the Palestinian Central Elections Commission (CEC), the National Democratic Institute (NDI), in partnership with The Carter Center, organized an 84-member international delegation to monitor the January 2006 Palestinian Legislative Council (PLC) elections. The delegation was led by former United States President Jimmy Carter, former Swedish Prime Minister Carl Bildt, former Albanian President Rexhep Meidani, and former Spanish Minister for Foreign Affairs Ana Palacio. The observation mission was supported by a grant from the United States Agency for International Development.

The observation mission was part of NDI's comprehensive effort to monitor Palestinian electoral processes. As part of this program, the Institute has observed voter registration processes, the 2005 presidential election and recent municipal elections in the West Bank and Gaza.[271]

After a "comprehensive effort to monitor the Palestinian electoral processes," the report concluded that "the CEC and electoral staff operated confidently, effectively and impartially, resulting in a process that compared favorably to international standards." The report did mention Israel's having placed limits on ballots cast in East Jerusalem but concluded that

the shortcomings in the electoral process had no material impact on the outcome of the elections. Consequently, the published results are believed to reflect the will of the Palestinian people.[272]

American states might wish for such a good report card. In the Palestinian elections there were no Floridian hanging chads of 2000,*,[273] no Iowa caucus debacle of 2020,[274] and the Supreme Court did not determine the president, as happened in the United States in 2000.

---

* "Hanging chad" refers to ballots that had to be carefully inspected in the 2000 United States presidential election. That president was ultimately determined by a Supreme Court ruling.

If democracy is a government where the people elect their leaders, then the PA would seem to meet that criterion. *Being aware of the electoral process for the Palestinian so-called government, it is difficult to still claim that Israel is the only democracy in the Middle East.*

But we can learn much more from these elections and the so-called "Palestinian Authority." We can learn how much Israel and the United States really support democracy.

The US government supported those elections. In fact, the US financed the monitoring of them, and even pushed for them, as mentioned in a 2006 *Washington Post* article:

> The Bush administration has spent nearly $500 million in the past year to bolster the Palestinian Authority and the ruling Fatah party, which was nonetheless crushed by Hamas at the polls. Against the advice of Israeli officials, the administration had pushed Palestinian President Mahmoud Abbas to hold the elections without delay, believing that the voting would strengthen his hand in disarming militia groups.[275]

The United States had invested heavily, financially and politically, in these elections, betting on and helping Fatah. We had done what we could to influence the elections—something we call "anti-democratic election meddling" when it is done to us.

The Israeli government also appeared to be more interested in influencing the elections than in honoring them. *The Guardian* described how just ten days before the elections, the Israeli government agreed to allow Palestinians to vote in East Jerusalem but vowed to prevent the participation of the militant group Hamas:

> Within hours of the decision, Israeli police arrested a group of Hamas political activists, including the second candidate on their list, on charges of illegal campaigning.[276]

The United States and Israel consider Hamas* a terrorist organization. Most of Hamas's activity in the occupied territories is in politics and social services. Going into the elections, Hamas was known to be a strong rival to the ruling Fatah party. The US did not appear to be deterred by Hamas being in the race, but it hoped that the people would choose President Abbas's Fatah faction. Israel was not so hands-off. Its police raided a supposed Hamas office and arrested four people. Soon thereafter, six Hamas members were arrested as they were getting ready to hold a press conference in East Jerusalem.

Israel also makes it more difficult for East Jerusalemites to vote:

> Israel is bound by prior agreements to allow the Palestinian residents of East Jerusalem to vote in Palestinian elections, as they cannot vote in Israeli polls. They have voted in previous elections in 1996 and 2005. But the matter is always contested by Israel as a way of emphasising its sovereignty over East Jerusalem, which was annexed by Israel in 1967.[277]

As an aside, notice that Israel claims sovereignty over East Jerusalem, yet the overwhelming majority of Palestinians who live there do not have Israeli citizenship or have the right to vote in Israeli parliamentary elections. Not only does Israel block their ability to vote for the Israeli Knesset by denying them citizenship, it also makes it difficult for East Jerusalemites to vote in Palestinian elections:

> Israel only allows around 5,000 votes to be cast [in the Palestinian elections] in East Jerusalem, and in the past only around 20% of those voters have exercised their right. Most voters travel to areas outside East Jerusalem to vote. The East Jerusalem ballots are conducted in Israeli post offices using post boxes and envelopes, as if they were postal ballots for a foreign country. The proposals to suspend the East Jerusalem vote had been criticised by the EU and the US.[278]

---

*   Hamas is covered in depth in chapter 13

It is worth unpacking this passage to better understand US and Israeli "democratic" values as reflected in their actions relative to Palestinian self-determination. In preparation for the elections, Israel arrested members of the party they didn't like, claiming illegal election campaigning. What makes the campaigning illegal? Israeli law, which trumps Palestinian law in Palestinian elections.

Israel further contested the ability for East Jerusalemites to vote and limited the votes to around 5,000 out of a population of around 250,000 Palestinians. Israel claimed that they had to vote by mail, since they would be voting from a "foreign country." But if East Jerusalem was a "foreign country," then why could Israel stop "foreigners" from voting in a "foreign country"? Does Israel also limit the number of Americans in Israel voting by mail in US elections? Occupation and democracy are like oil and water; they don't mix and always remain incompatible.

A clear sign of the authority of an organization is its level of control over the money. For a government, that means control of, and access to, tax revenues. The Paris Protocol (part of the first Oslo Accord) stipulated that the Israelis would collect taxes for the PA during the interim "confidence-building" period—until May 1999, when the final Israel-Palestine peace treaty was to be signed. However, after Yitzhak Rabin was assassinated, Benjamin Netanyahu became prime minister, and no final treaty was ever negotiated.

A 2016 World Bank report stated that Israel still collects the Palestinian taxes and withholds the money from the PA at will. It states that the Palestinian Authority does not even have the "authority" to define the value of Palestinian imports from other countries, let alone collect the taxes.[279] This withholding of tax revenue has been used repeatedly as a method of punishing the PA and Palestinians as a whole. For example, according to the *New York Times*, here is what Israel did after the 2006 elections:

> Israel transferred $100 million in Palestinian tax revenues to the office of the Palestinian president, Mahmoud Abbas, as part of a plan to bolster him and keep money out of the hands of

the Hamas government, Israeli officials said Friday [January 19, 2007].[280]

Note that the *New York Times* is admitting that Israel, not the PA, determines where the PA's money goes. Israel's actions reflect control over the PA (and the PA's submission to Israel) rather than democracy.

> Israel collects more than $50 million a month in taxes and customs money on behalf of the Palestinians under an arrangement dating from the 1990s, when the two sides were holding peace negotiations [the Paris Protocol].

> However, Israel began withholding the money after Hamas won the Palestinian elections a year ago, gaining control of the cabinet and legislature. Israel has not said precisely how much money it has withheld, but it is believed to be over $500 million.[281]

The fact that the PA does not have access to its money shows that it has little power. The fact that it does not even have access to an accounting of the money it is owed tells us that it has little choice but to be submissive.

> At a meeting last month, [Prime Minister] Olmert agreed to hand over $100 million as part of a package of moves designed to help Mr. Abbas in his power struggle with Hamas.[282]

Despite Fatah having lost the elections, Israel withheld money from the winning government and provided part of it to the losing party. Such undemocratic Israeli moves are common. And the Israeli government does not just subvert democracy during and after elections. They do it whenever the Palestinian so-called government doesn't fall in line with Israel's wishes.

When Hamas and Fatah reconciled in 2011, Israel suspended payments to the PA again—tax transfers that represent 70 percent of the PA's revenue. According to the BBC,

Israel has suspended tax transfers to the Palestinian Authority following a reconciliation deal between rival Palestinian factions Fatah and Hamas. ...

The sum, including customs and other levies, amounts to $94 million. ...

"I think the burden of proof is on the Palestinians, to make it certain, to give us guarantees that money delivered by Israel is not going to the Hamas, is not going to a terrorist organisation," said Israel's Finance Minister Yuval Steinitz.[283]

Five years after the elections, the "only democracy in the Middle East" still disregards the PA election results. The Israeli government also shows its occupation colors in its determination to undermine a Palestinian coalition government.

But failing to fall in line is more than just about Hamas. Four years later, a *Washington Post* article reported the following:

The Israeli government plans to withhold at least $127 million in tax revenue from the Palestinian Authority, an Israeli official confirmed Saturday, as tensions between the two sides escalated.

The move appears to be a response to Palestinian attempts to join the International Criminal Court in The Hague.

The decision comes after a week of what Israeli Prime Minister Benjamin Netanyahu described as "unilateral moves" by the Palestinians. They included trying to win passage of a UN resolution imposing a time frame for a peace accord and an Israeli withdrawal from occupied territory. The Palestinians have also said they will sign 16 international treaties, including one that would make them members of the ICC, as the international court is known.[284]

That Israel penalized Palestine for attempting to join the International Criminal Court (ICC) and sign international treaties shows us Israel's true objectives and weakness. The more state-like relationships Palestine has with other countries, the more difficult it will be for Israel to claim that there is no Palestine. If there is a Palestine, it is more difficult for Israel to violate Palestinian rights; the more international agreements that Palestine signs, the more it is protected by international law associated with those agreements and courts. To minimize these risks, Israel has to usurp any power the PA might have by exposing to the world that the "Palestinian Authority" has no authority. Israeli usurping any PA authority also exposes Israel's vulnerability: Palestinian self-determination. Israel cannot afford real self-determination or democracy, because it would mean Israel giving up either a Jewish majority or land.

Benjamin Netanyahu's criticism of Palestinian "unilateral moves" also shows us how the Israel language works. His statement creates a narrative implying that Palestinian moves should be coordinated or negotiated with Israel; otherwise, what would be wrong with "unilateral moves"? Using only language, Netanyahu is able to delegitimize "unilateral moves" by the "Palestinian Authority" and thereby delegitimize Palestinian self-determination. The Israel language shows us Israel's opposition to true democracy.

Israel's rejections of the PA's attempts to join international organizations and treaties are a sad reflection on Israel. The United States' rejections of Palestinian self-determination reflect poorly on us. When we criticize a government for wanting to sign international treaties, taking part in the international legal apparatus, and standing for human rights, we look uncivilized.

Of course, Israel's argument that decisions between the Palestinians and Israel need to be negotiated rather than unilateral is hypocritical. Israel oppresses Palestinians every day with its unilateral decisions. The occupation and the blockade are clearly not negotiated results. Neither is the unilateral Israeli decision to block refugees' Right of Return. When Israel can act unilaterally but Palestinians are required to negotiate a settlement with Israel for what they want, then *negotiated settlement* is Israelspeak for "submission."

Unilateral moves have their place. A unilateral move by Israel to grant citizenship to all Palestinians would be humane and provide the foundation for real democracy. Such a unilateral move would promote peace and lead toward equality. On the other hand, unilateral moves to continue demolishing Palestinian homes and expelling their inhabitants from their land while unilaterally subsidizing Jewish-only settlements lead us away from peace and subvert real democracy.

The PA serves at the pleasure of the Israeli government. That may be a strong statement, but the evidence is clear. We need only look at what happened to the Hamas politicians elected in 2006 whom Israel opposed. The results of the elections showed that the US position and support for Fatah was against the will of the Palestinian people:

> President Bush accepted the stunning election results in the Palestinian territories yesterday with a conciliatory tone, saying the landslide victory of the militant Islamic group Hamas was rejection of the "status quo" and a repudiation of the "old guard" that had failed to provide honest government and services.[285]

Many Americans believe that the Israel/Palestine conflict is about two peoples thousands of miles away who can't get along. In reality, and as mentioned earlier, we are involved in the conflict as well:

> The Bush administration has spent nearly $500 million in the past year to bolster the Palestinian Authority and the ruling Fatah party, which was nonetheless crushed by Hamas at the polls.[286]

Though we are told that foreign countries meddling in our elections are committing horrible crimes against democracy, that is exactly what we have done with Palestinians.

Israel's steps after the elections showed both the lack of authority of the "Palestinian Authority" and Israel's overall lack of support for democracy. Israel demonstrated the PA's lack of authority by arresting PA elected officials at will. It demonstrated its own lack of respect for democracy by unilaterally changing the balance of the Palestinian legislature. By the end of June of the year of the elections, Israeli forces had arrested one-third of the Hamas-led Palestinian cabinet and twenty lawmakers.[287]

Six years later, according to an Associated Press article, Palestinian elected officials were still in prison:

> Currently, 24 of 45 Hamas legislators from the West Bank are in Israeli detention on charges of membership in an illegal organization.
>
> Hamas lawmakers have been subject to arrest by Israel since the group competed in Palestinian parliament elections in 2006, defeating Fatah. Several lawmakers have been detained repeatedly.[288]

The "Palestinian Authority" is a misnomer when the occupier, Israel, can just go in and imprison (via "administrative detention": without any charge) those who won the elections whom it doesn't like. When the occupier determines which parties of the occupied are illegal and which officials of the occupied will be removed from office by imprisonment, then those actions violate the democratic claim of both the occupier and the occupied. *One knows that the "Palestinian Authority" is Israelspeak when the president of the so-called Palestinian Authority must obtain a permit from Israel in order to travel abroad.*[289]

The PA has power and authority only where it has Israeli implicit or explicit approval. Israel, with American support, allows the Palestinian security forces to have weapons that it can use against the Palestinian people. After Oslo, the PA and Israel developed and maintain "security cooperation" and "security coordination." Through this relationship, the PA shares intelligence information with Israeli authorities and neutralizes potential attacks against Israel. According to the *Middle East Monitor:*

Chief Palestinian negotiator Saeb Erekat said in one of the security meetings between Israel and the PA that the authority has been forced to kill its "own people" in order to prove that it was establishing law and order in territories under its control.[290]

According to the *Jerusalem Post*:

[The PA's] 6,000 officers make sure to remain in their barracks and their stations when the IDF [the Israeli Defense Forces, the name given to the military in Israel] pursues terrorists on the run or [makes] preventive arrests against those planning terrorist acts. Intelligence flows freely in meetings between senior Israeli IDF officers and their Palestinian counterparts in Abbas's security services. Often, such meetings embarrassingly show up in photos in the Hamas media, which condemn and deride them.[291]

The Israelis do not allow the existence of the PA in order to protect or represent Palestinians. Israel empowers the PA to support and enable the occupation.

The Israeli-PA relationship is what gives the "Palestinian Authority" power. The Palestinian ambassador to Egypt said it this way: "The end of [Israeli-PA] security cooperation equals the collapse of the PA."[292] The Israeli and American political, economic, and armed support gives the PA jurisdiction over the Palestinian people.

That power delegated from Israel and the United States to Mahmoud Abbas and his Fatah party leads to corruption and loss of credibility within Palestinian society. The popular Palestinian vote in 2006 for Hamas was a vote against Fatah corruption. Israel's detention of the newly elected officials made a farce of the elections. It also exposed how false were the Israeli and American claims of being supporters of democracy. There have been no presidential or parliamentary elections in the fifteen years since. There is no sense in having elections when Palestinians can see that the PA serves primarily at Israel's pleasure and that the officials Palestinians really want, and elect, will just be put in Israeli jails.

The US and Israel have helped Mahmoud Abbas weaken the other branches of the PA politically, economically, and through physical violence. The US Congress further undermines the Palestinian democratic system and supports Palestinian deference to Israel by approving $200 million for the Palestinians but requiring the money go through Israel or private groups rather than to the PA directly.[293]

The United States supported the overthrow of the democratically elected legislature by funding the training of thousands of members of Abbas's National Security Force and Presidential Guard under the leadership of US Army Lieutenant General Keith Dayton.[294] From 2007 through January 2019, the US has supported the Palestinian forces with more than $850 million.[295] This money has been used to fight Hamas and those who challenge Abbas's, and therefore Israel's, sovereignty.

Amnesty International included the following in its 2018 report on Palestine:

> Torture and other ill-treatment of [Palestinian] detainees [by Palestinian security forces] were commonly reported and were committed with impunity.[296]

Criticism of President Mahmoud Abbas lands Palestinians in jail. Even criticism of the policy that puts people in jail for criticizing President Abbas puts one behind bars. According to Amnesty International,

> Issa Amro, a founding member of the Youth Against Settlements group, was arrested by Palestinian security forces on 4 September 2017 after criticizing the Palestinian authorities on Facebook for arresting a journalist in Hebron who had been critical of President Mahmoud Abbas.[297]

A 2014 poll showed only "30 [percent] of the Palestinian public [said] people in the West Bank can criticize the [Palestinian] authority in the West Bank without fear" and that 55 percent believed that the PA had become a burden on the Palestinian people.[298]

Mahmoud Abbas gets funding and protection by doing Israel's and the US's dirty work. This fact casts doubt on the credibility of the PA as a democratic entity. Fourteen of the twenty-seven judges of the Palestinian Supreme Court resigned on September 5, 2018, in protest over a judicial authority law that would bring the judicial sector under the control of the president.[299] Mahmoud Abbas further announced the dissolution of the Palestinian Legislative Council (PLC) in December 2018.[300]

By choosing which Palestinian organizations are allowed to survive and in what form, by deciding which are illegal under Israeli laws rather than Palestinian or international laws, Israel undermines self-determination and democracy.

Even though the 2006 elections were internationally monitored, internationally approved, and exceeded US election standards, the arrest of winning politicians makes a joke of the Palestinian electoral process, the authority of the "Palestinian Authority," and Israel's claim to support or to be a democracy. The United States and Israel have successfully converted one of the most democratic institutions in the Middle East to another dictatorship.

Beyond "security coordination," the Israeli purpose of the PA is to impede Israeli citizenship for Palestinians while keeping control of the territory. This enables Israel to claim that Palestinians have representation in the PA, and Israel can therefore remain a Jewish-majority state.

The Israeli and Palestinian democracies have one thing in common: In both, Israel prevents Palestinian self-determination. Therefore, the reality is that neither is a democracy.

10

"People" in Israel

Much of the Israel language is about using English words but giving those words different meanings. The word *people* is treated differently in the Israel language. It just applies to one people and not another. One people is claimed to not exist, while the other is considered to be "God's chosen people."

"There Is No Such Thing as a Palestinian People"

There is no such thing as a Palestinian people. ... It is not as if we came and threw them out and took their country. They didn't exist.

Golda Meir, prime minister of Israel [301]
statement to London's Sunday Times, June 15, 1969

I have heard people claim, just as Golda Meir did in this section's epigraph, that there is no such thing as a Palestinian people. The Israel language can be confusing because although Israel recognizes the Palestinian Authority, many Israel supporters dispute the existence of a "Palestinian people."

By contrast, the International Court of Justice (ICJ) confirmed the legal existence of the "Palestinian people" and its right, as

157

a whole people, to self-determination in its 2004 advisory opinion on the separation wall in occupied Palestinian territory.[302] The ICJ pointed out that Israeli Prime Minister Yitzhak Rabin had replied to PLO (Palestine Liberation Organization) President Yasser Arafat's September 1993 correspondence recognizing "the right of the State of Israel to exist in peace and security" and asserting that "the Government of Israel has decided to recognize the PLO as the representative of the Palestinian people."[303]

The court opinion also pointed to a September 1995 Israeli-Palestinian Interim Agreement that also refers numerous times to the Palestinian people and their "legitimate rights." In addition, the court pointed to numerous United Nations resolutions that recognized those rights.[304]

Why is the existence of a Palestinian people important? If we believe in equality, then aren't all people just part of humanity? Does it not just confuse things to have different "peoples"? Furthermore, aren't human rights actually individual rights rather than collective rights? In the US it is unimportant whether one is of Italian, Irish, or Chinese heritage. Why all the fuss?

The reason for the fuss is that Israel is a country that calls itself an ethnic state and grants citizenship based on ethnicity. Once one has a country that claims to be ethnic, as Israel claims to be Jewish, then everyone else in that country also needs an identity; otherwise, these other people in effect disappear. Unnamed people can lose their national representation and have their individual rights violated. Acknowledging a "Palestinian people" provides a way for Palestinians to claim both their internationally recognized legal claim to their land and their self-determination. If there were no Palestinian people, then there would be no ability to collectively stand up in protest against the armed taking of the land.

Golda Meir claimed, "They didn't exist," yet they make up the second-largest refugee population in the world today. Despite her claim, she set up a covert Mossad group to assassinate members of the Palestinian group Black September. Black September took members of the 1972 Israeli Olympic team as hostages in Munich and asked to exchange them for 236 Palestinians held by Israel. Golda Meir is said to have declined, and nine hostages, five Black September hostage takers, and one German police officer were killed in a gun battle.[305]

Meir claimed that Palestinians didn't exist, yet she clearly recognized them, since she consciously treated them as different; they therefore need an identity. Israeli discrimination against Palestinians is racist, no matter what people Palestinians belong to. All people have a right to self-determination, especially in a country that claims to be democratic. Israel is violating that right just because Palestinians are not Jewish.

But depriving Palestinians of representation is even more sinister, for the following reasons:

- If there is no such thing as the Palestinian people, then it is easier to rewrite history. If there are no Palestinian people, then it is more plausible that Palestine was "a land without a people" when the Zionists arrived. If there were no people, then there could not have been an ethnic cleansing of the land. If there was no ethnic cleansing of the land, then the myth of Israel and the Zionists being defensive would finally make sense.

- The denial of Palestinians being a people is a way to invalidate any claim of refugee status. If Palestinians don't exist, then there can be no Palestinian refugees.

- To claim that a group of people don't exist is an additional tool to humiliate an oppressed people under occupation. One cannot be accused of discriminating against someone who doesn't exist.

- If there are no Palestinian people, then they don't need representation. If they have no representation, Israel can pick off one family or village at a time and expel them from their land with impunity. If the world does not hear the cry of an entire people, what are the chances the world will hear the cries of a family or village when each home is bulldozed, each of the families expelled, one at a time?

In this Orwellian language of Israel, the purpose of claiming that there is no such thing as a Palestinian people is to distract from the real issue. *By questioning the existence of the Palestinian people, Israel can divert attention from the main issue: the denial of human rights.* All people have a right to return to their homes, whether they are Palestinian or not. Freedom of movement is a right accorded to all human beings, whether Palestinian or otherwise. And collective punishment against a population is illegal, even if one claims that Palestinians don't exist.

People can choose to ignore the history of Palestinians, from their Canaanite roots, which preceded Abraham, to their official Palestinian passports and birth certificates issued before Israel became a country. People can turn a blind eye to Israeli agreements recognizing the "Palestinian people" and to international law. However, these denials do not give anyone the right to literally get away with land theft and murder.

God's "Chosen People"

> *For thou art an holy people unto the Lord thy God, and the Lord hath chosen thee to be a peculiar people unto himself, above all the nations that are upon the earth.*
>
> —*Deuteronomy 14:2, King James Bible*

Although Golda Meir and others have claimed that there is no such thing as the Palestinian people, many claim that the Jews are God's "Chosen People." Oftentimes, being a "Chosen People" is interpreted as being superior.

When a group of people believe that they are superior to others, that belief, and choice, has consequences. A belief in ethnic superiority has led to atrocity. This was true for the White settlers and slavers over the Native Americans and African Americans. Atrocities were also the result of German Nazis believing that

Aryans were superior. Similarly, the Japanese, according to Shinto doctrine, believed that they were superior.

I struggled with this concept of Chosen People because I did not want to believe in a racist God. Yet, if God is making certain people superior, especially people based on their ancestry, then God is being racist.

I choose to believe in an all-loving God and that we are all created in God's image. If God loves us all and we are images of God, then there is good reason to treat each other as ourselves. Equality is implicit if one accepts that we are all children of God. So how could I reconcile that with *chosen* being superior? After much thought, I realized that my struggle came back to language; my view of God depended on how I defined *chosen*.

After some reading I realized that *chosen* can also mean "enlightened," a trait that requires spiritual and moral work rather than the inheritance of certain genes. "Chosen People" started to make sense within my belief system.

If we interpret *chosen* to mean "selected for a responsibility," then the interpretation can also work in the context of equal rights. For example, we might say that Martin Luther King Jr. was "chosen" to lead the civil rights effort in the US in the 1960s. In the context of the Bible, it makes sense to say that Noah was "chosen" to build the ark. It further makes sense then that God would choose descendants of His closest followers to be responsible for spreading His message.

In Judaism, there is a concept of Light unto All Nations (in Hebrew, אור לגויים, *Or la'Goyim*). The concept is to be a moral beacon, an example for others to follow. The Bible has multiple verses (see Appendix: "The Promised Land") where the descendants of the Israelites that Moses led out of Egypt become unrecognized as the people of Israel. When they deviated from God's wishes, they were no longer "chosen" people, even though their genetic lineage remained the same. In cases as extreme as Achan son of Zerah in Joshua 7:24–25, some were stoned to death by their own tribe for having morally wandered.

Numbers 15:29–31 highlights the added burden to the Israelites. Israelites had to live by the same laws as others, but if they violated those laws, they were separated from their own:

> One and the same law applies to everyone who sins unintentionally, whether a native-born Israelite or a foreigner residing among you. But anyone who sins defiantly, whether native-born or foreigner, blasphemes the Lord and must be cut off from the people of Israel. Because they have despised the Lord's word and broken his commands, they must surely be cut off; their guilt remains on them.

I worry for children who are taught that they are part of the Chosen People because of their genes rather than because they treat others as equals in God's image. Being taught that one is "chosen" will likely make those children think they are different from, and potentially superior to, others. When that concept is in one's subconscious, how can it manifest itself other than in racist terms? Only by growing up believing that all children are chosen by God can we have peace.

To teach a child that he or she is better than others based on his or her ethnicity is racist. It is also hurtful to the child. If a child accepts the messaging of ethnic chosen-ness, then that teaching can easily lead that child to accept racism and potentially to become racist. We are still struggling with the repercussions of such teachings in the United States more than a century and a half after the Emancipation Proclamation.

True equality and love for one's fellow man was exemplified to me in a scene in the movie *Gandhi*. After the Muslims and Hindus stopped fighting and were asking Gandhi to stop his fast, a Hindu leader told Gandhi that he was living in hell. He said that he felt like he was in hell because he had killed (Muslim) children and because so many children had died. Gandhi told him that he knew a way out of hell for this man. He told the Hindu man to go find a Muslim orphan and raise him to be a good Muslim. Love is the respect of others as equals.

Gandhi, who was Hindu, viewed his religion as a tool to get closer to God(s) and to all human beings (including Muslims) rather than as a way to judge or separate people. He was following the Golden Rule; Gandhi did not want to treat another human being in a way that he would not want to be treated.

How close one gets to God is not based on one's religion but instead on one's chosen interpretation of religion. As a friend told me in college, "Don't let your dogma run over your karma."

Learning the distinctions in the different definitions of the word *chosen* was part of my learning the Israel language. Learning Israel helped me become aware of the major implications of word meanings.

This conscious distinction of the meaning of *chosen* is especially important for Jews. Jews have a history of both universalism (where we are all human beings) and ethnocentrism or separatism (where we are distinct as an ethnic group). These are two sides of the Jewish coin. The elder Rabbi Hillel (ca. 110 BCE–10 CE) captured both when he wrote, "If I am not for myself, who will be for me? If I am not for others, what am I? And if not now, when?"[306] Jews have a long history in universalist movements for social justice and equality. However, Jews have also supported Jewish ethnocentrism, separation, and distinctness from others, as evidenced by a "Jewish state."

These two opposing forces can be scary. Jews may fear universalism because in pure universalism all are equal and one can lose one's identity. On the other hand, pure ethnocentrism manifests itself as racism, and then one can no longer reflect the fundamental Jewish value of *Or la'Goyim*; as a racist one can no longer be the Light unto All Nations.

When it comes to Israel, it's hard to have a nonracist society if a large percentage of one ethnic group believes they are God's Chosen People because of their ethnicity. According to a 1993 Guttman Institute of Applied Social Research study, 50 percent of Israeli Jews "believe completely" that "the Jewish people was chosen among peoples"; 29 percent were not sure. Only 20 percent responded that they did not believe that to be true.[307]

Such views lead to openly racist positions. A survey by the Geocartography Institute published in March 2007 for the Center Against Racism found that 75 percent of Israeli Jews oppose Arabs and Jews living in the same apartment buildings, that most Jews would not want to be managed by an Arab at work, and that a Jewish woman marrying an Arab man amounts to "national treason." *The survey further reported that 55 percent of those Israeli Jews surveyed thought "Arabs and Jews should be separated at entertainment sites." Also reminiscent of historical segregation in the United States: 60 percent would not invite an Arab into their home. Of the five hundred Jewish respondents, 40 percent believed that Arab citizens of Israel should have their voting rights revoked in the "only democracy in the Middle East."*[308]

Our definition of *chosen people* is foundational to how we view our fellow human beings and the Israel/Palestine situation.

11

Gaza and "Gaza Wars"

Militants in the Gaza Strip fired a rocket at Israel as it celebrated its independence day on Thursday, the first such attack in months, causing no injuries or damage, Israeli authorities said.

Amir Cohen, [309]
Newsweek, April 23, 2015

But beyond the trench of the border [with Gaza] surges a sea of hatred and a lust for revenge...

IDF Chief of Staff Moshe Dayan [310]
April 30, 1956

I have never been to Gaza; what I have learned about Gaza is through people who have been there, through the media, and from personal research. In 2005 I saw on TV Israeli soldiers pulling Jewish families from their homes in Gaza; the families were clearly unhappy about being evicted when Israel declared its Gaza "disengagement." Based on media coverage, I had envisioned Gaza as a terrorist haven; it was where Hamas, which the State Department had called a terrorist organization, was in control. Palestinians in Gaza had a history of shooting rockets into Israel and killing or kidnapping Israeli soldiers, as they had with Gilad Shalit on June 25, 2006.

Years later I heard Noam Chomsky on the radio talking about the Gaza disengagement. He was saying that the settler expulsions were all an act.[311] He provided a perspective that I had not considered. He said that Israel did not need to expel the Gaza settlers; they would have left on their own had Israel just told them that all military support for them would be terminated by a certain date. I then realized a few things.

First, that comment helped me become aware of the high cost of occupation and settlements. Not only does Israel subsidize the settlers' housing and infrastructure, but there is an ongoing and extensive military protection cost as well. When I was in the West Bank, I saw soldiers at bus stops and at checkpoints. I saw soldiers just inside a settlement in a Palestinian neighborhood. I saw soldiers escorting settlers. I saw soldiers in vehicles. I even saw off-duty soldiers jogging in a neighborhood of Hebron. They are everywhere. That is the cost of having a colonial civilian population settling on other people's land.

In addition to the costs of settlements and all that is required to support them, there is the cost of the occupation itself. Besides military expenses for monitoring and controlling the occupied population, there are also administrative expenses. Israel issued 320,000 West Bank ID holder permits to enter East Jerusalem for Ramadan Friday prayers in May and June 2019; that does not count the permits that were rejected.[312] That is the administrative tip of the iceberg created by limiting a population from freedom of movement. In addition, there are the costs of managing checkpoints, military enforcement, adjudication, and detention that are elements of a system that requires the violation of the human right to freedom of movement.

It is a difficult task for a country to be burdened with the high costs of enabling and protecting a settler/colonizer population as well as controlling and restricting the larger indigenous population. Bearing that cost is easier, however, because the US government provides billions of dollars annually.

Second, Noam Chomsky's comment revealed Israel's sophistication and emphasis on the American media. His comment made me aware of how Israel's actions are choreographed to send a specific message. The US public would not have felt so sympathetic to the settlers had they just left on their own accord after protection was dismantled. Seeing them pulled by their own soldiers created a scene that would yield a much more sympathetic American reaction.

The argument that the pulling away of settlers was theater made sense when I learned that the Gaza settlers were going to receive compensation and that the number of settlers in the West Bank had already increased by more than nine thousand in that year alone.[313] That increase was more than the number of settlers leaving Gaza. The number of illegal settlers did not decrease that year; Israel had just moved them.

Gaza is in effect the largest prison in the world. In it can be seen the impact of ethnic cleansing of Palestinians from Israel, an occupation, regular bombings, and a blockade. Here are its primary statistics:

- **Population:** 2 million.[314] Gaza has almost as many people as one-quarter of Israel's citizen population.

- **Population density:** 5,479 per square kilometer[315]; by comparison, Boston has 5,143, and San Francisco has 6,659.[316] The fact that some of Gaza is farmland means that the population centers are even more densely populated; farms are not integral to the cities of Boston or San Francisco. By comparison, Israel has a population density of 353.[317] Gaza has therefore more than 15 times the people per square mile as Israel.

- **Median age:** 17.2.[318] *That means that most of the people in Gaza are children.*

- **Refugee status:** *Approximately 70 percent of the people in Gaza are officially refugees—Israel's refugees.*[319]

- **Unemployment rate:** 49 percent.[320]

Israeli and American officials describe the people of Gaza as foreign terrorists attacking Israel, but the statistics clearly show that the people in Gaza are mostly children and are overwhelmingly people internationally recognized as being refugees from Israel, who have been denied citizenship and the ability to live on their land in Israel.

Israel has a population of 8,675,475 on a land area of 21,497 square kilometers; the Gaza Strip has a population of 1,918,221 on a land area of 360 square kilometers. In other words, the population of Gaza is 22 percent of the population of Israel, yet Israel has concentrated the population onto a piece of land 1.67 percent the size of Israel.[321]

The United Nations Office for the Coordination of Humanitarian Affairs—Occupied Palestinian Territory (OCHA) and other sources highlight the extreme nature of the artificial crisis:

- 44 percent of households in Gaza are food insecure.[322]

- Most households in Gaza receive piped water only for six to eight hours every three to five days.[323] The people of Gaza had access to 79 liters per capita per day (2019 average), even though the World Health Organization's minimum recommended amount is 100.[324]

- 97 percent of water in Gaza is not fit for consumption.[325]

- 2019 saw an increase in electricity from an average of 6.6 to still only 12 hours per day.[326]

- 94 percent of schools in Gaza operate on double shifts due to lack of classroom space.[327]

- Gaza's public health system suffers from shortages in skilled personnel, drugs and disposables, and electricity supply. Many Palestinian patients need to be referred outside of Gaza for regular treatment; 46 percent of essential drugs are at zero stock level (less than a month's supply) with 43 percent completely depleted.[328]

- 110 million liters of raw, untreated sewage flow daily from Gaza into the Mediterranean Sea.[329]

The personal implications of the artificial crisis—a crisis deliberately manufactured by Israelis—are described in this 2015 Al Jazeera article:

Rula Abu Shammala, a 25-year-old English teacher from Khan Younis [in Gaza], has running water one or two hours a day. When the water comes, she turns on a motorized pump to direct the water to storage tanks on her roof. But the motor requires electricity, which is available in Gaza only four to six hours a day. The water schedule usually overlaps with the electricity schedule, but sometimes it doesn't, or no one is home to turn on the pump. On those occasions, Abu Shammala and her family will be without water to shower, clean the house, wash clothes or flush the toilet. It's worse in the summer. Without electricity and without the beach, showers are the only way to cool down, but that empties the water tank. The family runs out of water up to three times a week.[330]

Technology clearly exists to provide drinking water and to treat sewage. Unfortunately, these facilities require power to operate, and they get bombed. Israel restricts the electricity and does the bombing. Here is some of the infrastructure damaged by the Israeli bombing:

The three wars that Gaza has endured in the last six years have made an already intolerable situation worse. In last year's war [Operation Protective Edge in 2014], 26 municipal drinking wells and 183 agricultural wells were damaged or destroyed, as well as 20 to 30 percent of sanitation and water pipes, leading to streets being flooded with sewage. Most of the pipes remain under rubble and cannot be accessed for repair. Three sewage treatment centers were damaged, and 500 septic tanks were destroyed.[331]

Israel is systematically destroying the infrastructure to make Gaza unlivable. Non-potable water combined with raw sewage in the streets and minimal electricity is the formula for a health crisis.

A 2018 RAND Corporation study on Gaza's water crisis found that "more than a quarter of all reported disease in Gaza is due to poor water quality and access" and that "if present trends continue, Gaza and the surrounding region are at risk of a disease outbreak or another water-related public health crisis."[332]

The report mentions a 2010 survey that found some residents spend as much as one-third of their income on water.[333]

With 97 percent of the groundwater unfit for human consumption, the report concluded that "the first step in addressing Gaza's urgent water and sanitation deficits is to increase the quantity and consistency of Gaza's electricity supply."[334]

That this health crisis was premeditated and deliberately manufactured is validated by Gidon Bromberg, founder and Israel director of EcoPeace Middle East. The *Jerusalem Post* reported that he called on the Israeli government to approve the increased sale of water and electricity to Gaza.[335] An occupation is evident whenever the occupier requires all fuel and water be bought from the occupier.

Americans were told that we invaded Iraq in 2003 because of their weapons of mass destruction. Weapons of mass destruction include biological, chemical, and nuclear weapons. *Creating an environment where over 90 percent of the water is not drinkable is biological warfare against a civilian population.* Preventing sewage from being treated, thereby letting it flow in the streets and on the beaches, is biological warfare against civilians. Bombing a treatment facility may not seem like biological warfare; however, when one combines it with restriction of reconstruction supplies and power to operate the facility, then it becomes biological warfare.

In 2017 the United Nations Country Team in the Occupied Palestinian Territory provided a glimpse of life in Gaza:

> An 11-year-old child has not experienced more than 12 hours of electricity in a single day in his/her lifetime. No one remembers a time in recent memory when drinkable water reliably appeared out of the tap. Memories of ease of movement in and out of the Strip are also increasingly distant.[336]

Another passage showed how the factors combined to make life worse than normal prisons: "For most of us, with electricity only 2 hours a day as was the case recently, and youth unemployment at 60%, the 'unliveability' threshold has already been passed."[337]

Furthermore, the prospects for the future were forecast as bleak. Israel's blockade and infrastructure destruction has already led to Gaza's only water source being irreversibly depleted in spite of the disregarded warning "unless immediate remedial action is taken." Israel has destroyed the infrastructure, and the blockade has prevented its re-establishment, resulting in "de-development." This is not just a momentary situation: "Despite the warnings issued by the UN in 2012, Gaza has continued on its trajectory of de-development, in many cases even faster than the UN had originally projected."[338]

Electricity levels in Gaza vary; they have gone up and down since 2017. Gaza Electricity Distribution Company (GEDCO) reported an average of 6.6 hours of electricity per day in 2018, with a peak of 17 hours in November, when Qatari funds were allowed to be used for electricity. The average in 2019 was 12.5 hours per day through June.[339] During the last half of August 2020, Israel restricted Gaza's electricity to 6 hours per day, with some days dipping down to 3 to 4 hours.[340]

Collective punishment is a war crime under the Fourth Geneva Convention, Article 33:

> Collective penalties and likewise all measures of intimidation or of terrorism are prohibited. ... Reprisals against protected persons and their property are prohibited.[341]

Israel is punishing all the people of Gaza for not abandoning their cause, for staying in Gaza, and for demanding their right to return. To hide its collective punishment on the primarily child population, Israel implements its abuses in such a way as to minimize American media coverage. For example, the August 2020 drop in Gaza's electricity hours occurred while the US-brokered normalization of relations between Israel and the United Arab Emirates was making headlines. Similarly, on November 4, 2008, the day when Americans were consumed with the US presidential election, Israeli soldiers launched a raid into Gaza, killing six members of Hamas— an event that escalated into Operation Cast Lead, also known as the

Gaza Massacre, which lasted until January 18, 2009.[342] Following the pattern, on the day of the opening of the US embassy in Jerusalem (May 14, 2018), when the press was focused on the opening ceremony, Israel shot and killed 59 Palestinians in Gaza and wounded over 770 others. They also bombed seven Hamas targets.[343]

I had never seen the term *de-development* before. This de-development is clearly not accidental. It is the natural consequence of a systematic policy of regular bombings and a blockade to limit reconstruction. Starving a population and limiting their ability to import and export—and therefore to sustain themselves—can only lead to de-development.

The conflict between Israel and Gaza is nothing new. It preceded Hamas's forming by four decades. IDF Chief of Staff (and later Minister of Defense and member of the Knesset) Moshe Dayan summarized the Gaza conflict, and Israel's militaristic and aggressive "defense" overall, on April 30, 1956. In his famous eulogy for Ro'I Rotberg at the cemetery of Kibbutz Nachal Oz, on the edge of what had recently become the border with Gaza, he said:

> Millions of Jews, who were massacred because they lacked a country, look upon us from the ashes of Jewish history and command us to settle the land and to raise up a country for our people. But beyond the trench of the border surges a sea of hatred and a lust for revenge, which look forward to the day when the stillness will blunt our readiness, to the day when we shall listen to the ambassadors of malign hypocrisy who call upon us to lay down our arms.[344]

To Israel supporters, Dayan's speech is a rallying cry to "defend" Israel militarily. He predicted that they will need to do so for eternity—that they can never accept "stillness" as a reason to "blunt our readiness." Why? Because in his speech he confessed—by using the word *revenge*—that although they were the victims when it came to Germany, they were the aggressors when it came to Palestinians. He apparently surmised that their violence that resulted in ethnic cleansing and the theft of a people's possessions would have caused a "lust for revenge." The Gaza problem was caused by the Zionist movement over seventy years ago and continues to be exacerbated by Israel; most Israel supporters just hide it in Israelspeak that blames the victims.

Gaza Occupation versus "Disengagement"

It cannot be argued that Gaza is occupied. Israel left Gaza willingly [during the disengagement in 2005], yet they target our children as they are leaving for school.

—*President Shimon Peres,* [345]
November 18, 2012

The root cause of the violence that burst from Gaza is not Israel's occupation in Gaza, for a simple reason: Israel doesn't occupy Gaza. Israel left Gaza to the very last centimeter, to the very last inch. We uprooted all the settlements and vacated all the settlers.

—*Prime Minister Benjamin Netanyahu,*[346]
October 13, 2014

Before learning about the situation in Gaza and international law, I would have accepted these two quotes unequivocally. Yet as I learned about occupation and how Israel controls Gaza, I realized that these two statements are Israelspeak. Both statements create the narrative that no settlers means no occupation. They imply that only the presence of settlers is a sign of occupation.

It's as if Israel's Ministry of Truth* was proclaiming:

* George Orwell described the branch of government responsible for propaganda as the Ministry of Truth in his book *1984*. On the ministry's building were the words "WAR IS PEACE. FREEDOM IS SLAVERY. IGNORANCE IS STRENGTH."

SETTLEMENT IS OCCUPATION
REMOVAL OF SETTLERS IS FREEDOM FROM OCCUPATION

Neither of these statements is true, because settlers have nothing to do with occupation; they have to do with a colonial enterprise. If there were any relationship between legal settlement and occupation, it would be the opposite of these statements, since the Fourth Geneva Convention prohibits settlers in an occupied territory.

If Peres or Netanyahu meant that Israel is not occupying Gaza because soldiers have left, then that is also disingenuous. Israeli soldiers still control most aspects of life in Gaza, in the same way that prison guards control the life of prisoners. Even areas inside Gaza are controlled by Israel. Gaza is fenced in on land and further blockaded at sea. Israel has cleared a 300-meter zone on the Gaza side of the fence. Israel calls the area on the Gaza side of the fence the Access Restricted Areas (ARA) and thereby makes it a conflict zone. On the Israeli side of the fence are large berms, on top of which are perched Israeli soldiers. Snipers on the berms shoot Palestinians who are within that 300-meter band in Gaza. This ARA is the prime farmland of Gaza. Farmers who have not given up have to avoid being shot by Israeli snipers while they suffer the consequences of Israel spraying herbicides that kill Gaza crops.[347]

Israel is also present on the water, controlling Gaza territory. Gaza fishers are not allowed to go within one nautical mile of Egyptian or Israeli waters, even on the Gaza side of the borders. Israel restricts their fishing area to only 40 percent of the area allowed by the Oslo Accords, that allowance already having been limited. Even in that Israeli-approved area, Israeli forces shoot and kill fishermen. According to Human Rights Watch in June 2017:

> It is difficult to imagine the pain the Bakr family must have felt in July 2014, when an Israel Defense Force (IDF) missile killed four of their children, cousins Ismail, 9; Ahed, 10; Zakariya, 10; and Mohammad, 11, as they played football on the beach in Gaza.[348]

Gaza is home to over 1 million children. But that does not describe the situation. What describes the situation is that each of these children has a name, is a person, and wants to be free and play on the beach without getting assassinated.

> Today, they grieve again, after IDF forces fatally shot another family member, Mohammad Bakr, 25 years old and the father of two, while he fished with two brothers, Omran and Fadi, and a cousin on May 15.[349]

The blockade exposes the inhumanity required to maintain a Jewish-majority state. Supremacy is the only thing Israeli "Defense" Forces can be defending when they limit the livelihoods and end the lives of fishers with impunity.

> The Israeli patrol came beside them and soldiers fired live and rubber bullets at the boat. Mohammad clutched the engine, hoping to keep the Israelis from firing on it, Omran said. A bullet struck Mohammad in the chest. He died later that day.[350]

And Israel claims that there is no occupation of Gaza.

The opposite of occupation is independence, self-determination, and freedom. Gaza clearly has none of those. Instead, Israel controls their borders, their airspace, and their access to the sea. Israeli drones are ever-present above them.

Americans and Jews everywhere need to learn the Israel language so that important distinctions are understood. If two people use the same word, but each is applying a different meaning to that word, then that word is no longer a tool for effective communication. President Bill Clinton used a narrow definition of *sexual relations* when he said, "I did not have sexual relations with that woman, Miss Lewinsky."[351] The public ended up finding that statement misleading. To not be misled and to be a savvy media consumer on the subject of Gaza, we need to understand the term *occupation*. Israel claims that it is not occupying Gaza; others claim it is.

In 2017 the United Nations Country Team in the Occupied Palestinian Territory stated the following:

> Meanwhile, the numerous restrictions imposed by Israel on both movement of people and goods into and out of Gaza impede the enjoyment of a range of human rights such as the right to freedom of movement and a number of economic, social and cultural rights, including the right to health, education, work, adequate standard of living, and family life. ... Concerns persist as to the right to life and security of persons following the apparent use of excessive force in law enforcement operations within the ARA, including at sea. Given its jurisdiction and effective control exercised as the occupying power, Israel is bound by human rights obligations towards the population of Gaza.[352]

If one is performing "law enforcement" in the territory—as Israel is doing with the ARA—and those laws are Israel's laws, then Gaza is under occupation. And as occupier, Israel is responsible for the safety and health of its population in Gaza.

US officials rarely dispute Israel's claim that it no longer occupies Gaza, even though Palestinians need Israeli permits in order to leave Gaza, even for medical reasons. The US does not dispute the claim, even though Israeli navy boats continuously patrol and limit fishing in Gaza territorial waters. The US also supports Israel, even though Israeli forces commandeer and confiscate civilian ships trying to get to or leave Gaza, including ships with Americans on board. The Israeli navy consistently hijacks these ships in international waters and commandeers them to Israel.

The most notable case was the Turkish ship *Mavi Marmara*, part of the Gaza Freedom Flotilla in 2010. The UN Human Rights Council concluded that violations of international law, including international humanitarian and human rights law, were committed by the Israeli forces during the interception of the flotilla and during the detention of passengers in Israel prior to deportation.[353]

Nine people were killed during the raid and many others were injured. One of the passengers killed was a dual citizen of the United States and Turkey.

In its decision regarding the Israeli attack, the International Criminal Court concluded in November 2014, nine years after Israel had "disengaged" from Gaza, that

> the prevalent view within the international community is that Israel remains an occupying power in Gaza despite the 2005 disengagement ... based on the scope and degree of control that Israel has retained over the territory of Gaza following the 2005 disengagement.[354]

The control they referred to includes

> control over border crossings, the territorial sea adjacent to the Gaza Strip, and the airspace of Gaza; its periodic military incursions within Gaza; its enforcement of no-go areas within Gaza near the border where Israeli settlements used to be; and its regulation of the local monetary market based on the Israeli currency and control of taxes and customs duties. ... [The] authority retained by Israel amounts to effective control.[355]

The court emphasized that case law supports "that it is not a prerequisite that a State maintain continuous presence in a territory in order to qualify as an occupying power" but instead that it applies where a state has "the capacity to send troops within a reasonable time to make the authority of the occupying power felt."[356]

Whether it be from Israeli snipers enforcing the Israeli-defined ARA in Gaza, the navy shooting at fishers in Gaza waters, or major military actions, examples of Israeli incursions abound:

Since the start of 2015 through the end of October 2018, the Israeli army made 262 known ground incursions and operations to level land inside the Gaza Strip, including over 70 this year alone [2018]. This does not include the unknown number of covert operations like the one that went awry on Sunday [November 11].[357]

The most visible incursion after the "disengagement" was the Operation Cast Lead ground offensive, launched on December 27, 2008, when 9 Israeli soldiers were killed (including 4 from friendly fire). In contrast, 1,391 Palestinians were killed in that raid.[358] Imagine what a ground incursion looks like where invading soldiers kill 1,391 people, and those being invaded kill only 5 soldiers. That is not a war; that is a massacre.

American politicians agree with Israel's claim that Gaza is not occupied. My congressman told me in a meeting that he did not believe that Israel violates human rights. At least some world leaders know and state the truth, however; UN Secretary-General Ban Ki-moon succinctly described the occupation as one cause of the 2014 Gaza conflict:

We must not lose sight of the root causes of the recent hostilities: a restrictive occupation that has lasted almost half a century, the continued denial of Palestinian rights and the lack of tangible progress in peace negotiations.[359]

The term *occupation* has a legal definition; its legal implications need to be understood and reviewed. We therefore need to be careful to not confuse the legal definition with someone's attempted creation of a different usage definition. The word *occupation* is responded to in the Israel language not by defining what an occupation is but instead by promoting that the word does not apply to actions by the state of Israel (as we see in the statements by Netanyahu and Peres at the beginning of this section).

An occupation has legal ramifications if international law is enforced. Unfortunately, the United States ends up being the enforcer on many international issues, such as UN resolutions. When our government decides to ignore the law, as it does with Israel's violations of international law relative to Gaza, then civilians suffer. Our reputation as an even-handed mediator also suffers.

More important than a legal definition is what each of us as human beings consider to be fair and ethical. Gaza has been described as the largest open-air prison in the world. Is it exactly a prison? Not exactly. But as with a prison, Israel controls what comes in and what goes out, how much electricity Gaza gets, how much food it gets, where its people can fish, how many medical supplies it gets, and how much money it can earn.

As the occupation vise incrementally squeezes the Gaza population, results are apparent everywhere. *There is no PTSD (post-traumatic stress disorder) in Gaza, because there is no end to the trauma of war. Instead, there is CTSD (continuous traumatic stress disorder), which affects everyone.*

Almost half the children under the age of sixteen wet themselves in bed from constant fear.[360] That means that more than a fifth of the Gaza population has a bed-wetting problem.*[361] Moreover, 65 percent of those under thirty years old are unemployed.

According to a clinical psychologist from Vancouver, BC, who joined a Washington Physicians for Social Responsibility delegation into Gaza to help local mental health professionals work with trauma issues, "In one workshop of ten therapists, four had their homes demolished and three spoke of having family members killed in last summer's massacre."[362] And they are the ones trying to help other people with trauma.

The net result is a population with no opportunity but only desperation from regular brutal bombardment and a slow, inhumane poisoning. No wonder so many young people have no fear as they approach the fences lined with Israeli snipers shooting to kill and maim. The Great March of Return, a regular Gaza protest initiated by grassroot activists and joined by civil society and political factions started

---

* According to the CIA, 42.5 percent of the Gaza population is between zero and fourteen years old. If half that number is bed wetting, then that is 21 percent of the population.

on March 30, 2018. Palestinians commemorate March 30 as Land Day, when in 1976, six unarmed Palestinian Israeli citizens were killed; they were protesting Israel's decision to expropriate more Palestinian land.[363] Protestors have peacefully approached the fence where Israeli snipers await. As of October 4, 2019, 213 Palestinians were killed at the march, "including 46 children, two women, four paramedics, two journalists, and nine persons with disability. Another 18,460 persons have been wounded,"[364] including 4,649 children and 826 women, 222 paramedics, and 173 journalists. The Associated Press reported on:

> Nahed Qudih, a 17-year-old high school student, said he has nothing to lose by joining his peers in the seemingly futile and dangerous act of running toward armed soldiers who fire from behind a fence, some perched on high earthen berms providing cover.[365]

So, whether one calls it an occupation, a prison, or something else, the reality is that none of these restrictions would be in place if the Palestinians in Gaza happened to be Jewish. If the people in Gaza were Jewish, they would be free to return to their homes in Israel. They could import and export. They would have electricity, clean water, sewage systems, medical supplies, and foods of their choice. Israel unilaterally controls the situation; it has chosen to oppress, torture, and poison this mostly child population. Why? To assure a Jewish majority in Israel.

Gaza is a consequence of Israel's desire to be a Jewish-majority state. Gaza is part of the human cost of Israel's existence as a Jewish state. Because we, as Americans and Zionists throughout the world, support Israel, we need to understand that we are responsible for these crimes against the children in Gaza. *Our dream of a safe state for Jews is actually a promise of a lifelong nightmare for the indigenous people.*

Gilad Shalit

On June 25, 2006, the then 19-year-old corporal and his comrades were manning a post alongside the Israel-

Gaza border when Palestinian gunmen opened fire on their position. The gunmen had dug a tunnel underneath the Gaza barrier, allowing them to reach the position undetected. Two IDF soldiers were killed in the attack, three were wounded, and Shalit was led by his captors into Gaza. Three days after his abduction, IDF forces entered Gaza in an attempt to locate and retrieve him. In the operation, 277 Palestinians and five Israeli soldiers were killed, but Shalit was not returned.

Immediately following his capture, Hamas demanded the release of all female Palestinian prisoners and all prisoners under the age of 18 from Israeli jails in exchange for information on Shalit. Israel refused, and on July 1, 2006, his captors demanded the release of a further 1,000 Palestinian prisoners from Israeli prisons.

—Haaretz[366]

Hamas wants hundreds of Palestinian detainees freed from Israeli jails in exchange for the soldier. Israeli Prime Minister Benjamin Netanyahu has rejected the demand unless some of the worst offenders—including 450 with Israeli "blood on their hands"—are exiled. Hamas has rejected this condition.

—BBC[367]

Hamas captured [Israeli soldier] Shalit in a cross-border raid in 2006 but released him in October 2011 in exchange for 1,027 prisoners in Israel, most of them Palestinians. All five of his alleged guards, named by the group's military chief Mohammed Deif last week, have died since Shalit's release.

—Jack Moore, Newsweek[368]

Gilad Shalit was a young Israeli soldier who became a celebrity; his case also highlighted the one-sided nature of the Gaza-related conflicts. Here is a summary timeline I put together from the foregoing articles:

1. Palestinians from Gaza crossed the separation barrier into Israel through a tunnel on June 25, 2006, killed 2 Israeli soldiers who were enforcing the occupation (limiting Palestinian freedom of movement, denying the Right of Return, etc.), and wounded 3 others. The Palestinians captured 1 soldier, Gilad Shalit, and took him to Gaza.

2. Three days later, Israeli soldiers entered Gaza and killed 277 Palestinians. They were able to enter Gaza without needing to go through a tunnel and without permission from Palestinian authorities. During the invasion, 5 Israelis were killed. Note the scale of the imbalance of deaths: more than 55 to 1. No Israeli civilians were killed.

3. Hamas immediately asked for the release of detained women and children, not its fighters, in exchange for information about Shalit.

4. Israel declined to release the women and children.

5. Hamas followed up within a week, demanding the release of 1,000 more Palestinian prisoners, in addition to the previous demand for the release of women and children.

6. In June 2011, Prime Minister Netanyahu was willing to make the exchange as long as 450 out of the 1,000 would be exiled, meaning that they would be expelled from Israel and the occupied Palestinian territories. Hamas refused to exile Palestinian prisoners.

The one-sided nature is apparent, first in the ease of access to the other side's territory: The Palestinians had to dig a tunnel to get access to the Israeli military; the Israelis just opened the gate and went right into Gaza. The one-sided nature of respect for life is also evident: Palestinians killed 2 soldiers and kidnapped 1; Israelis entered Gaza and killed 277 people.

This exchange is important to analyze because it also exposes a little about each side's objectives:

- Hamas wanted women and children freed as a precondition for negotiation.

- Israel, however, wanted to keep Palestinian women and children incarcerated.

- The goal for the Israeli prime minister was to expel Palestinians beyond the occupied territories, to other countries.

- In contrast, the goal for Hamas was to let the prisoners be "free" in the occupied territories, a form of resistance from being expelled.

The case of Gilad Shalit shines a light on how Israel values Jews relative to its refugees. All armies value their soldiers more than the opposing side's. However, at least the US military faces public condemnation when we kill even a small number of civilians. Israel kills civilians with impunity and en masse.

We hear about the US position of requiring the parties to agree on a negotiated resolution. But the situation with Israel/ Palestine is so one-sided, with Israel's power so overwhelming over the Palestinians, that negotiating between such unbalanced parties without overarching rules, such as international law, is unreasonable. The enormous and continuous acts of impunity by Israel highlight both the one-sidedness of the situation and the unreasonableness of a negotiated settlement between only the two parties.

The Shalit affair offers an example of Israel's acts of impunity. After five years of Shalit's captivity, Israel and Hamas agreed to trade him for 1,027 Palestinians held by the Israelis.[369] However, as Israel prepared to attack Gaza three years later in the 2014 Operation Protective Edge, it rearrested prisoners it had released in the exchange. A few years after that operation, Hamas was still trying to get those prisoners re-released:

> According to the Hamas source, the group's position remains the same as it has been since the end of the war: Before beginning any negotiations, Israel must release the prisoners who were rearrested in the weeks before the 2014 conflict after being set free in the swap for IDF soldier Gilad Shalit deal. The official said that there

were only 58 such Hamas prisoners being held in Israel. "Israel put them back into prison and some of them were even returned to their life sentences. We are demanding that [Israel] honor the Shalit agreement of 2011 that was signed in Cairo."[370]

Israel and Hamas had made a deal, but then, after the prisoner swap, Israel rearrested dozens of the people it had just released.
From Merriam-Webster:

> **impunity.** *n.* Exemption or freedom from punishment, harm, or loss. *Example:* "Laws were flouted with impunity."[371]

Israel flouted agreements with impunity. Clearly, a third party needs to enforce any agreement.

The case of Gilad Shalit exposed a crack in the Israelspeak messaging. Benjamin Netanyahu said,

> The public pressure must be directed not at the government of Israel, but at Hamas—at this murderous terrorist organization that hasn't even allowed the Red Cross to visit Gilad Shalit even once.[372]

The crack is the importance of public pressure. Public pressure is the only thing that will change the situation for the people of Gaza. By contrast to Netanyahu's efforts to deflect blame to Hamas, Gilad Shalit's father, Noam Shalit, interviewed in March 2012, said, "If I were Palestinian I'd kidnap [Israeli] soldiers." He added, "We also kidnapped British soldiers when we were fighting for our freedom."[373]

Palestinian Segregation

Israel takes advantage of its different Palestinian populations. It plays one Palestinian group against another. Not only does it play Fatah against Hamas, but it also plays Palestinians against each other by geography: within Israel versus Jerusalem versus the West Bank versus Gaza versus elsewhere.

Israel wants Jerusalem as its capital, and that includes both West and East Jerusalem. After its 1967 occupation of East Jerusalem and the West Bank, Israel unilaterally gave the Palestinians in Jerusalem a right of residency in the city. That residency permit offered an optional conversion to Israeli citizenship. Palestinians in the West Bank and Gaza, however, were not given the same residency or conversion option.

This Jerusalem residency separated the Palestinians in Jerusalem from those in the West Bank. If Jerusalem Palestinians took Israeli citizenship, then Israel could claim that everyone in Jerusalem was an Israeli citizen. If all residents of Jerusalem were Israeli, then Israel could argue that all of Jerusalem should be part of Israel. If all of Jerusalem were part of Israel, then Palestine could not have East Jerusalem as its capital.

This creation of differing interests between Palestinians in Jerusalem versus those in the West Bank was a divide-and-conquer strategy. Only a small number of Jerusalem Palestinians have exercised the option, and of those, Israel has granted citizenship to only some. In talking with Palestinians during my trip, I was told that they stand in solidarity with one another and oppose the carving out of one small group of Palestinians from another. The net result of all these factors is that the vast majority of Palestinian Jerusalemites live there with residency permits only.

As to Gaza, Israel "disengaged" from Gaza in 2005 by dismantling the Jewish-only settlements it had built in Gaza. Yet Israel cannot fully free Gaza. To let Gaza go would enable it to trade with the rest of the world, since it borders on the Mediterranean Sea. If it were free to trade, it could have a thriving economy and become another beautiful beachfront resort spot. Palestinians in Gaza could then be better off than those under strict occupation in the West Bank. They could even be better off than East Jerusalemites who have some freedom to travel. Truly free Palestinians in Gaza might be better off than Palestinian citizens of Israel.

Israel parades Palestinian citizens of Israel as an example of its civility, equality, and Western values in general. Israel supporters claim that Palestinian Israeli citizens are better off than Palestinians elsewhere in the Middle East. Strangely, this argument is used as a rationalization for discounting the discrimination against Palestinians in Israel. Imagine what would happen if American Jews were told that they should not complain about discrimination in the US, because they have it better here than in parts of Europe. Imagine the response if African Americans were told that being discriminated against in the United States is still better than living in Africa. Or, for that matter, that Whites may be better off here than in their ancestors' homelands. ***All discrimination based on ethnicity is racist.***

This selective comparison of Palestinian Israeli citizens is part of the Israel language. Israel's blocking of the Right of Return is why Palestinians are in refugee camps in Lebanon, Syria, Jordan, Gaza, and the West Bank. Israel is the only party preventing their return to their homeland and blocking them from Israeli citizenship. Israel cannot claim to take good care of Palestinians by highlighting the few to whom it has granted citizenship while ignoring the overwhelming majority it has disenfranchised. Israel is still the cause of the refugee situation. Similarly, the United States cannot claim that we stood for equal rights of African Americans in 1800 by using as examples only free Black people who lived in some states in the North while ignoring the slaves in the South.

If Gaza were free, then even the shining star of the second-class Israeli citizen would lose its luster. The myth of equality of citizenship would be further exposed because one would have to wonder why such a concentrated Gaza population was doing better than the supposed lucky minority who had received Israeli citizenship. To maintain control of its oppressed populations and to support its myth of it being great for Palestinian citizens, Israel has to keep Gaza suffering. Furthermore, to prevent unrest in places where Palestinians live in close proximity with Jews, Gaza has to be the worst of the four options (Israeli citizens, Jerusalem residents, West Bank residents, and Gaza residents).

Gaza is also Israel's testing ground for world opinion and action. Israel can slowly ratchet up human rights violations until it reaches the maximum level of abuses that the international community will tolerate. Israel can gauge both European and US government reactions and press coverage to its bombing campaigns. It can see how much its bombing of hospitals and schools is covered in different media and countries relative to its just bombing apartment buildings. It can see how restricting fishing is covered and responded to relative to its restricting electricity or medical supplies.

Unfortunately for Palestinians, the international community has shown a high tolerance for Israeli human rights violations and crimes; no real sanctions have come about since the Gaza blockade. This impunity has convinced Israel that it can implement the same strategy in the West Bank. This is evidenced by the 2020 annexation plan and the Trump administration's "peace plan."

In perfect Israelspeak, the Trump plan was entitled "Peace to Prosperity: A Vision to Improve the Lives of the Palestinian and Israeli People,"[374] even though it was developed without any Palestinian involvement or approval. In fact, it was rejected by even the subservient Palestinian Authority. PA President Abbas said, "All our rights are not for sale and are not for bargain."[375] The plan allowed Israel to annex much of the West Bank, leaving only Palestinian enclaves that are completely surrounded and controlled by Israel. Like Gaza, the West Bank enclaves may show a Palestinian political face, but they are still a prison completely at the mercy and control of the Israeli government. The so-called "peace plan" was a way to make the occupation permanent while eliminating the protections of the Geneva Conventions and any claim to self-determination. Israeli journalist Amira Hass said it most succinctly: "The future of the children in those enclaves in the West Bank, ... their future is the present of the children in Gaza."[376]

Israel has to keep everyone in line:

- Palestinian citizens of Israel have to be in the number-one position (but below all Jews).

- Palestinians in Jerusalem have to be in the number-two position in order to legitimize Israel's acquisition of East Jerusalem. Since Jerusalemites are not taking the citizenship bait, Israel makes life more and more difficult for them by removing their residency permits and demolishing their homes. These seemingly administrative yet one-sided measures are forcing many Jerusalemite Palestinians to move to the West Bank or abroad. This puts many of them into position number three.

- Position number three is taken by the Palestinians in the West Bank, who die a slow death by systematically losing their land piece by piece to Jewish-only settlements. Their ability to move around the West Bank and their livelihood opportunities are also slowly being taken away until they become like the Palestinians in Gaza.

- The Palestinians in Gaza need to be in position number four, the worst off, in order to discourage the Palestinians in the West Bank from rising up and to keep Palestinian Israeli citizens looking privileged. Israel needs to keep Palestinians in the West Bank fearful that they could end up in or like those in Gaza, "the world's biggest prison."[377]

Managing these relative oppressions is difficult and resource-intensive.

The Gaza Blockade

In light of all these facts, not only is it obvious that there is no siege on Gaza, but it is also not reasonable to say that as a whole the Gaza Strip is under an Israeli blockade.

—Israel's Ministry of Foreign Affairs,[378]
August 17, 2014

From the United Nations Office for the Coordination of Humanitarian Affairs website:

The UN Secretary-General has found that the blockade and related restrictions contravene international humanitarian law as they target and impose hardship on the civilian population, effectively penalizing them for acts they have not committed.[379]

When UN Secretary-General Antonio Guterres was in Gaza in August 2017, he urged Israel to ease its blockade of the Gaza Strip.[380] How can Israel claim there is no blockade when the secretary-general urges Israel to ease it?

When the previously mentioned Turkish ship *Mavi Marmara* approached Gaza on May 30, 2010, and Israeli troops boarded it and killed nine people (an additional person died from injuries), including an American, and they wounded another fifty people; Israeli government officials said they were taking "all the necessary measures in order to enforce this blockade."[381] The Israeli military has further boarded and confiscated Freedom Flotilla boats attempting to reach Gaza in 2011, 2015, 2016, and 2018.

Perhaps the confusing use of Israel language, its Orwellian logic, is best described by *Haaretz* journalist Asher Schechter, who summarized the logic as follows:

> The Monty Python-esque absurdity of this policy is typical of Israel's conflicting positions regarding the Gaza blockade, in place since 2007, when Hamas took control of the Gaza Strip: officially, there is no blockade of Gaza—but Israel doesn't intend to lift it, and don't attempt to break it, or you'll be arrested.[382]

Similarly, George Orwell wrote in *1984*:

> This was not illegal (nothing was illegal, since there were no longer any laws), but if detected it was reasonably certain that it would be punished by death, or at least by twenty-five years in a forced-labour camp.[383]

Israeli officials deny the existence of a blockade, and yet there are the Freedom Flotilla Coalition boats to Gaza that keep getting intercepted and confiscated—taken by the Israeli military to Ashdod, Israel, against the will of the crews. Once in Ashdod, the crew and passengers are asked to sign a document confessing they entered Israel illegally. This is yet another example of Israelspeak: The pirates claim to be the victims because those whom they bound, kidnapped, and brought to Israel are accused, by the pirates who brought them there, of entering Israel illegally. Piracy is defined by Merriam-Webster as "an act of robbery on the high seas."[384]

The *New York Times* confirmed the blockade's existence and its enforcement in a 2016 article:

> Their chances of reaching the shores of Gaza were never high: Thirteen women on a yacht hoping to breach the years-old sea blockade of the Hamas-run Palestinian coastal territory enforced by the Israeli Navy.[385]

Israeli officials maintain that Israel needs to maintain the supposedly nonexistent blockade for Israel's security. A 2013 report by the UN secretary-general showed how the blockade covers far more than what would be normally covered for security. For example, the blockade included Gaza exports, the products sent from Gaza to other parts of the world:

> The blockade also continued to severely restrict Gaza's exports, preventing the population from maintaining their livelihoods. During the reporting period, Gaza exports equalled less than 2 per cent of the pre-blockade level.[386]

Blocking exports prevents an economy from generating revenue. The BBC described the extent of export restrictions in 2010:

> The closures have devastated the private sector. Before 2007, up to about 750 trucks of furniture, food products, textiles and agricultural produce left Gaza each month, worth half a million US dollars a day.

Under the blockade, the only exports allowed have been a small number of trucks of strawberries and flowers—although the situation improved slightly in early 2010, with 118 trucks leaving between December 2009 to April 2010.

Even production for local needs has come to a virtual standstill because raw materials are usually refused entry.[387]

Note that prior to the blockade, Gaza exported 750 trucks worth of merchandise per month; the "improvement" in 2010 was an increase to 118 trucks across four months, or an average of under 30 trucks per month. Another BBC piece said one truck per day was allowed out of Gaza in 2013, which is also about 30 trucks per month.[388] Furthermore, the people of Gaza can't produce goods, because they can't get raw materials.

Before learning to speak Israel, I thought that a "security blockade" would be deployed to prevent weapons from entering an area. But this blockade is also preventing commercial goods from leaving Gaza. Why would exporting goods be considered a security risk? Because in Israel, *security* means dominance rather than safety.

Here are two reasons for such harsh treatment of the Gaza civilian population:

- Israel does not want approximately 3 million Palestinians in the West Bank revolting against over 600,000 Israeli Jewish settlers there; a real conflict in the West Bank would be devastating, even though the minority Jews are the ones who are armed. The way to keep the West Bank Palestinians slightly appeased is if they think they have it better than Palestinians in Gaza and remain hopeful that one day they will have their own state.

- Israel is always afraid of the possibility of having to assimilate Palestinians to become citizens of Israel. People have said that the odds of that happening are extremely small; however, with the recent Great March of Return, they are bringing attention to the Right of Return issue. The 2 million Gaza Palestinians are more than the number of current Palestinian Israeli citizens. Just adding Gaza residents to Israel's citizen rolls would more than double the number of Palestinian Israeli citizens. If one's job is to "secure" a Jewish state, then diluting the Jewish population is a "security" risk.

As mentioned previously, Israel's solution to both of these issues is to make life so miserable, and Israel/Palestine so uninhabitable, that Palestinians just leave. Or as *The Economist* reported in 2019:

> Its "temporary" military occupation looks like the permanent subjugation of Palestinians under a separate law, even apartheid. ... Mr. Netanyahu pushed for an electoral pact with the hitherto untouchable far-right Jewish Power group, which wants to annex all the occupied territories and "encourage" Arabs, including Israeli citizens, to leave.[389]

The Economist used quotation marks around the words *temporary* and *encourage*; it recognizes Israelspeak.

But even the blockade import restrictions seem surreal. It is crazy to think that one has to smuggle animals in through tunnels for the local zoo.[390] It is dystopian for what we call a civilized nation to prevent children from going to school and to limit their access to school supplies, including paper, pens, and textbooks:

> More than a month into the school year, the Israeli restrictions have caused severe shortages that leave students unable to afford supplies such as notebooks. Students are obliged to share or take turns studying from used textbooks and workbooks. Some did not receive any books for this year's classes. Supplies smuggled through tunnels underneath Gaza's southern border with Egypt have failed to make up for the shortages caused by Israel's arbitrary restrictions on imports of educational materials.
>
> "Israel's blockade affects every aspect of life in Gaza, and is even preventing students from having basic school supplies," said Sarah Leah Whitson, Middle East and North Africa director at Human Rights Watch. ***"What possible justification can there be***

for blocking school supplies, which effectively deprives children of their right to an education?" [emphasis added].[391]

Poor countries may not be able to afford school supplies for their students. But why are we choosing to make our number-one recipient of foreign aid a country that blocks the access of such basic supplies to children? We need to think about what it means for Americans to support a blockade of items including soda, juice, spices, shaving cream, potato chips, cookies, and candy.[392] This is not just an issue about Israel; it is an issue about us and what we represent.

Egypt and Its Border with Gaza

Israel supporters say that there is no Israeli blockade, because Israel does not control all of Gaza's borders; they mention there is a fourteen-kilometer border with Egypt. That border has a single border crossing: the Rafah crossing, which they say is controlled by Egypt.

What happens at the Egyptian border—and specifically at the Rafah crossing—is complicated because of the many parties that influence and control that border. Typically, the two countries that control a border are the ones that share it. By contrast, the Egyptian border has many stakeholders.

When Egypt attacked Israel in the Yom Kippur War (or October War) of 1973, the United States had to defend Israel with airlift assistance. Since the 1979 Egypt-Israel peace treaty, the US has made Egypt the second-largest recipient of its foreign aid after Israel; the aid is in effect an annual payment to Egypt to not only not attack Israel but also to support it.

A large part of that American aid is military aid. The Egyptian military benefits tremendously from that aid, not only in its strength internationally but also domestically. The Egyptian military controls a large part of the Egyptian economy. With its support from the United States, the Egyptian military and its president have followed the US's wishes in the region.

193

On July 3, 2013, General Abdel Fattah al-Sisi (also spelled "Abdel Fattah el-Sisi"), the Egyptian minister of defense, overthrew his boss, Mohamed Morsi, a prominent member of the Muslim Brotherhood who had been democratically elected president following the Arab Spring overthrow of dictator Hosni Mubarak. Al-Sisi had been an Egyptian general under Mubarak and had attended the US Army War College.[393] He had regular conversations with US Defense Secretary Chuck Hagel at the Pentagon before and after the coup.[394]

Under al-Sisi's military rule, human rights violations have been worse than even under Mubarak; his regime has jailed tens of thousands of opponents and critics. The Egyptian constitution of 2012 was suspended by the Egyptian army.[395] Al-Sisi won the presidency in 2014 with 96 percent of the vote after having a number of his opponent's supporters arrested. In 2019 the Egyptian parliament approved constitutional amendments allowing him to remain president until 2034, making him head of the judiciary and maintaining the government under military "guardianship."[396]

The United States recognized the new military-led government shortly after the coup, thereby supporting a dictator over an Egyptian democracy. We also did not call it a coup; had we done so we would have had to stop aid to Egypt. The Egyptian military and president know who butters their bread; al-Sisi was the first foreign leader to congratulate Donald Trump on winning the presidential election of 2016.[397] At the 2019 G7 conference in Biarritz, France, President Trump called al-Sisi "my favorite dictator."[398]

Hamas in Gaza is an offshoot of the Muslim Brotherhood, the party that with Morsi had won the Egyptian election in 2012. The Muslim Brotherhood has been the greatest organized threat to Egyptian dictators. As a consequence, although Egypt sometimes plays an intermediary role between Gaza and Israel, Egypt's government is anti–Muslim Brotherhood and therefore anti-Hamas.

By contrast, the Egyptian public is anti-Israel. According to the *Jerusalem Post*, a September 2015 poll by the Egyptian Center for Public Opinion Research indicated that most of the Egyptian public view Israel as hostile. On a scale of 100 down to –100, where –100 is the

most hostile, Egyptians rated Israel as the most hostile, with a rating of
–88. The United States was the country rated as second-most hostile,
at –37.[399] Having the US be seen as the second-most hostile country in
the world and the most hostile country being our number-one ally in
the region does not help us in our "war on terror."

How does all this relate to the Egyptian border with Gaza? Even
though the Egyptian people are sympathetic to the Palestinians'
plight, their government has different interests.

When Israel "disengaged" from Gaza in 2005, it needed a way
to remain in control of the one crossing from Gaza into Egypt. In
November 2005, the government of Israel (GoI) and the Palestinian
Authority (PA) reached an agreement on Gaza called the Agreement
on Movement and Access (AMA), through which Israel would
have influence over, if not control of, the Gaza side of the Rafah
crossing.[400] US Secretary of State Condoleezza Rice facilitated this
agreement with the parties. In exchange for Gaza being allowed to
export products through Israel, start construction on a port, and
open an airport, the PA allowed Israel rights relative to the Rafah
crossing. However, although restrictions on Gaza movement and
access through the Rafah crossing have been in place since the AMA
was signed, the port and airport in Gaza have been stopped (the
airport was bombed) unilaterally by Israel. According to the AMA,

> use of the Rafah crossing will be restricted to Palestinian ID card
> holders and others by exception in agreed categories with prior
> notification to the GoI and approval of senior PA leadership.[401]

Note that Palestinian ID cards are issued only with Israel's
approval and supervision; the registry of approved Gaza cardholders
was held by Israel.[402]

The AMA confirmed the extent of Israel's control over the Gaza
population and its access to and from Gaza:

> Israel will provide the PA with all information needed to update
> the Palestinian population registry, including all information

on Palestinian ID card holders who are currently outside the country.[403]

The foregoing shows how little authority the "Palestinian Authority" really has; they do not even control who is a Gaza resident. Again, *democracy* and *self-determination* use Israel definitions when there is occupation—even after "disengagement."

Through the AMA, the PA was further restricted by a third party, the European Union:

> The 3rd party will review the PA's customs capacity in 12 months and make a recommendation to both sides for a joint decision regarding future arrangements. In the event of a disagreement, the US, in consultation with the GoI, the PA, and the 3rd party, will resolve the issue expeditiously.[404]

Not only did we Americans have a part in the agreement; the United States had the authority to resolve disagreements.

The AMA further described the Palestinians' authority over their border with Egypt:

> The 3rd party will have the authority to ensure that the PA complies with all applicable rules and regulations concerning the Rafah crossing point and the terms of this agreement. In case of non-compliance the 3rd party has the authority to order the re-examination and reassessment of any passenger, luggage, vehicle or goods. While the request is being processed, the person, luggage, vehicle or cargo in question will not be allowed to leave the premises of the Rafah crossing point.[405]

The bottom line on these complicated agreements was to ensure that the Palestinian Authority did not have "authority"; in this case, the PA did not even control its side of its border with Egypt.

The claim of Israel not controlling or being able to enforce a blockade because of the Rafah crossing is further undermined by reports that have been made public. The Israeli peace organization B'Tselem issued a report describing what happened after the Israeli soldier was taken prisoner in Gaza:

> On 25 June 2006, following the abduction of the soldier Gilad Shalit, Israel decided to close the [Rafah] crossing. It informed the European monitors that the crossing was closed for security reasons, and ceased to carry out its part of the agreement. Israel allowed the crossing to be opened only in isolated cases, and without giving advance notice.[406]

The preceding statement should make it clear as to who controlled the border with Egypt even after the "disengagement." Israel had control, and the Europeans enforced Israel's requests.

The abduction of Gilad Shalit and the takeover of Gaza by Hamas led to the Gaza blockade. To overcome the blockade, Palestinians in Gaza have built tunnels, especially between Gaza and the town of Rafah, on the other side of the Egyptian border.

Egypt under Hosni Mubarak had worked with the United States to find and stop the tunnels in 2008 and 2009. Mubarak's elected replacement, Mohamed Morsi, was more sympathetic to the people in Gaza. However, after al-Sisi's 2013 coup, Egyptian priorities changed back: The previously politically powerful Muslim Brotherhood needed to be weakened—along with its allies in Gaza.

In early 2008, the US gave Mubarak's Egypt $23 million to stop the tunnels. Shortly after Morsi's overthrow, the US Department of Defense awarded Egypt a contract for $10 million to provide tunnel detection technology.[407] These contracts are examples of the direct US involvement and complicity in the oppression and inhumane conditions in Gaza.

With US funding, the Egyptian military destroyed thousands of tunnels that crossed the border from Gaza into Egypt. In 2015 its engineering corps dug a fourteen-kilometer canal the whole length of its border with Gaza. Seawater then filled the tunnels. Egypt also moved the town of Rafah, which was on the border with

Gaza, a couple of kilometers away, thereby creating a "buffer zone." Imagine Egypt moving a town for US and Israeli purposes against the wishes of its people. Egypt gave more than 1,100 Egyptian families only forty-eight hours to leave their houses in the "buffer zone"; the buildings were then destroyed.[408]

To claim that the Egyptian border is controlled by Egypt is misleading. In many ways, Israel and the United States control the border. Egypt is controlled by its military. And that military does what is necessary to continue getting US aid. But that US aid is dependent on Israel blessing that aid. Egypt has had to lobby the US Congress because Israel was claiming that Egypt was not doing enough for Israel. According to a 2008 Congressional Research Service report,

> Egypt claims that Israel has not only exaggerated the threat posed by weapons smuggling, but is deliberately acting to "sabotage" US-Egyptian relations by demanding that the United States condition its annual $1.3 billion in military assistance on Egypt's efforts to thwart smuggling. Section 690 of P.L. 110-161, the Consolidated Appropriations Act, 2008, withholds the obligation of $100 million in Foreign Military Financing for Egypt until the Secretary of State certifies, among other things, that Egypt has taken concrete steps to "detect and destroy the smuggling network and tunnels that lead from Egypt to Gaza."[409]

This congressional research service report shows us who controls the Egyptian border with Gaza. Israel has the power to generate legislation in the US Congress that conditions Egypt getting US foreign aid as long as Egypt cooperates with Israel, especially as it relates to its border with Gaza. The result is that Egypt's military acts against the wishes of its people and instead does as Israel wishes. The Egyptian military has been bought by the United States, and our government follows the wishes of Israel supporters.

The prior paragraph may seem biased and accusatory until we research the evidence. Consider the example of our US Senate's actions during the US government shutdown of 2018/2019. The Israeli power over our Congress was evidenced by how the Senate gave preferential treatment for the funding of Israel over the United States in early 2019. While the United States government was in what became its longest shutdown in history, the Senate introduced its first bill, S.1, on January 3, 2019. *Instead of working to fund the US government, the Senate introduced a bill that extended payments to Israel through 2028 and changed the amount of funding from $3.3 billion annually to a minimum of that amount.*[410]

The United States is the power that politically, militarily, and financially supports the Egyptian military, which overthrew the democratically elected Egyptian government in 2013. The US influence is strong enough to cause the Egyptian government to act against the will of the Egyptian people. It is therefore reasonable to assert that the United States is the one that controls the Egypt-Gaza border—even if it does so on behalf of Israel.

The AMA, established shortly after Israel's disengagement from Gaza, was terminated when Hamas took over Gaza in 2007. Hamas replaced the PA on the border. But after ten years of erratic border openings, Egypt brokered a deal between Hamas and the PA to cede Gaza border control to the Israeli-restrained PA. In other words, even though Hamas still controlled Gaza internally, they could not control the Rafah crossing, because of external forces, whether they were Egyptian, Israeli, or American. On November 1, 2017, Hamas handed off its control of its border crossing with Egypt to its rival, the PA:

"We have handed over the crossings with honesty and responsibility, without bargaining and unconditionally," the Hamas leader, Ismail Haniyeh, said in a video address.

The Palestinian prime minister, Rami Hamdallah, said in a statement that taking charge of the crossings would help the PA fulfill its duty "to improve the living conditions of our people."[411]

A little more than one year later, in January 2019, the PA removed its border personnel:

> The Palestinian Authority (PA) says it is pulling its staff out of the Rafah border crossing between the Gaza Strip and Egypt, effectively closing the main exit point from the coastal territory.[412]

Egypt and the Israeli-supported PA have effectively closed the Rafah border with Gaza. Israel influences the United States, which influences Egypt's crossing with Gaza. Israel controls Gaza's airspace, Israel's border with Gaza, and the border Gaza has with no other country: its border with the Mediterranean Sea.

So, here is an attempt at defining the word *blockade* by and in Israel:

> **BLOCKADE.** *n.* Per some Israel supporters and politicians, it is a nonexistent blockage or significant restriction of movement of people, services, and goods in and out of Gaza. A blockade is overwhelmingly deployed by Israel not only on Israel's border with Gaza but also by its controlling Gaza's airspace and access to the sea. Blockage of the border with Egypt is significantly influenced by the United States, since Egypt has historically been the second-largest recipient of US foreign aid.

The foregoing is consistent with Dictionary.com's definition (other than the Israel claim that it does not exist):

> **blockade.** *n.* The isolating, closing off, or surrounding of a place, as a port, harbor, or city, by hostile ships or troops to prevent entrance or exit.[413]

Egypt is not stopping the people in Gaza from having an operating airport. Egypt has not stopped the ships that tried to leave Gaza or go into Gaza. Egypt has not blocked the opening of the Rafah crossing by preventing European Border Assistance Mission personnel from getting to the crossing.[414] Israel has done these things.

Someone may choose to believe the president and the prime minister of Israel when they say that there is no blockade. On the other hand, one can instead choose to believe what Prime Minister Netanyahu said in 2012 to the American Israel Public Affairs Committee (AIPAC):

> Ladies and gentleman, if it looks like a duck, if it walks like a duck, if it quacks like a duck, then what is it? ... That's right, it's a duck![415]

This treatment of Gaza's borders looks, walks, and quacks like a blockade.

I attended a foreign policy panel discussion at a local university and asked a retired American ambassador on the panel what he thought of doing an airlift to Gaza like we did for Berlin after World War II. During the 1948/1949 airlift, the United States provided food and medical supplies to the German civilian population of West Berlin. Here was his reply: "The Jewish state would not like that." That response told me that our politicians are more afraid of a small country of fewer than 9 million citizens than they were of the Soviet Union, which had single-handedly defeated the Nazis on the eastern front and had lost millions of lives doing it. His response also tells us how much power that small country of Israel has over our American politicians.

Stepping back, it is helpful to understand what led up to the Gaza blockade. The following timeline will include some of what we learned about the "Palestinian Authority" in chapter 9. It will also clarify the involvement and influence of the United States:

1. **1948-early 1950s:** Israel expelled Palestinians from their lands forcing many into an area now called Gaza. Israel called those trying to return to their land "infiltrators," expropriated their land and militarily supported Jewish settlement of that land while keeping Palestinians away. Although that ethnic cleansing and settlement project came into effect shortly after the UN Partition Plan passed in the General Assembly, it continues through today.

2. **March 19, 2003:** Mahmoud Abbas was nominated as the first prime minister of the PA, since the United States and Israel

would not work with elected president Yasser Arafat.[416] Abbas was regarded by some as a traitor and was forced to cancel a meeting with Israeli Prime Minister Ariel Sharon after the Fatah Central Committee criticized his negotiations with Israel.[417]

3. **November 11, 2004:** Yasser Arafat, chairman of the PLO and president of the PA, died. Swiss test results showed that he had high levels in his body of radioactive polonium, a rare element for which "a dose large enough to kill would likely have to come from a government with either civilian or military nuclear capabilities."[418] Mahmoud Abbas took over as PLO chairman. He was elected as president of the PA on January 9, 2005.

4. **February 2005:** Abbas made a deal with Sharon for a cease-fire.[419] Hamas stated that it was not a party to the agreement but would abide by it.

5. **September 2005:** Sharon pulled Israel out of Gaza and northern West Bank towns[420] but continued the expansion of settlements in the West Bank.[421] (There was no blockade at this point. Palestinians in Gaza could import and export.)

6. **January 26, 2006:** Palestinian elections were held, having been funded by the US and internationally monitored. Hamas won: Palestinians voted against the corrupt Fatah more than for Hamas.

7. **Early 2006:** Israel and the US cut off funding to the PA. Israel restricted movement from and in the West Bank.[422] Israel significantly cut back imports into Gaza with the closing of the Karni crossing for nearly one hundred days in 2006.[423] By March restrictions on food imports forced most bakeries in Gaza to close for a period, and the UNRWA became unable to do its emergency food distribution. Prices for rice and sugar more than doubled.[424] Although this situation was not yet the official Gaza blockade, it was its precursor. Israel, with US support, put economic sanctions on the PA, withholding tax revenues.[425] The United States and Israel did not recognize democracy when elections were won by candidates they didn't like.

8. **2006:** The United States urged Mahmoud Abbas to strengthen the power of the presidency in order to counter Hamas. US

Secretary of State Condoleezza Rice stated that she would "ask Congress for tens of millions of dollars to strengthen Abbas's security forces."[426]

9. **By June 2006,** Israel had arrested numerous Hamas elected officials, a third of the new Palestinian cabinet, and twenty lawmakers.[427] The United States continued to support the overthrow of the democratically elected government.

10. **June 25, 2006:** Hamas members crossed the Gaza fence through a tunnel, killed two soldiers, and captured Corporal Gilad Shalit and took him back to Gaza.

11. **June 28, 2006, and the ensuing months:** Israel unleashed Operation Summer Rains. It bombed the only electrical power plant operating in the Gaza Strip. After repeated bombings all six transformers were destroyed. For months to follow, people in Gaza could get water only two or three hours per day. Elevators in the tall apartment buildings were inoperable. Lack of refrigeration exposed many to food poisoning.[428] The Rafah border crossing with Egypt had been open per an agreement with Israel and the PA. It was now closed; crossings into Israel were severely restricted. From the end of June through November, Israeli forces killed 416 Palestinians, including 48 children.[429]

12. **June 2007:** Fatah held on to power with Israeli and US support, despite Hamas winning the election the prior year. In mid-June, Hamas took over Gaza from Fatah by force but was not able to do the same in the West Bank. Israel "tightened" the blockade.[430]

Gaza has been a prison ever since—largely because Hamas won an election against Israel's wishes.

As part of an event commemorating the tenth anniversary of Israel's attack on the Freedom Flotilla's *Mavi Marmara*, Israeli journalist Amira Hass stated the following:

Gaza is not the biggest prison in the world since 2007 but from much earlier on—actually since 1991, before the rockets, before the suicide attacks, before Hamas came to power, and even before the Palestinian Authority was established. Israel imposed the closure and put the Palestinians of Gaza under an unprecedented regime of movement restrictions back in 1991, not since 2007.[431]

Hass pointed out that Israel started the restrictions while the so called "peace" negotiations were going on, when the world expected Israel to withdraw from the territories occupied in 1967:

When talking about peace and the sweet words, first in Madrid, then in Oslo, Israel started designing its own solution to the situation.[432]

Americans have been, and continue to be, active enablers in the restriction of movement of the people in Gaza. We have enabled these violations of human rights through our support of the AMA and our support and protection of the Israeli and Egyptian governments despite their human rights violations.

Knowing that we are part of the problem of oppression is both bad and good. It is bad because we are guilty of being the enablers. The good news is that because we now know we are the enablers, we can change our ways and become disablers.

Is it worth doing something about it? Bishop Desmond Tutu said, "If you are neutral in situations of injustice, you have chosen the side of the oppressor."[433]

"Gaza Wars": Operations Cast Lead, Pillar of Defense, and Protective Edge

The IDF servicemen's purity of arms is their self-control in use of armed force. They will use their arms only for the purpose of achieving their mission, without inflicting unnecessary injury to human life or limb; dignity or property, of both soldiers and civilians, with special consideration for the defenseless, whether in wartime, or during routine security operations, or in the absence of combat, or times of peace.

—Israel Defense Forces Code of Ethics [434]

As one Israeli said, "It's a big mistake for Israel to say it 'won' the war, when there was no war. There were no battles ... no military enemy in the field."

—Norman Finkelstein [435]

News reports about rockets flying from Gaza often mention Israel needing to retaliate in order to defend itself. What has rarely been shown are pictures of the damage caused by the Gaza rockets on Israel. The lack of such footage was strange to me. The news always likes to have dramatic pictures and videos; why were they leaving out pictures of the damage to Israel? There was occasional video coverage and pictures of the leveling of multistory buildings in Gaza by Israeli weapons, yet the damage to Israel, which would be easier for Western reporters to access, was missing in the news.

Presidential candidate Barack Obama made a speech in Sderot, Israel, on July 23, 2008. Sderot is close to Gaza. Behind him were stacks of metal tubes, each approximately six inches in diameter. Here is from his speech:

> For seven years, they've [the residents of Sderot] endured constant threats to their security as demonstrated by this collection of rockets we see here today. [436]

Some of the cylinders behind Obama were more mangled than others. Clearly, no one would want one of those rockets coming down on one's house. Nonetheless, these rockets seemed small and amateurish. Maybe I had not seen damage on the news, because these rockets were simple projectiles, some even home-made, with unsophisticated controls and either poor or missing explosives.

I started looking online for pictures of Israeli damage. I did find some; they were of rockets about two or three feet long where they had broken through a patio or landed on a road. I saw one that had ended up in a house. However, the damage was so small that a handyman could have repaired it. I never saw one that had caused a large explosion or the leveling of a building.

The Israelis are exceptional public relations experts. If there had been pictures of significant damage, they would have paraded and highlighted them in news broadcasts. And yet the attacks *from* Israel, claimed to be in response to these Gaza rockets, were lethal and ruinous, resulting in large craters and the demolition of tall buildings. According to retired US Army Colonel Ann Wright,

> I went to Gaza for the first time in late January 2009, ten days after the brutal Israeli attack ended. As a twenty-nine-year U.S. Army veteran, I was stunned by the amount of destruction. The Israeli attack with American F-16 jets, drones, American Apache attack helicopters, American white phosphorus bombs, and American dense inert metal explosive bombs killed 1,440 Palestinians including 380 children. The attack also wounded over 5,000 and left 50,000 homeless.
>
> Entire areas had been systematically smashed with American-made weapons. Housing for over 50,000 had been blown up; people were living in tents and piled into family and friends' apartments that were very small and already crowded with their own immediate families. The electrical grid, and water and sewage systems had been destroyed. Schools and hospitals were severely damaged. Ambulances were destroyed. Ambulance crews risked their lives to take injured persons out of destroyed neighborhoods by wheelbarrow.[437]

So why would Hamas send up these measly rockets that can't be aimed accurately when they know that their rockets will do minimal, if any, damage and that Israel is going to respond with a barrage of high-powered weaponry and devastation? For the same reason that Gandhi supporters marched on the Dharasana salt depot on May 21, 1930. After worldwide coverage of the brutal attacks on the civilian marchers at the salt depot, Winston Churchill later stated that those protests and the response to enforce Britain's salt tax "inflicted such humiliation and defiance [on Britain] as has not been known since the British first trod the soil of India."[438]

Like the Indians, Palestinians are suffering under colonial rule. Even worse than with the Indians, however, Palestinians in Gaza are dying from being poisoned. The UN declared that Gaza is about to be unlivable. As mentioned earlier, regular bombing of civilian infrastructure and limitations on electrical power result in water that is not fit for consumption and sewage that lacks treatment. As of May 2019, more than one-fourth of all reported disease in Gaza is due to water issues.[439] Despite this horrific, slow death in the largest open-air prison in the world, the international media and governments overwhelmingly disregard this artificial catastrophe. The Palestinians under this continuous terrorism have two choices: to do nothing or to try to get media attention. If they do nothing, they die. If they do something, a few will die quicker, but there may be a glimmer of hope that someone will hear their cry and stop the oppression. As Haneen Zoabi, the Palestinian Israeli former Knesset member, said in an interview with TRT (Turkish public broadcast service): "Let us die in front of the camera and not within our houses without any camera portraying our suffering."[440] It appears that the only way to get the Western news media to cover the crimes against the 1 million adults and 1 million children in Gaza is to bait Israel and escalate the situation to the level of international newsworthiness.

It reminded me of when my kids were learning karate. One day as I was waiting for their lesson to end, I was speaking with one of the instructors about martial arts. He told me that different martial arts had been developed for the different parts of Japanese society:

The samurai tended to be on horseback, and they had swords and armor. The peasants, on the other hand, were disadvantaged: Not only were they swordless, they also had a height disadvantage from not being on a horse. Moreover, they did not have the samurai's protective helmet and armor. The instructor described the peasants' strategy: They had the advantage of numbers. When there was one samurai, there were dozens or more peasants. And once they could get that samurai off that horse and in combat, a group of them could defeat him. Unfortunately, that meant the sacrifice of a few peasants, who would die in compromising the horse and in blocking the sword. But they knew that if none of them acted sacrificially, to get the samurai off the horse or the sword out of the samurai's hand, then they would all lose.

Palestinians in Gaza seemed to be following the Japanese peasant martial art tactics. They are already dying a slow death from the Israeli restrictions on food, medicine, and other supplies as well as from the Israeli-imposed limits on clean water and freedom. The United Nations has already declared Gaza to be shortly unlivable. Like the Japanese peasants, the Palestinians are better off losing a few hundred people in an escalation with Israel if they get international attention than they are just by losing the same number of people from water poisoning or the inability to get food or medicine while getting no media attention. They might as well get value for those deaths.

Another analogy that struck me is that of Clint Eastwood in the movie *Gran Torino*. Near the end of the movie, he knows he is about to die from cancer, and he decides that he might as well have some good come of the end of his life. He goes to the house of a gang who had raped his neighbor, calls out to them from their front yard, and in plain sight of their neighbors pulls out a lighter. A number of the gang members in the house open fire and kill him, thinking he was pulling out a weapon. As a result, the gang members were caught committing murder with witnesses all around.

Palestinians in Gaza want witnesses to the death that Israel is committing. Dying from disease caused by bad water or sewage in the street is invisible. But by accelerating the process by baiting Israel's devastating response, they are making the death more visible.

The Israeli human rights organization B'Tselem reported the following on Israel's Operation Cast Lead:

On 27 December 2008, Israel launched Operation Cast Lead, which lasted until 18 January 2009. According to data collected by B'Tselem, Israel killed 1,391 Palestinians during the fighting, at least 759 of them civilians who had not taken part in the hostilities. Of these, 318 were under the age of 18. Israel also caused extensive damage to structures and to infrastructure, including electricity, water and sewage facilities that were on the brink of collapse even before the fighting and were now rendered completely dysfunctional. According to UN figures, Israel destroyed more than 3,500 homes, leaving tens of thousands of people without shelter or a home to return to. During the offensive, Palestinians fired rocket and mortar shells toward Israel, with the deliberate intention of harming civilians. Three Israeli civilians and one member of the Israeli security forces were killed as a result. In addition, nine Israeli soldiers were killed, four of them from friendly fire.[441]

These deadly attacks are actions by the military, which under international law is responsible for the safety of the people in Gaza.

Think about the relative use of force: 1,391 Palestinians killed, including 318 children, versus 3 Israeli civilians. There was 1 member of the security force killed by the Palestinians. The Palestinians killed 5 Israeli soldiers, and Israel killed 4 of its own soldiers. The Israeli military was so aggressive and undiscerning that almost half the Israeli soldiers killed were killed by their own fellow Israeli soldiers. Such indiscriminate killing is a massacre.

What made this massacre of around 1,400 people even more inhumane was how Israel used the chemical white phosphorus (WP) on the civilian population. Peter Kaiser, spokesman for the Chemical Weapons Convention (CWC), responded to being asked if WP is a chemical weapon by saying that smoke and camouflage are legitimate but that

> any chemicals used against humans or animals that cause harm or death through the toxic properties of the chemical are considered chemical weapons.[442]

In other words, if those weapons are used in civilian areas where the chemicals are likely to contact civilians, then they become "chemical weapons." The US is a party to the CWC, and Israel signed the convention on January 13, 1993, but has never ratified it.[443]

Here is from a report by Amnesty International:

> White phosphorus, a highly incendiary substance, was repeatedly fired indiscriminately over densely populated residential areas, killing and wounding civilians and destroying civilian property. It was often launched from artillery shells in air-burst mode, which aggravated the already devastating consequences of the attacks. Each shell ejected over a hundred felt wedges impregnated with highly incendiary white phosphorus, which rained down over houses and streets, igniting on exposure to oxygen and setting fire to people and property. Once their incendiary content had been discharged, the artillery shells often crashed into buildings causing further deaths and injuries. Repeated denials of the use of white phosphorus by Israeli officials during the conflict delayed or prevented appropriate treatment for people suffering agonizing burns. Some who died might otherwise have been saved.[444]

Doctors treated burns not knowing that they were from white phosphorus. Instead of the patients being relieved, the initial treatments were ineffective because the chemical kept burning inside the patients' bodies.

Artillery in general and white phosphorus shells in particular should never be used in populated areas.* Yet in Gaza Israeli forces repeatedly fired them into densely populated residential areas, knowing that such imprecise weapons would kill and injure civilians. Such attacks were indiscriminate and as such unlawful under international law.

The scale and intensity of the attacks were unprecedented, even in the context of the increasingly lethal Israeli military campaigns in Gaza in previous years. More Palestinians were killed and more properties were destroyed in the 22-day military campaign than in any previous Israeli offensive.[445]

Gaza is a densely populated area where most of the residents are children. This unprecedented assault had no strategic military objective. The report showed that the Israelis knew they were targeting and collectively punishing civilians and therefore children:

> Israeli forces could not conceivably have been unaware of the presence of civilians in locations which were repeatedly attacked, including with white phosphorus and other imprecise weapons, given that these areas were under close surveillance by Israeli drones.

> Even though Israeli officials knew from the first days of Operation "Cast Lead" that civilians were killed and wounded in significant numbers, Israeli forces continued to employ the same tactics for the entire duration of the 22-day offensive, resulting in growing numbers of civilian casualties. The pattern of attacks and the resulting high number of civilian fatalities and casualties showed elements of reckless conduct, disregard for civilian lives and property and a consistent failure to distinguish between military targets and civilians and civilian objects.[446]

---

* Population density in Gaza is some 4,200 people per square kilometer. The refugee camps have one of the highest population densities in the world. For example, over 82,000 refugees live in the al-Shati (Beach) camp, which is less than one square kilometer in size.

Remember that we had invaded Iraq half a decade earlier, based on the assertion that Iraq had chemical weapons. Here are excerpts from an article in *The Guardian* on the white phosphorus used in Operation Cast Lead:

> Israel has admitted—after mounting pressure—that its troops may have used white phosphorus shells in contravention of international law, during its three-week offensive in the Gaza Strip.
>
> One of the places most seriously affected by the use of white phosphorus was the main UN compound in Gaza City, which was hit by three shells on 15 January. The same munition was used in a strike on the al-Quds hospital in Gaza City the same day. ...
>
> "They obviously could not have gone on denying the use of phosphorus," Donatella Rovera, Amnesty researcher for Israel and the Occupied Territories, told the Guardian yesterday. "There are still phosphorus wedges burning all over Gaza including at the UN compound and at the school." ...
>
> Amnesty on Monday warned that Israel could be guilty of war crimes, saying the use of the shells in a civilian areas was "clear and undeniable." ...
>
> The admission that the shells may have been used improperly follows yesterday's demand by the UN secretary general Ban Ki-moon for an investigation into the targeting of UN facilities—including by phosphorus weapons.[447]

Not only did Israel use white phosphorus in a civilian area, it felt sufficiently confident of impunity to drop it on the main UN compound, a hospital, and a school. I had to reread the IDF Code of Ethics quoted at the beginning of this section: "They will use their arms only for the purpose of achieving their mission, without inflicting unnecessary injury to human life or limb." Either the

IDF's mission is to inflict unnecessary injury to Palestinians, or in Israel, the word *human* does not apply to Palestinians.

The next major operation occurred four years later. On November 14, 2012, Israel launched Operation Pillar of Defense. B'Tselem listed the results of the eight-day operation:

> Israel killed 167 Palestinians, at least 87 of whom had not participated in the fighting. Of these, 32 were under the age of 18. Over the course of the fighting, four Israeli civilians and two members of the security forces were killed by rockets that Palestinians fired from the Gaza Strip.[448]

These overwhelmingly one-sided massacres were followed two years later, in 2014, with Operation Protective Edge. The massacres were so horrific that UN Secretary-General Ban Ki-moon called out, "The massive death and destruction in Gaza have shocked and shamed the world."[449] According to the UN Relief and Works Agency for Palestine Refugees in the Near East (UNRWA):

> The scale of human loss, destruction, devastation and displacement caused by the 2014 conflict in Gaza—the third within seven years—was catastrophic, unprecedented and unparalleled in Gaza, since at least the start of the Israeli occupation in 1967 and further eroded whatever resilience the people in Gaza still have left. During the 50 days of hostilities lasting from 8 July until 26 August 2014, 2,251 Palestinians were killed; 1,462 of them are believed to be civilians, including 551 children and 299 women. 66 Israeli soldiers and five civilians, including one child, were also killed. Overall, 11,231 Palestinians were injured during the conflict, including 3,540 women and 3,436 children. Roughly one third of these children will have to cope with disabilities lasting throughout life as a result of their injuries.
>
> During the conflict, 118 UNRWA installations were damaged, including 83 schools and 10 health centres. In total, over 12,600

housing units were totally destroyed and almost 6,500 sustained severe damage. Almost 150,000 additional housing units sustained various degrees of damage and remained inhabitable. The conflict led to a massive displacement crisis in Gaza, with almost 500,000 persons internally displaced at its peak.[450]

UNRWA further reported that nearly 300,000 children needed humanitarian assistance, "including non-food-items, food, water, [and] psycho-social support."

One has to step back and allow these massacres to sink in. Gaza is a densely packed strip of land without a military and under blockade. People cannot get drinking water or regular electricity and medicines. And this mostly child population gets regularly bombed and massacred. And these numbers understate civilian casualties.* Israel uses Gaza as its military testing lab. The people of Gaza are Israel's guinea pigs.

Three years later, the UN Office for the Coordination of Humanitarian Affairs of the Palestinian territories (OCHAoPt) reported on the results of the 2014 hostilities:[451]

- One million tons of rubble have been removed in Gaza.

- Reconstruction of a hospital and three clinics that were totally destroyed is either pending or ongoing.

- 78 hospitals and clinics across Gaza were damaged but not destroyed, and have all been repaired.

- 299 women, including at least 16 pregnant, and 197 girls were killed.

---

* When contrasting Israeli civilian numbers with Palestinian ones, it is important to understand the definition of *civilian*. Israeli military personnel are not considered civilians. However, when Palestinians are attacked, civilians become "combatants" if they respond to being attacked. Since there is no Palestinian military, if Israel makes an incursion and starts killing people, those who hit a soldier over the head with something suddenly become combatants. This tends to understate the civilian casualties on the Palestinian side, both because of the level of incursions from Israel into Gaza relative to incursions from Gaza into Israel, and because Palestinians do not have a military. See chapter 12, where this is discussed further.

- At least 790 women were widowed.

- More than 2,000 women and hundreds of girls were injured.

- Some 900 Palestinians, a third of them children, became permanently disabled.

- About 100 injured Palestinians underwent amputation of limbs.

- Seven schools were destroyed; one of them has been rebuilt, and the rest are under reconstruction.

- 247 schools across Gaza were damaged but not destroyed, and all have been repaired.

- Over 160,000 Palestinian children are estimated to need continuous psychosocial support.

- Approximately 100,000 Palestinians had their homes destroyed or severely damaged.

- Two years on, 65,000 Palestinians in Gaza remain displaced.

- Delays in home reconstruction stem from import restrictions, funding gaps, lack of planning, and land ownership issues.

- Since the ceasefire, 17 civilians have been killed in Gaza, and 100 more have been injured, by explosive remnants of war.

- There is no funding for the repair of about a third of the damage to the water and sanitation infrastructure and equipment.

- So far, Israeli investigations on the 2014 hostilities have resulted in only one indictment issued for a case of looting.

Once one studies Gaza, the blockade, and these military operations, it becomes clear that *war* is not an apt description of these operations—unless *war* is an Israel word. In English, such a "war" can only be described as a "massacre."

The Merriam-Webster dictionary defines *massacre* as follows:

massacre. *n.*
1. the act or an instance of killing a number of usually helpless or unresisting human beings under circumstances of atrocity or cruelty
2. a cruel or wanton murder

3. a wholesale slaughter of animals
4. an act of complete destruction

Around 2003, after our "Shock and Awe" campaign in Iraq, I read Chris Hedges's book *War Is a Force That Gives Us Meaning*. In the introduction he describes his coverage of wars—from Central America, to Kosovo, to Gaza and the West Bank. Not only does he describe the horrors, the negative consequences to all involved, but he adds the following observation:

> Even as I detest the pestilence that is war and fear its deadly addiction, even as I see it lead states and groups towards self-immolation, even as I conceded that it is war that has left millions of dead and maimed across the planet, I, like most reporters in Sarajevo and Kosovo, desperately hoped for armed intervention. The poison that is war does not free us from the ethics of responsibility. There are times when we must take this poison—just as a person with cancer accepts chemotherapy to live. We can not succumb to despair. Force is and I suspect always will be part of the human condition. *There are times when the force wielded by one immoral faction must be countered by a faction that, while never moral, is perhaps less immoral* [emphasis added].[452]

Hedges is describing immorality as relative. It may be immoral to violently yank a child by the arm; yet when that is done to pull that child from an approaching car, then it is the right thing to do. In that case, the violent pulling of the child is less immoral than letting the car hit the child.

Rarely are two situations equally immoral. In fact, much of the language around Israel is about military actions being "defensive." Labeling actions as *defensive* rather than *offensive* gives the impression of moral superiority. How can we measure relative immorality? By analyzing who gets killed and injured: Is it the armed robber who broke into your house or the lady whose purse was stolen.

One way to compare relative immorality is to look at the injuries and deaths to civilians relative to soldiers and combatants. The killing of a child in bed, or while he or she is going to school, is very different from the killing of a soldier who is attacking you. Killing may be immoral, but these examples are not equally immoral. Stepping back from the Gaza situation and evaluating the relative immorality of each side, we get the following statistics from the 2014 events that Israel calls Operation Protective Edge:

2014 Gaza Operation Protective Edge

	Soldiers/Combatants	Civilians	Women	Children
Israeli casualties	93%	7%		1%
Palestinian deaths	35%	65%	13%	24%
Palestinian injuries			32%	31%

The Israeli government was willing to kill nearly two Palestinian civilians for each combatant. In other words, they were willing to kill nearly twice as many civilians as "enemy" fighters. By contrast, 93 percent of the Israelis killed by Palestinians in Gaza were soldiers. Hamas was immoral in killing Israeli civilians, but as Hedges points out, we need to compare the relative immorality of all the parties involved.

I went to a talk by an American military law professor who happened to mention Gaza in his presentation—Operation Protective Edge, in particular. He took the perspective that Israel had gone above and beyond the rules of armed conflict to protect civilians. He mentioned he had come to that conclusion after working with the Jewish Institute for National Security of America (JINSA) task force evaluating the Israeli army's actions after the war. That task force included a significant representation of retired American generals. Its executive summary included the following:

Contrary to accusations of widespread unlawful military conduct, we observed that Israel systemically applied established rules of conduct that adhered to or exceeded the Law of Armed Conflict (LOAC) in a virtually unprecedented effort to avoid inflicting civilian casualties, even when doing so would have been lawfully permitted, and to satisfy the concerns of critics. However, it is the conclusion of this Task Force that Israel's military restraint unintentionally empowered Hamas to distort both the law and facts for their own purposes to the ultimate detriment of civilians' safety, for which Hamas bears sole responsibility.[453]

This is an interesting conclusion, considering the hugely one-sided casualties documented by UNRWA: 1,462 Palestinians believed to be civilians, including 551 children and 299 women killed, versus 5 Israeli civilians, including 1 child.[454] It is interesting to note how the JINSA report was worded as "Hamas's strategy and Israel's response"[455] when Hamas itself was created in response to Israel's treatment of Palestinians.

A literal massacre and decimation of neighborhoods and infrastructure of a primarily refugee child population by one of the most powerful militaries in the world was rationalized as defensive. This justification of destruction was from the military that under international law was supposed to defend the same civilians it regularly attacks. The report left out that the military that bombed the civilian population was the military that created this refugee crisis. The same military that was being praised for its "restraint" was the one illegally preventing the civilians from returning to their homeland.

When a group of people view a civilian population in such a way as to justify the violation of human rights and to enforce oppression through violence, then the oppressors have lost their humanity. George Orwell wrote:

> In an intellectual way, Syme was venomously orthodox. He would talk with a disagreeable gloating satisfaction of helicopter raids on enemy villages, and trials and confessions of thought-criminals, the executions in the cellars of the Ministry of Love.[456]

I referred earlier to a 2017 article about Hamas and Israel negotiating prisoner exchanges. The article also mentioned the following:

> On Sunday Channel 2 news cited Israeli security sources saying that Hamas had raised new demands in the indirect talks,

including that Israel release thousands of Palestinians who were arrested in the lead-up to the summer 2014 war in the Strip.[457]

Note that the article mentions that there were thousands of prisoners taken in the lead-up to the summer 2014 war (Operation Protective Edge). The JINSA report, however, did not mention thousands of prisoners taken in the lead-up to the war. Is it possible that Hamas was "responding" to that Israeli action? Did the 2014 war really start when prisoners were taken or later, when Hamas acted? Which party was *retaliating* depends on when one claims the events started.

If the results are so devastating to the civilian population by the occupying power's bombing, then what does that tell us about what JINSA referred to as the "established rules of conduct" per the Law of Armed Conflict (LOAC)? Who writes those laws and to whose advantage? In this case, the advantage clearly went to the oppressing military rather than to the civilians.

Laws are written by those in power. They are often also written to support the maintenance of power. That explains the existence of slave laws and Jim Crow laws.* When laws are so egregious that they reveal their inhumanity and their ethical flaws, we as human beings have to take a stand against them. Consistent with a sign I saw at the Women's March on January 20, 2018, "When Injustice Becomes Law, Resistance Becomes Duty," I am thankful that the writers of the Declaration of Independence, Henry David Thoreau, Frederick Douglass, Susan B. Anthony, Eugene V. Debs, Rosa Parks, Martin Luther King Jr., and many others stood up against laws they thought were unjust.

Like these American heroes, who struggled for what they thought was justice, I was touched by a comment Haneen Zoabi made at an event I attended. She said that *she does not pursue her struggle for equality and human rights because she is optimistic or pessimistic; she pursues the struggle because to abandon the struggle would be to give up her humanity.*

---

* Jim Crow laws were state and local ordinances in the United States that limited the rights of African Americans and enforced segregation.

If a law justifies the mass killing of innocent civilians, including women and children, merely based on their ethnicity, then I would hope that everyone, including lawyers, would stand up against that law rather than enforce it. What we need are Americans standing up against, rather than hiding behind, such inhumane laws.

12

Terrorism

A deal is not a deal when you're dealing with terrorists. Have you ever negotiated with terrorists?

—Senator Marco Rubio,[458]
countering Donald Trump's approach to Israeli-Palestinian talks, implying that the Palestinians were terrorists, February 25, 2016

Somebody who is fighting against Israeli soldiers is an enemy and we will fight back, but I believe that this is not under the definition of terrorism, if the target is a soldier.

—Israeli cabinet member Tzipi Livni,[459]
March 2006

Turkish President Tayyip Erdogan called his Israeli counterpart Benjamin Netanyahu a "terrorist" on Sunday, escalating an exchange of insults that started after he criticized Israel's lethal military response to a demonstration on the Gazan border.

—Reuters,[460]
April 1, 2018

[Israeli Palestinian] Dareen Tatour was arrested in 2015 and held in house arrest for nearly three years for publishing a poem on Facebook. On Thursday morning, an Israeli court convicted her of incitement to violence and support for a terrorist organization.

+972 Magazine[461]
(Israeli Human Rights magazine[*,462]),
May 3, 2018

The whole world will hear what Israel's democracy is. A democracy for Jews only. Only Arabs go to jail. The court said I am convicted of terrorism. If that's my terrorism, I give the world a terrorism of love.

—Dareen Tatour,[463]
response to the verdict

What Is Terrorism?

I f the definition of terrorism seems confusing in the Middle East, it can also be confusing here in the United States. Consider this comparison from the *Los Angeles Times* in 2017:

When an assailant shot to death 49 people last year at the Pulse nightclub in Orlando, CNN called the massacre "the worst incident of domestic terrorism since 9/11." Last month, when a shooter killed 58 people at a music festival on the Las Vegas Strip, news outlets described him as a "granddad," a "gambler" and a "former accountant" — but not as a terrorist.[464]

---

*   *+972 Magazine* describes itself as a publication whose goal is "providing fresh, in-depth reporting and analysis directly from the ground in Israel-Palestine. The magazine is committed to human rights, democracy, and freedom of information, and actively opposes the Israeli occupation. However, +972 Magazine does not represent any outside organization, political party, or agenda."

The term *terrorism* became commonplace on 9/11 and during the ensuing "war on terror." Then, during the invasion of Iraq in 2003, I became aware that there was a problem with the term *terrorism*; I heard someone say, "One man's terrorist is another man's freedom fighter," and realized that I didn't know the definition of *terrorism*.

The term *terrorism* is used regularly by governments and the media. It is a term that is seldom defined. By not defining it clearly and precisely, individuals and governments are able to accuse individuals and groups of being terrorists without having to be held accountable for that accusation. Even worse, the lack of a clear definition enables those with the loudest voice to accuse others of being terrorists while covering up their own terrorism.

This chapter looks at the definition of *terrorism*. We look at how the language and framing can make us unaware of certain forms of terrorism. Even worse, language and framing has been used to convince people that certain forms of terrorism are not only not terrorism but instead are acceptable normality. Finally, this chapter looks at how the lack of specificity and clarity in one's definition of *terrorism* leads to such terms as *counterterrorism* being used to support, rather than oppose, terrorism and how these misleading concepts are broadcast in the media.

Once we have defined* terrorism*, we can recognize it; only then can we truly combat it.

One's definition of terrorism is extremely important. It can even affect our freedoms. For example, 18 US Code §2331(5)[465] defines *domestic terrorism* as activities that

> (A) involve acts dangerous to human life that are a violation of the criminal laws of the United States or of any State;
> (B) appear to be intended—
>> (i)   to intimidate or coerce a civilian population;
>> (ii) to influence the policy of a government by intimidation or coercion; or
>> (iii) to affect the conduct of a government by mass destruction, assassination, or kidnapping; and

(C) occur primarily within the territorial jurisdiction of the
United States.

This definition may seem reasonable until one notices that
acts of nonviolent protest can be categorized legally as terrorism.
Environmental and peace protesters can now be characterized as
terrorists when they participate in "acts dangerous to human life
that are a violation of the criminal laws of the United States" and
that are intended to "influence the policy of a government," even
when the lives they endanger are their own. With this definition,
walking into a military base unarmed and sitting on a bombing
field to protest the war economy is terrorism. Staying perched in
a national forest tree that logging companies are trying to cut down
can now officially and legally be called terrorism.

Some may say such concern is extreme. However, the FBI
website specifically names potential domestic terrorists as "those of
a political, religious, social, racial, or environmental nature."[466]

Our definition of *terrorism* is therefore extremely important. We
need to be conscious of where our freedom of speech is usurped
by charges of terrorism. We also need to be aware of a system of
repression that makes speaking out and peaceful protest onerous.
The American Civil Liberties Union (ACLU) states that Section
806 of the Patriot Act

> could result in the civil seizure of their [the protesters'] assets
> without a prior hearing, and without them ever being convicted of
> a crime. It is by far the most significant change of which political
> organizations need to be aware. Section 806 amended the civil
> asset forfeiture statute to authorize the government to seize and
> forfeit: all assets, foreign or domestic (i) of any individual, entity,
> or organization engaged in planning or perpetrating any act of
> domestic or international terrorism against the United States, or
> their property, and all assets, foreign or domestic, affording any
> person a source of influence over any such entity or organization.[467]

Such laws provide the government with the authority to significantly punish citizens for not falling in line. These kinds of laws lay the foundation for a government that is no longer of, by, and for the people. This one definition of *terrorism* suddenly strips us of quite a bit of freedom.

Then 18 US Code §2331(5) defines *international terrorism* similarly to *domestic terrorism*, primarily differentiating it by stating that its activities "occur primarily" outside the United States or "transcend national boundaries."[468]

According to Section 2656f(d) of Title 22 of the United States Code,

> (2) the term "terrorism" means premeditated, politically motivated violence perpetrated against non-combatant targets by subnational groups or clandestine agents.[469]

This definition might be preferable because it uses the word *violence* instead of "acts dangerous to human life"; it would be harder to call sitting in a tree violence. However, this definition provides another twist; it limits terrorists to only being "subnational groups or clandestine agents."

Therefore, according to the US government, it is not just what you do that makes you a terrorist; it is also who you are. Using this definition, neither the US government nor any other country's government can be called a terrorist organization.

These definitions of terrorism can have unintended consequences. Sometimes arbitrary definitions can put the United States in unexpected positions. The civil war in Syria is an example. The government of Syria was accused of dropping chemical weapons and bombing its own civilian population. According to Section 2656f(d) of Title 22, the Syrian government is not a terrorist organization, because it is a national government.

In that same conflict, the United States supported nongovernmental groups that were also committing violence against civilians. Therefore, using the same definition, the United States is supporting terrorists in that civil war. Writing the regulation to define a terrorist organization as nongovernmental would have seemed to provide the United States government with a "Get out of jail" card. In this case, however, it does the opposite because the (Syrian) government is committing atrocities and the US is supporting a nongovernmental unit.

The expression that one person's terrorist is another person's freedom fighter is also problematic, as I mentioned at the beginning of this chapter. Defining *terrorism* that way is to make it mean not much more than *enemy*.

To terrorism victims, who you are is not important. What you do to them is. Someone committing robbery, rape, or murder is a robber, rapist, or murderer whether they are your relative or a complete stranger from abroad. Likewise with terrorism: The problem is the crime, not whether it's local or foreign, or whether the perpetrator is an individual, an organization, or a government.

Language has consequences. If we include selective criteria for the offending party in the definition of *terrorism*, then our attention is distracted from the crime itself to whether or not the perpetrator is part of a group that gets off the hook.

Terrorism does not just include a specified set of tactics, such as suicide bombing. Terrorism is more about who the target is (civilians), what the strategy is (the threat or use of violence), and what the purpose is (financial or political).

For *terrorism* we need to avoid usage definitions and insist on dictionary or aspirational definitions. We need a definition that is not hypocritical; we need a definition that we would objectively agree with whether we might be the perpetrator or the victim. This leads me to the following aspirational definition:

> **terrorism.** *n.* The threat or use of violence against civilians for economic or political purposes.

It is very similar to a couple of dictionary definitions:

- In Dictionary.com: "The use of violence and threats to intimidate or coerce, especially for political purposes."[470]

- In FreeDictionary.com: "The use of violence or the threat of violence, especially against civilians, in the pursuit of political goals."[471]

Terrorism is a word that carries a lot of emotional energy. Terrorism is a "bad" thing. It carries much more bad energy than even *enemy* or the weaker word *adversary*.

With a clear definition we can identify true terrorism. Even better, because we can now identify terrorism more accurately and precisely, we can identify its causes. The only way to truly fight terrorism is to aim for its causes. Only with a clear and well-grounded definition of *terrorism* can we critically process the messaging we hear from the press and politicians. A clear definition is required to filter out propaganda.

As an exercise, let us review the US State Department coverage of Operation Cast Lead (also known as the 2008/2009 Gaza War or one of the Gaza massacres) and compare it to what actually happened. The archived Department of State web page describes the situation as follows:

> In response to a sharp increase in the number and frequency of rocket attacks into Israel prior to and following the expiration of Hamas' agreed period of "calm" on December 19, 2008, the Israeli Air Force launched Operation Cast Lead.[472]

These "rocket attacks" were violence against civilians in southern Israel. There were unfortunately three Israeli civilian deaths. Using our *terrorism* definition, Hamas committed terrorist acts that resulted in the Israeli civilian casualties.

Hamas partially justified these indiscriminate rocket launches into civilian areas based on Israel's occupation of Gaza. Israel has violated the human rights of Palestinians in Gaza and has occupied Gaza for more than fifty years. Occupation, including its violations of human rights, is violence against civilians; occupation therefore also meets our *terrorism* definition.

In addition, for over a decade the Israeli blockade of Gaza has been an additional form of violence against all 2 million Palestinians in Gaza. The blockade is a form of violence where force is used to block access to food and supplies, force is used to restrict freedom of movement, and force is used to destroy economic survival through significant restrictions on fishing, imports, and exports.[473] Therefore, Israel's blockade also meets our definition of *terrorism*.

Relative Terrorism

Israel's Operation Cast Lead resulted in civilian casualties. Close to 1,400 Palestinians, including over 750 civilians, died in the 2008/2009 operation.[474] In addition, Human Rights Watch reported that

> 3,540 homes, 268 factories and warehouses, as well as schools, vehicles, water wells, public infrastructure, greenhouses and large swathes of agricultural land, were destroyed, and 2,870 houses were severely damaged.[475]

So, yes, both sides committed terrorism using our definition. By learning about conflicts such as Operation Cast Lead, I also learned that determining whether a group was performing terrorism was not enough; I also needed to look at the level of terrorism committed by all parties. In this case, the scale of terrorism committed by each side is incomparable. Israel caused over 750 Palestinian civilian deaths, including over 300 children; Hamas caused 3 Israeli civilian deaths.

The occupation of Gaza is very violent. When Palestinians in Gaza, 70 percent of whom are refugees, try to return to their homeland, they get shot by the Israeli military. The Israeli demolition of homes in Gaza near the border is violence against civilians. The shooting of farmers working in their fields in Gaza is violence against civilians. The shooting at Gaza fishers by the Israeli navy is violence against civilians. The bombing of homes, schools, and hospitals is also violence against civilians.

If Gaza residents try to bring in blocked medical supplies, food, building supplies, and other basic necessities through tunnels, then

Israel's response is violent. If Gaza residents try to take their injured by boat for treatment, Israel has violently prevented them from doing so. When fishers take their boats beyond several nautical miles from shore for better fishing, they are shot at by the Israeli navy, and their boats are confiscated. When outsiders have tried to bring medical supplies by boat through freedom flotillas, those boats have been hijacked by the Israeli forces, the crews have been taken to Israel against their will, and the boats have been confiscated—all forms of violence against civilians.

But the definition of *terrorism* includes not only violence but also the threat of violence.

What keeps Palestinians from returning to their villages and towns in Israel is the threat of violence. That makes the blockade terrorism. The occupation and blockade are terrorist actions way beyond the casualties we may hear about in the news.

The evidence is clear that Hamas committed terrorism. Israel, though, committed much more significant terrorism not only based on the relative number of deaths but also because of its continuous threats of violence in enforcing the world's largest open-air prison.

When Palestinians killed only one more Israeli soldier than Israelis killed of their own from friendly fire during Operation Cast Lead, then how can the Israeli invasion be called defensive? How one-sided is this conflict when the group whose territory was being invaded kills 9 of the invader and the invader kills close to 1,400 and injures thousands more? Operation Cast Lead was layers of Israeli terrorism. The massacre of a mostly civilian population was terrorism. That massacre was a result of the terrorism of an invasion and a vastly disproportionate bombardment. That terrorism was on top of the terrorism from a blockade on top of terrorism of an occupation.

After I consciously defined the term *terrorism* and then used that definition to review situations, my view of terrorism evolved. Previously, I had considered only those nongovernment suicide bombers to be terrorists. With a more focused definition based on acts committed against civilians, I started to see who most terrorizes civilians. Shining a light on what makes up terrorism completely changed my view about who are the real terrorists.

With a clear, objective definition, I became focused on acts of violence and threats of violence against civilians. I then saw the Israeli military, which killed the unarmed, twenty-three-year-old American Rachel Corrie,[476] as a terrorist organization. I saw the driver of a bulletproof bulldozer who demolishes a Palestinian house and expels its civilian homeowners as a terrorist. The Israeli government's imposing limits on food, electricity, and clean water—limits that cause illness and death—became obvious terrorist acts.

When I saw the occupying power, which is by international law supposed to protect the occupied, instead bombing that population, then I saw who are the terrorists. When I saw a video of a child with an infected leg who was denied by the Israeli government an exit permit for medical treatment,[477] I saw terrorism through a new lens. This occupation is a form of terrorism against millions of people; its acts of terrorism occur twenty-four hours a day, every day of the year.

Normalizing Terrorism

There is no comparison between the suicidal terrorism of the desperate and the reasoned terrorism of an overarmed state.

—*Ilan Halevi,*[478,*]

Israel operates as if the occupation of the West Bank, East Jerusalem, Golan Heights, and Gaza are normal. They operate as if the Gaza blockade is normal. They operate as if the denial of the Right of Return is normal. They operate as if the ethnicity-related laws, even for Palestinian Israeli citizens, are normal. Accepting the denial of human rights (through the occupation, blockade, and

---

* Ilan Halevi (1943–2013) was a French-born Jewish writer who acted as the PLO vice minister of foreign affairs at the 1991 Madrid Conference. He described himself as "100 percent Jewish, 100 percent Arab."

racist laws) as normal has an ugly consequence: It makes violence to support these injustices normal. It also makes self-defense a crime.

Normalization of the occupation turns ethics and humanity on their head. *A normalized occupation changes the definition of terrorism, and with it who is the terrorist. Instead of the terrorist being the person who through violence forces someone to leave their home, the terrorist is redefined to be the civilian who is defending him or herself from the military invader.*

With a normalized occupation, the invading army stealing land and violently removing people from their homes and their land are merely considered a part of law enforcement.

Normalization of a brutal occupation changes the definition of *defensive.* People who were defending themselves against an invading military are merely redefined to be the aggressors against those whose job is to enforce the oppression. In George Orwell's *1984*, the Ministry of Truth had the party's three slogans inscribed on its building: "WAR IS PEACE. FREEDOM IS SLAVERY. IGNORANCE IS STRENGTH." When one normalizes occupation, one could add the following to the slogans: "OPPRESSION IS DEFENSIVE. SELF-PROTECTION IS TERRORISM."

The Israel language supports this normalization of the occupation. The language blurs lines and creates the illusion that the abnormal is normal. Israel hides actual terrorism and rewords it—in the process making actual terrorism normal. *A clear and precise definition of terrorism is needed in order to act as a light and yardstick. A clear definition is needed in order to highlight and measure the actual terrorism. A clear definition is needed to see when terrorism becomes normalized.*

The normality of terrorism can be so prevalent that one can miss it. Chapter 9 contained this quote from Israeli Finance Minister Yuval Steinitz:

> I think the burden of proof is on the Palestinians, to make it certain, to give us guarantees that money delivered by Israel is not going to the Hamas, is not going to a terrorist organisation.[479]

We can clearly understand Israel not wanting money, even if it is not theirs, going to Hamas. However, the finance minister's language is interesting in how it normalizes terrorism. The regime that occupies a people, that has control over 70 percent of the revenue of the occupied so-called government, that regularly murders and dispossesses its subjects, that violates their human rights every day, is calling an enemy of such a regime a terrorist organization. The minister who finances his own state's terrorism says he does not want money going to a terrorist organization! Who knows? He may even be oblivious to the irony of his statement—the irony that the larger terrorist organization is holding the money to prevent it from getting into the hands of smaller, less powerful terrorists. The occupier pot is calling the occupied kettle a terrorist.

I asked a Jewish acquaintance who lives in Israel if he was concerned about terrorism there. He replied that he was not worried about terrorism; he said he was far more likely to die in an automobile accident than from terrorism. This told me that the fear of terrorism promoted by our news media and politicians may not be based on reality. *The fear is promoted to Americans and Israelis to justify the oppression—to justify the state terrorism.*

On January 31, 2018, the BBC did follow-up TV coverage on the case of Ahed Tamimi, a sixteen-year-old girl who was arrested for slapping a soldier with her hand. The soldier had come onto and remained on her family's property in the West Bank. She had slapped the soldier shortly after another soldier had shot a rubber-coated metal bullet into her fifteen-year-old cousin's head in the same village. During the interview, BBC reporter Jeremy Bowen interviewed Israeli Knesset member Oren Hazan:[480]

HAZAN: If I was there, she would finish in the hospital. For sure. Nobody could stop me. I will kick, kick her face. Believe me.

BOWEN: She's a sixteen-year-old girl.

HAZAN: No, I don't look at it like this. Because today is a sixteen-year-old girl who punched a soldier; tomorrow she will stuck a knife in her [a soldier's] throat.

Note that the Knesset member considers kicking a sixteen-year-old girl in the face until she goes to the hospital an appropriate response to the girl slapping a soldier who had invaded her property. The logic he uses is a slippery one: He rationalizes actions that are far more violent than hers, based on what she might do in the future. Never mind that her actions are minuscule relative to the actions the soldiers had already committed against her and her family.

BOWEN: They say they are taking part in peaceful protest.

HAZAN: You see me smiling. If this is peaceful protest, I don't want to imagine what is not a peaceful protest.

BOWEN: A slap isn't terrorism.

HAZAN: No, a slap is terrorism. Believe me. A slap is a terrorism.

The term *terrorism* has been hijacked when it is used to describe a girl slapping a much taller, armed enemy soldier who has invaded her land. The term has also been hijacked when shooting an unarmed teenager in the face at close range is not called terrorism.

Definitions affect not only how we view a situation; they ultimately affect our actions. For this reason, it is important for each of us to consciously choose the aspirational definitions we believe most appropriate for terms. Those definitions will affect the kind of behavior that we, and ultimately our society, consider normal and acceptable.

It is also important that we are conscious of the usage definitions that are employed by others. Otherwise, we can be swayed.

A piece by Omar Rahman, an associate editor at World Politics Review, described how the language, tone, and content of the messaging we hear implies normalization of a very unbalanced situation:

> It has become senseless for Israelis and Palestinians to act like nothing is wrong with the status quo and carry-on with such projects. Normalization may be fine for those bridging the gaps between people in India and Pakistan or Venezuela and Colombia—where the two sides are on equal footing—but not in

Israel/Palestine where one side lives under the yoke and chain of the other. When we seek to normalize this relationship by giving each other equal standing and equal voice, we project an image of symmetry. Joint sports teams and theatre groups, hosting an Israeli orchestra in Ramallah or Nablus, all these things create a false sense of normality, like the issue is only a problem of recognizing each other as human beings. This, however, ignores the ongoing oppression, colonization, and denial of rights, committed by one side against the other.

Moreover, *normalization creates a false sense in the mind of Israelis that they are working for peace, while in actuality, though maybe unwittingly, they are contributing to the calcification of the status quo. Their energy is misdirected away from root causes and channeled into making the current situation more tolerable—largely for themselves—by helping them to cope with wider injustices occurring in their name.* Many Israelis who participate in normalization projects believe that they are detached, that they are not part of the problem, because they have some Palestinian friends or colleagues, even if they are doing nothing to rectify the actual injustices that have been committed by their society daily for over half a century. In the words of Israeli architectural theorist Eyal Weizman in his monumental work on the architecture of occupation, *Hollow Land*: *"The history of the occupation is full of liberal 'men of peace' who are responsible for, or who at least sweeten, the injustice committed by the occupation. The occupation would not have been possible without them"* [emphasis added].[481]

As Americans, we have sweetened the injustice by funding small infrastructure projects and sending money to the confined population. Unfortunately, we are also the ones who make the occupation and violation of human rights possible by funding the government whose wall confines that population, by providing the weapons that oppress the same people, by supplying the armored bulldozers that are used to demolish Palestinian homes and schools, and by vetoing Security Council resolutions intended to hold Israel accountable for its human rights violations.

With a clear definition of *terrorism*, I am now more conscious of the threats and violence committed against civilians. This makes me better able to identify terrorism. I am also now aware that terrorists' tools may be bulldozers as well as bombs. Terrorism may come from a soldier or a settler's gun as well as from knives or stones. Terrorism may even come from something that seems as mundane as a policy of denying building permits. Such a discriminatory policy results in the demolition of tens of thousands of houses. Such administrative language and procedures are the terrorist's weapon for taking farmland, for bulldozing schools, and for destroying the solar panels donated by European countries. I feel more at peace now in evaluating terrorism based on the actions committed rather than on the party performing those actions. Unfortunately, my new awareness often puts my government on the oppressor side of the equation.

Irish Senator Frances Black understands the twisted policies and how other countries are complicit by normalizing these crimes. She introduced the "Control of Economic Activity (Occupied Territories) Bill 2018." Here is her statement before the Seanad Éireann (Irish Senate):

> I saw the impact of settlement expansion when I visited the West Bank earlier this year. ... I witnessed the restrictions on movement, the shrinking space for housing and healthcare facilities, a chronic lack of supply of electricity and the crushing indignity of a Palestinian community having been cut off from its water supply, which had been diverted to support an Israeli chicken farm. That is horrendous and the injustice of it will stay with me forever. That commercial settlement built on stolen land beyond Israel's internationally recognised borders is a war crime. ... I ask my colleagues across the House whether the moral response is to condemn that action as illegal but then ask how much the eggs cost? There is deep hypocrisy in such a position.[482]

By doing something as mundane as buying eggs or hummus at the grocery store, we might be supporting terrorism. Unlike cigarette packs or cartons, egg containers don't have warning labels on them—labels such as "Product of Terrorism." Terrorism has been so normalized that we see it only if we know where to look.

The first step is to realize that terrorism is occurring and being normalized. The second step is to choose to oppose it.

And what is the best way to fight terrorism? Longtime Middle East reporter Robert Fisk said that the only way to overcome a violent institution such as Al-Qaeda is to produce justice.[483] Terrorism is able to recruit participants and supporters when it can convince those people of injustice. *If we want to fight terrorism, we have to produce justice rather than make institutionalized terrorism normal.*

"Settlements" and "Settlers"

Growing up, I had thought the word *settlement* referred to developing a place that had heretofore been uninhabited and therefore undeveloped. It seemed to me to have a good connotation. Why wouldn't one want people to settle a land?

The Hebrew term *Hitnachlut* (התנחלות) refers to settlements beyond the Green Line (West Bank, Golan Heights, and East Jerusalem). The word means "taking over one's inherited portion of land."[484] Would it not be normal to take what is yours?

The terms *settlement* and *Hitnachlut* create the illusion of normality. They are part of a whole framing and vocabulary that normalizes the taking of Palestinian land. Robert Fisk described the language used to cover for settlements:[28]

> And thus we were confronted by the special language of colonisation: "facts on the ground," a phrase coined by the Israelis, "new realities on the ground," said George W Bush in his infamous

2004 letter to Sharon, "settlements," "neighbourhoods," "suburbs," "population centres"—all in a West Bank no longer to be referred to as the "occupied territories" according to a prohibition by former US secretary of state Colin Powell, but rather: "disputed territories."[485]

I only recently realized the normality that the term *settler* creates and how I had been complicit in making it sound normal. I was talking to a friend about settlers, and he suggested that I always enclose the term *settler* within quotes in this book. He said that he saw it is a misnomer and euphemism. The word *settler* sounds normal and as such protects people who take part in violent action from accountability. He said that I needed to call settlers what they really were. He referred me to writings by Cornell University slavery historian Edward E. Baptist, who never uses the term *plantation* but instead refers to it as a "slave labor camp."[486]

Following Baptist's example, if we were to refer to settlers more accurately, we would probably call them "colonizers" and "perpetrators," or "accomplices of ethnic cleansing and violent property theft." That may sound harsh, but unfortunately, it is true: Settlers are people who move onto someone else's land—land taken based on the previous inhabitant's ethnicity. And unlike in the United States, where we have thankfully predominantly stopped those practices, those taking part in, and supporting moves into, settlements today are accomplices in the theft of that property.

Although I will continue to use the term *settler* in this book (and without quotes) to distinguish what they do from other forms of violent action, it seems appropriate to define the Israelspeak term *settler*:

SETTLER. *n.* A Jewish Israeli who
1. has moved, under the protection of the Israeli military and government, onto Palestinian land or into a Palestinian home;
2. has directly—or indirectly through the military or security forces—threatened or used violence against (Palestinian) civilians for political or economic purposes (in taking possession of the land or home).

B'Tselem reported that as of the end of 2017, over 600,000 settlers lived in the West Bank and East Jerusalem. The West Bank settler population growth rate was

> 1.75 times greater than that of the population of Israel: an annual increase of 3.5% in the settlements versus 2% in Israel. Approximately 60% of the increase in the settler population is accounted for by relocation by Israelis and the arrival of new immigrants to Israel who chose to live in settlements.[487]

Three-fourths of Israel's population of 8.84 million are Jewish,[488] so 10 percent of them are West Bank settlers. Almost 40 percent of the population of East Jerusalem are Jewish settlers.[489] All are illegal under international law.

Note the implication of the second part of my *settler* usage definition: Settlers threaten or use violence against Palestinian civilians, preventing the return of Palestinians to their lands. That fits the definition of *terrorist*.

The next question is, are settlers also civilians? As Israeli cabinet member Livni pointed out in the epigraph at the beginning of this chapter, attacking a soldier is not terrorism, but attacking civilians is. Therefore, it would be logical that the January 2002 Palestinian suicide bombing known as the Bat Mitzvah Massacre in Hadera, Israel, killing seven and injuring thirty-three was terrorism.[490] If that had been a military event rather than a bat mitzvah, then that would not have been terrorism.

But what if those victims had been settlers on confiscated Palestinian land? Views on who is a civilian vary. On one end of the spectrum are those who consider all Israeli Zionists who support Israel and its violent policies as non-civilians. Here is from a 2001 interview with Sheikh Ahmed Yassin, an imam and the spiritual leader and founder of Hamas:

> They're [Zionists are] the ones who are criminals. They took my house and my country. The soldier who attacks us, the pilot who

shells us, where do they live? All of Israel, Tel Aviv included, is occupied Palestine. So we're not actually targeting civilians—that would go against Islam.[491]

Sheikh Yassin's hometown of al-Jura was ethnically cleansed in 1948 and bulldozed by Israel. (The ruins of al-Jura are now part of the city of Ashkelon.) Yassin became a refugee in Gaza. He was assassinated at the age of sixty-seven in his wheelchair by a missile from an Israeli helicopter as he was leaving a Gaza mosque following early morning prayer.[492] Over 200,000 participated in his funeral procession.[493]

A slightly broader definition of *civilian* is held by those who consider people living in Israel proper (within the Green Line) civilians but not those who, against the Geneva Conventions, have moved onto occupied territory. Hussein al-Sheikh, a Fatah official, made the following statement on May 14, 2002:

> We sent a message to al-Aqsa: "Don't touch Israeli civilians. Never. Focus on the army and settlers. We don't consider settlers to be civilians."[494]

On the other hand, organizations such as Human Rights Watch consider settlers to be civilians. Its report states, "Israeli civilians living in the settlements, so long as they do not take up arms and take an active part in hostilities, are noncombatants."[495] According to Article 50 of the Protocol Additional to the Geneva Conventions of 12 August 1949, "in case of doubt whether a person is a civilian, that person shall be considered to be a civilian."[496]

In summary, not everyone agrees on who is an Israeli civilian. When using the word *civilian*, make sure you know which definition(s) the speaker and you are using.

Whether Palestinians are considered civilians is also debated. According to Article 51 (3) of the Protocols to the Geneva Conventions, "civilians shall enjoy the protection afforded by this Section, unless and for such time as they take a direct part in hostilities."[497] It would be hard to argue that someone shooting rockets into Israel is a civilian, although how else would civilians defend themselves in an air war such as Operation Pillar of Defense in 2012 (see chapters 11 and 13)? In the case when there is no military, as is the case with Palestine, who defends the civilians?

Although I agree with most international humanitarian law, I am concerned about the law redefining civilians when they are defending their property. If a thief breaks into my home and I attack him—or, in some states, even shoot him—then I am not considered the aggressor, because the event is occurring in my home. With this international law, however, civilians acting defensively against an invading military are suddenly converted to militants and lose their civilian status. Using this criterion, is the sixteen-year-old girl Ahed Tamimi, who slapped an invading soldier on her property, still a civilian, or did she become a combatant by slapping him? Is a teenager who throws a rock at a military vehicle as it enters his village a civilian or a combatant?

Either oppressed civilians need the right to defend themselves, or others need to take responsibility for their defense. It seems unjust to make the rules so that the only way for someone to retain civilian status is to do nothing as one is being invaded. If we are going to penalize civilians who try to defend their homes by forcing them to lose their civilian status and protections, then we need to rise and defend unarmed civilians against a powerful, oppressing military. Clearly, no major power has militarily defended the Palestinian civilians. No government has taken any military action, even something as peaceful as doing an airlift, to protect the civilians in Gaza during the past fifty years.

Some may consider the topic of who is a civilian to be black and white, but the more we look at it in detail, the more gray it can seem. Who is a "civilian" in a country such as Israel, where almost every young man and woman is required to serve in the military and support the oppression of the occupied? Who is a "civilian" when West Bank settler communities create their own armed militias and "vow to fight for land"?[498] Is *civilian* or *noncombatant* the most appropriate term to describe someone who depends on soldiers to expel Palestinians so that he or she can live in the Palestinians' home? Can one even call fourth- and fifth-grade settlers "civilians" when these ten-year-olds are trained in summer camps on how to use M16 rifles (with the IDF's approval) and they are taught the "values of Zionism … and values of the IDF without apology"?[499] Children ignorant to what is happening would be innocent civilians, but at what point in their lives do they become complicit aggressors?

Settlers who have been party to the expulsion of Palestinians, cut down or burned Palestinian olive trees, destroyed crops, poisoned water wells, destroyed cars and houses, or attacked Palestinians physically are rarely penalized or called "terrorists" by the authorities or media. In fact, many people call these terrorists "civilians." When we call people "civilians" who are conducting violence against civilians, we become complicit by protecting them with the *civilian* label.

The "civilian" categorization also affects how we hear about casualties. We are used to thinking that civilians are civilians and militants are militants. But because civilians who act defensively against an invading military are recategorized as militants or combatants, the number of civilian deaths is reduced—even if these victims had not been called militants or combatants before being attacked. The International Institute for Counter-Terrorism, an organization based in Israel, describes the situation in its 2009 executive summary on Operation Cast Lead,

> where many unaffiliated civilians become actively involved in confronting invading forces and thus become "ad hoc combatants."[500]

If anyone who defends him or herself against invaders becomes a "combatant," then the numbers are skewed in favor of the invader. A civilian supporting the military invading another party is considered a "civilian," but a civilian defending himself or his property against an invader is counted as a "militant."

Do we consider all settlers who live in West Bank settlements civilians? Many Palestinians do not. Do we consider all who live in Gaza civilians? Clearly, Israel does not.

Settlers and settlements do complicate the definitions of *terrorism* and *civilian*. Settlers have come to believe that their homes are in the West Bank. Although they are subsidized by the Israeli government, settlers also pay to live there. When a Palestinian returns and tries to take his land back, he is met with violence by settlers and the military protecting the settlers. If terrorism is "the threat or use of force against civilians," who is the terrorist when the Palestinian returns to his land and is met with violence? Who is the civilian? Does it matter if the Palestinian or the settler is armed? The answers to these questions can be difficult and may vary, depending on each person's level of complicity.

The words *terrorism* and *civilian* are intertwined. That is because the words *Zionism* and *settler* are interdependent. There would not be a question as to whether a settler is, or is not, a civilian if the land had not been taken by force against international law. There would not be that question if Israel had followed UN Security Council Resolution 242 (1967), stating the need for "withdrawal of Israel armed forces from territories occupied in the recent conflict."[501] There would not be a question as to whether a settler is, or is not, a civilian if Israel had followed the 1949 Fourth Geneva Convention's Article 49, which stipulates that "the Occupying Power shall not deport or transfer parts of its own civilian population into the territory it occupies."[502] If that resolution or the Geneva Conventions had been honored, then there would be no settlers in the West Bank.

Each of those acts by the state of Israel was "the use of violence against civilians for economic or political purposes"; each of those acts was and continues to be acts of terrorism. Settlers and settlements are the evidence of the terrorism.

"Counterterrorism"

I defined *terrorism* as the threat or use of violence against civilians for political or economic purposes. So then, what is *counterterrorism*?

On June 15, 2016, the Knesset passed the "Combatting Terrorism Law, 5776-2016":[503]

> The Law defines a "terrorist action as an action that:
> 1. is driven by a political, religious, or ideological motive;
> 2. is carried out with the goal of instilling in the public fear or anxiety, or of forcing the Israeli government or another governmental agency, including an agency of a foreign country, or an international organization to do or refrain from doing an act; or
> 3. involves an actual act or a real threat to inflict severe harm on one of the following:
>   a. a person's body or liberty;
>   b. public security or health;
>   c. property, where the circumstances involved entail an intention or a real possibility to inflict severe harm on individuals or public safety and liberty;
>   d. religious sites, burial places, and religious paraphernalia; or
>   e. infrastructure, public systems or essential services, or the state economy or environment."

It is important to note that Israel's War of Independence, the Zionist movement, the occupation, and the blockade all meet this definition of a terrorist action. Therefore, a real "counterterrorism" law or effort would be against all of those movements and actions.

The problem is that this law applies only to groups that Israel defines as "terrorist organizations." Like the US Department of State's definition of terrorism applying only to non-American and nongovernmental organizations, the Israeli law protects the organization committing the majority of the terrorist activities: itself.

Adalah, the Legal Center for Arab Minority Rights in Israel, described the result of this law:

> The law includes draconian measures for investigating detainees accused of security offenses; provides for the extensive use of secret

evidence in court; limits detainees' access to judicial review; lowers the evidentiary requirements of the state in such cases; creates new criminal offenses, including for any public expression of support for or sympathy with a terrorist group; and sharply increases the maximum sentences for people convicted of security offenses. ...

The law substantially strengthens and expands the powers of the police and the General Security Services (GSS, or Shabak/ Shin Bet) to suppress legitimate protest activities by Palestinian citizens of Israel and Palestinian residents of the OPT [occupied Palestinian territories]. It adds to a pre-existing system that provides fertile ground for the security agencies to employ illegal methods in the interrogation room, which includes a "temporary order" that exempts the security agencies from producing audio or visual documentation of interrogations of security detainees.[504]

In their June 19, 2016, press release, Adalah stated the following:

"This new law marks Palestinian citizens of Israel as suspects due simply to the fact that they are Arab. ... ... The newly-approved Anti-Terror Law integrates British Mandate–era Emergency Regulations and other emergency guidelines into the Israeli law books. It paints the political activities and expression of Arabs in Israel—including those of a social, humanitarian and charitable nature—with a hostile and war-like façade, reclassifying them as acts of terror. This law essentially criminalizes the social and political affinity that Palestinian citizens of Israel feel with the Palestinian people and their just struggle against the occupation."

In 2014, the UN Human Rights Committee in its concluding observations on Israel (para. 11) raised concerns about "the definition of terrorism, and the legal safeguards afforded to persons suspected of, or charged with, a terrorist or related crime contained in the draft law currently under consideration." It urged Israel to ensure that the legislation fully complies with its obligations under the International Covenant on Civil and Political Rights, which Israel ratified in 1991.[505]

The UN understands that Israel is a language. The UN Human Rights Committee has concerns with Israel's definition of *terrorism*.

In the English language, *counterterrorism* is the opposition, reduction or elimination of terrorism. In the Israel language, however, *counterterrorism* is the elimination of the rights to resist oppression. Such rights to resist oppression are covered in the Declaration of the Rights of Man, as approved in the French National Assembly in 1789. Here are Articles 1 and 2 of that declaration:[506]

1. Men are born and remain free and equal in rights. Social distinctions may be founded only upon the general good.

2. The aim of all political association is the preservation of the natural and imprescriptible rights of man. These rights are liberty, property, security, and resistance to oppression.

These rights were reaffirmed in the adoption of the Universal Declaration of Human Rights in the third session of the UN General Assembly in 1948. Eleanor Roosevelt chaired the Universal Declaration of Human Rights Drafting Committee. The declaration's preamble states that the

> recognition of the inherent dignity and of the equal and inalienable rights of all members of the human family is the foundation of freedom, justice and peace in the world.[507]

It further states that it is "essential ... that human rights should be protected by the rule of law"; otherwise, man's "recourse" is "rebellion against tyranny and oppression."[508] In the Israel language, the human right to "rebellion against tyranny and oppression" is called "terrorism."

In English, *terrorism* is the violation of human rights. In Israel, that is *counterterrorism*.

Terrorism in the News

Fear is a disease that eats away at logic and makes man inhuman.

—*Marian Anderson, singer* [509]

The word *terrorism* is founded in fear. And that fear can overpower logic. How can a society that gives preferential citizenship based on ethnicity not realize that it is racist? Fear provides a set of blinders.

Many messages fertilize and nurture that fear. Regular accusations of politicians and public figures of anti-Semitism foster a fear of hatred toward Jews. The constant movies, stories, and programs about the Holocaust remind Jews and others of its racist atrocities. Mass shootings in churches, synagogues, and mosques infect people with the disease of fear, which "eats away at logic and makes man inhuman." Terrorism in the news spreads this fear disease.

As I became more aware of the details and facts around the situation in Israel, the West Bank, and Gaza, I became a sharper consumer of the media. By knowing more of the facts about the situation than were presented in news programs, I could see what was emphasized and what was being left out. I could see how the media was selectively fomenting fear.

When there were instances of mass murder in the United States, such as the 1995 Oklahoma City bombing, the 1999 Columbine shooting, the 2012 Newtown school shooting, the 2015 Charleston church shooting, or the 2017 Las Vegas shooting, they were described as shootings or bombings. When we learned about the perpetrator, if he was not Muslim, we would not be told his religion. However, when the event was perpetrated by one or more Muslims, as in the 2013 Boston Marathon bombing or the 2015 San Bernardino shooting, then it would be called a terrorist event, and we would be told that the perpetrators were Muslim. This is an interesting bias of the media. This creates fear of Muslims, even though many more deaths were caused by non-Muslims.

Why is it that the only American police officer whose religion we know of is the Minnesota officer of Somali descent? Mohamed Noor shot the young Australian lady Justine Damond (née Ruszczyk) on July 16, 2017.[510] We have more than 400 fatal police shootings every year,[511] yet we know the religion of only one officer. Do we know Dylann Roof's religion after his mass murder of 9 people in the Emanuel African Methodist Episcopal Church in Charleston, South Carolina, on July 17, 2015? Do we know the religion of Adam Lanza, the man who massacred 20 children and 6 adult staff members on December 14, 2012, at Sandy Hook Elementary School in Newtown, Connecticut, or Stephen Paddock, who killed over 50 and injured over 860 people in Las Vegas on October 1, 2017? What was the religion of Timothy McVeigh, responsible for the 1995 Oklahoma City bombing, which killed 168 people and injured more than 680? We always hear the religion in the media when it is a Muslim but rarely when it is anyone else.

The news has conditioned us to associate terrorism with Muslims. Even our schools teach Americans that terrorism is associated with religion—and Islam specifically: The Texas high school standards for teaching world history use the word *terrorism* only when it is preceded by "radical Islamic."[512] The narrative we create for ourselves is that religion is a significant cause of terrorism.

Professor Robert Pape, a University of Chicago specialist in suicide bombers, tested this premise in his book *Dying to Win: The Strategic Logic of Suicide Terrorism*.[513] The book is based on research he and his team did on every suicide bomber from 1980 through 2003. His team's goal was to better understand what suicide bombers had in common and what motivated them. Their analysis showed that the largest number of suicide bombers had not been from an Islamic group but instead were Tamil Tigers, a secular group out of Sri Lanka.[514] Furthermore, Pape's team calculated that the most statistically significant common trait among suicide bombers was not their religion but instead their goal "to compel democracies to withdraw military forces from the terrorists' national homeland."[515] The news tells us only that the terrorists were Muslim. We rarely learn why they committed the acts; instead, we are left to create our own narrative: that it was because of religion. According to Pape,

> more than 95 percent of all suicide attacks are in response to foreign occupation, according to extensive research that we conducted at the University of Chicago's Project on Security and Terrorism, where we examined every one of the over 2,200 suicide attacks across the world from 1980 to the present day.[516]

Learning that religion was not the common thread of these suicide bombers made me that much more critical and discerning of the American media. I noticed that I would usually hear the words *Islamic* and *terrorist* used together. I noticed how pundits shared the myth of Islam being the motivator time and again. Knowing that Israel was the most significant terrorist organization in the Gaza massacre known as Operation Cast Lead, I was thankful that I never heard Judaism being claimed as a motivator for Israel's terrorism.

It was interesting how the news media paradoxically played what seemed to be a Ministry of Truth discourse. They claimed that the occupied population was the aggressor, motivated by religion. They followed up the narrative with the more powerful, oppressive, and destructive side being "defensive."

While taking a journalism course in college, I realized I had been a poor consumer of the media and had been extremely vulnerable to biased messaging. I learned that good journalists either describe what they personally witnessed or attribute the source for something they are told. Because they are there to report, good reporters abstain from stating someone's motivation, because motivation is not observable. Good journalists will report that "John *said* that he hit Bill because Bill had taken something from John." By contrast, a good journalist would not write, "John hit Bill because Bill had taken something from John"; John's real motivation cannot be proved. A journalist who makes that motivation assertion has stepped over the boundary from reporting to opinion. This distinction is extremely important. A news consumer who is not conscious of this distinction can interpret a statement of motivation as a fact when in reality it is an opinion, a guess, or propaganda.

As I processed the media coverage of Operation Cast Lead and other conflicts in the region, I noticed the press using such terms as "retaliates" and "responds to." These expressions were opinions rather than reporting, yet they were used extensively in the media when describing Israel's actions against Gaza. Repeating the State Department description referenced earlier, note the phrase "in response to" at the beginning:

> In response to a sharp increase in the number and frequency of rocket attacks into Israel prior to and following the expiration of Hamas' agreed period of "calm" on December 19, 2008, the Israeli Air Force launched Operation Cast Lead.[517]

This sentence exhibits three characteristics of misreporting:

- **Asserting motivation as fact.** The motivation assertion is evident in the use of "in response to."

- **Omission of relevant facts.** The omitted fact is that Israel had previously mounted an offensive on Gaza during the "calm."

- **Leaving out context.** There is no mention of the context of Gaza being under occupation* and a crippling siege known as the blockade.

The wording of this article further distorts the scene: For example, the Hamas rockets, which did little damage, are referred to as "attacks," whereas the beginning of the devastating Israeli military campaign is referred to as a "launch."

Reporters on multiple sides of an argument are guilty of these mistakes. What is important is that we as news consumers are able to recognize these biases and influencers when we encounter them.

---

* Even though Israel "disengaged" in 2005 by removing its settlers from Gaza, the International Criminal Court still determined in a 2014 decision that Gaza was under occupation. See "Gaza Occupation versus 'Disengagement'" for more details.

Only by recognizing these journalistic deviations can we consciously resist being swayed by them.

Of the three characteristics of misreporting, implied or asserted motivation is the easiest to catch.

A month and a half before the end of the mutually agreed-upon "calm" period,[518] a reporter described Israel's invasion and the killing of six Hamas people. The reporter also implies motivation, this time in justifying Hamas's actions:

> A four-month ceasefire between Israel and Palestinian militants in Gaza was in jeopardy today after Israeli troops killed six Hamas gunmen in a raid into the territory.

> Hamas responded by firing a wave of rockets into southern Israel, although no one was injured. The violence represented the most serious break in a ceasefire agreed in mid-June, yet both sides suggested they wanted to return to [an] atmosphere of calm.[519]

A practice of poor journalism that is harder to catch is the omission of relevant facts or context. I cover many facts in this book, so that you, as a consumer of the media, will be able to detect the omission of facts and context when you are faced with future news on this subject. For example, the article just quoted mentioned that Israeli troops killed six Hamas gunmen in a Gaza raid. This was a violation of the mid-June ceasefire agreement between Hamas and Israel. That violation occurred during the supposed "calm," before the Gaza rockets mentioned in the State Department summary. That summary, and most of the American press, left out the fact that Israel had broken the ceasefire agreement. The State Department's description of a "sharp increase in the number and frequency of rocket attacks into Israel prior to and following the expiration of Hamas' agreed period of 'calm,'"[520] implies that Hamas had broken the agreement. In fact, it had been broken by Israel a month and a half earlier, when Israeli troops invaded Gaza and killed six Hamas members.

Like many of us, reporters have daily pressures that can result in accidental mistakes. However, when the mistakes show a pattern, then one needs to take notice of the pattern. American media sources were misleading when they did not mention Israel invading and murdering six Hamas people in Gaza before the rockets were launched. Examples such as this of what the news covered and did not cover, and when it was covered, show a pattern. It is a pattern of attempting to manipulate Americans' perception of the situation.

(Another technique Israel uses for handling terrorism in the news is to conduct aggressive strikes when the US media is distracted. The Israeli invasion occurred hours after the American presidential election, when the US news media was focused on election results.[*,521])

A more recent example of the media completely missing important facts occurred while I was in Israel and the West Bank. We went to the northern part of the West Bank on highway 60, the main north–south highway in the West Bank. On our return, we had to take a detour because the highway had been closed. A protest on that road had become violent with a settler shooting two Palestinians. One of the Palestinians was killed and the other, a reporter, was injured. I was curious as to what had happened. I searched for videos on YouTube as well as news articles in the US and locally. Here is how a *New York Times* article with the headline "Israeli Fires on Palestinian Protesters in the West Bank, Killing One" starts off:

> An Israeli settler whose car was caught up in a pro-Palestinian street demonstration in the West Bank on Thursday opened fire on the protesters, killing a 23-year-old Palestinian man and wounding a news photographer.
>
> The protest, held in support of Palestinian prisoners on a hunger strike that has now lasted 32 days, was one of several marred by violence recently.[522]

---

* Similarly, on November 3, 2020, the day of another US presidential election, Israeli bulldozers demolished, for the first time in seven years, an entire Palestinian village in the West Bank. The demolition of Khirbet Humsa left 74 people, including 41 minors, homeless.

Videos of the event show cars stopped as the protesters blocked the road with their signs and flags. At one point a car in the front row plows into the protesters, ultimately running into and damaging a parked ambulance. The protesters started throwing stones at the car. Within seconds an army jeep came onto the scene, and the crowd scattered, running. Soldiers shot tear gas into the area. They were focused on the crowd and paid no attention to the car, even though they were right next to it. Once the crowd was far from the car and the driver was protected by the army, one can see the driver taking a gun and shooting out of his rear window. He then drove off while the army remained focused on the crowd.

The article did not mention that the Israeli settler had accelerated and plowed his car into the crowd. It did not mention that he had driven into and damaged a parked ambulance. It did not mention that the settler was perfectly safe, that no one was near him when he started shooting.

How can one talk about anti-racism activist Heather Heyer's death and the injury of more than 30 others in Charlottesville, Virginia, on August 12, 2017, at the "Unite the Right" White Nationalist protests without mentioning that James Alex Fields Jr. accelerated his car into the crowd? One needs to be wary when an article describes one party as just "caught up" in a situation. Again, the *New York Times* article referred to "an Israeli settler whose car was caught up in a pro-Palestinian street demonstration." How come his car was the only one "caught up"? There were a lot of cars there. Why does the reporter not explain why his car was literally "caught up" in the ambulance?

Another difference between the Charlottesville killing and the West Bank killing was that the Israeli murderer was not arrested. Instead, he voluntarily went to a police station, where he filed a complaint with the police and walked out.[523,][*,][524] A man, without any risk to his life, after crowds had been dispersed and while the military was there protecting him, pulled out a gun and shot into the crowd, only to go

---

* It is interesting to compare the two aforementioned articles with two videos of the event.

and file a complaint. The police station then let him leave without filing any charge against him. For any US media to have left out these important contextual facts was misleading at best.

Years ago, I was about to have a discussion on US domestic policy with an uncle of mine. He said he would enjoy such a discussion, but he had one requirement: Any argument I made supporting a position, I had to be willing to accept the same argument in return. Based on that concept, I often test language and arguments from the other perspective. Taking the State Department's description of Operation Cast Lead, for example, we can reverse the language and bias to see what it would look like and how it would resonate.

In the article, Gaza's actions were described as

> a sharp increase in the number and frequency of rocket attacks into Israel

Rewriting that sentence fragment to take the other side would produce something like the following:

> Gaza Palestinians responded to the crippling blockade, recent deadly Israeli invasion, and violation of the ceasefire agreement with rockets.

This replacement sentence creates a completely different narrative as to who is the offender and who is the victim. This huge difference highlights how the public can be manipulated by the media's reporting. Who the "terrorist" is can suddenly change sides. This is just another example that shows why everyone needs to be vigilant and careful in news analysis. And careful analysis requires knowledge of history, the current situation, and clear word definitions.

As previously described, the problem with many articles in the US media about events in Israel/Palestine is that they leave out crucial facts. The movie *The Occupation of the American Mind* describes how Rachel Maddow, often described as one of the most liberal TV personalities, never mentioned the blockade or occupation in any of her reporting of Operation Cast Lead. *Describing a potential motivation for one side and none for the other is biased reporting. Leaving out context altogether is deceptive.*

So, with the education and sensitivity for noticing when reporters are infusing such motivation language as "retaliate" or "respond to," I noticed how often the media stepped over the journalism boundary and whether they did it for one side or both.

I also looked more closely at how often the news media described bombings or shootings as being a terrorist action depending on whether the perpetrator was Muslim or non-Muslim.

I noticed how often an Israeli spokesperson was interviewed versus a Palestinian spokesperson. In the case of the Gaza bombings, I looked at how often a representative of Hamas was actually interviewed. Most of the times, none were. Yet Israel's officials were constantly represented. When the occasional Palestinian representative was interviewed, he or she would be followed by the Israeli representative—as though the Israeli always had the last say and could "correct" the Palestinian. Rarely would a reporter correct the Israeli—or translate, since the representative was speaking Israel.

I heard dozens of descriptions by news pundits describing what motivates Islamic terrorists, but only once or twice did I hear a description of what Osama bin Laden actually wrote in his letter explaining his motivations for 9/11. It's not that I believe everything Osama bin Laden said. However, I tend to put more weight on someone's stated motivations, especially if they match his actions, than someone who has never met the man nor spoken with him about his motivations. *Yet our media overwhelmingly ignores the original sources of our adversaries and employs the so-called pundits to speak on their behalf. As news consumers, we need to be conscious of these deceptive tactics.*

Hamas is defined by our government as a terrorist organization. Often in the news media I have heard that Hamas vows for the destruction of Israel.[525] The Hamas charter is often interpreted by American pundits as advocating the killing of Jews rather than advocating the destruction of a racist state. The destruction of the state of Israel was in the original charter, but Hamas dropped that clause from its manifesto before the 2006 Palestinian parliamentary elections and its Document of General Principles and Policies, issued in May 2017.[526] (For more on Hamas, see chapter 13.)

It is important to notice that the media allows their own pundits to state Hamas's position rather than ask a Hamas representative to speak for Hamas itself. Sharing partial information can lead an audience to incorrect conclusions. Pundits refer to Hamas's founding document rather than the most current one. Using original documents as the guiding principles of an entity is dangerous; if we did the same for the United States, people would believe we support slavery.

In the American mass media, Hamas is described as a terrorist organization, yet the government that violently takes children from their parents at night, forces people off their land at gunpoint, and violates human rights is not.

After I saw the extensive Israeli settlement infrastructure in the West Bank, it was obvious to me that Israel plans the destruction of a meaningful Palestinian state. Yet we rarely hear criticism by US politicians or the largest American media channels of the systematic and continuous actions that Israel takes to undermine any possibility of a Palestinian state.

Instead, the media fires commentators who take a stand for equality and freedom. On November 29, 2018, CNN fired Temple University Professor Marc Lamont Hill after he spoke at the United Nations. His speech highlighted that as the world celebrated the seventieth anniversary of the Universal Declaration of Human Rights, for those same seventy years,

the Palestinian people have been deprived of the most fundamental of [those rights] … We have an opportunity to not just offer solidarity in words but to commit to political action, grassroots action, local action, and international action that will give us what justice requires—and that is a free Palestine from the river to the sea.[527]

I hear people say that the Palestinian government does not recognize Israel, even though it did as part of the Oslo Accords. Meanwhile, the news does not mention that Israel and the United States are in the minority of countries that do not recognize Palestine as a state. A 2014 opinion piece in *Haaretz* was entitled "How Many Times Must the Palestinians Recognize Israel?" and here was the subtitle: "Netanyahu's new 'Jewish state' mantra negates the fact that Palestinians recognized Israel more than twenty years ago. They're still waiting for Israel to recognize Palestine."[528] This imbalance of coverage affects US public opinion.

We should be concerned that few people publicly push back against politicians and media coverage despite it being so one-sided. Here is a passage from *The Guardian* on May 1, 2017:

> Ed Royce, the chair of the House foreign relations committee, said: "Until Hamas recognises Israel's right to exist, its words are meaningless. I will see to it that Hamas remains designated a terrorist organisation as long as it continues to launch rocket attacks against Israeli civilians, remains an Iranian proxy, and engages in other acts that threaten the US and Israel."[529]

Playing Mad Libs and switching the players (Israel for Hamas, Palestine for Israel, etc.), in the previous statement shows how one-sided it is:

> Ed Royce, the chair of the House foreign relations committee, said: "Until Israel recognises Palestine's right to exist, its words are meaningless. I will see to it that Israel remains designated a terrorist organisation as long as it continues to launch rocket attacks against Palestinian civilians, remains an American proxy, and engages in other acts that threaten Hamas [the democratically elected government of the Palestinians] and Palestine."

The media's job is to hold those in power accountable. The media airing such one-sided messaging without context is not news or journalism; it crosses the line into propaganda dissemination.

Jon Stewart had a scene in one of *The Daily Show* episodes where he described the coverage of Operation Cast Lead. He showed TV news segments of interviews with different American political figures commenting on the conflict.[530] President George W. Bush said, "I understand Israel's desire to protect itself." Senator Harry Reid said, "I think what the Israelis are doing is very important." Mitt Romney said, "Israel has no choice but to take military action." Senator Mitch McConnell said, "The Israelis are doing the only thing they can possibly do to defend their population." Governor Jon Corzine said, "The missile firings into Israel, I think, brought a proper response from the Israelis." Stewart continued saying that the analogies always flowed only one way. There was no explanation for why rockets were coming from Gaza.

George Will followed, saying, "All Americans know what we would be doing if rockets were landing in San Diego from Tijuana." Governor Mark Sanford used a similar analogy, saying that if Cuba sent projectiles to South Florida, we would retaliate. Then to summarize, Stewart showed a video clip of Mayor Michael Bloomberg, who asked what you would do if some emotionally disturbed person were banging on your door, screaming, "I'm going to come through this door and kill you." He continued, "Do you want us to respond with one police officer, which is proportional, or with all the resources at our command?" Stewart responded, "I guess it depends if I forced that guy to live in my hallway and make him go through checkpoints every time he has to take a [*bleep*]."

Stewart's reaction was brave. He was willing to expose Israel's mythical emperor as wearing no clothes. He was showing his disgust in the twisted, one-sided, propagandist mantra that our politicians and media were promoting, a messaging that is required to keep the Israel "defensive" myth alive and credible. None of the politicians had mentioned the occupation or the blockade and the related human rights abuses. None had mentioned the horrendous bombings and attacks by a military against a primarily child and refugee population with no military. It took a Jewish comedian to do what American politicians and media did not have the integrity or courage to do. Jon Stewart identified the real terrorist that American politicians and the American media would not.

Years later, there was another Jon Stewart segment of *The Daily Show* of another Gaza massacre. Again, Israel was claiming its massive Israeli bombardment was defensive against Gaza aggression. In this July 14, 2014, segment entitled "(500) Crazies of Summer,"[531] Stewart showed how one-sided the aggression was, especially relative to the story described in our media: "Perhaps nothing sums up the asymmetrical nature of this conflict more than a quick check-in with the correspondents assigned to the respective beats." He then showed a screen shot of the two NBC correspondents side by side in their different locations—the relaxed man in Tel Aviv in his orange polo shirt, contrasting with the fully covered man in Gaza up to his neck in a heavy blue outfit including a protective vest marked PRESS.[532] That picture of the two reporters made it clear who was being terrorized and how the news was twisting the story.

One moment of awakening for me was when years before the Gaza wars, I heard that a significantly higher number of Palestinians had been killed than Israelis over a period of time. This surprised me because I had remembered hearing in the news about more Jewish casualties than Palestinian ones. It turns out the news had covered in great detail and with multiple stories about the Jewish casualties but only summary coverage of a small percentage of the Palestinian casualties. This tactic gives the impression that more Jews were being killed.

The media had not lied. They had very selectively picked what to cover and how to cover it, creating a mirage.

I researched the number of casualties on such human-rights-oriented sites as IfAmericansKnew.org and Btselem.org, and, sure enough, there were many times more Palestinian deaths than Jewish

Israeli ones. And of course, the Israeli deaths were described as deaths by terrorists, even if against the military, whereas the deaths of civilian Palestinians rarely were.

On May 9, 2018, President Trump announced that the United States was backing out of the 2015 Iran nuclear deal, formally known as the Joint Comprehensive Plan of Action (JCPOA). The next morning, Iranian forces fired rockets from Syria into the Israeli-occupied Golan Heights. Here was some of the coverage on National Public Radio's *Morning Edition*:

> DAVID GREENE: "Sirens there as Iranian forces in Syria fired about 20 rockets into the Golan Heights, targeting the Israeli military. Israel responded with what's described as its largest ever attack on Iranian military targets in Syria. Now, let's learn all we can here from Jane Ferguson. She's a special correspondent for the "PBS NewsHour" in Jerusalem. Good morning, Jane."[533]

Notice the setup. Which party initiated action and which "responded"? The piece went on to describe the impact on tourists and school schedules on only the Israeli side of the conflict, connecting the listener emotionally with the Israeli side. Since violence was being threatened against civilians, that had to mean that terrorism was taking place:

> DAVID GREENE: "Well, can you tell us more about this escalation in violence? ... It seems like the latest event in what's been escalating for a couple weeks now."

> JANE FERGUSON: "It has been escalating for months actually across the border in Syria under the guise of the very complex, bloody civil war. ... So the Israelis have actually been conducting airstrikes in Syria for some time now. Those airstrikes have been increasing in frequency and they've become more deadly, killing Iranian military commanders or military members inside Syria. So we have, for some time, been expecting some sort of Iranian

response to that. And that appears to have been what we have seen last night."[534]

Notice how David Greene's setup mentioned Israel's having "responded" to Iranian rockets, whereas Jane Ferguson actually told us that Israel had been bombing Iranian installations in Syria for months, inflicting casualties, and that the Israelis had been expecting a "response." So, the newsclip clearly started with Israel responding to Iran, but by the end of the clip, it was sounding like Iran and Syria were responding to Israel.

Ferguson and Greene were also different in their reporting: Ferguson mentioned that the Golan Heights was occupied territory. Who was really "responding," and who was terrorizing, given that the Golan Heights was Syrian territory occupied by Israel? How much mention was there of Syrian civilians? If the media did not mention civilians, then it would be harder for the news consumer to associate the months of attacks as terrorism.

Another example of terrorism in the news is the coverage of the Gaza Palestinians' "Great March of Return." It is interesting to note how our administration brings in terrorism by naming a "terrorist" organization. As background, the Great March of Return is the overwhelmingly nonviolent protest against Israel's blocking of Palestinian refugees in Gaza from returning to their land, as guaranteed by international law. On May 14, 2018, 58 Palestinians participating in the march, including 6 children, died in Gaza from Israeli gunfire. More died later from wounds received that day. The day's Israeli attacks resulted in the injury of over 2,700 Palestinians in Gaza, including 1,359 from live Israeli ammunition. Israel committed these violent acts on the same day as the US opened its embassy in Jerusalem—again, a time when the US media would be distracted. Here is how the *Washington Post* reported the event:

> Israeli snipers were determined not to allow a breach, and ambulances soon began screaming back and forth from the fence as gunshots rang out. No Israeli soldiers were injured, though,

and Israel drew widespread condemnation for an excessive use of force. ...

The United Nations said that "those responsible for outrageous human rights violations must be held to account," and Human Rights Watch described the killings as a "bloodbath." Palestinian Authority President Mahmoud Abbas condemned a continuing "massacre" of the Palestinian people. Turkey and South Africa announced they were recalling their ambassadors from Israel.[535]

Here is how Canadian Prime Minister Justin Trudeau responded to the massacre:

Canada deplores and is gravely concerned by the violence in the Gaza Strip that has led to a tragic loss of life and injured countless people. We are appalled that Dr. Tarek Loubani, a Canadian citizen, is among the wounded—along with so many unarmed people, including civilians, members of the media, first responders, and children.

We are doing everything we can to assist Dr. Loubani and his family, and to determine how a Canadian citizen came to be injured. We are engaging with Israeli officials to get to the bottom of these events.[536]

By contrast, here is how White House Principal Deputy Press Secretary Raj Shah answered a reporter's question "Is the President concerned about the demonstrations there [in Gaza] and Israel's response to people trying to climb over the fence?":

Well, we're aware of the reports of continued violence in Gaza today. The responsibility for these tragic deaths rests squarely with Hamas. Hamas is intentionally and cynically provoking this response. And as the Secretary of State said, Israel has the right to defend itself.[537]

People were killed trying to go home. The United Nations and Human Rights Watch called out the human rights violations. The Canadian prime minister condemned the injuring of a health worker and countless others. By contrast, the United States condemned Hamas rather than those who pulled the triggers.

Notice how our White House deputy press secretary told the news media that the soldiers had a right to "defend" themselves by killing unarmed civilians in Gaza.

The US is associating public protests for freedom and human rights, against an occupation and a blockade, as part of a terrorist organization's efforts. Hamas did not prevent the return of refugees and enforce a blockade. Hamas was formed two decades after Palestinians were occupied and almost four decades after they had become refugees. Without the background and context knowledge, someone might think Mr. Shah's statements were in English; in fact, they were in Israel.

In summary, when we consume the news about terrorism and the state of Israel, we need the foundation of a clear definition of *terrorism* and a knowledge of the situation. Only then can we translate what is said and not said in the news from Israel into English.

We should be concerned when the American media and our politicians describe a one-sided massacre of 58 unarmed people in their own land and another 2,700 injured as a "clash" or "defensive action"; those are Israel terms. We should be further concerned with our media when they do not challenge, but instead repeat, that occupying forces have a right to aggressively "defend themselves" from unarmed civilians demanding their rights be honored. Our media further shows its corruptness and collusion when it leaves out that civilians under occupation and blockade have a right to defend themselves against the oppressing military forces.

This one-sided reporting of terrorism in Israel/Palestine is a symptom of how our American media and politicians have failed us. It shows how they have undermined a crucial pillar of a democratic society: accurate information. True democracy requires accuracy in reporting (freedom of the press), a knowledgeable electorate (free education), and the right to vote. If either of the first two is missing, then we make decisions, including voting decisions, based on a false understanding of the world. *When we as Americans do not stand firm for accuracy in reporting and a strong civics education, then we leave ourselves open to manipulation. When that happens, propaganda and manipulation of the public wins and real democracy loses.*

George Orwell's Thought Police is alive and strong; it is therefore urgent that we learn to speak Israel. If we don't, what we think is democracy is merely an illusion.

13

Hamas:
A Terrorist Organization

U.S. District Judge Jorge A. Solis sentenced the Holy Land Foundation for Relief and Development (HLF) and five of its leaders following their convictions by a federal jury in November 2008 on charges of providing material support to Hamas, a designated foreign terrorist organization.

—Federal Bureau of Investigation, Dallas Division, press release,[538]
May 27, 2009

I had always known that Hamas was a terrorist organization. I had heard repeatedly that in their charter they called on Israel's destruction and the killing of Jews. They had been behind suicide bombers in the early 2000s. People kept telling me that yes, Israel committed violations of human rights, but what about Hamas? I had to confront that legitimate question. That question led me to learn about Hamas.

Hamas is a Palestinian Islamic resistance organization that was formed in 1987, at the beginning of the First Intifada. To understand Hamas, I wanted to learn about its formation, and that meant that I had to learn about the First Intifada.

The First Intifada

On December 8, 1987, a traffic accident near the Jabalia refugee camp in Gaza triggered the First Intifada.[539] The word *intifāḍa* is Arabic (انتفاضة) for "uprising," or "shaking off." The term has been used for decades across the Middle East to refer to resistance against oppression, or to an uprising to "shake off" oppression.[540] The traffic accident involved an Israeli tank transporter colliding with Palestinian cars, killing four passengers. Rumors spread that it had been an intentional act, and protests started. The Israeli military fired on the protesters with live ammunition, killing unarmed protesters. During the next few weeks, no Israelis were killed, but 22 Palestinians were killed, including 5 under the age of seventeen.[541]

Wendy Pearlman described the Israeli response to the protests in her book *Violence, Nonviolence, and the Palestinian National Movement*:

> No sooner had riots begun in 1987 than Israel resolved to restore order. To that end, it deployed some seventy thousand soldiers in the occupied territories in 1988 alone. When the United Nations Security Council condemned Israel's use of live ammunition against civilians, the army outfitted soldiers with clubs. In the words of Minister of Defense Yitzhak Rabin, they could then "break Palestinians' bones." In the assessment of leading Israeli journalists, soldiers' beatings of unarmed protesters became systematic.[542]

As I read passages like this one, I thought about what such policies tell us about a society and about American support for such policies. I couldn't study Hamas without understanding the context of the violence perpetrated against people based on their ethnicity.

> [Israel] also carried out a legal crackdown, arresting or imprisoning some fifty thousand Palestinians. ... By the end of 1988, about ten thousand Palestinians were held without charge or trial in

administrative detention, a six-month incarceration eligible for renewal. Investigations found that detainees routinely met with harsh interrogation and ill-treatment falling within accepted definitions of torture.[543]

It is under this backdrop of occupation, widespread state violence, imprisonment, and torture against a civilian population that Hamas was formed and grew.

The First Intifada dragged on for another six years—years of violence in Israeli and Palestinian streets, years of condemnation of Israel's violent response by world governments. Worn down by the conflict, Israeli voters in 1992 gave Yitzhak Rabin a mandate to find peace.[544] Israel began secret discussions with the PLO and a year later signed a peace agreement with the Palestinians—the Oslo Accords. Both sides appeared to see the agreement as a prospect for actual peace, and the Intifada died out. During the violence, the Israeli military had killed 1,500 Palestinians; Hamas and its associates had killed 300 Israeli civilians.[545]

In March 1998, Israel Labor Party leader Ehud Barak, who became prime minister the following year, said in a TV interview with Gideon Levy of *Haaretz*,

> If I was [a Palestinian] at the right age, at some stage I would have entered one of the terror organizations and have fought from there.[546]

This admission told me a lot. It was an admission that the Palestinian response is logical and that it is based on their condition and Israel's actions rather than on religious or ethnic traits.

The Hamas Organization

Ḥamās (حماس) is an Arabic acronym for حركة المقاومة الاسلامية, *Ḥarakat al-Muqāwamah al-'Islāmiyyah*, "Islamic Resistance Movement." As a movement, it includes a number of organizations. Not only does Hamas have an armed wing, the Izz ad-Din al-Qassam Brigades, but it is also associated with many Islamic social services organizations and charities—a dual role that has brought Hamas credibility in Palestinian society. Its standing for Palestinian rights earns it respect from Palestinians, and its social services organizations have supported Palestinians who have needed assistance in their daily lives. Hamas-related organizations offer everything from dental services and quality medical clinics to orphanages, summer camps, and soup kitchens.

Hamas has been declared a terrorist organization by the United States and the European Union[547] among others. This "terrorist" designation makes it difficult for the movement to receive international donations. Hamas therefore distances itself financially from these social service affiliations so as not to jeopardize the charities' funding sources. Despite the absence of visible financial ties with Hamas, Hamas representatives are still prominent on the boards of the public service charity organizations.[548]

Since 2005 Hamas has also been prominent on the Palestinian political scene. As covered in chapter 9, Hamas won in the internationally monitored and US-funded Palestinian Authority legislative election in January 2006. After the election, Israel arrested a number of the newly elected officials. The United States supported Israel's withholding of Palestinian tax revenues and its refusal to provide the funds to the newly elected government. Israel and the United States have continued to deny relations with a Palestinian Authority run by elected Hamas officials.

Hamas as a Terrorist Organization

The following is from Article 7 of the 1988 Hamas Covenant (Charter):

The Islamic Resistance Movement aspires to realize the promise of Allah, no matter how long it takes. The Prophet, Allah's prayer and peace be upon him, says: "The hour of judgment shall not come until the Muslims fight the Jews and kill them, so that the Jews hide behind trees and stones, and each tree and stone will say: 'Oh Muslim, oh servant of Allah, there is a Jew behind me, come and kill him,' except for the Gharqad tree, for it is the tree of the Jews." (Recorded in the Hadith collections of Bukhari and Muslim).[549]

Consistent with its charter, Hamas has fought and killed Jews. It is therefore not surprising that Hamas has been designated as a terrorist organization.[550] And this designation is warranted whether one uses the US Department of State definition or the definition used in this book.

Hamas's most deadly weapon has been suicide bombers. The first suicide attack against Israeli civilians was the Afula bus suicide bombing on April 6, 1994. Hamas stated that it carried out the attack in response to the killing of 29 praying Muslims in the Ibrahimi Mosque in Hebron, a couple of months prior, by settler Baruch Goldstein.[551],* Later that year Hamas was responsible for the Dizengoff Street bus bombing, "one of the deadliest terrorist attacks in Israeli history" where 20 civilians were killed and 48 people were injured.[552] Other attacks on buses continued in 1995, when two Hamas bombings killed a total of 10 civilians plus a police chief; over 100 people were injured.[553]

Between 1994 and September 2000, 120 Israelis died from Palestinian attacks. Hamas took responsibility for many of those attacks.*

In September 2000, the Second Intifada broke out. It is also called the Al-Aqsa Intifada, since it was the Palestinian uprising triggered by Prime Minister Ariel Sharon's September 28, 2000,

---

* See the "'If They Would Only Not Teach Them to Hate'" section in the sequel to this book, *Speak Equality: Revealing the Root of the Israel/Palestine Struggle*.

** From a language perspective, it is interesting to note that our media uses the phrase "took responsibility for the attack." We don't usually hear that language used for actions by states. For example, Israel does not "claim responsibility" for its attacks; it often claims that Hamas is responsible for Israeli bombings.

visit to the Temple Mount, which Muslims refer to as Al-Aqsa. Palestinians considered the Israeli prime minister visiting the third-holiest site in Islam provocative. It was also a time when the Oslo Accords were past due for transitioning more autonomy and control of the West Bank and Gaza to the Palestinians.

During the Second Intifada—more precisely from September 2000 through September 2005—Palestinians killed 444 civilians in Israel. Another 223 Israeli civilians were killed in the West Bank and Gaza.[554] Hamas was responsible for a large number of the terrorist acts; again, suicide bombings were the most deadly.

During the same time period, the Israeli military killed 3,218 Palestinians in the West Bank and Gaza, 657 of whom were children (under the age of eighteen). (Note that Israelis killed almost five times as many Palestinians as Palestinians killed Israelis and that Israelis killed approximately the same number of Palestinian children as Palestinians killed Israeli civilians.) Hamas was clearly a target of the Israeli government. Israel conducted 187 extrajudicial executions of Palestinians during that time (included in the 3,218 number just cited). At least 29 of the Israeli extrajudicial executions were children.[555]

The peak year of suicide bombings from numerous Palestinian organizations—including Hamas, Fatah, Palestinian Islamic Jihad, and Al-Aqsa Martyrs' Brigade—was 2002; 457 Israelis were killed in Israel and the occupied territories in that year alone.[556]

On February 8, 2005, Palestinian Authority President Mahmoud Abbas and Israeli Prime Minister Ariel Sharon agreed to a ceasefire at the Egyptian resort of Sharm el-Sheikh, ending the Second Intifada. Hamas announced that it would abide by the ceasefire but that it would also not be bound by it. After having been absent for four years, the Egyptian and Jordanian ambassadors returned to Israel.[557]

Hamas's next tactic was sending rockets into Israel. In 2004 an Israeli civilian was killed by a rocket from Gaza. Since then, thousands of rockets have been fired by Hamas and other groups in Gaza.

During the eight days of Operation Pillar of Defense (November 14–21, 2012), 1,500 rockets were fired from Gaza.[558] Approximately 50 percent of the rockets fired into Israel were short-range, reaching up to twenty kilometers. Slightly fewer than half were medium-range, landing up to sixty kilometers away. Fewer than 1 percent went beyond sixty kilometers.

Of the 1,500 rockets, 60 hit populated areas, killing 4 Israeli civilians, including 1 Palestinian Bedouin. At least 103 Palestinian civilians in Gaza died in the fighting, more than 25 times the number of Israeli civilians killed.[559] The following is from Human Rights Watch on December 24, 2012:

> Under international humanitarian law, or the laws of war, civilians and civilian structures may not be subject to deliberate attacks or attacks that do not discriminate between civilians and military targets. Anyone who commits serious laws-of-war violations intentionally or recklessly is responsible for war crimes.[560]

That means that Gaza's use of rockets is a violation of international humanitarian law because Hamas's rockets are so crude.

> Many of the rockets fired by Hamas—including locally-made rockets, more advanced Soviet-designed "Grad" rockets, and reportedly longer-range Iranian "Fajr" rockets—are considered to be so inaccurate as to be incapable of being aimed in a manner to discriminate between military targets and civilian objects, at least when, as has been the case, they are directed at populated areas. Statements from Palestinian armed groups indicate that they are directing their rockets at Israeli population centers. The use of such rockets against civilian areas violates the prohibition on deliberate and indiscriminate attacks.[561]

Hamas violated international humanitarian law because it did not have weapons that were sophisticated enough to distinguish civilian from military targets. Israel by contrast claimed that it was in compliance with international humanitarian law because it had warned civilians of upcoming bombings and because it had targeted only "legitimate targets" with its sophisticated weapons.

It seems ironic that the organization with the unguided rockets, which ended up killing 4 civilians, was chided as violating humanitarian law because they did not have the capability to avoid civilians, whereas the organization with precision-targeted missiles and bombs that ended up killing 103 civilians was considered as having used restraint and as having kept in compliance with international law.[562]

If these positions are correct and Hamas was the only violator of international humanitarian law in this conflict, then does the law serve people? How was a population of primarily children and overwhelmingly refugees, with no military, expected to defend itself from one of the most powerful militaries in the world, which by international law was supposed to be protecting them? If weapons were not being permitted to be imported by world powers to the people of Gaza, especially weapons that would have enabled the people to target the oppressive military that was violating their human rights, then what were the people in Gaza supposed to do?

Operation Pillar of Defense was an Israeli air campaign. Israel did not send ground troops into Gaza. Therefore, there was no way for the people of Gaza to defend themselves except by trying to send projectiles themselves. However, if they were not allowed to import defensive weapons or projectiles that could be aimed accurately enough to pick out only military targets, then by international law they were not allowed to defend themselves. That left the population of Gaza with only one legal option: to die without fighting back.

During the fifteen years from 2004 through July 7, 2019, all the rockets and mortars from Gaza killed a total of 28 Jewish civilians in Israel.[563] The killing of civilians for political or economic purposes is terrorism, and Hamas is clearly guilty of terrorism.

The low number of deaths from Gaza rockets begs one to wonder why Hamas continues to launch them. If Hamas's objective has been to kill civilians, then rockets have clearly been relatively ineffective and expensive; again, in fifteen years they killed 28 Israeli civilians with thousands of rockets.

Maybe Hamas's goal has not been to kill civilians. Maybe its goal has been to get media attention, attention from the international community, on which it depends to survive. **When Gaza is not in the news, the atrocities from the occupation and blockade continue unnoticed. When Gaza is not in the news, the occupation and blockade become accepted by the world as normal, as not being a problem.**

Another motive for Hamas launching rockets is popular support. A December 2014 survey showed that just a few months after Operation Protective Edge, Hamas was still strong in the Palestinian polls. Results showed that if there had been a presidential or legislative election at that time, Hamas would have won both (Fatah is in control and there has been no such elections since 2006).

> Most Palestinians continue to believe that Hamas won the war [Operation Protective Edge]. Moreover, an overwhelming majority of Palestinians continues to support launching of rockets from the Gaza Strip if the blockade is not lifted.[564]

Popular support does not justify terrorism. And we have already ascertained that Hamas has committed acts of terrorism. Therefore, one might assume that it makes sense that the United States, Israel, and the European Union designate Hamas as a terrorist organization, as they have done. After all, **Hamas was responsible for 39.9 percent of the suicide attacks between September 2000 and August 2005* during the al-Aqsa or Second Intifada.**[565]

---

* Statistics are from a sample of Palestinian-led suicide attacks during that time period where the target was identified. The suicide attacks that are included account for 98 percent of all the Israelis killed by suicide attacks during that period.

Such a terrorist designation would make sense, except that during the same period, 26.4 percent of the suicide attacks were by Fatah. Fatah currently runs the Palestinian Authority and commits human rights abuses against Palestinians. The PA's security services have been condemned for their use of torture (see chapter 9). So why does the United States not consider Fatah a terrorist organization as well? Why is the United States willing to provide Fatah financial support and training by our military? American criteria for determining whether an organization is a terrorist organization appear to be more based on whether they are doing what we want rather than whether they commit terrorism.

The Hamas Charter

Earlier in this chapter, I quoted part of the 1988 Hamas charter. The very incendiary passage in Article 7 is quoted by Israel supporters to communicate that even if an outside enemy such as Iran does not intend to kill the Jews in Palestine, then surely Hamas does. The Article 7 passage is proof.

Since 1988, Hamas appears to have found this language in its charter counterproductive. The organization's feeling of embarrassment is evident in a document posted on its website:

> That document [the 1988 charter] was a practical response to an oppressive occupation. It reflected the views of one of the movement's elder leaders; and it was ratified during the unique circumstances of the Uprising [the First Intifada] in 1988 as a necessary framework for dealing with a relentless occupation. There was little opportunity, at that time, to pore over the minutia of either its religious and political terminology or the broader perspective of international law.[566]

This may come as a surprise to Hamas, but many Jews don't consider terminology related to killing Jews "minutia." Just as one should refrain from food shopping when one is hungry, a time of rage or anger may not be the best time to write one's charter.

A couple of decades later, Hamas issued its newer Document of General Principles and Policies.[567] An updated document made sense; the organization had changed from just being a militant organization fighting an occupation to an elected party and provider of government services.

US history is similar. George Washington started out violating laws and killing British law enforcement officers. He also led militias against the state (Great Britain). But the revolutionaries evolved and became a government. As an elected official, George Washington likely had a different view of the importance of following the rule of law.

Looking at Hamas as an evolving organization seems appropriate based on the statement on their website:

> Despite the group's evolution, it is an inescapable fact that the charter represents a milestone in the struggle against an irredentist occupation. At any rate, historical statements remain a testament to the past; and the charter, as a document written over two decades ago, retains its authoritative value. However, it is not a constitution drafted as law; and cannot be construed to demand literal interpretation. In fact, the movement has to a certain degree moved on from its content simply by participating in the political process, accepting a Palestinian state within the 1967 borders and publicly declaring a readiness to explore political solutions with the international community. The claim of an intransigent organization simply does not tally with the reality of a group opening up to its regional environment; and one which participated in a national parliament borne of the Oslo Accords, having won a majority vote through participatory elections in 2006.[568]

Since Hamas is a prominent player in Palestinian politics and is mentioned regularly by American and Israeli politicians and in the press, it is important to understand how Hamas itself describes its role and objectives. The following is from the preamble to Hamas's Document of General Principles and Policies:

> Palestine is the cause of a people who have been let down by a world that fails to secure their rights and restore to them what has been usurped from them, a people whose land continues to suffer one of the worst types of occupation in this world.

> Palestine is a land that was seized by a racist, anti-human and colonial Zionist project that was founded on a false promise (the Balfour Declaration), on recognition of a usurping entity and on imposing a fait accompli by force.

> Palestine symbolizes the resistance that shall continue until liberation is accomplished, until the return is fulfilled and until a fully sovereign state is established with Jerusalem as its capital.

> Palestine is the true partnership among Palestinians of all affiliations for the sublime objective of liberation.[569]

This summarizes Hamas's story about itself. We all have our stories. Stories are helpful in knowing how an individual, a group, or a country wants to be viewed. Stories are not necessarily true, but they do provide us with a yardstick against which we can measure. The story of the United States includes the assertion that our forefathers wanted freedom, yet we know that that story was not fully accurate, because we started our new, "free" country with slaves.

I wanted first to understand how Hamas sees itself and then determine how it lives up to that image. The Document of General Principles and Policies helped me understand that Hamas wants to be viewed as an organization supporting a group of people who have been let down by the world, resisting a racist colonial project.

Because *Hamas* is an Arabic acronym for a full name that translates to "Islamic Resistance Movement," it is important to understand how Hamas views Islam. The newer Document of Principles and Policies tells us the following:

8. ... Islam is a religion of peace and tolerance. It provides an umbrella for the followers of other creeds and religions who can practice their beliefs in security and safety. Hamas also believes that Palestine has always been and will always be a model of coexistence, tolerance and civilizational innovation.

9. Hamas believes that the message of Islam upholds the values of truth, justice, freedom and dignity and prohibits all forms of injustice and incriminates oppressors irrespective of their religion, race, gender or nationality. Islam is against all forms of religious, ethnic or sectarian extremism and bigotry. It is the religion that inculcates in its followers the value of standing up to aggression and of supporting the oppressed; it motivates them to give generously and make sacrifices in defence of their dignity, their land, their peoples and their holy places.[570]

The document is also interesting from a language perspective; it tells us how Hamas defines other terms, including *Palestinian*, *Palestine*, and *Right of Return*:

6. The Palestinian people are one people, made up of all Palestinians, inside and outside of Palestine, irrespective of their religion, culture or political affiliation. ...

12. *The Palestinian cause in its essence is a cause of an occupied land and a displaced people. The right of the Palestinian refugees and the displaced to return to their homes from which they were banished or were banned from returning to— whether in the lands occupied in 1948 or in 1967 (that is the whole of Palestine), is a natural right, both individual and collective. This right is confirmed by all divine laws as well as by the basic principles of human rights and international*

law. It is an inalienable right and cannot be dispensed with by any party, whether Palestinian, Arab or international.

13. Hamas rejects all attempts to erase the rights of the refugees, including the attempts to settle them outside Palestine and through the projects of the alternative homeland. Compensation to the Palestinian refugees for the harm they have suffered as a consequence of banishing them and occupying their land is an absolute right that goes hand in hand with their right to return. They are to receive compensation upon their return and this does not negate or diminish their right to return.[571]

In reading the document, I realized that I had never known what values Hamas proclaimed it stood for; I had only heard talking heads on the news saying that Hamas was a terrorist organization against Jews. The document told a different story, one of standing for freedom, self-determination, and equality.

14. The Zionist project is a racist, aggressive, colonial and expansionist project based on seizing the properties of others; it is hostile to the Palestinian people and to their aspiration for freedom, liberation, return and self-determination. The Israeli entity is the plaything of the Zionist project and its base of aggression. ...

16. Hamas affirms that its conflict is with the Zionist project not with the Jews because of their religion. Hamas does not wage a struggle against the Jews because they are Jewish but wages a struggle against the Zionists who occupy Palestine. Yet, it is the Zionists who constantly identify Judaism and the Jews with their own colonial project and illegal entity.

17. Hamas rejects the persecution of any human being or the undermining of his or her rights on nationalist, religious or sectarian grounds.[572]

The document also highlights the Israel language. In the following paragraph, Hamas calls out the Israelspeak use of the word *peace*:

23. ***Hamas stresses that transgression against the Palestinian people, usurping their land and banishing them from their homeland cannot be called peace.*** Any settlements reached on this basis will not lead to peace. Resistance and jihad for the liberation of Palestine will remain a legitimate right, a duty and an honour for all the sons and daughters of our people and our Ummah.[573],*

As I was going through the document, it seemed to me more like our Declaration of Independence or a United Nations document than a terrorist manifesto.

25. ***Resisting the occupation with all means and methods is a legitimate right guaranteed by divine laws and by international norms and laws.*** At the heart of these lies armed resistance, which is regarded as the strategic choice for protecting the principles and the rights of the Palestinian people. ...

30. Hamas stresses the necessity of building Palestinian national institutions on sound democratic principles, foremost among them are free and fair elections. ...

38. The Palestinian issue is one that has major humanitarian and international dimensions. Supporting and backing this cause is a humanitarian and civilizational task that is required by the prerequisites of truth, justice and common humanitarian values.

39. From a legal and humanitarian perspective, the liberation of Palestine is a legitimate activity, it is an act of self-defence, and it is the expression of the natural right of all peoples to self-determination.

---

* *Ummah* (Arabic أمة) means "community," specifically the Islamic community.

40. In its relations with world nations and peoples, Hamas believes in the values of cooperation, justice, freedom and respect of the will of the people.

41. Hamas welcomes the stances of states, organisations and institutions that support the rights of the Palestinian people. It salutes the free peoples of the world who support the Palestinian cause. At the same time, it denounces the support granted by any party to the Zionist entity or the attempts to cover up its crimes and aggression against the Palestinians and calls for the prosecution of Zionist war criminals.[574]

Through its May 2017 declaration, Hamas still stands by its right to militaristic actions. Hamas states it more diplomatically—not as hatred toward a people but as a response to a system that is violating human rights and universal values, including self-determination. *Hamas does not seem to have anything against self-determination of Jews—just not on Arab land at the expense of another people. Hamas states that no confiscation of land or oppression is acceptable.*

As far as it being a terrorist organization, Hamas claims to oppose an occupation and the theft of land. That could involve fighting the military that is enforcing the occupation.

Since this book defines a terrorist organization as a group that threatens or uses violence against civilians for economic or political purposes, Hamas would not be considered a terrorist organization as long as it only fought the occupying military. Attacking Israeli civilians is what makes it deserve the terrorist designation.

Hamas and Relative Terrorism

Knowing Hamas's claimed story and objectives is helpful. However, to determine if an organization or government is a terrorist organization, we need to look at its actions more than its public relations material. In looking at the organization's actions, we need to acknowledge its crimes but understand them in context. The US bombing of Dresden, Tokyo, Hiroshima, and Nagasaki in World War II were clearly acts of violence against civilians for political purposes—in other words, terrorism. However, they were in the context of a war against parties that first declared and engaged war against us. Having been attacked by a party that declared war against us does not vindicate actions; it merely provides context.

Hamas has committed violence against Israeli civilians with its suicide bombings and well-publicized rocket launches. Those actions meet our definition of terrorism. Other Hamas actions, such as the building of tunnels for the importation of goods, do not meet the definition of terrorism. Even the importation of weapons through tunnels is not terrorism, since importation is not a threat or use of violence against civilians.

Our society tends to oversimplify the "terrorism" label. We talk about whether or not an organization is a terrorist organization rather than about how much terror they produce and the context for it. Just like one has to take into context a 350-pound sumo wrestler telling someone who weighs 250 pounds that they are overweight, *we also need to take into relative context governments that call organizations terrorists when those governments are far worse offenders.*

The accuser and the accused are both responsible for protecting civilians and for refraining from violence against civilians. Having said that, we need to be careful and determine the worst offenders rather than let ourselves be distracted and look only at the ones in the spotlight.

Civilians Killed[575]

	Israeli	Palestinian
Operation Cast Lead (2008/2009)	3	759
Operation Pillar of Defense (2012)	4	87
Operation Protective Edge (2014)	5	1,462
Total:	12	2,308

When considering relative terrorism, we need to look at the records of Hamas and Israel relative to each other. The preceding table shows the Israeli and Palestinian civilian deaths from the three "Gaza Wars."[576] During these three "operations," or wars, 12 Israeli civilians were killed from Gaza rockets, whereas 2,308 Palestinian noncombatant civilians, including 845 children, were killed by the Israeli soldiers.

The occupation and the Gaza blockade are clear forms of violence against civilian populations. The operations are merely consequences of the oppressive occupation and blockade; none of them would have occurred had Palestinians had equal rights. The occupation has been going on for more than fifty years, the blockade for more than ten, and operations continue.

The number of civilian deaths from the aforementioned "operations" have been extremely one-sided, almost reaching a civilian death ratio of 200 Palestinians to every Israeli.

But the ratio of civilian deaths to militant/military deaths is also important to note. *Israel wounds and kills a much higher percentage of Palestinian civilians relative to Hamas, which wounds and kills a higher percentage of soldiers.*

These different results reflect each organization's objectives. Hamas states that it is trying to right a wrong between the two parties:

- Palestinians want to get rid of the Zionist movement (the Israeli government), which has wronged Palestinians. They are asking for the rule of international law to be upheld with what they call "divine laws." Hamas is asking for liberation and self-determination, not terrorism.

- Israel, on the other hand, claims to be trying to right a wrong from such third parties as Nazi Germany. It just so happens that Zionists are creating a wrong in the process of righting another wrong; they are creating Israel at the expense of the Palestinians. And since Palestinians don't want to voluntarily pay for Germany's sins, the only way a Zionist movement can be successful in establishing a country on Palestinian land is through violence against Palestinians—especially against civilians.

This explains why Israel inflicts such a high percentage of its casualties and injuries on civilians; Palestinian civilians are its primary threat. The more Palestinian civilians there are, the more Israel is at risk of not being a Jewish state. Palestinian civilians, rather than Hamas, are Israel's primary enemy.

By contrast, Hamas's primary opponent is the Israeli military; they are the ones preventing Palestinians from going home, blocking their freedom of movement, and otherwise violating their human rights.

Israel requires terrorism to survive because civilians are its necessary target. That violence has included the forced displacement of Palestinians during the Nakba, as it continues through today. That required violence necessitates the violation of human rights, including the occupation, blockade, property seizure, and related enforcement mechanisms. Without violence against the Palestinians, Israel cannot survive as a Jewish state.

If Israel does not violently stop Palestinians from returning to their homelands in Israel, then Jews will become a minority in Israel. And a democratic state with a Jewish minority would be the end of the Zionist project as it is most often described.

We can condemn Hamas for committing terrorism. However, Israel cannot rightfully do so without acknowledging its own terrorism. As Israeli human rights lawyer Lea Tsemel said, "On what moral grounds should I judge the people who resist my occupation?"[577]

In summary, Hamas has committed terrorism. But to only ask if Hamas is a terrorist organization deflects condemnation of the most egregious terrorist organization in Israel/Palestine. *Not comparing Hamas's terrorism with the state of Israel's terrorism is to be complicit in the injustice.*

The contrasting levels of terrorism by the two organizations is immense. Hamas does not need terrorism to survive; Israel as a Jewish state does. The occupation and blockade show us which organization uses terrorism for its daily sustenance.

It does not look good for Israel when its opponent, Hamas, is demanding real equality, real democracy, and the support of international laws. Hamas, not Israel, openly opposes oppression.

This goes to show that the United States government is fluent in Israel; it defines only Hamas as the terrorist organization while defending Israel's actions.

14

Christians and the Holy Land

As I mentioned in the preceding chapter, I was surprised by how much Hamas's charter and its Document of General Principles and Policies sounded like declarations of independence or other political documents. I had expected to find much more religious emphasis in their documents. I thought about why I had had that bias and concluded that it was both because terrorism in the United States is usually described in the context of Islam (see "Terrorism in the News" in chapter 12) and because so many Americans look at the situation in Israel from a religious perspective. For example, American Christian Zionists represent one of the largest groups of Israel supporters.

"Christian" Zionism

Not all Zionists are Jewish. In fact, there are more Christian Zionists in the United States than Jewish Zionists. Trump administration Vice President Mike Pence and Secretary of State Mike Pompeo are Christian Zionists. For centuries, groups of Christians have studied the biblical references about the return of the Jews to the land of Israel, such as this passage from the book of Isaiah:

He will raise a banner for the nations and gather the exiles of Israel; he will assemble the scattered people of Judah from the four quarters of the earth. [Isa. 11:12 (NIV)]

Lord Arthur James Balfour, author of the Balfour Declaration, was a Christian Zionist.

Christian Zionism has especially grown in the United States since 2006, when Pastor John Hagee of the Cornerstone Church, an 18,000-member megachurch in San Antonio, Texas, began building up Christians United for Israel (CUFI). The organization now claims over 7 million members.[578] (By comparison, the American Israel Public Affairs Committee [AIPAC] claims it has 100,000 members.[579])

John Hagee has published a number of books, including *Jerusalem Countdown: A Warning to the World* and *In Defense of Israel*. He considers the creation of the state of Israel part of the biblical prophecies and that Hitler was part of God's plan to make Israel become a Jewish state.[580] In an interview aired in September 2006, Hagee said that the end times and the Second Coming of the Messiah are imminent, that no other prophecies need to happen before the Rapture, that there will be a great battle, and

the enemies of Israel are going to be crushed in such a dramatic fashion, quite similar to Pharaoh in the Red Sea, that all of Israel will recognize that the God of Abraham, Isaac, and Jacob is indeed the Lord.[581]

Hagee also does not believe any of the land of biblical Israel should be divided, including through a peace treaty. He not only opposes Gaza and the West Bank being outside of Israel, he also opposes Israel having given up land in Lebanon, the Sinai, and Jordan. He quoted the book of Joel and summarized that any nation that divides the land of biblical Israel "will experience the judgment of God."[582]

Hagee said in the interview that one has to believe in Jesus Christ in order to go to heaven during the Rapture. He referred to Revelation 14 and how God will send down angels to preach the Gospel across the Earth "so that everyone will have the opportunity of knowing who Jesus Christ is." Hagee went on to say that per Zechariah, Jews "are not going to believe that Jesus Christ is the Messiah until they see him." After the Rapture and the Second Coming of Christ, God will then judge "all nations" and that Jews, because they then will believe in Jesus Christ, will be saved.[583]

Hagee is careful not to widely broadcast what happens to Jews who do not convert to Christianity; other Evangelical Christian Zionists are more direct and proclaim that Jews who don't convert will go to hell.[584] On the one hand, Hagee and other Christian Zionists trumpet being pro-Jewish, yet they appear to actively help get Jews to Israel so that the Rapture can occur, resulting in the deaths of the Jews who do not convert.

John Hagee is a leader in the Christian Zionist movement, but he is not alone. At the dedication of the American embassy in Jerusalem on May 14, 2018, where Hagee gave the closing benediction, he was joined by fellow Christian Zionist Pastor Robert Jeffress, who gave a prayer as well. Jeffress also leads a megachurch in Texas; he is senior pastor of the 13,000-member First Baptist Church in Dallas. He is also an adjunct professor at Dallas Theological Seminary. He is blunter in his statements about Jews and others. Instead of evading what happens to Jews after the Rapture, he said in 2017 that people who imply that there is any way to be saved other than through Jesus are "leading people to hell because [they] are suggesting there is another opening somewhere."[585] Here is what Jeffress said with respect to Jews:

> Judaism—you can't be saved being a Jew. You know who said that, by the way? The three greatest Jews in the New Testament: Peter, Paul and Jesus Christ. They all said Judaism won't do it. It's faith in Jesus Christ.[586]

Here is from a sermon of Jeffress's in 2008:

Not only do religions like Mormonism, Islam, Judaism, Hinduism —
not only do they lead people away from the true God, they lead
people to an eternity of separation from God in hell.[587]

Hagee and other Evangelical Christian Zionists are vehemently
anti-Islam. Hagee believes that the Qur'an teaches "very clearly" that
all Muslims have a mandate to kill Christians and Jews. When he
describes the impending end times, he describes Muslims invading.[588]

These Christian Zionists do not look at Jews as equals. Instead,
they openly share how Jews are merely pieces on the Christian
Zionist chessboard. Their goal is to get all the pieces in place so
that God can declare checkmate.

Yet despite using Jews for this Christian Zionist plan of
destruction, Hagee is very popular with Jewish organizations. He
was the first non-Jew to receive the Humanitarian of the Year Award
from the San Antonio B'nai B'rith council.[589] Pastor Hagee has
been presented the Zionist Organization of America (ZOA) Adelson
Defender of Israel Award as well as the ZOA Service Award.[590]

Not all Christians are Zionists. In fact, the National Council of
Churches issued the following response to Christian Zionism:

On August 22, 2006 the highest ranking Christian leaders of
Jerusalem issued a statement of concern about the rising popularity
of modern Christian theologies and political movements that
embrace the extreme ideological positions of Christian Zionism.
It said in part:

"The Christian Zionist programme provides a worldview where
the Gospel is identified with the ideology of empire, colonialism
and militarism. In its extreme form, it places an emphasis on
apocalyptic events leading to the end of history rather than living
Christ's love and justice today. We categorically reject Christian
Zionist doctrines as false teaching that corrupts the biblical
message of love, justice and reconciliation." ...

Christian Zionism is flourishing in part because of the lack of knowledge and popularly accessible alternative Christian theologies of the end-times.[591]

I have named this section of the chapter "'Christian' Zionism," where the word *Christian* is in quotes because people who consider themselves Christian have very different views. All Christians are not in agreement.

American Christians are very polarized on issues from capital punishment to treatment of the poor and from military occupation to divorce. These differing Christian views exist despite Jesus having made His views known on each of these topics in the Bible. People who consider themselves Christian interpret the Bible differently. Some claim to read the Bible literally. However, even those who claim to read the Bible literally acknowledge some symbolism. Pastor Hagee is quite a literalist in reading about the Rapture. However, when talking about Revelation 13, he explains in sermons the symbolism of the beast and its numerous heads and horns. Similarly, when Pastor Jeffress said (quoting Jesus), "Nobody comes to the Father except through me,"[592] he probably meant that metaphorically rather than literally (physically).

The book of Revelation is believed to have been written around 96 CE by "John the Elder" while he was in exile on the island of Patmos. The book is believed by numerous scholars to be a coded way of describing the evil nature of the Roman Empire. He did not want the authorities to know that he was criticizing them. Scholars associate, for example, the seven hills in Revelation 17:9 as the seven hills of Rome. They also associate Revelation 17:10–11 to Roman emperors:

They are also seven kings. Five have fallen, one is, the other has not yet come; but when he does come, he must remain for only a little while. The beast who once was, and now is not, is an eighth king. He belongs to the seven and is going to his destruction.

The five "fallen" ones were Augustus, Tiberius, Gaius (Caligula), Claudius, and Nero, all of whom had died by the time John was in exile. Vespasian was the emperor "who is," Titus "has not yet come," and Domitian is the eighth mentioned.[593]

This is not the only interpretation of Revelation. Each Christian chooses which part of the Bible is metaphorical and to what extent. Some Christians read these chapters and verses as a coded historical forecast of the fall of the Roman Empire, while others interpret the battles and beasts as Pastor Hagee does: literal future battles with metaphorical beasts.

Then there are those who interpret the battles as internal and personal; they see these battles and beasts as struggles we all go through as we grow spiritually. These struggles appear as we are tempted and follow such idols as fame, lust, money, and power. At some point we realize the earthly pleasures are merely a distraction; they lead us away from rather than toward peace. One's rebirth leads us to our personal place of peace, our own "Jerusalem." For some Christians, Jerusalem is only a city in the Middle East; for other Christians it is also a metaphor for the personal place of peace we reach as part of our tumultuous spiritual journey where the Spirit in us is born again.

For both Zionist and non-Zionist Christians, Bible prophecies can be self-fulfilling. Those who see that battle as internal can face it internally and can consciously identify the "beasts." By reading the Bible, they are given tools to identify the idols and find the path to inner peace and salvation. On the other hand, those Christians who choose to believe that the battle is a physical battle between countries are encouraging, whether they like it or not, such a battle to occur. They, like John Hagee, support the taking of land from people (the Palestinians). They aggressively stand for and promote the military attacks on Muslim-majority countries, such as Iran. They support Israel's violation of human rights by denying non-Jews a right to any of the land. All those positions and actions will most likely lead to war. What response would one expect to the taking of land and expulsion of people?

Palestinian Christians also lose because of a Christian Zionist inconsistency in interpreting a passage from Paul's Epistle to the Galatians:

If you belong to Christ, then you are Abraham's seed, and heirs according to the promise. [Gal. 3:29 (NIV)]

If Christians are also Abraham's seed, then Palestinian Christians should have equal rights to the land of Israel. If Christians are also Abraham's seed, then should not Israel be called a Jewish-Christian state rather than merely a Jewish state? So why would Christian Zionists support Israel's discrimination against Palestinian Christians? Why would they not insist that their brothers and sisters in Christ be treated as Abraham's seed?

Every Christian has created an image of Jesus in his or her mind. What would your Jesus do in today's situation? Would He expel people from the land? Would He discriminate against those of different ethnicities, or would He follow the Golden Rule as He suggested in the parable of the Good Samaritan? Does your Jesus act more like a Crusader or like Mother Teresa? Does your Jesus yearn for war and biblical genocide, or does your Jesus stand for peace and the oppressed? Each Christian benefits by thinking through these trade-offs consciously; it is easy to get swayed by one biblical passage, especially when it is taken out of context. Taking a passage without using the context of a loving God can be tragic, both for the individual whose perspective and beliefs are diverted from loving one's neighbor as oneself, as well as for the neighbor. (For a light biblical and religious institutional analysis, see Appendix: "The Promised Land.")

The book of Genesis states the following:

So God created man in his own image, in the image of God created he him; male and female created he them. [Gen. 1:27 (RSV)]

I heard Rabbi Arik Ascherman say that *the ultimate idolatry is when the holiness of the land prevents someone from seeing the holiness in another human being.*

What is "Christian" Zionism today? A large and growing organized effort to support the state of Israel despite its persecution of Christians (among others) whose families date back to Jesus himself. These "Christian" Zionists do not consider Palestinians to be seed of Abraham, and they do not treat them as their neighbor. Instead, Christian Zionists consider Palestinian Christians collateral damage.

Palestinian Christians' Struggle

Pilgrims have been coming here since 1106 AD to wash themselves in the holy fire, to celebrate the founding miracle of Christianity. They will certainly continue to do so. But how many will be coming from the neighborhood? That's not a religious question anymore. It's political.

—Israeli Ambassador Michael Oren,[594]
60 Minutes, April 22, 2012

In December, amid reports Trump was planning to change Jerusalem's status, thirteen church leaders from 13 denominations signed an open letter warning of "irreparable harm" to the Holy City if the US implemented the change. ...

So, it is arresting to hear one of Jerusalem's highest-ranking Christian figures declare that the most pressing threat facing Christians in the Middle East is not from a terror group, but rather the White House. ...

Driving away Christians from the Holy Land, say local clergy, is the perceived preferential treatment the US shows toward Israel, and the occupation of Palestinian lands, which means restrictions on the lives, movements, and opportunities of Palestinian Christians, as well as Muslims.

—Ian Lee, CNN[595]

Kairos Palestine is a Palestinian Christian movement, born out of the Kairos Document, which advocates for ending the Israeli occupation and achieving a just solution to the conflict. The Kairos Document is a cry from Palestinian Christians to the world about what is happening in Palestine. It describes how Kairos Palestine interprets Christianity, an interpretation especially pertinent to the situation in Israel/Palestine:

> We, a group of Christian Palestinians, after prayer, reflection and an exchange of opinion, cry out from within the suffering in our country, under the Israeli occupation. ... We proclaim our word based on our Christian faith and our sense of Palestinian belonging—a word of faith, hope and love. ...

> The aggression against the Palestinian people which is the Israeli occupation ... is an evil and a sin that must be resisted and removed. Primary responsibility for this rests with the Palestinians themselves suffering occupation. Christian love invites us to resist it. However, love puts an end to evil by walking in the ways of justice. Responsibility lies also with the international community, because international law regulates relations between peoples today. Finally responsibility lies with the perpetrators of the injustice; they must liberate themselves from the evil that is in them and the injustice they have imposed on others.[596]

The Christian Zionists focus on one prophetic interpretation of the Bible. In contrast, the Kairos Document focuses on justice and love versus evil:

We say to our Christian brothers and sisters: ... The communion
of love says to every believer in spirit and in truth: if my brother
is a prisoner I am a prisoner; if his home is destroyed, my home
is destroyed; when my brother is killed, then I too am killed. ...
Perhaps, as individuals or as heads of Churches, we were silent
when we should have raised our voices to condemn the injustice
and share in the suffering. ...

Our word to the Churches of the world is firstly a word of
gratitude for the solidarity you have shown toward us in word,
deed and presence among us. It is a word of praise for the many
Churches and Christians who support the right of the Palestinian
people for self determination. It is a message of solidarity with
those Christians and Churches who have suffered because of their
advocacy for law and justice.[597]

The Kairos Document expresses appreciation to others for their
law-and-justice solidarity. However, it also highlights how theological
interpretation is dividing, rather than uniting, Christians:

However, it is also a call to repentance; to revisit fundamentalist
theological positions that support certain unjust political options
with regard to the Palestinian people. It is a call to stand
alongside the oppressed and preserve the word of God as good
news for all rather than to turn it into a weapon with which to
slay the oppressed. The word of God is a word of love for all His
creation. God is not the ally of one against the other, nor the
opponent of one in the face of the other. God is the Lord of all
and loves all, demanding justice from all and issuing to all of us
the same commandments. We ask our sister Churches not to offer
a theological cover-up for the injustice we suffer, for the sin of
the occupation imposed upon us. Our question to our brothers
and sisters in the Churches today is: Are you able to help us get
our freedom back, for this is the only way you can help the two
peoples attain justice, peace, security and love?[598]

Christians need to decide if they stand for a prophecy or for loving their neighbors as themselves. Christians need to decide if their God is one who is for love and justice or for mass destruction because of people's beliefs.

On February 26, 2017, Rev. Dr. Olav Fykse Tveit, the general secretary of the World Council of Churches (WCC), met with President Mahmoud Abbas. Here is what he said relative to Palestine:

> No people should be denied their rights and, certainly, no people should be denied their rights for generations. The unresolved conflict in Israel and Palestine is primarily about justice, and until the requirement of justice is met, peace cannot be established. ...
> As Israel's occupation of East Jerusalem, the West Bank, and Gaza nears the 50-year mark, generations have been suffering under this reality.[599]

Christians also need to determine if the ethnic cleansing of Christians from the Holy Land—the consequence of Christian Zionist actions—is part of their faith.

In April 2016, Nicola Khamis, the mayor of the predominantly Christian town of Beit Jala, just six miles south of Jerusalem, said, "Without this land all the Christians will leave this country."[600] He added, "It is impossible to build in Beit Jala. We want to widen Beit Jala." He said this because most of Beit Jala's land is in Area C, under administration by the state of Israel. Extremely few building permits are granted to Palestinians in Area C, even though it is in the West Bank and is Palestinian land. The separation wall cuts off Beit Jala residents from their land. Mayor Khamis also said,

> We want people outside to come and say "enough is enough."...
> Christians all over the world must stop being silent. ... What Israel is doing here is against peace.[601]

A 2015 BBC article reported:

> Foreign dignitaries have also expressed their concerns to Israeli authorities, listing the separation barrier among pressures that are pushing Christians to leave the Holy Land.[602]

American Christians have to decide if their faith stands for the oppression of others, including members of their own faith. American Christians need to decide if their faith stands for the oppression of others merely for who they are and not for anything they have done. Is it Christian to violate human rights, and even kill one's own fellow believing Christians, in the name of Christianity?

We have to take ownership of our language and our faiths. We are responsible for the consequences of what we choose to believe. We have to define the terms *Christian* and *Jewish* as they relate to how we treat our fellow human beings. Do we want our faiths to reflect treating others as subjugated or as our brothers and sisters? Do we want our faiths to represent abuse or love? We need to be vigilant in making sure the terms *Christian* and *Jewish* are not kidnapped and used to promote hatred.

We can choose to believe in a God who is racist or a God who is not racist. The Bible has been used to justify both. The choice is ours.

15

"America's Greatest Ally"

Israel is our greatest ally, and a true friend to the United States.

—*Texas Congressman John Culberson* [603]

There is no greater friend and reliable ally to the United States than Israel.

—*New York Congressman Lee Zeldin* [604]

As you know by having read this far into this book, the United States is intimately involved in the Israel project. That had not been my understanding before I started to learn how to speak Israel. I had always thought that the US was a cheerleader and protector of the Jewish state from its aggressive neighbors. I also knew of the US playing a major role in peace talks between Israel and the Palestinians. However, it was only through my research that I learned the depth of the US involvement in the Zionist project. In this book I have detailed the commitment and support Americans have given Israel, from the extensive foreign aid to military support to vetoes in the United Nations. To summarize, Israel has historically been the largest recipient of US foreign aid. The US has guaranteed Israel military superiority over all its neighbors combined. The UN vetoes have protected Israel from answering for its human rights violations and war crimes. These are significant acts of "friendship" and loyalty by the United States toward Israel.

Our Congress also strongly supports Israel. The 113th Congress listed the following caucuses directly related to Israel: the Congressional Hellenic Israel Alliance, the Congressional Israel Allies Caucus, the Democratic Israel Working Group, the House Israel Solution Caucus, and the House Republican Israel Caucus. By contrast, there was only one United Kingdom caucus and one Germany caucus and no France caucus as of 2014.[605] It is to be expected that we would have allies and opponents and that we would treat our allies better than we would our opponents. However, Germany and France are not our opponents. By contrast, Israel's influence has so permeated the political, power, and money structure of the United States that its advocates have corrupted our politicians into compromising the American values of democracy, equality, and freedom.

We have compromised our value of equality by giving preferential treatment to one country and one ethnic group; we have become racist by selectively and preferentially adopting a unique definition of only one form of racism in the Department of State: *anti-Semitism*. No other country or ethnic group has that protection. As mentioned earlier in this book, someone who criticizes Iran does not get labeled anti-Persian. This State Department definition of *anti-Semitism* creates an Orwellian twist, where people who stand for equality—and therefore are critics of Israel for its racist policies— are often labeled as anti-Semitic. ***Our United States government has taken a page out of George Orwell's Newspeak: We have codified standing for equality as racism.***

Others may say that no system is perfect and no system is completely free of corruption, but the case of Israel is exceptional. We do not cover up an attack against our military by any other ally as we do for Israel. Israel conducted an air and naval attack on the USS *Liberty*, an American intelligence-gathering ship, on June 8, 1967, killing 34 American sailors and wounding 173. The ship was sold for scrap.[606] As of October 2020, Congress has yet to request an investigation of the attack.

Israel in the US Government

Israel has infiltrated our government at many levels, as exemplified by the infamous Israeli spy Jonathan Pollard. Pollard was a former US naval intelligence analyst who was given a life sentence in 1987 for stealing tens of thousands of US secrets for Israel. Israel and pro-Israel groups in the US lobbied administrations for his release. He was granted parole in 2015. Hardly embarrassed about Pollard, Israel granted Pollard citizenship in 1996[607] and renamed Paris Square in Jerusalem to Pollard Square.[608] Upon his release from parole in November 2020, Pollard and his wife were flown to Israel on a private jet owned by Sheldon Adelson, the man that every 2016 Republican presidential candidate visited in Las Vegas (more on Adelson later in the chapter); the Pollards were personally greeted by Prime Minister Netanyahu and were given Israeli ID cards.[609] According to Paul Pillar, former CIA national intelligence officer for the Near East and South Asia,

> they're [the Israelis are] incredibly aggressive. They're aggressive in all aspects of their relationship with the United States. Why would their intelligence relationship with us be any different?[610]

Additional Israeli spies have been convicted in US courts.

Israel's power within and over the United States is extensive, and its operatives work with impunity. According to I. C. Smith, former top FBI counterintelligence specialist,

> in the early 1980s, dealing with the Israelis was, for those assigned that area, extremely frustrating. The Israelis were supremely confident that they had the clout, especially on the Hill, to basically get [away] with just about anything.[611]

We raise concerns about Russian meddling with social media and influencing US election results, but we do not hear concerns about a foreign country's influence throughout our government. As revealed in this chapter's epigraphs and reinforced in the FBI counterintelligence specialist's statement, our politicians enable, rather than restrict, Israel's actions. American politicians have in essence been bought. In a completely polarized Congress that can get little done, one issue that always passes is aid to Israel.

I wrote a letter to Texas Senator John Cornyn with my concerns about US policy toward Israel and the treatment of Palestinians. His response, dated July 31, 2019, is worth analyzing from a language perspective. It included the following:

> The Middle East region is critical to our national security, and the United States remains committed to achieving peace between Israel and Palestine. Since its founding in 1948, Israel has been a strong and faithful ally to the United States in the Middle East. In a region characterized by instability and violence, Israel stands alone in its commitment to democracy, individual liberty, and free-market principles. Meanwhile, the Palestinian faction Hamas refuses to recognize Israel's right to exist and continues to endanger the lives of Israelis by launching rockets and terror attacks, reaching as far north as Tel Aviv and Jerusalem.
>
> The United States and Israel have developed bonds based on our shared values—including our strong cultural, religious, and political ties. The United States has joined with Israel in fighting terrorism, and we remain resolute in pursuing our shared goals. By continuing our strategic alliance with Israel, we can end the scourge of extremism and usher in a new chapter in the peace process.[612]

Unpacking this carefully worded letter, we start with "the United States remains committed to achieving peace between Israel and Palestine." If we were truly committed to peace, then we would require that all people have equal rights, and we would enforce international human rights laws. There can be no peace with an occupation, with a blockade, and without equality. Peace requires justice. Justice requires equality. Equality means a right of return for everyone equally. When it comes to Israel/Palestine, the United States has not shown any commitment to equality.

The letter continues: "In a region characterized by instability and violence, Israel stands alone in its commitment to democracy, individual liberty, and free-market principles." Israel is anti-democratic because it will not give equal rights to all its people. When Israel does not even recognize the indigenous people of the land as its own, we cannot regard it as a democracy. Israel is a country that denies citizenship to a significant portion of the population from the territory it occupies, that denies the right to vote for the government that controls their lives; when we call that country a democracy, we are complicit in the deception.

An occupation, a blockade, and Israel's restrictions on movement of Palestinians are examples of how Israel stands against, rather than for, individual liberty. What did it say about Israel's stand for individual liberty when it required US Congresswoman Rashida Tlaib to sign a document limiting her free speech when she would go to Palestine? An occupying government was asking an American congresswoman to sign away individual liberties?

A real democracy requires liberty. Yet Senator Cornyn was calling this occupying government a "democracy." My senator was asking for recognition and legitimization of an apartheid state dependent on racism and the violation of human rights while he condemned victims fighting for equality, freedom, and justice:

> Meanwhile, the Palestinian faction Hamas refuses to recognize Israel's right to exist and continues to endanger the lives of Israelis by launching rockets and terror attacks.

My senator talked about endangering lives while he disregarded the vast majority of the people who have been killed. We have looked at the number of casualties from the rockets my senator referred to; they were minuscule relative to the killing of children by the Israeli forces. The extreme lopsidedness of his and most American legislators' stand on the issue—taking a position against democracy and human rights in favor of an ethnic supremacy state—highlights our government's misinformation efforts.

Finally, his promotion of misleading messaging showed the depth of the complicity:

> The United States has joined with Israel in fighting terrorism, and we remain resolute in pursuing our shared goals. By continuing our strategic alliance with Israel, we can end the scourge of extremism and usher in a new chapter in the peace process.

The reality is that Israel is extremism, and yet he said that with our "strategic alliance with Israel, we can end the scourge of extremism." The most effective tool for fighting terrorism is justice. The United States and Israel actively stand against justice and equality in this region.

Unfortunately, because the United States stands against justice and equality in the region, Americans are the ones who foster terrorism. ***Without Israel's terrorism there would have been no need for Hamas.***

The senator referred to extremism as if those who were fighting for freedom and human rights were extremists. Extremism is when a US president tweeted to the prime minister of a foreign country that the prime minister "would show great weakness," by letting two elected American congresswomen entry into Israel, as he did relative to Representatives Rashida Tlaib of Michigan and Ilhan Omar of Minnesota on August 15, 2019.[613] Extremism is when an American president said,

> the only real winner here is Tlaib's grandmother. She doesn't have to see her [own granddaughter] now![614]

Extremism is obvious when one looks at the disproportionate lists of people killed in Israel/Palestine. Taking twenty seconds to scan the Israel-Palestine Timeline tells us the human cost of extremism and which side is the most extreme.[615] Continuing our alliance with Israel builds, rather than ends, the scourge of extremism and terrorism.

Senator Cornyn's position is representative of the position of many, if not most, members of Congress. His misleading letter showed the corruption of our political system. I have met with members of his staff in Texas and in Washington. They are smart people. They know what is happening. Therefore, to so openly twist the situation and take a position against our foundational values of equality and freedom (including the freedom of speech) highlighted the duplicity within our system of media and government.

And this corruption of our political officials goes to the highest level. In the 2016 presidential election, all Republican and Democratic candidates, except for Bernie Sanders, went in front of AIPAC, the American Israel Public Affairs Committee. That is, *all but one major-party presidential candidate went in front of an organization whose objectives are to support a foreign country. Those American candidates pledged their support to that foreign country, Israel.* Imagine if they had done that for Germany, England, or even Canada. Here is Merriam-Webster's definition of *treachery*:[616]

treachery. *n.*
1. violation of allegiance or of faith and confidence
2. an act of perfidy or treason

Moreover, all the 2016 Republican presidential candidates came out to Las Vegas to visit casino magnate Sheldon Adelson to ask for his campaign contributions. Adelson said, "I am a one-issue person. That issue is Israel." That quote is believable, considering that he also stated in 2010 that "the [United States] uniform that I wore in the military, unfortunately, was not an Israeli uniform."[617][618] As mentioned earlier in this chapter, Adelson provided a private plane for Jonathan Pollard, who had been convicted of spying for Israel against the United States, to fly to Israel. Adelson's contributions, especially to the Republican Party, have been immense:

The Adelsons were in Jerusalem for their victory lap, just as they had spent the inauguration with Trump. Recently, we learned of an over $30 million donation—some might say payoff—to the Republican Party on top of the estimated $82 million spent on Trump and the GOP in 2016.[619]

The Democratic Party was also on the take for Israel. *Forbes* reported that nearly 80 percent of the $75.9 million raised by Hillary Clinton's Priorities USA Action super PAC (January 1, 2015, to April 30, 2016) came from just twenty donors. The article claims Haim and Cheryl Saban to be at the top of the list, donating $10 million as well as $10 million to the Clinton Foundation.

> What Saban, born to a Jewish family in Egypt, and Clinton have in common is their pro-Israel stance.[620]

Other sources show Donald Sussman, involved with the Israel Policy Forum, giving Clinton's PAC over $18 million.[621] A number of the other million-dollar-plus donors are also known to be strong supporters of Israel.

Hillary Clinton wrote a letter to Haim Saban in July 2015, taking a position against Americans' free speech rights. She committed to fight BDS, the Palestinian call to boycott, divest, and sanction Israel until Palestinians are treated equally, they have their Right of Return honored, and the occupation is ended. Clinton also described her loyalty to Israel by preventing Palestine from becoming a state without Israel's accord. Here was how she started her letter:

> I am writing to express my alarm over the Boycott, Divestment, and Sanction movement, or "BDS," a global effort to isolate the State of Israel by ending commercial and academic exchanges. I know you agree that we need to make countering BDS a priority. [622]

Note that this was an American presidential candidate taking a position against Americans' freedom of speech; the Supreme Court had ruled in 1982 that boycotting is a form of constitutionally protected speech in *NAACP v. Claiborne Hardware Co.*

More from Clinton's letter:

> BDS is the latest attempt to single out Israel on the world stage, but we've seen this sort of attack before, at the UN and elsewhere. As Senator and Secretary of State, I saw how crucial it is for America to defend Israel at every turn. I have opposed dozens of anti-Israel resolutions at the UN, the Human Rights Council, and other international organizations. I condemned the biased Goldstone Report, making it clear that Israel must be allowed to defend itself like any other country. And I made sure the United States blocked Palestinian attempts at the UN to unilaterally declare statehood. Time after time, no matter the venue, I have made it clear that America will always stand up for Israel—and that's what I'll always do as President.[623]

Note that Clinton was well versed in speaking Israel. She followed a sentence about BDS with one stating "how crucial it is for America to defend Israel at every turn." It is hard to translate her letter from Israel into English in any other way than to say she was offering to sacrifice Americans' constitutional freedom of speech (reflected in boycotts, divestments, and sanctions) for the benefit of the foreign country Israel. The foregoing paragraph from her letter may sound reasonable to anyone unfamiliar with the situation or new to speaking Israel. Let's look at one of the sentences:

> I condemned the biased Goldstone Report, making it clear that Israel must be allowed to defend itself like any other country.

The United Nations Fact-Finding Mission on the Gaza Conflict was headed by Judge Richard Goldstone, a South African Jewish Zionist, and its findings are known as "the Goldstone Report."[624] If there was any bias in the report, as Clinton asserted in her sentence, it would have been in favor of Israel. However, despite being Zionist and Jewish, Goldstone faced a lack of cooperation from Israel during the mission. Israel blocked those doing the investigation access to Gaza from Israel, forcing them to travel via Egypt. The Israeli government even blocked the investigators from going to the West Bank to meet with members of the Palestinian Authority; PA representatives ended up going to Jordan, where they were able to meet. In addition:

> Israel refused to engage with the mission and denied it any understanding of Israel's motives in attacking the Gaza Strip.[625]

Pressure on Judge Goldstone was so intense after the report was issued that he was not allowed to attend his grandson's bar mitzvah in South Africa. In summary, in contrast with Clinton's letter, Israel was allowed "to defend itself" but instead chose to block the investigation in multiple ways.

Clinton was speaking Israel because she described the Goldstone Report as biased, as if it were biased against Israel, even though the mission had been headed by a Zionist. In fact, it is the United States that has become biased: We pressure the United Nations to rescind condemnations against Israel but not against Saudi Arabia, Yemen, Egypt, Syria, and others for their human rights violations. (I am not suggesting we encourage the UN to rescind condemnations of the others too!)

Unfortunately, Clinton was not the only corrupted politician standing up for a foreign country at Americans' expense. While serving as secretary of state, she had experienced a lot of pressure from other American politicians on this issue. More than one hundred members of Congress had written her a letter urging the Obama administration to prevent the Goldstone Report from reaching the International Court of Justice in The Hague.[626] This level of corruption is exceptional: Over one hundred members of Congress had gone on record to prevent a report, which if anything would have been biased in favor of Israel because it was led by a Zionist judge, from reaching a court of justice because it was still too critical of Israel.

Stepping back, I saw a level of corruption in my government that I had not previously fathomed. Here was a presidential candidate, and previous secretary of state, asking for money from a donor whose primary interest was the support of a foreign country. She and more than one hundred congresspeople wanted the United States to take a stand against human rights (and ultimately against constituents' free speech rights). And in the language of Israel, the stand for human rights was considered "biased."

Interestingly, Clinton also stated the following in the Israel language: "And I made sure the United States blocked Palestinian attempts at the UN to unilaterally declare statehood." The bias appeared in this sentence as well. Israel had declared its own statehood unilaterally in 1948. Is it not biased for one "people" to have self-determination while denying that same right to another "people"? The United States and Israel, against the Charter of the United Nations, regularly vote against the self-determination of a people. Despite the United States having claimed that it supports a two-state solution for decades, it has consistently blocked the statehood of Palestine and has threatened and defunded organizations that do support statehood. The United States has joined Israel against an overwhelming majority of the countries of the world in opposing Palestinian statehood.

One might translate Clinton's sentences into English as follows:

> And I was even willing to compromise the reputation and values of the United States and violate Article 1 of the United Nations Charter,[*,627] in order to protect Israel from needing to answer for its violations of Palestinian rights under international law and the Geneva Conventions. I took a stand against self-determination

---

* Among the purposes and principles stipulated in Chapter I, Article 1.2 of the Charter of the United Nations is the following: "To **develop friendly relations among nations based on respect for the principle of equal rights and self-determination of peoples.**" And stipulated in Article 1.3: "To achieve international co-operation in solving international problems of an economic, social, cultural, or humanitarian character, and in promoting and encouraging **respect for human rights and for fundamental freedoms for all without distinction as to race,** sex, language, or religion."

and used American power to let Israel rather than international law determine how Palestinians will or will not be represented. I used the political capital of the United States to overpower the votes of a majority of countries of the world.

She capped her appeal by pledging allegiance: "Time after time, no matter the venue, I have made it clear that America will always stand up for Israel—and that's what I'll always do as President."[628]

Israelspeak from the US Government to Americans

Israel has developed this language of deception, a form of propaganda resulting in the violation of American values, rights, and fortune through the corruption of our politicians. This shameless misleading of the public is what I became more and more aware of as I learned to speak Israel. The awakening of the American public may be what ultimately causes the reversal of US support.

This Israel language has permeated American society. The Texas State Board of Education is influential in determining the content of school textbooks in the United States because of the size of the Texas market. It approved in its six-year curriculum, starting with the school year 2011/2012, the world history standard for high school students. Its coverage of the Israel/Palestine situation is included in one standard; students are asked to explain how "Arab rejection of the State of Israel has led to ongoing conflict."[629] No mention of the second-largest refugee population in the world nor of the seventy-plus-year violation of human rights in blocking refugee return.

Israelspeak can turn arguments on their head. In the Texas curriculum, instead of ethnic cleansing and human rights violations being the problem, it is the Arab rejection of these abuses that is defined to be the cause for conflict. Children are indoctrinated with this skewed misconception of the situation; this view is then supported with the Israelspeak we hear from our politicians and media.

The following is from Jeffrey Goldberg, correspondent for *The Atlantic*, in 2011:

> The Arab revolts have inspired many Americans who will soon look at the West Bank and see unfree Arabs. Then they will look at who is suppressing these Arabs and see Israel; and then they will become confused by this, because they have heard many times that Israel is the only democracy in the Middle East.[630]

Israel, whose supporters have to deceive us to maintain our support, is the country that our politicians call our greatest ally.

16

A Call to Action

Extremism in the defense of liberty is no vice. And moderation in the pursuit of justice is no virtue.

—Senator Barry Goldwater[631]

Rosa Parks was the queen mother of a movement whose single act of heroism sparked the movement for freedom, justice and equality. Her greatest contribution is that she told us a regular person can make a difference.

—Marc Morial,[632] *president of the National Urban League*

Not to speak is to speak. Not to act is to act.[633]

We are not to simply bandage the wounds of victims beneath the wheels of injustice, we are to drive a spoke into the wheel itself.[634]

—Dietrich Bonhoeffer

We cannot bring the victims of historical atrocities back to life. We can only stop atrocities from happening today and in the future. Our first step toward responsible action is to know what is happening. Hopefully, this book has provided historical context and information about the current situation.

Our second step is to call out the misinformation and misleading framing. As long as the deceiving messaging persists, atrocities will continue. The best way to collapse the mythology is by reframing the Israel/Palestine situation. We need to reframe it in a more accurate way so that the light shines on the misleading messaging.

A Palestinian Narrative

This book started with the Israeli and American narratives I knew growing up. I have since learned what I now think of as a Palestinian narrative. I call it a Palestinian narrative not because it is representative of what Palestinians believe; I won't speak for them. I call it a Palestinian narrative because it acknowledges their existence and their history. I include it here because I believe it is important for us to vocalize an alternative narrative to the ones we hear in our schools, in our media, and from our politicians. With a more accurate narrative we can consciously frame our conversations, analyze conversation validity, and move toward solving the real problems rather than merely being distracted by symptoms. Narratives affect perspective, and if we want to help enable peace in the region, we need to operate from a framing that enables such a future. To have any hope for peace and justice, we need to insist on integrity in conversations on Israel/Palestine.

The city of Jericho in the West Bank has archeological evidence dating back to 9000 BCE; it is one of the oldest continuously inhabited cities of the world.[635] Some Palestinians claim to be descendants of the Canaanites, the name given to those who lived in the land as far back as 4500 BCE, long before Abraham, and therefore long before God could have given him the land.[636] Jews talk about returning to the land of their forefathers as if Jews were from the area. From a Palestinian perspective, the Israelites were one of many invaders over the centuries who came through Palestine. The land has been called Palestine (or the variations on the term including Peleset, Pilistu, Palaestina, Philistia, Filastin) for most of the time since the late Bronze Age, including before anyone called it the land of Israel.[637] Abraham is known as Abraham of Ur (in Mesopotamia).

To understand the Palestinian perspective, it is helpful to get a flavor of the number of rulers over the centuries. Skipping ahead a few thousand years from 4500 BCE, I learned that the land came under Egyptian control in the 14th century BCE. Israelites are known to have settled in the area around the 13th century BCE. For approximately 100 years, starting around 1020 BCE, the kingdom of Israel ruled. Then it was divided into two independent Hebrew kingdoms, the southern one called Judah and the northern one still called Israel.[638] Around 925 BCE, the Egyptians were back. Then the Assyrians conquered the northern kingdom in 721 BCE and a couple of decades later territory from Judah. By around 600 BCE, the Babylonians had replaced the Assyrians controlling the region. Then the Persians took over around the beginning of the 5th century BCE. In 330 BCE, Alexander the Great took control. The year 63 BCE brought the beginning of the Roman period. From the 7th century CE, the Muslim caliphs ruled. Around 1100 CE, the Christian Crusaders from Europe took over Palestine and ruled until Saladin took it over in 1187.[639] Prior to World War I, the Ottoman Empire had ruled Palestine for 402 years. Then the British controlled the land during the Mandate period for about 25 years. And this is a rough, abbreviated sampling of the political shifts of the region![640]

With this context, Palestinians find it unreasonable for one of the relatively short-lived invaders of a few thousand years ago to lay claim to the land today when Palestinian ancestors preceded those conquerors and have remained on the land for thousands of years.

The end of World War II brought the Nuremberg trials and the United Nations. World War II—and the Holocaust in particular— focused attention on human rights, culminating in the Universal Declaration of Human Rights. The commission drafting that declaration was chaired by the American president's widow and human rights advocate Eleanor Roosevelt.

However, Palestinians argue that the human rights standards have been applied for the benefit of others but not for them. Since 1947, the Zionists have been ethnically cleansing the land of the Palestinian population. Even according to Israeli historians, most of the Palestinians who lived in what became Israel in 1948 had been forced out by 1949.[641] This period of upheaval, called the *Nakba* (Arabic النكبة, *al-Nakbah*, "the Catastrophe"), resulted in approximately 750,000 Palestinian refugees.[642] Since then, this narrative goes, Israel has continued to take Palestinian land piece by piece, using numerous tactics, including terror, forced evictions, house demolitions, and the construction of Jewish-only settlements on Palestinian land. The infamous Israeli wall and fence cuts up land, enabling Israel to steal more Palestinian land by making access for Palestinians difficult if not impossible.

Palestinians understand and sympathize with the Jewish loss from the Holocaust; most just don't think that Palestinians should be the ones to pay for what the Germans did. Just because Germany robbed from and killed Jews does not give Jews the right to rob from and kill Palestinians.

Although many Palestinians resent the fact that so many Jewish Zionist immigrants have come in and changed their homeland, many have come to accept that those immigrants, and their recent descendants, will not go away. These Palestinians just want equality. They want the same rights as Jews. They want to be able to live in their homes, work their fields and groves, and not be forced into ghettos. They want freedom of movement and to be allowed to use the same roads as Israelis rather than being forced to go through humiliating, clogged checkpoints. They want the apartheid to end. They want equal access to, and pricing of, public services, including such necessities as water. They want to be under the same civilian laws rather than under military law and occupation. They want equal citizenship—one person, one vote—independent of ethnic background, whether they live in Gaza City, Nazareth, Jerusalem, or Hebron. They want self-determination and freedom. They want free commerce rather than being forced to beg for international aid because their economy is completely controlled and crushed by occupier laws, restrictions, and a blockade.

Many Palestinians would argue that the United States has always favored the Zionists over the indigenous Palestinian population. The US pushed for carving up Palestine in 1947 in order to give control of most of the land to the minority Jewish population. Then, although it condemned the ethnic cleansing of the land's population when Israel was formed, the US never enforced the Right of Return, as referenced in UN General Assembly Resolution 194 and subsequent Security Council resolutions.[643] In 1967, when Israel invaded the Golan Heights, East Jerusalem, the West Bank, Gaza, and the Sinai Peninsula, the US condemned Israel's taking land by force with its support for Security Council resolution 242;[644] however, the US never enforced the return of the land (only the Sinai Peninsula was returned to Egypt, more than a decade later through a peace treaty between Israel and Egypt).

Palestinians believe that taking land by force and blocking their Right of Return is against international law. They wish the United States would support humanitarian law rather than protect the oppressor. To Palestinians, the US appears hypocritical: It has stated for decades that it supports a two-state solution, but it has always voted against Palestinian statehood in the United Nations. The US, they say, tries to satiate the Palestinians with aid, as if one's freedom and rights were for sale.

Although the United States was never an evenhanded mediator in so-called peace negotiations, its pretense in playing such a role was completely discarded by the Trump administration. Palestinians regard the US recognition of Israel's possession of the Golan Heights, of the Israeli settlements in the West Bank, and of East Jerusalem as Israeli territory as a violation of international law. They now regard any illusion of American balance, legality, and morality on this issue as shattered.

To Palestinians, the American complicity in Israel's crimes is evident every time an American-made Israeli jet drops a bomb on Gaza or every time Palestinians face a tear gas canister labeled "Made in Pennsylvania."

That is my version of a Palestinian narrative. It is now for us to decide as Americans how we want future paragraphs of this narrative to read, especially as it relates to the US involvement.

The Ball Is in Our Court

The situation in Israel/Palestine is not just about violations to human beings decades ago. As Americans, we are complicit in supporting a system that violates human rights today. Even worse, we have an active role in worsening that situation. Israeli journalist Amira Hass has described Israel's policy as "the Palestinian enclaves" solution, a policy of cramming Palestinians into a small space and then slowly cutting off their livelihoods and ability to survive economically, emotionally, and physically. Gaza was the initial experiment. As mentioned in chapter 11, she was quoted in an event commemorating the tenth anniversary of the deadly assault on the Freedom Flotilla's *Mavi Marmara*:

> The future of the children in those enclaves in the West Bank ...
> is the present of the children in Gaza.[645]

If we do not act, that is the future for which we will be responsible.

Once we identify the problem, we can fix it. Fixing it will require many people. Therefore, we need to share this information with others, so that we can create a movement for justice and peace. Clearly, our media and politicians will not lead this change. The only way for peace to come to the region and ultimately here at home is for us to lead. As anthropologist Margaret Mead is reputed to have said, "Never doubt that a small group of thoughtful, committed citizens can change the world. Indeed, it is the only thing that ever has."

The goal is not to label anyone as "bad" but instead to stop actions that are against our values. We need to require of everyone that the truth be told; we need to disallow Israelspeak. We need to follow the West Point Cadet and Texas A&M honor codes and not lie, cheat, or steal—nor tolerate those who do.

As Americans, we need to know that it is our money and weaponry that are used to violate human rights and kill civilians. It is our political might that prevents Security Council resolutions from stopping Israel from illegally taking land from Palestinians. It is our military that provides intelligence on where to bomb civilian targets in Gaza and how to oppress civilians. It is even our tax money that helps provide the bulletproof bulldozers used to demolish thousands of civilian homes, including the one that killed the young, principled, and courageous American Rachel Corrie.

So, who needs to take action? Everyone—but especially:

- Christians, because the largest pro-Israel group in the United States is now Christians United for Israel (CUFI), which claims 7 million members.[646] Only Christians can claim that organizations such as CUFI do not reflect Christian values; Buddhists can't make that claim. Only Christians can speak out and say that their religion is one of love rather than supporting the destruction of an ethnic group unless they convert.

- Jews, because Israel claims to operate on behalf of Jews. Others are accused of being anti-Semitic when they dare to criticize Israel. This does not mean that someone who happens to be Jewish is responsible for what Israel does. However, the reality is that Israel's claim to act on behalf of, and to represent, Jews gives Jews privilege and responsibility. Only Jews can claim that Israel does not act on their behalf; nobody else can make that claim. Only Jews can claim that organizations such as CUFI are racist against Jews rather than supportive of Jewish interests.

- Americans, because we provide the military, political, and financial support that enables the occupation and related human rights violations while we protect Israel from international law and repercussions. Only Americans can hold our political representatives accountable. Only Americans can take a stand for what our values are.

Both Israelis and Americans have the power through the ballot box to stop the human rights violations and bring equality and freedom for all. In the early twentieth century, it was men who had to pass the Nineteenth Amendment to the Constitution so that women could vote; women could not do that. African Americans protested against racism, from slavery to Jim Crow laws, but White people had to eliminate those racist laws because only Whites had the voting rights. Similarly, Palestinians can protest, but it is only Israelis and Americans who can bring about equality and freedom in that region.

It is time for Jews and Christians across the world, and all Americans, to stand against racism by publicly denouncing the racist state of Israel. As mentioned earlier, Rabbi Hillel once wrote, "If I am not for myself, who will be for me? If I am not for others, what am I? And if not now, when?"[647]

So, what can you do to make a difference?

- **Become fluent in speaking Israel.** The more you get into conversations with people about Israel, the more you will hear Israel myths and propaganda. Be prepared with these books from **HowToSpeakIsrael.com**:

  ▶ *When They Speak Israel: A Guide to Clarity in Conversations about Israel* (a shorter guide, with specific tips for conversations). This is a handy pocket guide for getting to the bottom of often-repeated Israel expressions. The guide unpacks each of those expressions, identifies its core issue, and provides queries to ask a conversation partner. These queries are intended to develop relationships while remaining clear on core values, including equality and human rights. This guide highlights the faulty logic of Israel expressions.

  ▶ *Speak Equality: Revealing the Root of the Israel/Palestine Struggle* is a continuation of this book, covering less history and many more Israelspeak expressions. *Speak Equality* equips you to clearly see the faults in more Israeli narratives. The sequel focuses on the fundamental issue that defenders of the state don't want you to see: its dependence on racism. The sequel equips you to counter the standard rhetoric we hear in the news and from politicians, from those who are trying to deceive and from those who believe Israelspeak. The sequel provides the knowledge needed to call out the real issue in our conversation with others; it equips you with the background and clarity to neutralize Israelspeak when you hear it, both factually and logically.

Both books provide resources for responding to such questions and statements as the following:

▸ "That comment is so anti-Semitic."

▸ "Palestinians are taught to hate."

▸ "What we need is a Palestinian Gandhi."

▸ "Arabs are better off in Israel than in Arab countries."

▸ "BDS is anti-Semitic."

▸ "The UN gave Jews Israel."

▸ "Do you believe Israel has a right to exist?"

▸ "Doesn't Israel have a right to defend itself?"

▸ "Israel needs a good faith negotiating partner."

▸ "Palestinians never miss an opportunity to miss an opportunity."

▸ "But Arab countries are not assimilating Palestinians."

• **Regularly communicate with your representative, senators, president, and other government officials** to demand that the funding for military and other financial and military support for Israel is cut until Israel ends the occupation and the Gaza blockade and gives Palestinians the same rights as those enjoyed by Jews.

• **Do not let anyone talk about Israel without also mentioning the occupation, the blockade, and the violation of human rights** (including the Right of Return). Silence is complicity, and we do not want to stand idly by as the misleading messaging persists. Make sure politicians and school history teachers talk about the region and the conflict today within the context of the occupation, blockade, and human rights violations.

- **Support organizations personally and financially.** Since we can't change the world alone, I am providing a list of organizations with whom you can be active, you can support, and whose materials you can share to raise awareness. The following is a small list of many organizations:

  ▸ **Palestinian organizations:**
  - BDS—Boycott, Divestment, Sanctions (BDSMovement.net)
  - Defense for Children International—Palestine (DCI-Palestine.org)
  - Adalah—The Legal Center for Arab Minority Rights in Israel (adalah.org/en)
  - Al Mezan Center for Human Rights (Mezan.org/en)
  - Palestinian Centre for Human Rights (pchrgaza.org/en)
  - We Are Not Numbers (WeAreNotNumbers.org)

  ▸ **Israeli organizations:**
  - B'Tselem, the Israeli Information Center for Human Rights in the Occupied Territories (BTselem.org)
  - ICAHD-USA, the Israeli Committee against House Demolitions–USA (ICAHDUSA.org)
  - Zochrot Organization (Zochrot.org/en)
  - MachsomWatch, Women for Human Rights and against the Occupation (MachsomWatch.org/en)
  - Breaking the Silence (BreakingTheSilence.org.il)

  ▸ **Jewish organizations in the US:**
  - Jewish Voice for Peace (JVP.org)
  - If Not Now (IfNotNowMovement.org)
  - Center for Jewish Nonviolence (CJNV.org)

  ▸ **Peace and human rights organizations:**
  - CODEPINK (CodePink.org)
  - Amnesty International (Amnesty.org)
  - Human Rights Watch (HRW.org)

  ▸ **Palestinian solidarity organizations:**
  - Eyewitness Palestine (EyewitnessPalestine.org)

- The "No Way to Treat a Child" campaign of Defense for Children International–Palestine and American Friends Service Committee (NoWayToTreatAChild.org)
- US Boats to Gaza, a partner of the International Freedom Flotilla Coalition (USBoatsToGaza.org)
- If Americans Knew (IfAmericansKnew.org)
- US Campaign for Palestinian Rights (USCPR.org)
- Visualizing Palestine (visualizingpalestine.org/impact)

▸ **Religious organizations:**
  - American Friends Service Committee (AFSC.org)
  - American Muslims for Palestine (AMPalestine.org)
  - Friends of Sabeel North America: A Christian Voice for Palestine (FOSNA.org)
  - Kairos Palestine (KairosPalestine.ps)
  - Torat Tzedek: Torah of Justice (https://torat-tzedek.org.il/)

▸ **Take a trip to the occupied Palestinian territories.** Spend some time with people living under occupation to understand what that means in their daily life. Do not take a "Holy Land" tour that hides the occupation from visitors. Instead, visit with organizations such as CODEPINK, Eyewitness Palestine, and others that take you to Hebron, refugee camps, and communities affected directly by the wall and settlements, and that take you through major Palestinian checkpoints.

▸ **Open the discussion in your communities.** Invite speakers on the subject to share about life under occupation. The following movies are a great way to get the community learning about Israel/Palestine: *Occupation 101: Voices of the Silenced Majority*, *The Occupation of the American Mind*, *The Wanted 18*, *5 Broken Cameras*, *1948—Creation & Catastrophe*, *On the Side of the Road*, and many others. A great movie on the Great March of Return in Gaza is the documentary *Gaza Fights for Freedom*.

▸ **Take a stand!** If you have influence in your community, whatever that community, and want to stand for justice, please reach out for information and join one or more of the organizations previously listed.

We need to remember that the only way for a government of the people, by the people, and for the people to succeed is by keeping the people accurately informed. Since the information in this book differs from the message we get from our politicians and media, please share what you have learned here with other Americans. It would not hurt my feelings if you gave copies of this book to your friends who also care about our great country. Get a book at **HowToSpeakIsrael.com** and let me know how you would like to get involved.

Thank you for doing your part in making the United States stand for freedom, equality, and dignity for all. May your fluency in Israel make the world a better place.

Acknowledgments

The deception I experienced was the seed for writing this book. However, a seed can't grow on its own; it took many people to provide the soil, nutrients, and water to nurture what was originally just an idea to grow into a book. Many people helped me see different perspectives on the Israel/Palestine issue. It also took many kind people to read through my drafts and provide feedback. A number of people were gracious enough to read through and provide additional historical information and make me aware of issues of which I had been ignorant.

A number of friends spent a lot of time going through the whole manuscript and provided extremely detailed feedback. For their dedication and insights, I am grateful beyond measure. A number of others read sections and helped me see my writing through different perspectives.

To protect these great people from the abuse and retribution that is described in this book, and is all too commonly directed toward people who expose information on Israel, I will not name them here. Nonetheless, I would like to share my admiration and gratitude for their love for all people and for human rights generally; they are truly inspiring. I am honored to walk for peace and justice with them.

When people accuse me of picking on Israel, here is another example of how Israel is different. Critics of China, Egypt, Iran, Russia, Saudi Arabia, and Turkey are known to have been severely punished and even killed. However, rarely are the American critics of those regimes punished. Israel is different. Americans get regularly punished for criticizing Israel. That is why I believe this book is needed.

Thanks again to all who helped me along this journey.

Peace to all.

APPENDIX

"The Promised Land"

You say the Bible is not a property deed. But I say the opposite; the Bible is our mandate, the Bible is our deed.

—Benjamin Netanyahu,[648]
October 6, 1995

And so today, as I stand in Abraham's "Promised Land," I believe that all who cherish freedom, and seek a brighter future, should cast their eyes here to this place and marvel at what they behold.

—Vice President Mike Pence,[649]
in a special session of the Knesset,
January 22, 2018

On a flight between Florida and Texas, I shared an early version of my manuscript with a lady seated next to me. She kindly read the first thirty or so pages before I had to stow my laptop for landing. I asked her what she thought of the manuscript. She replied, "But God gave them that land." This appendix is for those who have accepted a similar belief, who are willing to learn about passages from the Bible, and who are open to hearing what people of faith with a different perspective have said on the subject. The goal of this appendix chapter is not to convince you that any particular belief is correct or incorrect—only that the Bible and religious leaders are not as clearly supportive of this position as we are led to believe.

I am no biblical scholar, so I can't tell you which Bible interpretation is correct. I have met many Jews and Christians with different perspectives on this subject. After some research, I have concluded that the Bible can be used to support each position, just as it was used to both support and oppose slavery in our country. Each of us needs to make our own interpretation choice; each of us also has to live with the consequences of our choice.

After studying the subject, I determined that those who believe that God gave the land to the Jews need to consider two issues:

- If one takes the position that God gave Jews the exclusive or supreme rights to the land, then one logically is taking a position that God supports the subjugation or removal of non-Jewish people from that land. If one believes that God intended the land to be for one ethnic group and not another, then removing the undesirable group would be acceptable in God's eyes. In modern English, this is called racial discrimination, or ethnic cleansing. In English, the ethnic cleansing of people is also called the violation of human rights. And before one chooses to follow a scripture interpretation that endorses the violation of human rights—including ethnic discrimination, or racism—then one might want to double-check what the Bible says to make sure we are following God's will rather than taking a verse out of context.

- If one takes the position that God gave the land to the Jews because the Jews were His followers, then what promise did God make to Jews who no longer followed Him? If one accepts this interpretation of the Bible, then the promise was not ethnic but instead spiritual or religious.

To believe that God promised Abraham and others of His followers safety in the land of Israel as long as they exemplified righteous living is to believe in a God Who wants us to follow God's laws. By contrast, if one chooses the interpretation that God gave the land exclusively to ethnic Jews (as opposed to only religious followers of God), one is then choosing to believe in a God Who is racist; it is to accept racism as godly. These are very different gods, and each of us gets to choose which one we want to follow.

To insinuate that God is racist can be considered sacrilegious. My goal is not to be irreverent in any way; on the contrary, my goal is to highlight how language and teachings can convince us that actions that kindergartners know to be evil can be interpreted by some as holy, and vice versa. Throughout history we can find crimes committed in the name of God. Each of us needs to determine what is moral and what is not—and therefore what we believe God stands for and what God opposes. Let's start by looking at what the Bible actually says.

Genesis 17:7–8 (King James Version):

> And I will establish my covenant between me and thee and thy seed after thee in their generations for an everlasting covenant, to be a God unto thee, and to thy seed after thee.
>
> And I will give unto thee, and to thy seed after thee, the land wherein thou art a stranger, all the land of Canaan, for an everlasting possession; and I will be their God.

Genesis 15:18 (NIV) describes the land:

> On that day the Lord made a covenant with Abram and said, "To your descendants I give this land, from the Wadi [the Wadi al-'Arish River in Egypt] of Egypt to the great river, the Euphrates."

That can be interpreted to include land that is today part of Egypt, Iraq, and Saudi Arabia, as well as all of Israel, Palestine, Jordan, Syria, Lebanon, and Kuwait.

Although it does not appear that the Jewish descendants of Abraham ever exclusively had possession of all this land, we get passages that tell us that God's promises were fulfilled—for example, 1 Kings 8:56 (King James Version):

> Blessed be the Lord, that hath given rest unto his people Israel, according to all that he promised: there hath not failed one word of all his good promise, which he promised by the hand of Moses his servant.

And according to Joshua 11:23 (NIV), all of the land was taken:

> So Joshua took the **entire** [emphasis added] land, just as the Lord had directed Moses, and he gave it as an inheritance to Israel according to their tribal divisions. Then the land had rest from war.

Joshua claimed to have had all the land, yet it is not clear that there were only people of Israel on the whole region from the Mediterranean to the Euphrates.

The book of Joshua describes how genocide was committed by Israel (the people [the Israelites], not the state)—the annihilation of the people of Ai in Joshua 8:21–26 being one example. The Bible gives the impression that God supported those acts. On the one hand, it appears that God supported murder and taking land by force. On the other hand, the book of Joshua emphasizes the need for the people of Israel to follow God's law. God's support for the people of Israel was contingent on their obeying God's law. That requirement becomes clear in Joshua 7:7–12, where Joshua asked God why He had put Israel (the people) at the mercy of the Amorites in the Promised Land. Here was God's response (Josh. 7:11–12 [NIV]):

> Israel has sinned; they have violated my covenant, which I commanded them to keep. They have taken some of the devoted things; they have stolen, they have lied, they have put them with their own possessions. That is why the Israelites cannot stand against their enemies; they turn their backs and run because they have been made liable to destruction. *I will not be with you*

anymore unless you destroy whatever among you is to destruction
[emphasis added].

We are given examples of how this covenant was contingent on living morally. Later Joshua found out that Achan had stolen property when they moved into the land. Joshua interpreted God's saying, "I will not be with you anymore unless you destroy whatever among you is devoted to destruction" as a charge that the Israelites needed to kill their own:

> Then Joshua, together with all Israel, took Achan son of Zerah, the silver, the robe, the gold bar, his sons and daughters, his cattle, donkeys and sheep, his tent and all that he had, to the Valley of Achor. Joshua said, "Why have you brought this trouble on us? The Lord will bring trouble on you today."
>
> Then all Israel stoned him, and after they had stoned the rest, they burned them. [Josh. 7:24–25 (NIV)]

Achan was of the tribe of Judah, one of the twelve tribes of Israel. To please God, other members of the tribe felt obliged to kill their own because of Achan's moral misbehavior.

Here is more from the book of Joshua:

> But just as all the good things the Lord your God has promised you have come to you, so he will bring on you all the evil things he has threatened, until the Lord your God has destroyed you from this good land he has given you. If you violate the covenant of the Lord your God, which he commanded you, and go and serve other gods and bow down to them, the Lord's anger will burn against you, and you will quickly perish from the good land he has given you. [Josh. 23:15–16 (NIV)]

So, according to the book of Joshua, it appears that it was Israel's responsibility to act in accordance with God's law, and if they deviated, God would not protect them. God had no sympathy for Israel, nor any feeling of the Israelites' rights to land while they were sinning. It was Israel's job to keep all of their members obedient to God's law. The book of Judges has more on this:

> Therefore the Lord was very angry with Israel and said, "Because this nation has violated the covenant I ordained for their ancestors and has not listened to me, I will no longer drive out before them any of the nations Joshua left when he died. I will use them to test Israel and see whether they will keep the way of the Lord and walk in it as their ancestors did." The Lord had allowed those nations to remain; he did not drive them out at once by giving them into the hands of Joshua. [Judg. 2:20–23 (NIV)]

God chose to no longer drive out non-Jews. Instead, he wanted the non-Jews to be a test for the descendants of Joshua. God was using these non-Jews as a tool to see if Joshua's descendants would follow God as their ancestors had done. God's intent appeared to be to make the land nonexclusive to descendants of Joshua. The primary criterion for control of the land was not heredity but moral conduct.

There was a whole series of Israel sinning and then making up. Each time Israel sinned, God took away the land and made someone else the ruler. Judges 3:12–14 offers another example where the Israelites were subject to Eglon, king of Moab, for eighteen years.

The "promise" seems similar to the parents' promise of a car to their teenager; the promise is valid until school grades suffer or the kid gets into trouble. This interpretation is supported also by the Orthodox Jewish view that

> the entire People of Israel is required to obey the Torah, and whoever doesn't want to, ceases to be part of the congregation of Israel.[650]

In other words, the land would be ruled by those who obey the Torah rather than those who are direct descendants.

According to Neturei Karta International (Jews United against Zionism), a minority Jewish group:

> the so-called "State of Israel" is diametrically opposed and completely contradictory to the true essence and foundation of the People of Israel. ... The only time that the People of Israel were permitted to have a state was two thousand years ago when the glory of the creator was upon us, and likewise in the future when the glory of the creator will once more be revealed, and the whole world will serve Him, then He Himself (without any human effort or force of arms) will grant us a kingdom founded on Divine Service. However, a worldly state, like those possessed by other peoples, is contradictory to the true essence of the People of Israel. Whoever calls this the salvation of Israel shows that he denies the essence of the People of Israel, and substitutes another nature, a worldly materialistic nature, and therefore sets before them, a worldly materialistic "salvation," and the means of achieving this "salvation" is also worldly and materialistic i.e. to organize a land and army. However, the true salvation of the People of Israel is to draw close to the Creator. This is not done by organization and force of arms. Rather it is done by occupation to Torah and good deeds.[651]

This interpretation seems consistent with how God viewed Abraham and those who followed him:

> Abraham will surely become a great and powerful nation, and all nations on earth will be blessed through him. For I have chosen him, so that he will direct his children and his household after him to keep the way of the Lord by doing what is right and just, so that the Lord will bring about for Abraham what he has promised him. [Gen. 18:18–19 (NIV)]

Note that God considered "nation" as people and that all nations (all people) would be blessed through Abraham because of Abraham's followers doing what was right and just. Abraham had been "chosen" by God to direct others "to keep the way of the Lord"; God's plan did not appear to be an entitlement program based on ethnicity.

Since "Israel" is the name of both a people and now a modern state, some may think that they are the same or related. The Bible informs us that the biblical Israel was a people, and a moral people at that. Even when children of the moral people deviated, they became outcasts and no longer the people of Israel. Even worse, as we saw with the invasion of Ai, God punished all of Israel because one (Achan) had sinned. Following God's laws appears not to be only an individual responsibility but also a communal responsibility.

The New Testament also states that all nations were blessed through Abraham, that those who followed God would become "children" of Abraham:

> *Understand, then, that those who have faith are children of Abraham* [Gal. 3:7 (NIV); emphasis added].

The definition of "child" or "descendant" also loses its genetic meaning:

> So in Christ Jesus you are all children of God through faith. [Gal. 3:26 (NIV)]

Paul's Epistle to the Galatians continues:

> If you belong to Christ, then you are Abraham's seed, and heirs according to the promise. [Gal. 3:29 (NIV)]

According to this Bible passage, Jews and Christians have equal rights to the land of Israel, since they are both believers; Israel is not a Jewish state but a Jewish-Christian state (and this was written before Islam existed, so today one might claim it is then a Jewish-Christian-Muslim state).

As mentioned earlier in this chapter, the state of Israel and the people of Israel are not synonymous in the Bible. *It is counter to the Bible that the nation-state of Israel, which is systematically oppressing people, taking their land and violating their human rights, is in any way related to the people of Israel following God's law.*

It would be hard to call Israeli government actions Jewish, or worthy of the name Israel, based on elder Rabbi Hillel's summary description of the Torah:

> That which is hateful to you do not do to another; that is the entire Torah, and the rest is interpretation.[652]

Rabbi Hillel's summary of the Torah is consistent with the book of Numbers:

> The community is to have the same rules for you and for the foreigner residing among you; this is a lasting ordinance for the generations to come. You and the foreigner shall be the same before the Lord: The same laws and regulations will apply both to you and to the foreigner residing among you. [Num. 15:15–16 (NIV)]

This verse in Numbers makes sense only if the land were not exclusively for Jews. One can't have a Jewish-only state if there are "foreigners residing among you." One can't discriminate against the "foreigner" if the same laws and regulations "apply both to you and to the foreigner."

And with the book of Deuteronomy:

> If you pay attention to these laws and are careful to follow them, then the Lord your God will keep his covenant of love with you, as he swore to your ancestors. [Deut. 7:12 (NIV)]

Deuteronomy also implies that God's grant is conditional:

Follow justice and justice alone, so that you may live and possess the land the Lord your God is giving you. [Deut. 16:20 (NIV)]

Based on these Bible passages, it would appear that the land does not belong to ethnic Jews but instead to those who follow God's laws, to those who follow justice. But the state of Israel is a secular state and grants citizenship primarily based on ethnicity.

The claim that God gave the land to ethnic Jews is part of the Israel house of cards. If one chooses to believe that God gave the land to ethnic Jews, then God is racist (giving preferential treatment to one ethnic group over another). If one chooses to believe in a racist God, then one chooses to be racist. If God is racist, then there can be no Golden Rule, a foundational Abrahamic belief: Racism and the commandment to "do to others what you would have them do to you"* are incompatible.

This vicious circle shows how powerful the con is: *Good people following what they thought was Christian or Jewish teaching have been conned into compromising a foundational value of their faith. By giving up the Golden Rule, one replaces the possibility of peace with racism.*

Despite some of the recently quoted verses, some believers may think that if the land is not promised by God to ethnic Jews, then it may be promised exclusively for religious Jews. If religious Jews have exclusive rights to the land, then one needs to decide if God's will is to expel the millions of ethnic Jews and Arabs from the Promised Land. Choosing that interpretation entails support for the ethnic cleansing of probably most Israeli citizens from the state of Israel. Choosing that interpretation entails support for expelling the

---

* The Jewish version of this Christian precept (Matt. 7:12 [NIV]) is from Rabbi Hillel (ca. 110 BCE–10 CE): "That which is hateful to you do not do to another; that is the entire Torah, and the rest is interpretation," which is a summary from Leviticus: "Do not seek revenge or bear a grudge against anyone among your people, but love your neighbor as yourself. I am the LORD."

overwhelming majority from the West Bank, Gaza, East Jerusalem, and the Golan Heights as well.

But one cannot stop there, or that would be hypocritical; if one believes that the Promised Land is for religious Jews only, then one cannot claim that only part of it is for Jews only. One therefore also needs to ethnically cleanse non-Jews from Jordan, Lebanon, Syria, Kuwait, parts of Egypt, parts of Saudi Arabia, and parts of Iraq, since some claim that they are also part of the Promised Land, the biblical land of Israel. To do anything short would be inconsistent with that interpretation of scripture. Lebanon has a population of nearly 5.5 million, Jordan has over 10 million people, and Syria has close to 20 million; Egypt has over 100 million people, and Iraq has nearly 40 million, although most of them do not live in the biblical land of Israel.[653] In stark contrast, there are only approximately 7 million ethnic Jews in Israel (and religious Jews are far fewer) with a similar number of Arabs under Israeli control. If one chooses to believe that all of biblical Israel is exclusively for religious Jews (the same rule applies for those who believe the land is exclusively for ethnic Jews), then one has to accept that such a belief requires the belief that God wants to remove many tens of millions of people for 7 million people. One also has to decide where God wants the Lebanese, Syrians, Jordanians, and others to live.

But saying that the land is only for religious Jews and not for other followers of God—and, in particular, not for followers of the other Abrahamic faiths—is a narrow viewpoint. Christians, Muslims, and others also believe they follow God's laws. Who determines which laws are really God's laws?

Explaining the exclusivity of land to only one of the Abrahamic faiths would be extremely difficult. Clearly, it would be difficult to convince the majority Muslim population. It would also be difficult to convince the 2 million Lebanese Christians and the 10 million Egyptian Christians,[654] in addition to the Palestinian Christians. *It is already difficult to explain to historically local Christians and Muslims that it is God's will that they cannot access their sacred sites, such as those in Jerusalem, without*

getting permission from a secular entity that claims to have religious rights to the land.

Any compromise on any of this territory begs the question: If not all the land, then why only part of the land? If there is a religious or moral stand for the land of Israel for religious Jews only, one then has to apply that criterion to the whole land, not just parts; otherwise, one is defying God. Does God really want that?

Having looked at scripture and demonstrated that multiple interpretations can be made relative to God's intent for the land of biblical Israel, I researched and found positions of a number of Jewish, Christian, and Muslim groups and individuals, all followers of a form of the Old Testament, who oppose Israeli policies. For example, I found a position by the Catholic Church in 2010:

> Bishops from the Middle East who were summoned to Rome by the pope demanded on Saturday that Israel accept UN resolutions calling for an end to its "occupation" of Arab lands. In a final joint communique, the bishops also told Israel it shouldn't use the Bible to justify "injustices" against the Palestinians.[655]

One can't talk about bishops opposing Israel's occupation of the Holy Land without mentioning Archbishop Hilarion Capucci. He became bishop of the Roman Catholic Church in Jerusalem in 1965. He was arrested in 1974 for smuggling rifles and dynamite for the Palestinians in his Mercedes with Vatican diplomatic plates. He was sentenced to twelve years of prison time in Israel. Israel expelled him in 1978, after Pope Paul VI requested his release and agreed to the condition that Capucci leave the region. Capucci remained politically active, though; he went to Iraq in 1990 to free sixty-eight Italians from Saddam Hussein's government after the invasion of Kuwait. In 2009 he was aboard a ship that tried to break the Gaza blockade. The next year, at the age of eighty-seven, he sailed again, this time on the *Mavi Marmara*; he was aboard when Israeli troops boarded the ship and killed nine civilians.[656,*,657]

---

* A tenth civilian went into a coma and died four years later.

Against Israel's wishes, the Vatican recognized Palestine as a state in 2015, when it signed a treaty with Palestine.[658]

South African Archbishop Desmond Tutu wrote the following in an op-ed:

> Nelson Mandela famously said that South Africans would not feel free until Palestinians were free. He might have added that the liberation of Palestine will liberate Israel, too.[659]

Beyond taking a stand against a biblical interpretation of Jews exclusively owning the land, a number of churches have taken a much stronger stand against Israel, officially becoming part of the Boycott, Divestment, Sanctions (BDS) movement against Israel's occupation. They include Presbyterian Church (U.S.A.), the United Church of Christ, and the United Methodist Church (UMC) among others.[660]

So, the "Promised Land" can be defined biblically and aspirationally as follows:

> **Promised Land.** *n.* A territory from the Wadi (the Wadi al-'Arish River in Egypt) to the Euphrates that is believed to cover parts of modern-day Egypt, Saudi Arabia, and Iraq, and all of Israel, Palestine, Jordan, Lebanon, Kuwait, and Syria. This land was originally "promised" in the Old Testament by God to Abraham. God also allows the people of Israel (and therefore the land of Israel) to be ruled by others when the people of Israel fail to obey His laws. The Old Testament disenfranchises nonbelievers, including Jewish descendants, negating the concept of a secular ethnic Jewish state of Israel. Not only does God not promise exclusivity to any group, He stands for equality: "You and the foreigner shall be the same before the Lord" (Num. 15:15 [NIV]) and He stipulates that "the same laws and regulations will apply both to you and to the foreigner residing among you" (Num. 15:16 [NIV]).

The choice is ours. Based on scripture, we can choose to believe in a God Who wants the oppression of others or in a God Who wants equality and justice. We have to decide if we agree with Salam Fayyad, a man who was instrumental in changing the Palestinian opposition to occupation from being violent to being peaceful. In 2007, when he was the Palestinian Authority prime minister, he said,

> It's the responsibility of men of religion to ... present religion as a way of tolerance, not as a cover for bloodshed.[661]

We have to decide if our God looks more favorably on someone like Salam Fayyad or the leaders or soldiers responsible for occupying and terrorizing women and children. Does our God want us to violate others' human rights in order to enforce a supposed deed? Here is what Jesus said about our choices:

> Woe to you, teachers of the law and Pharisees, you hypocrites! You give a tenth of your spices—mint, dill and cumin. But you have neglected the more important matters of the law—justice, mercy and faithfulness. [Matt. 23:23 (NIV)]

If we choose to believe in a God of justice, then we need to stand for justice too. Without equality, there is no justice. Without human rights, there is no justice.

As Christians, Jews—and Americans overall—we have been complicit in supporting misleading messaging. We have protected from accountability the government of Israel's robbery of Palestinians' justice, including the robbery of their human rights and their land. Not only have Christian, Jewish—and American—leaders protected Israel and claimed that Israel is only acting defensively, we have also blamed the Palestinian victims. Here is a warning from the book of Proverbs:

> Whoever says to the guilty, "You are innocent," will be cursed by peoples and denounced by nations. [Prov. 24:24 (NIV)]

We are seeing the consequences of claiming that the guilty are innocent and that the innocent are guilty. We have seen the repercussions in increased terrorism. American Jews and non-Jews have also experienced disdain because of our complicity.

If we want to proclaim the scriptures as coming from a loving, just God, then the message we should be focusing on is what the Bible encourages throughout: to support those who are oppressed and seek justice:

Learn to do right; seek justice. Defend the oppressed. [Isa. 1:17 (NIV)]

Consider again these words from Genesis:

So God created man in his own image, in the image of God created he him; male and female created he them. [Gen. 1:27 (RSV)]

And again what I heard Rabbi Arik Ascherman say, that *the ultimate idolatry is when the holiness of the land prevents someone from seeing the holiness in another human being.*

The Good News, or the Gospel of Jesus, is said to be about love. Even when He was harassed, hanging from a cross, what came from His mouth was not racism, hatred, or fear. Instead, He said,

Father, forgive them, for they do not know what they are doing. [Luke 23:34 (NIV)]

We need to make sure we know what we are doing and why. We need to choose what kind of God we want to believe in.

Glossary

This glossary contains a list of terms and abbreviations used throughout this book. Organizations are given a brief description under their full name; their abbreviation provides only the organization's full name. This glossary also includes certain dictionary definitions for easy reference. Please refer to the Israel-English Dictionary, immediately following this glossary, for Israel terms and the English usage definitions.

Adalah. The Legal Center for Arab Minority Rights in Israel.

ADL. *See* Anti-Defamation League (ADL).

AIPAC. *See* American Israel Public Affairs Committee (AIPAC).

aliyah (עליה). *n.* The immigration of Jews to Israel.

Al Jazeera. An international news organization based in Doha, Qatar.

American Israel Public Affairs Committee (AIPAC). An organization that describes itself as "America's pro-Israel lobby." Its website also proclaims: "We engage with and educate decision-makers about the bonds that unite the two countries, and how it is in America's best interest to help ensure that the Jewish state remains safe, strong and secure."[662]

anti-BDS laws. Laws (including in states across the United States) that penalize individuals and/or companies that participate in a boycott of Israeli products or services or divest in related companies.

Anti-Defamation League (ADL). An organization founded in 1913 that works "to stop the defamation of the Jewish people, and to secure justice and fair treatment to all." The ADL is a defender of Israel and its policies. Its website states, "We will defend Israel's right to exist, calling out those who delegitimize and demonize her."[663]

anti-Israel. *adj.* Descriptive of those who place a higher value on equality, freedom, and human rights—even if the consequence is a multiethnic (rather than a Jewish) state in the land that Israel controls.

anti-Semitism. *n.* According to Merriam-Webster, "hostility toward or discrimination against Jews as a religious, ethnic, or racial group."[664]

There are many definitions for this term. This book tries to avoid using the term because different definitions conflict and it has become a term in the Israel language.

apartheid. *n.* According to the International Convention on the Suppression and Punishment of the Crime of Apartheid, apartheid is a crime that applies to "policies and practices of racial segregation and discrimination" and "inhuman acts committed for the purpose of establishing and maintaining domination by one racial group of persons over any other racial group of persons and systematically oppressing them."[665] The convention refers to the UN Charter, the Universal Declaration of Human Rights, and the International Convention on the Elimination of All Forms of Racial Discrimination. One example of apartheid is in Article II (c):

> Any legislative measures and other measures calculated to prevent a racial group or groups from participation in the political, social, economic and cultural life of the country and the deliberate creation of conditions preventing the full development of such a group or groups, in particular by denying to members of a racial group or groups basic human rights and freedoms, ... the right to leave and to return to their country, the right to a nationality, the right to freedom of movement and residence, the right to freedom of opinion and expression, and the right to freedom of peaceful assembly and association.[666]

This word is not defined in the Israel-English Dictionary, since it does not apply to Israel per Israel supporters. This denial is despite international organizations calling it out.

BBC. *See* British Broadcasting Corporation (BBC).

BDS. *See* Boycott, Divestment, Sanctions (BDS).

blockade. *n.* Blockage or significant restriction of movement of people, services, and goods in and out of Gaza. A blockade is overwhelmingly deployed by Israel not only on Israel's border with Gaza but also by its controlling Gaza's airspace and access to the sea. Blockage of the border with Egypt is significantly influenced by the United States, since Egypt has historically been the second-largest recipient of US foreign aid. This word is not defined in the Israel-English Dictionary, since Israeli politicians have historically stated that there is no blockade of Gaza despite reality showing us otherwise.

Boycott, Divestment, Sanctions (BDS). A Palestinian-led movement that asks people to not support companies and activities (concerts, conferences, etc.) that support the Israeli occupation and denial of Palestinian human rights.[667] Some people interpret the BDS movement to target only entities and activities that directly support the Israeli occupation, such as Caterpillar's armored bulldozers that are used to destroy Palestinian homes. Others apply the BDS concept more broadly and include all Israeli companies and activities, since the policies of occupation, blockade, and violation of human rights are decided by the Israeli government (in Israel rather than in the occupied Palestinian territories) and the people who elect those government leaders.

British Broadcasting Corporation (BBC). A British public service broadcaster that is said to be the largest broadcaster in the world by number of employees.

B'Tselem. An Israeli organization that describes itself as the "Israeli Information Center for Human Rights in the Occupied Territories."[668]

Christians United for Israel (CUFI). An American Christian pro-Israel organization led by John Hagee, founder of the Cornerstone Church in San Antonio, Texas.

CUFI. *See* Christians United for Israel (CUFI).

democracy. *n.* According to Merriam-Webster,[669]
1. a: government by the people, *especially:* rule by the majority
   b: a government in which the supreme power is vested in the people and exercised by them directly or indirectly through a system of representation usually involving periodically held free elections
2. a political unit that has a democratic government
3. the absence of hereditary or arbitrary class distinctions or privileges

This word is also an Israel word (*See* Israel-English Dictionary).

equality. *n.* The state of having equal rights. Quoting James Wilson, a signer of the Declaration of Independence and an original justice of the United States Supreme Court:

> When we say, that all men are equal; we mean not to apply this equality to their virtues, their talents, their dispositions, or their acquirements. ... There is still one aspect, in which all men in society, previous to civil government, are equal. With regard to all, there is an equality in rights and in

obligations; there is that "jus aequum," that equal law, in which the Romans placed true freedom. The natural rights and duties of man belong equally to all.[670]

This word is also an Israel word (*See* Israel-English Dictionary).

ESCWA. *See* United Nations Economic and Social Commission for Western Asia (ESCWA).

ethnic cleansing. *n.* According to Dictionary.com, "the elimination of an unwanted ethnic group or groups from a society, as by genocide or forced emigration."[671]

Green Line. The internationally recognized de facto borders of Israel based on the 1949 Armistice Agreements between Israel and its neighbors. The Green Line(s) separate(s) internationally recognized Israel from the West Bank and Gaza. Independent of the Green Line, the border with Egypt was confirmed in the 1979 Egypt-Israel peace treaty, and the border with Jordan was confirmed in the 1994 Israel-Jordan peace treaty.

The Guardian. A British daily newspaper.

Haaretz. An Israeli newspaper, founded in 1918, that is published in Hebrew and English.

Herzl. Theodor Herzl (1860–1904), known as the father of modern political Zionism.

ICJ. *See* International Court of Justice (ICJ).

ICTY. *See* International Criminal Tribunal for the former Yugoslavia (ICTY).

IDF. *See* Israeli Defense Forces (IDF) in the Israel-English Dictionary.

illegal. *adj.*
1. *As used by Israel:* Against Israeli law.
2. *As used by Palestinians (and most of the world):* Against international law, such as the Geneva Conventions and international humanitarian law.

Example: Construction in Area C of the West Bank, in the occupied Palestinian territories under Israeli administrative and military control, is illegal (under Israeli law) without Israeli permits. Permits to build on this Palestinian land are granted overwhelmingly to settlements that are illegal under international law. These same building permits are not granted to the local indigenous population, who are there legally by international and Israeli law, many of whose families have been there for hundreds, if not thousands, of years. As a result, Israel is demolishing Palestinian buildings against international law but in accordance with Israeli law in the Palestinian territories.

impunity. *n.* Exemption or freedom from punishment, harm, or loss. *Example:* "Laws were flouted with impunity."[672]

International Court of Justice (ICJ). The primary United Nations judicial body. According to its website, "the Court's role is to settle, in accordance with international law, legal disputes submitted to it by States and to give advisory opinions on legal questions referred to it by authorized United Nations organs and specialized agencies."[673]

International Criminal Tribunal for the Former Yugoslavia (ICTY). A United Nations court of law, lasting from 1993 through 2017, that dealt with war crimes committed in the Balkans during the 1990s.

international law. Law based on agreements between and among countries.

Intifada. *n.* An Arabic term meaning "uprising." It refers to Palestinian uprisings against the Israeli occupation. The First Intifada lasted from December 1987 to 1991 (the Madrid Conference) or as late as 1993 (the signing of the Oslo Accords); the Second Intifada went from 2000 into 2005.

IOF. The name given by many anti-Zionists for the Israeli military. IOF is an abbreviation for Israeli Occupation Forces (IOF). *See* ISRAELI DEFENSE FORCES (IDF) in the Israel-English Dictionary.

ISIL. The Islamic State of Iraq and the Levant (ISIL). *See* Islamic State of Iraq and Syria (ISIS).

ISIS. *See* Islamic State of Iraq and Syria (ISIS).

Islamic State of Iraq and the Levant (ISIL). *See* Islamic State of Iraq and Syria (ISIS).

Islamic State of Iraq and Syria (ISIS). *Also known as* the Islamic State of Iraq and the Levant (ISIL) and Daesh (its Arabic name), a militant group and quasi-state that has fought against the United States and its allies throughout the Middle East. It is designated as a terrorist organization by the United Nations and numerous countries.

Israel. *n.* A term used in this book to mean a number of concepts: a language, the country, its government, its citizenry, and a people, depending on the context of the sentence. The term is used as a reference to a language that uses English words yet appears to have nontraditional and even misleading definitions.

Israeli. *adj.* Descriptive of something from Israel (i.e., Israeli company, Israeli newspaper).

n. A citizen of Israel. Note that this book includes many passages from the media where politicians and others often refer to an Israeli as being Jewish, ignoring or discounting Palestinian Israelis. Broadly, the term *Israeli* can refer to a large group of, but not necessarily all, Israeli citizens. The term *Israelis* might be used similarly to the term *Americans* in the sentence "Americans chose Donald Trump as their president," which would not mean that all Americans chose Donald Trump.

Israeli Occupation Forces (IOF). *See* ISRAELI DEFENSE FORCES (IDF) in the Israel-English Dictionary.

Israel opponents. *n.* Those who place a higher value on equality, freedom, and human rights—even if the consequence is a multiethnic (rather than a Jewish) state in the land that Israel controls. Although anti-racists clearly oppose Israel as a state that gives preferential rights to one ethnic group at the expense of another, there are also people who are antagonistic toward Israel for racist reasons—because they choose to be racist against Jews—however, this book does not represent their views, and they are not who this book refers to as "Israel opponents."

Israel/Palestine. *n.* A piece of land for which there is currently no universally accepted name. The term *Israel/Palestine* also applies to the people residing on that land. The term *Israel* is inadequate, because the state of Israel, which has never defined its borders, claims and controls land that the international community calls "the occupied Palestinian territories" while it denies the population it controls in those territories Israeli citizenship and rights under its civilian legal system. The term *Palestine* is also inadequate to describe the land covered in this book, because although most of the countries of the world recognize the state of Palestine, that state is not contiguous with historic Palestine under the British mandate (1923–1948).

Israel supporters. *n.* People who support a state with a Jewish-majority citizenship and therefore a Jewish control over the country, often described as a "Jewish state." Supporters are either unaware of, or accept, the consequences of that choice: racist policies. Such policies include unequal rights to citizenship and the violation of human rights on the land that Israel currently controls.

Jerusalem Post. An Israeli newspaper based in Jerusalem, founded in 1932, and published in English and French.

Jew. *n. or* **Jewish,** *adj.* Primarily, someone who is of Jewish descent, although in some situations, the term may be referring to someone of the Jewish faith.

Jewish Institute for National Security of America (JINSA). An organization dedicated to educating Congressional, military and civilian national security decision-makers on American defense and strategic interests, primarily in the Middle East, the cornerstone of which is a robust U.S.-Israeli security cooperation. JINSA believes that a strong American military and national security posture is the best guarantor of peace and the survival of our values and civilization.[674]

Jewish National Fund (JNF). A nonprofit organization and United Nations NGO (nongovernmental organization), founded in 1901, that (according to its website[675]) gives all generations of Jews a unique voice in building a prosperous future for the land of Israel and its people. It buys and develops land for Jewish settlement. It is responsible for planting hundreds of millions of trees and creating parks, many on top of demolished Arab villages that had been depopulated in 1948.

JINSA. *See* Jewish Institute for National Security of America (JINSA).

JNF. *See* Jewish National Fund (JNF).

Knesset. The Israeli parliament.

massacre. *n.* According to Merriam-Webster,[676]
1. the act or an instance of killing a number of usually helpless or unresisting human beings under circumstances of atrocity or cruelty
2. a cruel or wanton murder
3. a wholesale slaughter of animals
4. an act of complete destruction

Nakba. *n.* An Arabic term meaning "catastrophe." The term typically refers to the period from the end of 1947 through 1949, during which approximately 750,000 Palestinians, the majority population in what became Israel, were forced to leave and not be allowed to return. Many Palestinians say that the Nakba continues through today because Palestinians continue to be forced from their homes and are prevented from returning.

Newspeak. *n.* A term coined by George Orwell in his novel *1984.* Newspeak provided a way of speaking that formed "mental habits" and made "all other modes of thought impossible."[677] Words were deliberately constructed for political purposes: words, that is to say, which not only had in every case a political implication, but were intended to impose a desirable mental attitude upon the person using them.[678]

Newspeak was a language developed by the government to frame the issues of the day in a desirable way and in a way to minimize thought.

occupied Palestinian territories (oPt). Gaza and the West Bank, including East Jerusalem. References to oPt sometimes include the Golan Heights although it is occupied Syrian territory.

OCHA. *See* United Nations Office for the Coordination of Humanitarian Affairs (OCHA).

OCHA oPt. *See* United Nations Office for the Coordination of Humanitarian Affairs: Occupied Palestinian Territory (OCHA oPt).

oPt. Occupied Palestinian territories.

PA. Palestinian National Authority.

Palestine. *n.* Depending on the context, this term can refer to the area that was defined as Palestine under the British mandate from 1922 into May 1948, or the state as recognized by UN members.

Palestinian. *n.* For this book, someone whose ancestors came from Palestine— generally, Arabs (Muslim, Christian, and Jewish) whose ancestors lived in or were from Palestine prior to 1948. This book defines *Palestinian* to exclude Zionists, partly to distinguish Zionists from Palestinians but also because Zionists who had Palestinian passports prior to the creation of the state of Israel do not consider themselves Palestinians.

Palestinian National Authority (PA) *or* **Palestinian Authority (PA).** The interim self-government body that exercises partial civil control over the Gaza Strip and enclaves in the West Bank known as Area A and Area B.

piracy. *n.* An act of robbery on the high seas; *also*, an act resembling such a robbery.[679]

Promised Land. A territory from the Wadi (the Wadi al-'Arish River in Egypt) to the Euphrates that is believed to cover parts of modern-day Egypt, Saudi Arabia, and Iraq, and all of Israel, Palestine, Jordan, Lebanon, Kuwait, and Syria. This land was originally "promised" in the Old Testament by God to Abraham. God also allows the people of Israel (and therefore the land of Israel) to be ruled by others when the people of Israel fail to obey His laws. The Old Testament disenfranchises nonbelievers, including Jewish descendants, negating the concept of a secular ethnic Jewish state of Israel. Not only does God not promise exclusivity to any group, He stands for equality: "You and the foreigner shall be the same before the Lord" (Num. 15:15 [NIV]) and in the next verse, He stipulates that "the same laws and regulations will apply both to you and to the foreigner residing among you."

Purim. *n.* A Jewish spring festival commemorating the defeat of a plot to massacre Jews. Purim is based on the book of Esther in the Bible, which describes how Queen Esther and Mordecai dismantled the plot and then used the king's seal to kill 75,000 Jewish enemies.

QME. *See* qualitative military edge (QME).

qualitative military edge (QME). Israel's military superiority codified in the US Naval Vessel Transfer Act of 2008. The act limits sales of arms to states in the region such that Israel always has the ability to counter and defeat any military threat from those states and non-state actors.

racism. *n.* The preferential treatment of one group over another based on national or ethnic origin or descent. Here is how the International Convention on the Elimination of All Forms of Racial Discrimination starts its definition of racial discrimination:

> In this Convention, the term "racial discrimination" shall mean any distinction, exclusion, restriction or preference based on race, colour, descent, or national or ethnic origin which has the purpose or effect of nullifying or impairing the recognition, enjoyment or exercise, on an equal footing, of human rights and fundamental freedoms in the political, economic, social, cultural or any other field of public life.[680]

See the chapter on racism in this book's sequel: *Speak Equality: Revealing the Root of the Israel/Palestine Struggle.*

refugee. *n.* Primarily, someone who is registered with the United Nations as a refugee, including descendants of original refugees, who are themselves also refugees.

Right of Return. A principle codified in international law that guarantees everyone's right of voluntary return to, or reentry to, their country of origin or of citizenship. The Right of Return is part of the broader human rights concept of freedom of movement.[681] The principle is based on a concept documented hundreds of years BCE, during the time of ancient Sparta and Persia's Cyrus the Great. Numerous international treaties and national laws have included the concept from the Magna Carta in 1215 to the Universal Declaration of Human Rights in 1948, the Fourth Geneva Convention (1949), and the Convention on the Elimination of All Forms of Racial Discrimination (1969). As an example, Article 13 of the Universal Declaration of Human Rights includes the following: "Everyone has the right to leave any country, including his own, and to return to his country."[682] The term *Right of Return* should not be confused with Israel's Law of Return.

settler. *n.* A Jewish Israeli who
1. has moved, under the protection of the Israeli military and government, onto Palestinian land or into a Palestinian home;
2. has directly—or indirectly through the military or security forces—threatened or used violence against (Palestinian) civilians for political or economic purposes (in taking possession of the land or home). Note the similarity of this definition with the definition of *terrorism*.

steal. *v.* To take the property of another wrongfully and especially as a habitual or regular practice.[683]

terrorism. *n.* The threat or use of violence against civilians for economic or political purposes. *See* chapter 12.

treachery. *n.* According to Merriam-Webster,[684]
1. violation of allegiance or of faith and confidence
2. an act of perfidy or treason

UNESCO. *See* United Nations Educational, Scientific and Cultural Organization (UNESCO).

UNHCR. *See* United Nations High Commissioner for Refugees (UNHCR).

United Nations Economic and Social Commission for Western Asia (ESCWA). A commission established on August 9, 1973, pursuant to Economic and Social Council's Resolution 1818 (LV) to stimulate economic activity in member countries (Algeria, Bahrain, Egypt, Iraq, Jordan, Kuwait, Lebanon, Libya, Mauritania, Morocco, Oman, the state of Palestine, Qatar, Saudi Arabia, Somalia, the Sudan, the Syrian Arab Republic, Tunisia, the United Arab Emirates, and Yemen), strengthen cooperation between them, and promote development.[685]

United Nations Educational, Scientific and Cultural Organization (UNESCO). A United Nations organization that seeks to build peace through international cooperation in education, the sciences, and culture.[686]

United Nations High Commissioner for Refugees (UNHCR). An agency established in 1950 for non-Palestinian refugees. Palestinian refugees are managed by the United Nations Relief and Works Agency (UNRWA), which was formed in 1949.

United Nations Office for the Coordination of Humanitarian Affairs (OCHA). A United Nations body established in 1991 by the General Assembly to strengthen the international response to complex emergencies and natural disasters.[687] Among other duties, OCHA provides maps of the area, showing areas of control and limitations on freedom of movement.

United Nations Office for the Coordination of Humanitarian Affairs: Occupied Palestinian Territory (OCHA oPt). An organization established in 2002 by the UN Office for the Coordination of Humanitarian Affairs (OCHA) in the occupied Palestinian territory (oPt), occupied by Israel since the 1967 war, in order to support international efforts to respond to the humanitarian situation in the West Bank, including East Jerusalem, and in the Gaza Strip.[688]

United Nations Relief and Works Agency (UNRWA). An organization formed in 1949 by the United Nations General Assembly in response to the large number of Palestinian refugees from the Israeli War of Independence, referred to by Palestinians as the Nakba.[689]

United Nations Resolution 181. A resolution passed in 1947 by the UN General Assembly calling for a Palestine Partition Plan, dividing the British mandate into an Arab state and a Jewish state.

United Nations Resolution 194. A resolution passed in 1948 by the UN General Assembly to deal with refugees, stipulating that refugees wishing to return to their homes and live at peace with their neighbours should be permitted to do so at the earliest practicable date, and that compensation should be paid for the property of those choosing not to return and for loss of or damage to property which, under principles of international law or in equity, should be made good by the Governments or authorities responsible.[690]

United Nations Resolution 242. A UN Security Council resolution passed in response to the 1967 Six-Day War. The resolution emphasized "the inadmissibility of the acquisition of territory by war" and states that a just and lasting peace requires the "withdrawal of Israel armed forces from territories occupied in the recent conflict." The resolution also affirmed the necessity "for achieving a just settlement of the refugee problem."[691]

UNRWA. *See* United Nations Relief and Works Agency (UNRWA).

wall. *n. See* security fence in the Israel-English Dictionary.

Zionist. *n. or* **Zionism.** According to Merriam-Webster, a follower of an international movement originally for the establishment of a Jewish national or religious community in Palestine and later for the support of modern Israel.[692] There are a number of definitions of *Zionist* and *Zionism*, and although the distinctions may seem minute, they can have great implications. *Political Zionists* believe in an ethnic and/or religious Jewish state. *Religious Zionists* advocate religious Jews moving to historical Palestine but nonetheless do not support a Jewish state. *Cultural Zionists* want a state where all people have equal rights but where historical Jewish culture is promoted and respected. Zionists can be Jewish, but they can also be Christian. Jews may or may not be Zionist. One is typically born Jewish, but one is Zionist by choice. This book generally uses the terms *Zionist* and *political Zionist* interchangeably.

Zionist Occupation Forces. *See* Israeli Defense Forces (IDF) in the Israel-English Dictionary.

Israel-English Dictionary

ANTI-SEMITIC. *adj.*

1. Racist against Jews.

2. Not racist enough; not willing to support preferential treatment of Jews over another ethnic group (such as in Israel).

APARTHEID. *n.* This word is not defined in the Israel-English Dictionary, since it does not apply to Israel per Israel supporters. This denial is despite international organizations calling it out.

BLOCKADE. *n.* This word is not defined in the Israel-English Dictionary, since Israeli politicians have historically stated that there is no blockade of Gaza despite reality showing us otherwise.

BOYCOTT, DIVESTMENT, SANCTIONS (BDS). An anti-racism (equal rights) campaign that is portrayed by Zionists as a racist campaign (against Jews) to destroy Israel.

COUNTERTERRORISM. *n.* The elimination of the rights to resist oppression.

DEFENSIVE. *adj.* Descriptive of a comprehensive international campaign and lobbying effort to have world powers draw borders in such a way as to give a minority population the majority of the land. The campaign and effort is followed by an armed seizure of the land, the forcible expulsion of its civilian indigenous population, the destruction of their villages and towns, the confiscation of their property, and the blocking and killing of returning refugees—all in violation of international law. Racist local laws prevent the remaining indigenous majority population from ever becoming equal citizens or having proportionate political power.

DEMOCRACY. *n.* A form of government that provides rights, including citizenship and the right to vote, primarily based on ethnicity; is based on the expulsion of the majority of the indigenous population during its founding, causing the previous majority to become a minority; is dependent on the violation of international law by obstructing the return of the indigenous refugees, thereby maintaining a majority of the minority; and discriminates based on ethnicity, resulting in the further decrease in citizenship rights of certain ethnic group(s).

EQUALITY. *n.* The state of having equal rights only some of the time and in some situations. Equality usually does not apply to housing, where one can live, government benefits (from school funding and infrastructure to building permits), one's spousal and children's rights, representation in government, freedom of speech, or freedom of assembly. Because the term means sometimes equal and sometimes not, the word is fundamentally meaningless in Israel.

ISRAELI DEFENSE FORCES (IDF). Official name of the military forces of the state of Israel. Due to its aggressive, rather than defensive, role in maintaining an ongoing occupation and blockade and in enforcing the violation of human rights, it is also called Israeli Occupation Forces (IOF) or Zionist Occupation Forces by opponents.

ILLEGAL. *adj.*

1. *As used by Israel:* Against Israeli law.

2. *As used by Palestinians (and most of the world):* Against international law, such as the Geneva Conventions and international humanitarian law.

Example: Construction in Area C of the West Bank, in the occupied Palestinian territories under Israeli administrative and military control, is illegal (under Israeli law) without Israeli permits. Permits to build on this Palestinian land are granted overwhelmingly to settlements that are illegal under international law. These same building permits are not granted to the local indigenous population, who are there legally by international and Israeli law, many of whose families have been there for hundreds, if not thousands, of years. As a result, Israel is demolishing Palestinian buildings against international law but in accordance with Israeli law in the Palestinian territories.

INTERNATIONAL LAW. Law agreed to by countries through treaties and agreements. Most countries have supported UN resolutions that point out Israel's violations of international law; Israel claims to be in compliance or disregards these accusations.

LAW OF RETURN. An Israeli law that provides citizenship to immigrating Jews. The term *Law of Return* should not be confused with the term Right of Return. Unlike the international Right of Return, the Israeli Law of Return is not used by people who are returning. Those wanting to return—namely, Palestinians and their direct descendants—are denied their right to do so.

NAKBA. *n.* This term is not defined in the Israel-English dictionary, because Israel punishes parties financially that recognize the Nakba.

RIGHT OF RETURN. Although Right of Return is an internationally recognized right, it does not exist in Israel, and therefore it has no definition in this dictionary.

SECURITY FENCE. *n.* A barrier, typically in the form of a metal fence or concrete wall, that protects the party taking land from civilians by force rather than protecting the victims from the aggressor. The metal fence is electrified in segments and/or contains razor-wire sections. The concrete wall can exceed 26 feet in height and has occasional observation towers (by contrast, the Berlin Wall was less than 12 feet tall). The "security fence," or wall, cuts off and impedes Palestinians from reaching their agricultural lands, schools, and markets. It creates ghettos. It limits movement and trade, thereby crippling the Palestinian economy. It limits freedom of movement in the West Bank and to East Jerusalem, including to the Christian and Muslim religious sites. The "security fence" then enables the newly conscripted land to be developed for Jewish-only colonial settlements without impediments from its displaced Palestinian owners.

START. *n.* A continuation.

v. To continue.

Example: The War of Independence started in May 1948.

TRANSFER. *v.* A euphemism for "force out" or "expel." Also described as *voluntary transfer*.

WAR OF INDEPENDENCE. An organized, financed, and armed offensive, primarily by relatively recent Jewish immigrants from foreign lands, against the indigenous population. The Zionist militias and Israeli forces purged the land of a majority of its non-Jewish inhabitants. Unlike the US, Israel's major opponent in its "War of Independence" was not its colonial power.

Endnotes

Introduction.

1 Diana Muir, "A Land without a People for a People without a Land," Middle East Quarterly 15, no. 2 (Spring 2008), 55–62, accessed November 18, 2020, https://www.meforum.org/1877/a-land-without-a-people-for-a-people-without.

2 Nazila Fathi, "Wipe Israel 'Off the Map' Iranian says," *New York Times*, last modified October 27, 2005, accessed June 23, 2018, https://www.nytimes.com/2005/10/27/world/africa/wipe-israel-off-the-map-iranian-says.html; "Text of Mahmoud Ahmadinejad's Speech," trans. Nazila Fathi, *New York Times*, last modified October 30, 2005, accessed June 23, 2018, https://www.nytimes.com/2005/10/30/weekinreview/text-of-mahmoud-ahmadinejads-speech.html.

3 Middle East Media Research Institute, "The Covenant of the Islamic Resistance Movement: Hamas" (translation of the Hamas Covenant, written in 1988), Palestine Special Dispatch 1092, February 14, 2006, accessed August 16, 2019, https://www.memri.org/reports/covenant-islamic-resistance-movement-%E2%80%93-hamas.

4 Douglas Bloomfield, "Washington Watch: Panic Attack," *Jerusalem Post*, last modified May 10, 2017, accessed April 25, 2019, https://www.jpost.com/Opinion/Washington-Watch-Panic-attack-490364.

1. Israel Is Also a Language

5 Robert Green McCloskey, ed., *The Works of James Wilson*, vol. 1, chap. 15 ("Equality"), doc. 48 ("Of Man, as a Member of Society, Lectures on Law," *Works* 1:240–241 [1791]) (Cambridge, MA: Belknap Press of Harvard University Press, 1967), accessed November 18, 2020, https://press-pubs.uchicago.edu/founders/documents/v1ch15s48.html.

6 UN General Assembly, Resolution 3068 (XXVIII), International Convention on the Suppression and Punishment of the Crime of *Apartheid* (in force July 18, 1976), accessed November 18, 2020, https://www.un.org/en/genocideprevention/documents/atrocity-crimes/Doc.10_International%20Convention%20on%20the%20Suppression%20and%20Punishment%20of%20the%20Crime%20of%20Apartheid.pdf.

2. The "Security Fence"/Barrier/Wall

7 "Netanyahu Says West Bank Barrier to Stay for Now," *Reuters*, last modified July 22, 2009, accessed June 6, 2019, https://www.reuters.com/article/us-

palestinians-israel-barrier/netanyahu-says-west-bank-barrier-to-stay-for-now-idUSTRE56L39W20090722.

8   "Suicide and Other Bombing Attacks in Israel Since the Declaration of Principles (Sept 1993)," Israel Ministry of Foreign Affairs, accessed March 2, 2020, https://mfa.gov.il/mfa/foreignpolicy/terrorism/palestinian/pages/suicide%20and%20other%20bombing%20attacks%20in%20israel%20since.aspx.

9   "Maps," UN Office for the Coordination of Humanitarian Affairs (OCHA): Occupied Palestinian Territory, accessed November 19, 2020, https://www.ochaopt.org/maps.

10 "International Court of Justice Advisory Opinion Finds Israel's Construction of Wall 'Contrary to International Law,'" United Nations, Meetings Coverage and Press Releases, July 9, 2004, accessed November 19, 2020, https://www.un.org/press/en/2004/icj616.doc.htm.

11 "International Court of Justice Advisory Opinion Finds Israel's Construction of Wall 'Contrary to International Law.'"

12 Seumas Milne and Ian Black, "Palestine Papers: MI6 Plan Proposed Internment—and Hotline to Israelis," *Guardian*, last modified January 25, 2011, accessed May 24, 2019, https://www.theguardian.com/world/2011/jan/25/mi6-palestinian-papers-rejectionists-plan.

13 Milne and Black, "Palestine Papers."

14 Milne and Black, "Palestine Papers."

15 Milne and Black, "Palestine Papers."

16 Arieh O'Sullivan, "Palestinian Non-Violent Resistance Catching On," *Jerusalem Post*, last modified February 15, 2012, accessed January 29, 2018, https://www.jpost.com/Features/In-Thespotlight/Palestinian-non-violent-resistance-catching-on.

17 Daniella Peled, "Palestinian Tactics Set to Change," *Institute for War and Peace Reporting*, June 21, 2011, https://iwpr.net/global-voices/palestinian-tactics-set-change; Daoud Kuttab, "A New Palestinian Strategy," *Cairo Review of Global Affairs* (Spring 2014), https://www.thecairoreview.com/essays/a-new-palestinian-strategy/; "With Peace Talks Frozen, Palestinians Back Protests," *Asharq Al-Aswat*, last modified January 24, 2010, https://eng-archive.aawsat.com/theaawsat/news-middle-east/with-peace-talks-frozen-palestinians-back-protests.

18 "Threat of Demolitions in East Jerusalem," UN Office for the Coordination of Humanitarian Affairs (OCHA): Occupied Palestinian Territory, July 9, 2019, accessed October 22, 2019, https://www.ochaopt.org/content/threat-demolitions-east-jerusalem.

19 Visualizing Palestine, accessed January 17, 2021, https://visualizingpalestine.org/visuals/segregated-roads-west-bank.

3. Home Demolitions.

20 United Nations Human Rights Committee, "International Covenant on Civil and Political Rights," CCPR/C/ISR/CO/4, November 21, 2014, UN Treaty Body

Database, Office of the High Commissioner, Human Rights, United Nations, accessed July 12, 2018, http://tbinternet.ohchr.org/_layouts/treatybodyexternal/Download.aspx?symbolno=CCPR/C/ISR/CO/4&Lang=En.

21 "Off the Map: Land and Housing Rights Violations in Israel's Unrecognized Bedouin Villages," Human Rights Watch, March 30, 2008, accessed June 24, 2019, https://www.hrw.org/report/2008/03/30/map/land-and-housing-rights-violations-israels-unrecognized-bedouin-villages.

22 "Off the Map: Land and Housing Rights Violations."

23 "Negev: Demolition of Al-Araqeeb Village for 119th Time," *Middle East Monitor*, October 3, 2017, accessed January 12, 2021, https://www.middleeastmonitor.com/20171003-negev-demolition-of-al-araqeeb-village-for-119th-time/.

24 Ramzy Baroud, "Al-Araqeeb Village: Palestinian Bedouins Refuse to Surrender 116 Times," *CounterPunch*, August 17, 2017, accessed March 25, 2019, https://www.counterpunch.org/2017/08/17/al-araqeeb-village-palestinian-bedouins-refuse-to-surrender-116-times/.

25 "Record Number of Demolitions, Including Self-Demolitions, in East Jerusalem in April 2019," UN Office for the Coordination of Humanitarian Affairs (OCHA): Occupied Palestinian Territory, May 14, 2019, accessed October 22, 2019, https://www.ochaopt.org/content/record-number-demolitions-including-self-demolitions-east-jerusalem-april-2019.

26 "Dangerous Implications of Israeli Supreme Court Decision to Allow Forced Displacement of Atir-Umm al-Hiran for Remaining Unrecognized Bedouin Villages in Naqab," Adalah: Legal Center for Arab Minority Rights in Israel, September 26, 2017, accessed October 13, 2017, https://www.adalah.org/en/content/view/9243.

27 "Area C," UN Office for the Coordination of Humanitarian Affairs (OCHA): Occupied Palestinian Territory, accessed November 23, 2020, https://www.ochaopt.org/location/area-c#:~:text=Over%2060%20per%20cent%20of,the%20expense%20of%20Palestinian%20communities.

28 "Record Number of Demolitions and Displacements in the West Bank during 2016," UN Office for the Coordination of Humanitarian Affairs (OCHA): Occupied Palestinian Territory, February 10, 2017, accessed October 16, 2017, https://www.ochaopt.org/content/record-number-demolitions-and-displacements-west-bank-during-2016.

29 "West Bank Demolitions and Displacement: An Overview," UN Office for the Coordination of Humanitarian Affairs (OCHA), September 2019, accessed June 4, 2020, https://www.ochaopt.org/sites/default/files/demolition_monthly_report_september_2019.pdf.

30 "100-year-old Bedouin Woman Left Homeless as Israel Continues Negev Demolitions," *Ma'an News Agency*, last modified February 9, 2017, accessed October 16, 2017, http://www.maannews.com/Content.aspx?id=775366, archived at https://web.archive.org/web/20170220110542/http://www.maannews.com/Content.aspx?id=775366.

31 "West Bank Demolitions and Displacement: An Overview."

32 Abeer Salman, "Israel Demolishes Schools for Palestinians, Citing Lack of Permits," *CNN World*, last modified August 29, 2017, accessed October 16, 2017, http://www.cnn.com/2017/08/29/middleeast/israel-demolishes-palestinian-schools/index.html.

33 Salman, "Israel Demolishes Schools for Palestinians."

34 Salman, "Israel Demolishes Schools for Palestinians."

35 Abeer Salman, "With Bricks—Not Metal—Palestinians Rebuild School Demolished by Israel," *CNN World*, last modified September 20, 2017, accessed October 16, 2017, https://www.cnn.com/2017/09/20/middleeast/palestinian-schools-rebuilt/index.html.

36 "Israel Confiscated Classroom Chairs and Tables at Elementary School in the Palestinian Community of Ras al-Tin," B'Tselem: The Israeli Information Center for Human Rights in the Occupied Territories, September 10, 2020, accessed October 29, 2020, https://www.btselem.org/facing_expulsion_blog?community=213062&nid=213075.

4. It's Not Just about Israel; It's about Us

37 Jeremy M. Sharp, "U.S. Foreign Aid to Israel," Congressional Research Service, RL33222, April 10, 2018, accessed December 7, 2018, https://fas.org/sgp/crs/mideast/RL33222.pdf; Nick Thompson, "Seventy-Five Percent of U.S. Foreign Military Financing Goes to Two Countries," *CNN Politics*, last modified November 11, 2015, accessed December 7, 2018, https://www.cnn.com/2015/11/11/politics/us-foreign-aid-report/index.html; "Foreign Aid Explorer," USAID, February 20, 2020, accessed 2 March 2020, https://explorer.usaid.gov/reports and https://explorer.usaid.gov/cd/ISR.

38 *Foreign Relations of the United States, 1969–1976*, vol. 26, *Arab-Israeli Dispute, 1974–1976*, "227. Memoranda of Agreement," Office of the Historian, US Department of State, September 1, 1975 (Library of Congress, Manuscript Division, Kissinger Papers, CL 159, Geopolitical File, Israel, September 1–17, 1975. Secret), accessed November 23, 2020, https://history.state.gov/historicaldocuments/frus1969-76v26/d227.

39 "Security Council—Veto List (in Reverse Chronological order)," The United Nations Dag Hammarskjöld Library, accessed December 7, 2018, http://research.un.org/en/docs/sc/quick/veto; "U.N. Security Council: U.S. Vetoes of Resolutions Critical to Israel (1972–Present)," Jewish Virtual Library, American-Israeli Cooperative Enterprise (AICE), accessed December 7, 2018, https://www.jewishvirtuallibrary.org/u-s-vetoes-of-un-security-council-resolutions-critical-to-israel; Donald Neff, "U.S. Vetoes of U.N. Resolutions on Behalf of Israel," If Americans Knew: What Every American Needs to Know about Israel-Palestine, accessed December 7, 2018, https://ifamericansknew.org/us_ints/p-neff-veto.html.

40 US House of Representatives, United States Code 287e, "Authorization of Appropriations; Payment of Expenses," Title 22 (Foreign Relations and

Intercourse), Chapter 7 (International Bureaus, Congresses, etc.), Subchapter 16 (United Nations Organization), accessed June 5, 2019, https://uscode.house.gov/view.xhtml?req=USC+287e+palestine&f=treesort&fq=true&num=1&hl=true&edition=prelim&granuleId=USC-prelim-title22-section287e#.

41 "Constitution of the United Nations Educational, Scientific and Cultural Organization," Basic Texts, United Nations Educational, Scientific and Cultural Organization (UNESCO), 2018 Edition, accessed February 20, 2020, https://unesdoc.unesco.org/ark:/48223/pf0000261751.page=6.

42 Jonathan Easley, "US Stops Funding UNESCO over Palestine," *The Hill*, last modified October 31, 2011, accessed December 7, 2018, https://thehill.com/blogs/blog-briefing-room/news/190803-us-stops-funding-unesco-over-palestine.

43 "State of Palestine Flag to Fly at United Nations Headquarters, Offices as General Assembly Adopts Resolution on Non-Member Observer States," UN General Assembly (Meetings Coverage and Press Releases), September 10, 2015, accessed December 7, 2018, https://www.un.org/press/en/2015/ga11676.doc.htm.

44 Zena Agha, "Israel Can't Hide Evidence of Its Occupation Anymore," *Foreign Policy*, August 3, 2020, accessed January 12, 2021, https://foreignpolicy.com/2020/08/03/israel-cant-hide-evidence-of-its-occupation-anymore/.

45 "Defining Anti-Semitism," US Department of State, Office of the Special Envoy to Monitor and Combat Anti-Semitism, May 26, 2016, accessed October 28, 2019, https://www.state.gov/defining-anti-semitism/, archived at https://web.archive.org/web/20181207180133/https://www.state.gov/s/rga/resources/267538.htm.

46 *Merriam-Webster Dictionary*, s.v. "Zionism," accessed November 24, 2020, https://www.merriam-webster.com/dictionary/Zionism.

47 "Global Anti-Semitism Review Act," US Department of State Archive, October 8, 2004, accessed December 7, 2018, https://2001-2009.state.gov/g/drl/rls/79640.htm.

48 Erica L. Green, "Education Dept. Reopens Rutgers Case Charging Discrimination against Jewish Students," *New York Times*, September 11, 2018, https://www.nytimes.com/2018/09/11/us/politics/rutgers-jewish-education-civil-rights.html.

49 "Tennessee," Palestine Legal, last modified April 16, 2019, accessed November 24, 2020, https://palestinelegal.org/tennessee.

50 "CS/CS/HB 741: Anti-Semitism," Florida House of Representatives, effective May 31, 2019 (per https://www.flsenate.gov/Session/Bill/2019/00741), accessed June 5, 2019, https://www.flsenate.gov/Session/Bill/2019/741/BillText/c2/PDF.

51 "Executive Order on Combating Anti-Semitism," WhiteHouse.gov: Law & Justice, December 11, 2019, accessed February 14, 2020, https://www.whitehouse.gov/presidential-actions/executive-order-combating-anti-semitism/; Michael Warren, "Trump's Anti-Semitism Executive Order, Explained," *CNN Politics*, last modified December 12, 2019, accessed February 14, 2020, https://www.cnn.com/2019/12/12/politics/trump-anti-semitism-executive-order-explained/index.html.

52 Karen DeYoung, "Trump Picks a Supporter of West Bank Settlements for Ambassador to Israel," *Washington Post*, last modified December 15, 2016,

accessed March 19, 2018, https://www.washingtonpost.com/world/national-security/trump-picks-a-supporter-of-west-bank-settlements-for-ambassador-to-israel/2016/12/15/1a50c03c-c32e-11e6-9a51-cd56ea1c2bb7_story.html.

53 Jeremy Diamond and Elise Labott, "Trump Recognizes Jerusalem as Israel's Capital," CNN Politics, last modified December 6, 2017, accessed March 19, 2018, https://www.cnn.com/2017/12/06/politics/president-donald-trump-jerusalem/index.html.

54 "Amid Divisions over Jerusalem, Korean Nuclear Programme, General Assembly Hears Defence of Diplomacy, Dialogue to End Crisis, Put World on Sustainable Path," UN General Assembly (Meetings Coverage and Press Releases), December 29, 2017, accessed March 19, 2018, https://www.un.org/press/en/2017/ga11998.doc.htm.

55 "Amid Divisions over Jerusalem, Korean Nuclear Programme."

56 "Amid Divisions over Jerusalem, Korean Nuclear Programme."

57 "Bringing Israel to North America's Jewish Summer Camps," The Jewish Agency for Israel, accessed December 23, 2020, https://www.jewishagency.org/bringing-israel-to-north-americas-jewish-summer-camps/.

58 Laura E. Adkins, "Israeli, French and American Jews Agree on Almost Everything—Except Trump," *Jewish Telegraphic Agency*, June 2, 2019, accessed August 26, 2019, https://www.jta.org/2019/06/02/israel/israeli-french-and-american-jews-agree-on-almost-everything-except-trump.

59 William Cummings, "Trump Criticized for Calling Netanyahu 'Your Prime Minister' at Jewish Republican Event," *USA Today*, April 8, 2019, accessed August 26, 2019, https://www.usatoday.com/story/news/politics/2019/04/08/trump-calls-netanyahu-your-prime-minister-jewish-american-event/3398487002/.

60 Jordan Weissmann, "What Republicans Really Mean When They Call Jews Disloyal," *Slate*, August 22, 2019, accessed August 25, 2019, https://slate.com/news-and-politics/2019/08/what-republicans-really-mean-when-they-call-jews-disloyal.html.

61 "Defining Anti-Semitism."

62 Stephen M. Walt, "Petraeus & Me (a Non-Story)," *Foreign Policy*, March 19, 2010, accessed March 18, 2020, https://foreignpolicy.com/2010/03/19/petraeus-me-a-non-story/; "Statement of General David H. Petraeus, U.S. Army Commander, U.S. Central Command, before the Senate Armed Services Committee on the Posture of U.S. Central Command, 16 MAR 2010," Senate Armed Service Committee, March 16, 2010, accessed March 18, 2020, https://web.archive.org/web/20100331012029/http://armed-services.senate.gov/statemnt/2010/03%20March/Petraeus%2003-16-10.pdf.

63 Jason Burke, "Osama Issues New Call to Arms," *Guardian*, last modified November 24, 2002, accessed July 25, 2018, https://www.theguardian.com/world/2002/nov/24/alqaida.terrorism; "Full Text: Bin Laden's 'Letter to America,'" *Guardian*, last modified November 24, 2002, accessed July 25, 2018, https://www.theguardian.com/world/2002/nov/24/theobserver.

64 "Transcript of Bin Laden's October Interview," *CNN*, last modified February 5, 2002, accessed July 25, 2018, http://edition.cnn.com/2002/WORLD/asiapcf/south/02/05/binladen.transcript/.

65 Rebecca Shabad, "Letter Sent by Alleged 9/11 Mastermind to Obama Surfaces," *CBS News*, last modified February 8, 2017, accessed July 25, 2018, https://www.cbsnews.com/news/9-11-mastermind-letter-to-obama/.

66 "Press Availability with Jordanian Foreign Minister Ayman Safadi," US Department of State, April 30, 2018, accessed May 1, 2018, https://www.state.gov/press-availability-with-jordanian-foreign-minister-ayman-safadi/.

67 Greg Myre, "Which Nations Hate the U.S.? Often Those Receiving U.S. Aid," *Parallels: Many Stories, One World*, National Public Radio, July 23, 2013, accessed September 2, 2019, https://www.npr.org/sections/parallels/2013/07/22/204516430/which-nations-hate-the-u-s-often-those-receiving-u-s-aid?t=1565179807452.

68 Andrew Kohut et al., "America's Global Image Remains More Positive Than China's: But Many See China Becoming World's Leading Power," Pew Research Center, July 18, 2013, accessed September 2, 2019, https://www.pewresearch.org/global/wp-content/uploads/sites/2/2013/07/Pew-Research-Global-Attitudes-Project-Balance-of-Power-Report-FINAL-July-18-2013.pdf.

69 David Brog, "The End of Evangelical Support for Israel?" *Middle East Quarterly* 21, no. 2 (Spring 2014), accessed July 25, 2018, https://www.meforum.org/3769/israel-evangelical-support.

70 JTA, "Jewish Pro-BDS Group Endorses Anti-Israel Black Lives Matter Platform," *Times of Israel*, last modified August 6, 2016, accessed July 25, 2018, https://www.timesofisrael.com/jewish-pro-bds-group-endorses-anti-israel-black-lives-matter-platform/.

71 "More Than Half of NFL Players Booked for Israel PR Trip Withdraw," *Guardian*, last modified February 15, 2017, accessed July 25, 2018, https://www.theguardian.com/sport/2017/feb/15/nfl-players-israel-trip-michael-bennett.

72 Hadas Thier, "Peter Beinart on the End of the Two-State Solution for Israel and Palestine," *Jacobin*, July 13, 2020, accessed October 28, 2020, https://jacobinmag.com/2020/07/two-state-solution-peter-beinart-israel-palestine/.

73 "News: Ranking the Top 10 Anti-Israel Groups in 2013," Anti-Defamation League, October 21, 2013, accessed July 25, 2018, https://www.adl.org/news/press-releases/news-ranking-the-top-10-anti-israel-groups-in-2013-adl.

74 *BDS*, Palestinian BDS National Committee (BNC) and Palestinian Campaign for the Academic and Cultural Boycott of Israel (PACBI), accessed July 25, 2018, https://bdsmovement.net.

75 "As Mideast Violence Continues, a Wide Partisan Gap in Israel-Palestine Sympathies," Pew Research Center, last modified July 15, 2014, https://www.people-press.org/2014/07/15/as-mideast-violence-continues-a-wide-partisan-gap-in-israel-palestinian-sympathies/.

76 Samantha Smith and Carroll Doherty, "5 Facts about how Americans View the Israeli-Palestinian Conflict," Pew Research Center, last modified May 23, 2016, https://www.pewresearch.org/fact-tank/2016/05/23/5-facts-about-how-americans-view-the-israeli-palestinian-conflict/.

77 Michael Wilner, "South Carolina Becomes First US State to Take Action against Anti-Israel Boycotts," *Jerusalem Post*, last modified June 5, 2015, https://www.jpost.com/Diaspora/South-Carolina-becomes-first-US-state-to-take-action-against-anti-Israel-boycotts-405120.

78 "Anti-BDS Legislation by State," Palestine Legal, accessed July 25, 2018, https://palestinelegal.org/righttoboycott.

79 Richard Parker, "*NAACP v. Claiborne Hardware Co.* (1982)," *The First Amendment Encyclopedia*, accessed August 7, 2020, https://mtsu.edu/first-amendment/article/288/naacp-v-claiborne-hardware-co.

80 Oren Liebermann, Abeer Salman, and Michael Schwartz, "Israel Bars Democratic Congresswomen from Entering Country," *CNN Politics*, August 15, 2019, accessed on August 16, 2019, https://www.cnn.com/2019/08/15/politics/israel-visit-ilhan-omar-rashida-tlaib-intl/index.html.

81 Oren Liebermann, Amir Tal, and Lauren Said-Moorhouse, "Rep. Rashida Tlaib Says She Won't Visit Israel After Being Allowed to Enter on Humanitarian Grounds," *CNN Politics*, August 16, 2019, accessed August 16, 2019, https://www.cnn.com/2019/08/16/politics/rashida-tlaib-israel-visit-intl/index.html.

82 "FBI Charges Florida Professor with Terrorist Activities," *CNN*, February 20, 2003, accessed January 12, 2021, https://www.cnn.com/2003/US/South/02/20/professor.arrest/.

83 Hillary Mann Leverett and Flynt Leverett, "US Deports Professor Sami Al-Arian for Criticizing Israel and Backing Palestinian Rights," *Truthout*, last modified February 7, 2015, accessed January 12, 2021, https://truthout.org/articles/us-deports-professor-sami-al-arian-for-criticizing-israel-and-backing-palestinian-rights/#15041139831791; "Exclusive: Deported Palestinian Scholar Sami Al-Arian on His Chilling Post-9/11 Prosecution," *Democracy Now!* last modified February 6, 2015, accessed January 12, 2021, https://www.democracynow.org/2015/2/6/exclusive_deported_palestinian_scholar_sami_al; Murtaza Hussain and Glenn Greenwald, "Exclusive Interview: Sami Al-Arian, Professor Who Defeated Controversial Terrorism Charges, Is Deported from US," *Intercept*, last modified February 5, 2015, accessed January 12, 2021, https://theintercept.com/2015/02/05/sami-al-arian-charged-terrorism-never-convicted-deported-today-u-s/; Jennifer Steinhauer, "Palestinian to Be Imprisoned before Deportation," *New York Times*, last modified May 1, 2006, accessed January 12, 2021, https://www.nytimes.com/2006/05/01/us/01cnd-islamic.html.

84 Yaakov Katz, "American Israel Critic Denied Entry to Country," *Jerusalem Post*, May 25, 2008, accessed March 2, 2020, https://www.jpost.com/Israel/American-Israel-critic-denied-entry-to-country; Toni O'Loughlin, "US Academic Deported and Banned for Criticising Israel," *Guardian*, May 25, 2008, accessed March 2, 2020, https://www.theguardian.com/world/2008/may/26/israelandthepalestinians.usa.

85 "*Salaita v. Kennedy, et al.*," Center for Constitutional Rights, accessed January 16, 2019, https://ccrjustice.org/home/what-we-do/our-cases/salaita-v-kennedy-et-al.

86 Mark Guarino, "Professor Fired for Israel Criticism Urges University of Illinois to Reinstate Him," *Guardian*, last modified September 9, 2014, accessed January 13,

2021, https://www.theguardian.com/education/2014/sep/09/professor-israel-criticism-twitter-university-illinois; Ryan Weber, "University of Illinois Professor Loses His Job after Anti-Israel Tweets," *Washington Post*, last modified August 14, 2014, accessed January 13, 2021, https://www.washingtonpost.com/news/morning-mix/wp/2014/08/14/university-of-illinois-professor-loses-his-job-after-anti-israel-tweets/; "Jewish Letter to U. of Illinois Leadership: Just As We Work to Oppose Israeli Ethnic Cleansing of Palestinians in Our Name, We Will Ensure the Silencing of Professor Salaita Does Not Take Place in Our Name Either," *Mondoweiss*, last modified September 4, 2014, accessed January 13, 2021, https://mondoweiss.net/2014/09/leadership-palestinians-professor/; Jodi S. Cohen, "University of Illinois OKs $875,000 Settlement to End Steven Salaita Dispute," *Chicago Tribune*, last modified November 12, 2015, accessed January 13, 2021, https://www.chicagotribune.com/news/breaking/ct-steven-salaita-settlement-met-20151112-story.html; Robert Mackey, "Professor's Angry Tweets on Gaza Cost Him a Job," *New York Times*, last modified September 12, 2014, accessed January 13, 2021, https://www.nytimes.com/2014/09/13/world/middleeast/professors-angry-tweets-on-gaza-cost-him-a-job.html.

87 Emma Pettit, "'Ousted' from Academe, Steven Salaita Says He's Driving a School Bus to Make Ends Meet," *Chronicle of Higher Education*, last modified February 19, 2019, accessed January 13, 2021, https://www.chronicle.com/article/Ousted-From-Academe/245732.

88 Teresa Watanabe, "How a Casino Tycoon Is Trying to Combat an Exploding Pro-Palestinian Movement on Campuses," *Los Angeles Times*, last modified August 21, 2016, accessed December 28, 2020, https://www.latimes.com/local/la-me-uc-israel-palestinian-adv-snap-story.html; Clark Mindock, "Sheldon Adelson to Hold College Anti-Semitism Meeting to Tackle Israel Critics," *International Business Times*, last modified June 1, 2015, accessed December 28, 2020, https://www.ibtimes.com/sheldon-adelson-hold-college-anti-semitism-meeting-tackle-israel-critics-1947322; Nathan Guttman, "Secret Sheldon Adelson Summit Raises up to $50M for Strident Anti-BDS Push," *Forward*, last modified June 9, 2015, accessed December 28, 2020, https://forward.com/news/israel/309676/secret-sheldon-adelson-summit-raises-up-to-50m-for-strident-anti-bds-push/; Jerry Kang, "Dialogue over Demagoguery," UCLA Office of Equity, Diversity and Inclusion, April 19, 2016, accessed December 28, 2020, https://equity.ucla.edu/crosscheck/dialogue-over-demagoguery/.

89 "U.N. General Assembly Votes to Recognize Palestinian State," *CBS News*, last modified November 30, 2012, accessed July 25, 2018, https://www.cbsnews.com/news/un-general-assembly-votes-to-recognize-palestinian-state/; "General Assembly Votes Overwhelmingly to Accord Palestine 'Non-Member Observer State' Status in United Nations," UN General Assembly (Meetings Coverage and Press Releases), November 29, 2012, accessed July 25, 2018, https://www.un.org/press/en/2012/ga11317.doc.htm.

5. Zionism and the "Jewish State"

90 Diana Muir, "A Land without a People for a People without a Land," *Middle East Quarterly* 15, no. 2 (Spring 2008): 55–62, accessed January 24, 2019, https://www.meforum.org/1877/a-land-without-a-people-for-a-people-without#_ftnref21.

91 Monika Richarz, "The History of the Jews in Europe during the Nineteenth and Early Twentieth Centuries," *Remembrance and Beyond Discussion Papers Journal*, vol. 1, ch. 8, The Holocaust and the United Nations Outreach Programme, 2008, accessed September 2, 2019, https://www.un.org/en/holocaustremembrance/docs/pdf/Volume%20I/The_History_of_the_Jews_in_Europe.pdf.

92 *Dictionary.com*, s.v. "pogrom," accessed September 2, 2019, https://www.dictionary.com/browse/pogrom.

93 Elizabeth Nix, "What Was the Dreyfus Affair?" History.com, updated August 22, 2018, accessed September 2, 2019, https://www.history.com/news/what-was-the-dreyfus-affair.

94 John Ehrman, "The Dreyfus Affair: Enduring CI Lessons," *Studies in Intelligence* 55, no. 1 (Extracts, March 2011), accessed September 2, 2019, https://www.cia.gov/library/center-for-the-study-of-intelligence/csi-publications/csi-studies/studies/vol.-55-no.-1/pdfs/CleanedEhrman-Review%20of%20Dreyfus.pdf.

95 Jean-Denis Bredin, *The Affair* (New York: George Braziller, 1986), 434, 480.

96 Liam Hoare, "Did Dreyfus Affair Really Inspire Herzl?" *Forward*, February 26, 2014, accessed September 2, 2019, https://forward.com/schmooze/193316/did-dreyfus-affair-really-inspire-herzl/.

97 "Neo-Völkisch," Southern Poverty Law Center, accessed September 2, 2019, https://www.splcenter.org/fighting-hate/extremist-files/ideology/neo-volkisch.

98 David Ben-Gurion, "Theodor Herzl: Austrian Zionist Leader," Encyclopædia Britannica, June 29, 2019, accessed September 2, 2020, https://www.britannica.com/biography/Theodor-Herzl#accordion-article-history.

99 Ben-Gurion, "Theodor Herzl."

100 Hayim Herring, "New Findings about Pew Study: Simplification, Complification or Obfuscation," last modified November 19, 2013, accessed November 26, 2020, https://hayimherring.com/new-findings-pew-study/.

101 "Pre-State Israel: Under Ottoman Rule (1517–1917)," Jewish Virtual Library, American-Israeli Cooperative Enterprise (AICE), accessed November 26, 2020, https://www.jewishvirtuallibrary.org/ottoman-rule-1517-1917.

102 Angela Woollacott, *On Her Their Lives Depend: Munitions Workers in the Great War* (Berkeley, Los Angeles, London: University of California Press, 1994), 90.

103 "Chaim Weizmann's Acetone Patent Turns 100: A Centennial of Entrepreneurship," *Weizmann Magazine* 8 (September 27, 2015), accessed January 24, 2019, https://weizmann.ac.il/WeizmannCompass/sections/people-behind-the-science/chaim-weizmann's-acetone-patent-turns-100; Frances E. Hughes, "Local Industry Owes Much to Weizmann," Wayback Machine, accessed November 26, 2020, https://www.scribd.com/document/20112627/Local-Industry-Owes-Much-to-Weizmann.

104 "Chaim Weizmann's Acetone Patent Turns 100: A Centennial of Entrepreneurship."

105 Nabeel Shaath, "Britain Must Atone for Its Sins in Palestine: Ever Since the Balfour Declaration of 1917, Britain Has Denied Our People Their Rights," *Telegraph*, last modified October 31, 2012, accessed January 22, 2019, https://

www.telegraph.co.uk/news/worldnews/middleeast/palestinianauthority/9645925/Britain-must-atone-for-its-sins-in-Palestine.html.

106 "Pre-State Israel: The Hussein-McMahon Correspondence (July [19]15–August 1916)," Jewish Virtual Library, American-Israeli Cooperative Enterprise (AICE), accessed August 20, 2020, https://www.jewishvirtuallibrary.org/the-hussein-mcmahon-correspondence-july-1915-august-1916.

107 Fourteenth Meeting of the Arab and UK Delegations to the Conferences on Palestine on 17 March 1939, "United Nations Report of a Committee Set Up to Consider Certain Correspondence between Sir Henry McMahon (His Majesty's High Commissioner in Egypt) and the Sharif of Mecca in 1915 and 1916," His Majesty's Stationery Office, accessed August 19, 2020, https://unispal.un.org/UNISPAL.NSF/0/4C4F7515DC39195185256CF7006F878C.

108 "Memorandum of Edwin Montagu on the Anti-Semitism of the Present (British) Government: Submitted to the British Cabinet, August, 1917," The Balfour Project, last modified October 22, 2012, accessed January 22, 2019, http://www.balfourproject.org/edwin-montagu-and-zionism-1917/.

109 "Memorandum of Edwin Montagu on the Anti-Semitism of the Present (British) Government."

110 "The Covenant of the League of Nations (Including Amendments Adopted to December, 1924)," Yale Law School Lillian Goldman Law Library: Avalon Project, accessed January 22, 2019, https://avalon.law.yale.edu/20th_century/leagcov.asp.

111 F. P. Walter, A History of the League of Nations (New York: Oxford University Press, 1952), 32.

112 "League of Nations Mandate," Saylor Academy, accessed November 27, 2020, https://resources.saylor.org/wwwresources/archived/site/wp-content/uploads/2011/06/League-of-Nations-Mandate.pdf.

113 "The Covenant of the League of Nations (Including Amendments Adopted to December, 1924)."

114 "League of Nations: Mandate for Palestine," League of Nations, August 12, 1922, accessed January 22, 2019, https://unispal.un.org/DPA/DPR/unispal.nsf/0/2FCA2C68106F11AB05256BCF007BF3CB.

115 Jimmy Carter, Palestine: Peace Not Apartheid (New York: Simon & Schuster, 2006), 58.

116 "Palestine under the British Mandate," Palestinian Academic Society for the Study of International Affairs (PASSIA), accessed October 28, 2020, http://www.passia.org/maps/view/6.

117 Carter, Palestine: Peace Not Apartheid.

118 Matthew Hughes, "From Law and Order to Pacification: Britain's Suppression of the Arab Revolt in Palestine, 1936–39," Journal of Palestine Studies 39, no. 2 (Winter 2010): 6–22, accessed January 24, 2019, https://www.palestine-studies.org/sites/default/files/jps-articles/From%20Law%20and%20Order%20to%20Pacification-%20Britain%27s%20Suppression%20of%20the%20Arab%20Revolt%20in%20Palestine%2C.pdf.

119 Dan Horowitz, "Before the State: Communal Politics in Palestine under the Mandate," in *The Israeli State and Society: Boundaries and Frontiers*, ed. Baruch Kimmerling (Albany, NY: SUNY Press, 1989), 38.

120 "The Anglo-American Committee of Inquiry: Appendix IV, Palestine: Historical Background," Yale Law School Lillian Goldman Law Library: Avalon Project, accessed January 23, 2019, https://avalon.law.yale.edu/20th_century/angap04.asp.

121 Hughes, "From Law and Order to Pacification: Britain's Suppression of the Arab Revolt in Palestine, 1936–39."

122 Matthew Hughes, "A Very British Affair? British Armed Forces and the Repression of the Arab Revolt in Palestine, 1936–39 (Part Two)," *Journal of the Society for Army Historical Research* 87, no. 352 (Winter 2009), 357–373, accessed January 24, 2019, https://bura.brunel.ac.uk/bitstream/2438/3866/1/Fulltext.pdf.

123 Sam Katz, *Israeli Elite Units since 1948* (Oxford, UK: Osprey Publishing, 1988), 3–4.

124 "Question of Palestine/Partition Recommendation—UN Special Committee on Palestine (UNSCOP)—Report Addendum 1 (Annexes, Appendix and Maps)," Appendix, III. Special Note by Sir Abdur Rahman, Representative of India, (II) The Mandate and Balfour Declaration in Their Historical Setting, United Nations, The Question of Palestine, accessed January 20, 2021, https://www.un.org/unispal/document/auto-insert-186346/.

125 "Recruitment of Jews," UK Parliament—*Historic Hansard* HL Deb vol 123 cols 179–210, accessed January 23, 2019, https://api.parliament.uk/historic-hansard/lords/1942/jun/09/recruitment-of-jews#S5LV0123P0-00335.

126 *Merriam-Webster Dictionary*, s.v. "*aliyah*," accessed November 27, 2020, https://www.merriam-webster.com/dictionary/aliyah.

127 Joanna Saidel, "Yitzhak Shamir: Why We Killed Lord Moyne," *Times of Israel*, July 5, 2012, accessed September 29, 2019, https://www.timesofisrael.com/yitzhak-shamir-why-we-killed-lord-moyne/.

128 Rabbi Dr. Tzvi Hersh Weinreb, "The Unburied Corpse," *Arutz Sheva: Israel National News*, May 17, 2016, accessed October 7, 2019, http://www.israelnationalnews.com/Articles/Article.aspx/18884.

129 "Notorious Massacres of Palestinians between 1937 & 1948," *Middle East Monitor*, Fact Sheet, May 2013, accessed October 7, 2019, https://www.middleeastmonitor.com/wp-content/uploads/downloads/factsheets/ZionistMassacres_1937-48.pdf.

130 *A Survey of Palestine, Volume II* (Washington, DC: The Institute for Palestine Studies, 1991), 566.

131 Antonio Flores, "How the US Hispanic Population Is Changing," Pew Center FactTank News in the Numbers, last modified September 18, 2017, accessed February 4, 2019, https://www.pewresearch.org/fact-tank/2017/09/18/how-the-u-s-hispanic-population-is-changing/.

132 UN General Assembly, "Official Records of the Second Session of the General Assembly," supplement no. 11, United Nations Special Committee on Palestine,

Report to the General Assembly, vol. 1, A/364, ch. 2, item 122, September 3, 1947, accessed January 23, 2019, https://unispal.un.org/UNISPAL. NSF/0/07175de9fa2de563852568d3006e10f3.

133 UN General Assembly, "Official Records of the Second Session of the General Assembly," ch. 1, item 12.

134 UN General Assembly, "Official Records of the Second Session of the General Assembly," ch. 1, item 3.

135 UN General Assembly, "Official Records of the Second Session of the General Assembly," ch. 2, item 19.

136 "Memorandum of Edwin Montagu on the Anti-Semitism of the Present (British) Government: Submitted to the British Cabinet, August, 1917."

137 UN General Assembly, "Official Records of the Second Session of the General Assembly," ch. 2, item 127.

138 UN General Assembly, "Official Records of the Second Session of the General Assembly," ch. 2, item 75.

139 UN General Assembly, "Official Records of the Second Session of the General Assembly," ch. 2, item 77.

140 UN General Assembly, "Official Records of the Second Session of the General Assembly," ch. 2, items 76, 78.

141 UN General Assembly, "Official Records of the Second Session of the General Assembly," ch. 4, part 2, item 5.

142 "Chapter 3 of the Report of Sub-Committee 2 to the Ad Hoc Committee on the Palestinian Question of the UN General Assembly 1947," accessed January 23, 2019, http://www.mlwerke.de/NatLib/Pal/UN1947_Palestine-Minority-Report_Chapter3.htm#Chap3Sec03.

143 "Chapter 3 of the Report of Sub-Committee 2 to the Ad Hoc Committee on the Palestinian Question of the UN General Assembly 1947."

144 "Binationalism Not Partition," in *From Haven to Conquest: Readings in Zionism and the Palestine Problem until 1948*, ed. Walid Khalidi (Beirut: Institute for Palestine Studies, 1971), 645–702.

145 "Binationalism Not Partition," 675–677; Simha Flapan, *The Birth of Israel: Myths and Realities* (New York: Pantheon Books, 1987), 83, n. 2.

146 UN General Assembly, "Official Records of the Second Session of the General Assembly," ch. 2, items 10–19.

147 UN General Assembly, Resolution 181 (II), Future Government of Palestine (November 29, 1947), accessed September 29, 2020, https://unispal.un.org/UNISPAL.NSF/5ba47a5c6cef541b802563e000493b8c/7f0af2bd897689b-785256c330061d253?OpenDocument.

148 Michael J. Cohen, *Truman and Israel* (Berkeley: University of California Press, 1990), 157, 169–170.

149 John B, Quigley, *Palestine and Israel: A Challenge to Justice* (Durham, NC: Duke University Press, 1990), 37.

6. Israel's "War of Independence" and "Defensive Wars"

150 "About the War of Independence," The Knesset, accessed April 17, 2018, https://knesset.gov.il/holidays/eng/independence_day_war.htm.

151 Francine Klagsbrun, "Golda: A Force of Nature," *Hadassah Magazine*, Israeli Scene, September 2017, accessed February 4, 2019, https://www.hadassahmagazine.org/2017/09/27/golda-force-nature/.

152 Benny Morris, *The Birth of the Palestinian Refugee Problem Revisited* (Cambridge, UK: Cambridge University Press, 2004), 99.

153 Michael Elliott, "The War That Never Ends Begins a Violent New Chapter," *Time*, July 16, 2006, accessed September 29, 2019, http://content.time.com/time/magazine/article/0,9171,1214968,00.html.

154 Jimmy Carter, *Palestine: Peace Not Apartheid* (New York: Simon & Schuster, 2006), 58.

155 Neil Caplan, "*No End of Conflict: Rethinking Israel-Palestine* by Yossi Alpher (Review)," *Middle East Journal* 70, no. 4 (Autumn 2016), 677–678, accessed September 29, 2019, https://muse.jhu.edu/article/634697/summary.

156 "MLK at Western: Guide Detailing Dr. Martin Luther King, Jr.'s, December 18, 1963, Speech at Western Michigan University," Western Michigan University Libraries Databases, accessed February 4, 2019, https://libguides.wmich.edu/mlkatwmu/excerpts.

157 "About the War of Independence."

158 Morris, *The Birth of the Palestinian Refugee Problem Revisited*, xiv–xviii; "Mansurat al-Khayt," *Zochrot*, accessed February 4, 2019, https://www.zochrot.org/village/view?id=49262.

159 Benny Morris, *Righteous Victims: A History of the Zionist-Arab Conflict, 1881–2001* (New York: Vintage Books, 2001), 208.

160 Morris, *The Birth of the Palestinian Refugee Problem Revisited*, 311–312.

161 "We Are JNF," Jewish National Fund, accessed October 2, 2019, https://www.jnf.org/menu-3/about-jnf.

162 "Our History," Jewish National Fund, accessed October 2, 2019, https://www.jnf.org/menu-3/our-history.

163 "Israel Society & Culture: Israel Lands—Privatization or National Ownership?" Jewish Virtual Library, American-Israeli Cooperative Enterprise (AICE), accessed October 2, 2019, https://www.jewishvirtuallibrary.org/israel-lands-privatization-or-national-ownership.

164 David Margolick "Endless War," *New York Times*, last modified May 4, 2008, accessed January 13, 2021, https://www.nytimes.com/2008/05/04/books/review/Margolick-t.html.

165 "Benny Morris: What Caused the Palestinians to Flee in 1948?" Med Israel for Fred (MIFF), September 27, 2014, accessed August 19, 2016, https://www.youtube.com/watch?v=n4RA_zIqf0g.

166 "The Nakba Did Not Start or End in 1948: Key Facts and Figures on the Ethnic Cleansing of Palestine," *Al Jazeera*, last modified May 23, 2017, accessed December 4, 2017, https://www.aljazeera.com/indepth/features/2017/05/nakba-start-1948-170522073908625.html; Morris, *The Birth of the Palestinian Refugee Problem Revisited*, 596.

167 Morris, *The Birth of the Palestinian Refugee Problem Revisited*, 39.

168 "About the War of Independence."

169 "About the War of Independence."

170 "Jewish Refugees of the Israeli-Palestinian Conflict," Mideast Web, accessed March 3, 2020, http://www.mideastweb.org/refugees4.htm; "Jewish Communities Lost in the War of Independence," Israel Ministry of Foreign Affairs, accessed February 4, 2019, https://www.mfa.gov.il/MFA/AboutIsrael/Maps/Pages/Jewish%20Communities%20Lost%20in%20the%20War%20of%20Independence.aspx.

171 "Remembering the Nakba: Israeli Group Puts 1948 Palestine Back on the Map," *Guardian*, last modified May 2, 2014, accessed September 5, 2017, https://www.theguardian.com/world/2014/may/02/nakba-israel-palestine-zochrot-history; "The Nakba Did Not Start or End in 1948."

172 "Nakba Map," Zochrot Organization, accessed February 17, 2021, https://zochrot.org/en/site/nakbaMap; "Flight and Expulsion of the Palestinians in 1948," *The Nakba: Exhibition Catalogue for the Exhibition of That Name*, Zochrot Organization, 17 (n1), accessed February 19, 2021, https://zochrot.org/uploads/uploads/aa0d1cda57550fb0ad815d606cb1ccb1.pdf.

173 Benny Morris, "The New Historiography: Israel Confronts Its Past," in *Making Israel*, ed. Benny Morris (Ann Arbor: University of Michigan Press, 2007), 11–12, accessed September 22, 2019, https://www.press.umich.edu/pdf/9780472115419-ch1.pdf.

174 Ilan Pappé, *The Ethnic Cleansing of Palestine* (London: Oneworld Publications, 2014), xii-xiii.

175 "About the War of Independence."

176 Lawrence Joffe, "Yitzhak Shamir Obituary: Rightwing Prime Minister of Israel Who Took a Hardline Stance on Palestine," *Guardian*, July 1, 2012, accessed October 3, 2019, https://www.theguardian.com/world/2012/jul/01/yitzhak-shamir.

177 UN General Assembly, "Progress Report of the United Nations Mediator on Palestine Submitted to the Secretary-General for Transmission to the Members of the United Nations," September 16, 1948, accessed October 3, 2019, https://unispal.un.org/DPA/DPR/unispal.nsf/53936ddf3dd093a1852575530073f2e6/ab14d4aafc4e1bb985256204004f55fa.

178 UN General Assembly, "Progress Report of the United Nations Mediator on Palestine."

179 UN General Assembly, "Progress Report of the United Nations Mediator on Palestine."

180 UN General Assembly, "Progress Report of the United Nations Mediator on Palestine."

181 "General Lundstrom Gives Eyewitness Account of Bernadotte's Death," United Nations Department of Public Information, Press Release PAL/298, September

18, 1948, accessed October 3, 2019, https://unispal.un.org/UNISPAL. NSF/0/23E5F866FE7393B585256A680061B348.

182 Matt Plen, "Israel's War of Independence: Establishing a New Nation and Defending It," *My Jewish Learning,* accessed January 28, 2019, https://www.myjewishlearning.com/article/israels-war-of-independence/.

183 "Aeschylus (525 BC–456 BC): Greek Tragic Dramatist," *The Quotations Page,* accessed February 15, 2019, http://www.quotationspage.com/quotes/Aeschylus/.

184 "About the War of Independence."

185 "Israel's War of Independence (1947–1949)," Israel Ministry of Foreign Affairs, accessed March 3, 2020, https://www.mfa.gov.il/MFA/AboutIsrael/History/Pages/Israels%20War%20of%20Independence%20-%201947%20-%201949.aspx; "Israeli War of Independence: Background & Overview (1947–1949)," Jewish Virtual Library, American-Israeli Cooperative Enterprise (AICE), accessed March 3, 2020, https://www.jewishvirtuallibrary.org/background-and-overview-israel-war-of-independence; Plen, "Israel's War of Independence."

186 "The 1947 UN Partition Plan," Europe Israel Press Association (EIPA), accessed January 28, 2019, http://eipa.eu.com/category/information-centre/history-independence/the-un-partition-plan/.

187 *A Survey of Palestine, Volume II. and Supplement* (Washington, DC: Institute for Palestine Studies, 1991), 566.

188 *Dictionary.com,* s.v. "ethnic cleansing," accessed February 16, 2021, https://www.dictionary.com/browse/ethnic-cleansing.

189 "The Arab-Israeli War of 1948," Office of the Historian, US Department of State, accessed June 21, 2019, https://history.state.gov/milestones/1945-1952/arab-israeli-war.

190 "The Arab-Israeli War of 1948"; "Creation of Israel, 1948," Office of the Historian, US Department of State, accessed June 22, 2018, https://history.state.gov/milestones/1945-1952/creation-israel.

191 Mohammed Haddad, "Ethnic Cleansing of Palestine," Humanitarian Crises, *Al Jazeera,* last modified May 15, 2015, accessed October 16, 2017, https://www.aljazeera.com/indepth/interactive/2015/05/ethnic-cleansing-palestine-150514130231067.html; "The Nakba Did Not Start or End in 1948."

192 UN General Assembly, "Report of the Commissioner-General of the United Nations Relief and Works Agency for Palestine Refugees in the Near East (1 January–31 December 2007)," A/63/13, July 31, 2008, accessed October 16, 2017, https://www.unrwa.org/userfiles/20100118141933.pdf; "Quick Facts: The Palestinian Nakba," Institute for Middle East Understanding, last modified May 13, 2015, accessed October 16, 2017, https://imeu.org/article/quick-facts-the-palestinian-nakba.

193 Yosef Weitz, "A Solution to the Refugee Problem" (1940), cited in Maxime Rodinson, *Israel: A Colonial-Settler State?* (New York: Pathfinder Press, 1973), 15.

194 Yosef Weitz, *Retroactive Transfer: A Scheme for the Solution of the Arab Question in the State of Israel* (1948), cited in Morris, *The Birth of the Palestinian Refugee Problem Revisited*, 313.

195 Dominique Vidal, "The Expulsion of the Palestinians Re-examined," *Le Monde Diplomatique*, December 1997, accessed October 18, 2019, https://mondediplo.com/1997/12/palestine.

196 Morris, *Righteous Victims*, 139–140.

197 "Nuremberg Trial Proceedings Vol. 1: Charter of the International Military Tribunal," Yale Law School Lillian Goldman Law Library: Avalon Project, accessed October 2, 2019, https://avalon.law.yale.edu/imt/imtconst.asp#sec1.

198 "Nuremberg Trial Proceedings Vol. 1: Charter of the International Military Tribunal."

199 "The Nuremberg Trials," *Holocaust Encyclopedia*, United States Holocaust Memorial Museum, accessed October 2, 2019, https://encyclopedia.ushmm.org/content/en/article/the-nuremberg-trials.

200 Crispin Bates, "The Hidden Story of Partition and Its Legacies," *BBC, British History*, March 3, 2011, accessed October 2, 2019, http://www.bbc.co.uk/history/british/modern/partition1947_01.shtml.

201 International Law Commission, "The Charter and Judgment of the Nürnberg Tribunal: History and Analysis (Memorandum Submitted by the Secretary-General)," United Nations, A/CN.4/5, 1949, Introduction, p. v, accessed October 1, 2019, https://legal.un.org/ilc/documentation/english/a_cn4_5.pdf.

202 International Law Commission, "The Charter and Judgment of the Nürnberg Tribunal: History and Analysis (Memorandum Submitted by the Secretary-General)," 5. War Crimes, A. Definition, Article 6(b), p. 61.

203 International Law Commission, "The Charter and Judgment of the Nürnberg Tribunal: History and Analysis (Memorandum Submitted by the Secretary-General)," 6. Crimes against Humanity, A. Definition, Article 6(c), p. 65.

204 Rome Statute of the International Criminal Court, United Nations, Treaty Series, vol. 2187, no. 38544, in force on July 1, 2002, accessed October 2, 2019, https://www.icc-cpi.int/NR/rdonlyres/EA9AEFF7-5752-4F84-BE94-0A655EB30E16/0/Rome_Statute_English.pdf.

205 UN General Assembly, Resolution 181 (II), Future Government of Palestine (November 29, 1947).

206 Morris, *The Birth of the Palestinian Refugee Problem Revisited*, 318.

207 Brian Kelly, "Where There Are Refugees There Is Persecution and Inhuman Injustice," Catholicism.org, June 15, 2010, accessed October 1, 2019, https://catholicism.org/where-there-are-refugees-there-is-persecution-and-inhuman-injustice.html.

208 "Kushner Said Pushing to Close UNRWA, End Refugee Status for Palestinian Millions," *Times of Israel*, August 4, 2018, accessed January 30, 2019, https://www.timesofisrael.com/kushner-said-pushing-to-end-refugee-status-for-millions-of-palestinians/.

209 "Refugees," United Nations (Peace, Dignity and Equality on a Healthy Planet), accessed January 30, 2019, https://www.un.org/en/sections/issues-depth/refugees/.

210 Imogen Foulkes, "Global Refugee Figures Highest Since WW2, UN Says," *BBC News,* last modified June 20, 2014, accessed March 3, 2020, https://www.bbc.com/news/world-27921938; "Palestine Refugees: Locations and Numbers," Migration, *New Humanitarian,* last modified January 16, 2010, accessed March 3, 2020, http://www.thenewhumanitarian.org/report/89571/middle-east-palestinian-refugee-numberswhereabouts.

211 Syria Regional Refugee Response, Operational Portal—Refugee Situations, UNHCR, last updated September 12, 2019, accessed September 22, 2019, https://data2.unhcr.org/en/situations/syria.

212 *Merriam-Webster Dictionary,* s.v. "steal," accessed March 18, 2019, https://www.merriam-webster.com/dictionary/steal.

213 "Benny Morris: I Haven't Found Evidence of Arab Radio Broadcast Asking Palestinians to Flee in 1948," Med Israel for Fred (MIFF), September 27, 2014, accessed August 13, 2016, https://www.youtube.com/watch?v=eNwTk2lpBtU.

214 "Total Immigration to Israel by Continent and Year (1948–Present)," Jewish Virtual Library, American-Israeli Cooperative Enterprise (AICE), accessed January 11, 2019, https://www.jewishvirtuallibrary.org/total-immigration-to-israel-by-continent-per-year.

215 David Green, "Arab Jews and Myths of Expulsion and Exchange," *Palestine Chronicle,* December 20, 2009, accessed January 11, 2019, www.palestinechronicle.com/arab-jews-and-myths-of-expulsion-and-exchange/.

216 "Immigration to Israel: Total Immigration, by Country of Origin (1948–Present)," Jewish Virtual Library, American-Israeli Cooperative Enterprise (AICE), accessed January 11, 2019, www.jewishvirtuallibrary.org/total-immigration-to-israel-by-country-of-origin.

217 Mohamed Chtatou, "Moroccan Jews' Departure to Israel Regretted in Morocco," *African Exponent,* last modified January 10, 2017, accessed November 27, 2017, https://www.africanexponent.com/bpost/4528-moroccan-jews-departure-to-israel-regretted-in-morocco.

218 Green, "Arab Jews and Myths of Expulsion and Exchange."

219 "Jews in Islamic Countries: Morocco," Jewish Virtual Library, American-Israeli Cooperative Enterprise (AICE), accessed March 4, 2020, https://www.jewishvirtuallibrary.org/jews-of-morocco.

220 "Return to Morocco," *Al Jazeera,* last modified January 21, 2015, accessed November 27, 2017, https://www.aljazeera.com/programmes/aljazeeraworld/2015/01/return-morocco-2015120124346751467.html.

221 *They Were Promised the Sea: Arab Jews between Homeland and Promised Land,* directed by Kathy Wazana (Toronto: BiCom Productions, 2013).

222 "King of Morocco Lifts Ban on Jewish Emigration; Announcement Issued," *Jewish Telegraphic Agency—Daily News Bulletin* 28, no. 37 (February 23, 1961), accessed September 11, 2020, http://pdfs.jta.org/1961/1961-02-23_037.pdf.

223 Esther Meir-Glitzenstein, "Operation Magic Carpet: Constructing the Myth of the Magical Immigration of Yemenite Jews to Israel," *Israel Studies* 16, no. 3 (Fall 2011), 149–173, accessed November 27, 2017, http://muse.jhu.edu/article/448679.

224 "55 Address by Prime Minister Begin at the National Defense College, 8 August 1982," Volume 8: 1982–1984, Israel Ministry of Foreign Affairs, August 8, 1982, accessed September 28, 2019, https://www.mfa.gov.il/mfa/foreignpolicy/mfadocuments/yearbook6/pages/55%20address%20by%20prime%20minister%20begin%20at%20the%20national.aspx.

225 Amir Oren, "Israel Deceived the World in 1967, and Paid the Price for It in 1973," *Haaretz*, June 5, 2017, accessed June 13, 2020, https://www.haaretz.com/israel-news/.premium.MAGAZINE-israel-deceived-the-world-in-67-and-paid-the-price-in-73-1.5479696.

226 Joseph Finklestone, "Obituary: General Matti Peled," *The Independent*, March 16, 1995, accessed June 13, 2020, https://www.independent.co.uk/news/people/obituary-general-matti-peled-1611418.html.

227 "Six-Day War" *Encyclopædia Britannica*, May 29, 2019, accessed November 7, 2019, https://www.britannica.com/print/article/850855.

228 "Recruitment of Jews."

229 Jeremy Dean, "The Illusion of Truth," PsyBlog, December 2010, accessed March 4, 2020, https://www.spring.org.uk/2010/12/the-illusion-of-truth.php.

230 Ben Sales, "Palestinian Activists Don't Understand Why They Can't Enter the US," *Jewish Telegraphic Agency*, May 15, 2019, accessed July 30, 2019, https://www.jta.org/2019/05/15/israel/palestinian-activists-dont-understand-why-they-cant-enter-the-us; Associated Press, "Senior Palestinian Official Denied US Visa Blames 'Pettiness and Vindictiveness,'" *Washington Times*, May 13, 2019, accessed July 30, 2019, https://www.washingtontimes.com/news/2019/may/13/hanan-ashrawi-senior-palestinian-official-denied-u/.

7. Stepping Back: Why Is Israel Different?

231 "Watchdog Accuses Amnesty International of Anti-Semitic Campaign against Israel's Tourism Industry," *Jewish News Syndicate*, January 29, 2019, accessed October 4, 2019, https://www.jns.org/watchdog-accuses-amnesty-international-of-anti-semitic-campaign-against-israels-tourism-industry/.

232 "Making Peace: Fifty Years after the Prize," *Chronicles of Quaker Education* (Fall 1997), last modified August 4, 2004, accessed December 4, 2020, https://resources.finalsite.net/images/v1539221559/friendscouncilorg/dakoqqjzatvudtppkvql/636748036668302005Fall_199702005.pdf.

233 Jack Moore, "Israel Just Blacklisted a Group That Helped Jews under Nazi Rule in World War II—Here's Why," *Newsweek*, January 18, 2018, accessed October 4, 2019, https://www.newsweek.com/israel-just-blacklisted-group-helped-jewish-and-christian-nazi-victims-world-773792.

234 "FBI Urged to Reopen Probe into 1985 Assassination of Arab-American Leader Alex Odeh in California," *Democracy Now!* last modified October 17, 2013, accessed April 6, 2018, https://www.democracynow.org/2013/10/17/fbi_urged_to_reopen_probe_into.

235 Michael King, "The Uneasy Death of Riad Hamad: Investigation Continues in the Mysterious Death of an Austin Peace Activist," *Austin Chronicle*, last modified May 9, 2008, accessed July 25, 2018, https://www.austinchronicle.com/news/2008-05-09/621848/.

236 "Who We Are," If Not Now, accessed August 21, 2020, https://www.ifnotnowmovement.org/about.

237 Thomas Jefferson, *In Congress, July 4, 1776: The Unanimous Declaration of the Thirteen United States of America*, Independence Hall Association, https://www.ushistory.org/declaration/document/.

238 "McCain in His Own Words," Obituaries, National Public Radio, last modified August 26, 2018, https://www.npr.org/2018/08/26/642008005/mccain-in-his-own-words.

239 "The Palestine Exception to Free Speech: A Movement under Attack in the US," Center for Constitutional Rights, September 30, 2015, accessed October 4, 2019, https://ccrjustice.org/the-palestine-exception; "The Palestine Exception: Executive Summary," Palestine Legal, accessed October 4, 2019, https://palestinelegal.org/the-palestine-exception.

8. "The Only Democracy in the Middle East"

240 Raphael Ahren, "Netanyahu to Meet Trump at White House on February 15," *Times of Israel*, last modified January 30, 2017, accessed January 11, 2018, https://www.timesofisrael.com/netanyahu-to-meet-trump-at-white-house-on-february-15/.

241 "Full Text: George Bush's Speech to the American Enterprise Institute," *Guardian*, last modified February 27, 2003, accessed January 11, 2018, https://www.theguardian.com/world/2003/feb/27/usa.iraq2.

242 "Israel," *World Factbook*, Central Intelligence Agency, accessed January 11, 2018, https://www.cia.gov/library/publications/the-world-factbook/geos/is.html.

243 "Lebanon," *World Factbook*, Central Intelligence Agency, accessed January 11, 2018, https://www.cia.gov/library/publications/the-world-factbook/geos/le.html.

244 "United States," *World Factbook*, Central Intelligence Agency, accessed January 11, 2018, https://www.cia.gov/library/publications/the-world-factbook/geos/us.html.

245 "Turkey," *World Factbook*, Central Intelligence Agency, accessed January 11, 2018, http://teacherlink.ed.usu.edu/tlresources/reference/factbook/geos/tu.html.

246 "Iran," *World Factbook*, Central Intelligence Agency, accessed January 11, 2018, http://teacherlink.ed.usu.edu/tlresources/reference/factbook/geos/ir.html.

247 "Democracy vs. Republic," Diffen, accessed January 4, 2021, https://www.diffen.com/difference/Democracy_vs_Republic.

248 "Democracy vs. Republic."

249 "Saddam 'Wins 100% of Vote,'" *BBC News*, last modified October 16, 2002, accessed January 12, 2018, http://news.bbc.co.uk/2/hi/2331951.stm.

250 David Wasserman, "2012 National House Popular Vote Tracker," Google Sheets, Cook Political Report, 2012, accessed December 11, 2018, https://docs.google.com/spreadsheets/d/1dC1t1lUqkKTDRAWimeq8gN9UN7Zbl3X_3cN2aUkAxj0/edit#gid=0.

251 W. Gardner Selby, "Republicans Won More House Seats Than More Popular Democrats, Though Not Entirely Because of How Districts Were Drawn," *Politifact Texas*, last modified November 26, 2013, accessed January 12, 2018, https://www.politifact.com/texas/statements/2013/nov/26/lloyd-doggett/democrats-outpolled-republicans-who-landed-33-seat/.

252 *Merriam-Webster Dictionary*, s.v. "democracy," accessed January 12, 2018, https://www.merriam-webster.com/dictionary/democracy.

253 "Extract from Thomas Jefferson to William C. Jarvis," Jefferson Quotes & Family Letters, Papers of Thomas Jefferson: Retirement Series, Thomas Jefferson Foundation, Inc., September 28, 1820, accessed January 19, 2018, http://tjrs.monticello.org/letter/382.

254 "Keeping the State Archives Secret," Editorial, *Haaretz*, last modified January 18, 2018, accessed January 30, 2018, https://www.haaretz.com/opinion/editorial/.premium-keeping-the-state-archives-secret-1.5744833.

255 "Keeping the State Archives Secret."

256 Hagai El-Ad, "What Kind of Democracy Deports Human Rights Workers?" *+972 Magazine*, April 28, 2019, accessed May 4, 2019, https://972mag.com/democracy-deports-human-rights-workers/141206/.

257 Gershom Gorenberg, "How Occupation Has Damaged Israel's Democracy," *Washington Post*, last modified June 4, 2017, accessed January 12, 2018, https://www.washingtonpost.com/news/global-opinions/wp/2017/06/04/how-occupation-has-damaged-israels-democracy.

258 *Merriam-Webster Dictionary*, s.v. "Bantustan," accessed December 5, 2020, https://www.merriam-webster.com/dictionary/Bantustan.

259 United Nations Human Rights Committee, "Israeli Annexation of Parts of the Palestinian West Bank Would Break International Law: UN Experts Call on the International Community to Ensure Accountability," Office of the High Commissioner, Human Rights, United Nations, June 16, 2020, accessed January 13, 2021, https://www.ohchr.org/EN/NewsEvents/Pages/DisplayNews.aspx?NewsID=25960&LangID=E.

260 "Israel's Election Outcome Remains Unclear, But the 'Ultimate Loser' Will Be Palestinians," *Democracy Now*, September 18, 2019, accessed September 18, 2019, https://www.democracynow.org/2019/9/18/israeli_election_results_netanyahu_gantz.

261 Noura Erakat, @4noura, Twitter.com, September 17, 2019, accessed September 18, 2019, https://twitter.com/4noura/status/1173965986346803201.

262 "Knesset Approves Bill That Prevents Division of Jerusalem," *World Israel News*, last modified January 2, 2018, accessed January 19, 2018, https://worldisraelnews.com/knesset-approves-bill-prevents-division-jerusalem/.

263 Noa Landau, "Israeli Arab Lawmakers Forcefully Removed after Protesting Pence Speech," *Haaretz*, January 22, 2018, accessed December 5, 2020, https://www.haaretz.com/israel-news/watch-the-moment-israeli-arab-lawmakers-protested-pence-1.5750910, https://www.youtube.com/embed/Rd1nY9Z5QnM.

264 United Nations Security Council, "Resolution 2334 (2016)," S/RES/2334 (2016), December 23, 2016, accessed January 19, 2018, https://www.un.org/webcast/pdfs/SRES2334-2016.pdf.

265 Associated Press, "John Kerry Defends UN's Israel Vote during Farewell Speech," *Fortune*, last modified December 28, 2016, accessed January 17, 2018, https://fortune.com/2016/12/28/john-kerry-speech-israel/.

266 "Haneen Zoabi MK Talks about Israel Apartheid and Lack of Democracy," iDirectMovies, August 8, 2012, accessed March 4, 2020, https://www.youtube.com/watch?v=OEHk1bLJCBw.

267 Ruth Eglash, "20 Groups That Advocate Boycotting Israel Will Now Be Denied Entry," *Chicago Tribune*, last modified January 7, 2018, accessed January 11, 2018, https://www.chicagotribune.com/nation-world/ct-bds-organizations-banned-from-israel-20180107-story.html.

268 "AFSC among Human Rights Orgs Barred from Israel," American Friends Service Committee, January 8, 2018, accessed January 11, 2018, https://www.afsc.org/story/afsc-among-human-rights-orgs-barred-israel.

269 Yara Hawari, "Israel Is Supposedly The Only Democracy in the Middle East, Yet 4.5 Million Palestinians under Its Control Can't Vote," *The Independent*, March 17, 2015, accessed January 11, 2018, https://www.independent.co.uk/voices/comment/israel-is-supposedly-the-only-democracy-in-the-middle-east-yet-45-million-palestinians-under-its-10113950.html.

270 Tom Richardson ("Tomthepipersson"), comment to Jakob Reimann, "Israel Is an Apartheid State (Even If the UN Report Has Been Withdrawn)," *Foreign Policy Journal*, March 31, 2017, accessed January 27, 2021, https://www.foreignpolicyjournal.com/2017/03/31/israel-is-an-apartheid-state-even-if-the-un-report-has-been-withdrawn/.

9. "The Palestinian Authority"

271 "Final Report on the Palestinian Legislative Council Elections," National Democratic Institute for International Affairs, January 25, 2006, accessed January 17, 2018, https://www.ndi.org/sites/default/files/2068_ps_elect_012506.pdf.

272 "Final Report on the Palestinian Legislative Council Elections."

273 "The Florida Recount of 2000: A Nightmare That Goes On Haunting," National Public Radio, last modified November 12, 2018, accessed November 26, 2019, https://www.npr.org/2018/11/12/666812854/the-florida-recount-of-2000-a-nightmare-that-goes-on-haunting.

274 Kate Fazzini, "Iowa Caucus Debacle Is One of the Most Stunning Tech Failures Ever," *CNBC*, last modified February 4, 2020, accessed November 2, 2020, https://www.cnbc.com/2020/02/04/iowa-caucus-app-debacle-is-one-of-the-most-stunning-it-failures-ever.html.

275 Glenn Kessler, "Bush Is Conciliatory in Accepting Victory of Hamas," *Washington Post*, January 27, 2006, accessed October 4, 2019, http://www.washingtonpost.com/wp-dyn/content/article/2006/01/26/AR2006012601009_pf.html.

276 Conal Urquhart, "Palestinians Allowed to Vote in East Jerusalem, But Israel Bars Hamas from Election," *Guardian*, last modified January 15, 2006, accessed January 17, 2018, https://www.theguardian.com/world/2006/jan/16/israel.

277 Urquhart, "Palestinians Allowed to Vote in East Jerusalem, But Israel Bars Hamas from Election."

278 Urquhart, "Palestinians Allowed to Vote in East Jerusalem, But Israel Bars Hamas from Election."

279 The World Bank, "Economic Monitoring Report to the Ad Hoc Liaison Committee," April 19, 2016, accessed August 5, 2019, http://documents.worldbank.org/curated/en/780371468179658043/pdf/104808-WP-v1-2nd-revision-PUBLIC-AHLC-report-April-19-2016.pdf.

280 Greg Myre, "Israel Releases $100 Million Withheld from Palestinians," *New York Times*, January 20, 2007, accessed January 17, 2018, https://www.nytimes.com/2007/01/20/world/middleeast/20mideast.html.

281 Myre, "Israel Releases $100 Million Withheld from Palestinians."

282 Myre, "Israel Releases $100 Million Withheld from Palestinians."

283 "Israel Suspends Cash to Palestinians after Hamas Deal," *BBC News*, last modified May 1, 2011, accessed January 17, 2018, https://www.bbc.com/news/world-middle-east-13254155.

284 Ruth Eglash, "Israel Withholds Tax Revenue from Palestinian Authority as Dispute Escalates," *Washington Post*, last modified January 3, 2015, accessed January 17, 2018, https://www.washingtonpost.com/world/middle_east/israel-withholds-tax-revenues-from-palestinian-authority-as-dispute-escalates/2015/01/03/3718e5c4-9378-11e4-a66f-0ca5037a597d_story.html?utm_term=.ec56cbc437e8.

285 Glenn Kessler, "Bush Is Conciliatory in Accepting Victory of Hamas," *Washington Post*, last modified January 27, 2006, accessed January 17, 2018 http://www.washingtonpost.com/wp-dyn/content/article/2006/01/26/AR2006012601009.html.

286 Kessler, "Bush Is Conciliatory in Accepting Victory of Hamas."

287 "Israel arrests top Hamas officials," *Chicago Tribune*, last modified June 29, 2006, accessed January 8, 2021, http://articles.chicagotribune.com/2006-06-29/news/0606300358_1_hamas-leaders-gaza-israeli-tanks-and-bulldozers.

288 Associated Press, "Israel Arrests Another Hamas Lawmaker in West Bank," *Deseret News*, last modified January 24, 2012, accessed January 17, 2018, https://

www.deseretnews.com/article/700218377/Israel-arrests-another-Hamas-lawmaker-in-West-Bank.html.

289 Noura Erakat, @4noura, Twitter.com, September 17, 2019, accessed September 18, 2019, https://twitter.com/4noura/status/1173981171103031296.

290 Jessica Purkiss and Ahmad Nafi, "Palestinian Security Cooperation with Israel" *Middle East Monitor*, Fact Sheet, October 28, 2015, accessed October 4, 2019, https://www.middleeastmonitor.com/wp-content/uploads/downloads/factsheets/20151028_FactSheet-PalestinianSecurityCooperationWithIsrael-web.pdf.

291 Hillel Frisch, "Israel and Abbas: The Fruits of Security Cooperation," *Jerusalem Post*, December 18, 2018, accessed October 5, 2019, https://www.jpost.com/Opinion/Israel-and-Abbas-The-fruits-of-security-cooperation-574722.

292 Neri Zilber, "What Will Happen If the Palestinians Really End Security Cooperation?" *The Tower*, no. 25 (April 2015), accessed October 4, 2019, http://www.thetower.org/article/what-will-happen-if-the-palestinians-really-end-security-cooperation/.

293 Steven R. Weisman, "Sharon: Pullout Will Proceed," *Chicago Tribune*, May 25, 2005, accessed January 8, 2021, https://www.chicagotribune.com/news/ct-xpm-2005-05-25-0505250215-story.html.

294 Mohammed Assadi, "U.S. Plans to Expand Program for Abbas's Forces," *Reuters*, last modified April 27, 2009, accessed August 9, 2019, https://www.reuters.com/article/us-palestinians-usa-security-sb/u-s-plans-to-expand-program-for-abbass-forces-idUKTRE53Q5ZD20090427.

295 Agencies, "Israeli-Palestinian Security Ties Likely to Continue Despite US Aid Freeze," *Times of Israel*, February 1, 2019, accessed October 5, 2019, https://www.timesofisrael.com/israeli-palestinian-security-ties-likely-to-continue-despite-us-aid-freeze/.

296 "Palestine (State of) 2018," Amnesty International, accessed August 9, 2019, https://www.amnesty.org/en/countries/middle-east-and-north-africa/palestine-state-of/report-palestine-state-of/.

297 "Palestine: Authorities Must Drop Charges against Human Rights Defender Issa Amro for Peaceful Criticism," Amnesty International, 27 March 2019, accessed August 9, 2019, https://www.amnesty.org/en/latest/news/2019/03/palestine-authorities-must-drop-charges-against-human-rights-defender-issa-amro-for-peaceful-criticism/.

298 "Palestinian Public Opinion Poll No (54)," Palestinian Center for Policy and Survey Research (PSR), January 15, 2015, accessed August 14, 2019, http://www.pcpsr.org/sites/default/files/poll-54-Dec2014-English%20new.pdf.

299 "15 Palestinian Supreme Court Justices Resigned," *Middle East Monitor*, September 7, 2018, accessed August 9, 2019, https://www.middleeastmonitor.com/20180907-15-palestinian-supreme-court-justices-resigned/.

300 "Hamas Rejects Abbas's Plan to Dissolve Palestinian Parliament," *Al-Jazeera*, December 23, 2018, accessed August 9, 2019, https://www.aljazeera.com/news/2018/12/hamas-rejects-abbas-plan-dissolve-palestinian-parliament-181223101257989.html.

10. "People" in Israel

301 Onnesha Roychoudhuri, "Made in Palestine: Is It Possible to Speak Openly in America about the Palestinian Plight? The Reaction towards One Art Exhibit Suggests Not," *Mother Jones*, last modified May 11, 2005, accessed April 24, 2018, https://www.motherjones.com/media/2005/05/made-palestine-1/.

302 "ICJ Advisory Opinion on the Legal Consequences of the Construction of a Wall in the OPT—Full Text," The Question of Palestine, United Nations, 2004, accessed September 3, 2020, https://www.un.org/unispal/document/auto-insert-178825/.

303 "ICJ Advisory Opinion on the Legal Consequences of the Construction of a Wall in the OPT—Full Text," paragraph 118.

304 "ICJ Advisory Opinion on the Legal Consequences of the Construction of a Wall in the OPT—Full Text," paragraph 118.

305 Adel Darwish, "Abu Daoud: Palestinian Terrorist Who Masterminded the 1972 Olympic Massacre," *The Independent*, July 6, 2010, accessed August 5, 2019, https://www.independent.co.uk/news/obituaries/abu-daoud-palestinian-terrorist-who-masterminded-the-1972-olympic-massacre-2019092.html.

306 Carolyn L. Karcher, ed., *Reclaiming Judaism from Zionism: Stories of Personal Transformation* (Northampton, MA: Olive Branch Press, 2019), 70.

307 Daniel J. Elazar, "How Religious Are Israeli Jews?," Jerusalem Center for Public Affairs, accessed August 8, 2018, http://www.jcpa.org/dje/articles2/howrelisr.htm.

308 Roee Nahmias, "'Marriage to an Arab Is National Treason,'" *Ynet News*, March 27, 2007, accessed September 2, 2019, https://www.ynetnews.com/articles/0,7340,L-3381978,00.html.

11. Gaza and "Gaza Wars"

309 Amir Cohen (Reuters), "Rocket Fired from Gaza on Israel's Independence Day," *Newsweek*, last modified April 23, 2015, accessed April 17, 2018, https://www.newsweek.com/rocket-fired-gaza-israels-independence-day-324537.

310 Allan Arkush, "Moshe Dayan: Eulogy for Ro'i Rotberg," Tikvah Society, February 11, 2021, accessed April 5, 2021, https://tikvahfund.org/collegiate-forum/moshe-dayan-eulogy-for-roi-rothberg/.

311 Noam Chomsky, "Noam Chomsky on Finkelstein's Gaza Book," NormanFinkelstein.com, October 3, 2018, accessed August 8, 2019, http://normanfinkelstein.com/2018/10/03/noam-chomsky-on-finkelsteins-gaza-book/; Noam Chomsky, "'A Hideous Atrocity': Noam Chomsky on Israel's Assault on Gaza & U.S. Support for the Occupation," interview by Amy Goodman and Juan González, *Democracy Now*, August 7, 2014, accessed August 8, 2019, https://www.democracynow.org/2014/8/7/a_hideous_atrocity_noam_chomsky_on.

312 "Some 320,000 West Bank ID Holders Permitted into East Jerusalem for Ramadan Friday Prayers," UN Office for the Coordination of Humanitarian Affairs (OCHA), Occupied Palestinian Territory, last modified July 16, 2019, accessed February 2, 2021, https://www.ochaopt.org/content/some-320000-west-bank-id-holders-permitted-east-jerusalem-ramadan-friday-prayers.

313 "Number of W Bank Settlers Rises," *BBC News*, last modified August 26, 2005, accessed August 12, 2019, http://news.bbc.co.uk/2/hi/middle_east/4188216.stm.

314 "Gaza Ten Years Later," United Nations, UN Country Team in the Occupied Palestinian Territory, July 2017, accessed December 10, 2020, https://unsco.unmissions.org/sites/default/files/gaza_10_years_later_-_11_july_2017.pdf.

315 "Gaza Ten Years Later."

316 "List of United States Cities by Population Density," Wikipedia, accessed October 4, 2017, https://en.wikipedia.org/wiki/List_of_United_States_cities_by_population_density.

317 Danielle Ziri, "Israeli Population Density on the Rise, CBS Report Shows," *Jerusalem Post*, last modified September 17, 2013, accessed October 18, 2017, http://www.jpost.com/National-News/Israeli-population-density-on-the-rise-CBS-report-shows-326322.

318 "Country Comparison: Median Age," *World Factbook*, Central Intelligence Agency, accessed December 10, 2020, https://www.cia.gov/library/publications/the-world-factbook/rankorder/2177rank.html#gz.

319 United Nations Relief and Works Agency for Palestine Refugees in the Near East (UNRWA), "Where We Work: Gaza Strip," accessed October, 10, 2017, https://www.unrwa.org/where-we-work/gaza-strip.

320 Gisha: Legal Center for Freedom of Movement, "Gaza Unemployment Rate in the Second Quarter of 2020: 49.1%," UN Office for the Coordination of Humanitarian Affairs (OCHA): OCHA Services Reliefweb, last modified October 3, 2020, accessed December 10, 2020, https://reliefweb.int/report/occupied-palestinian-territory/gaza-unemployment-rate-second-quarter-2020-491#:~:text=According%20to%20figures%20(Arabic)%20by,%2C%20now%20standing%20at%2049.1%25.

321 "Israel," *World Factbook*, Central Intelligence Agency, accessed September 9, 2020, https://www.cia.gov/library/publications/the-world-factbook/geos/is.html; "Gaza Strip," *World Factbook*, Central Intelligence Agency, accessed September 9, 2020, https://www.cia.gov/library/publications/the-world-factbook/geos/gz.html.

322 "Gaza Strip: Early Warning Indicators—December 2019," UN Office for the Coordination of Humanitarian Affairs (OCHA): Occupied Palestinian Territory, January 13, 2020, accessed March 14, 2020, https://www.ochaopt.org/sites/default/files/early_warning_indicator_december_2019.pdf.

323 "2017 Gaza Crisis: Urgent Funding Appeal," United Nations Office for the Coordination of Humanitarian Affairs, Humanitarian Country Team, accessed March 14, 2020, https://www.ochaopt.org/sites/default/files/gaza_urgent_humanitarian_funding_v5_3july2017_10am_1.pdf.

324 "Gaza Strip: Early Warning Indicators—December 2019."

325 "Study Warns Water Sanitation Crisis in Gaza May Cause Disease Outbreak and Possible Epidemic," UN Office for the Coordination of Humanitarian Affairs (OCHA): Occupied Palestinian Territory, last modified November 16, 2018, accessed March 14, 2020, https://www.ochaopt.org/content/study-warns-water-sanitation-crisis-gaza-may-cause-disease-outbreak-and-possible-epidemic.

326 "Gaza Strip: Early Warning Indicators—December 2019."

327 "Israel-Palestinian Conflict: Life in the Gaza Strip," *BBC News*, May 15, 2018, accessed March 14, 2020, https://www.bbc.com/news/world-middle-east-20415675.

328 "Occupied Palestinian Territory—Gaza," Health Cluster Bulletin, November–December 2019, World Health Organization, UN Office for the Coordination of Humanitarian Affairs (OCHA): OCHA Services Reliefweb, accessed February 2, 2021, https://reliefweb.int/report/occupied-palestinian-territory/occupied-palestinian-territory-gaza-health-cluster-bulletin-0.

329 Fred de Sam Lazaro, "Water Crisis May Make Gaza Strip Uninhabitable by 2020," *PBS News Hour*, January 1, 2019, accessed March 14, 2020, https://www.pbs.org/newshour/show/water-crisis-may-make-gaza-strip-uninhabitable-by-2020.

330 Jen Marlowe, "Parting the Brown Sea: Sewage Crisis Threatens Gaza's Access to Water," *Al Jazeera America*, April 18, 2015, accessed August 8, 2019, http://america.aljazeera.com/articles/2015/4/18/sewage-crisis-threatens-gazas-access-to-water.html.

331 Marlowe, "Parting the Brown Sea."

332 Shira Efron, Jordan R. Fischbach, Ilana Blum, Rouslan I. Karimov, and Melinda Moore, "The Public Health Impacts of Gaza's Water Crisis: Analysis and Policy Options," RAND Corporation, 2018, accessed August 8, 2019, https://www.rand.org/pubs/research_reports/RR2515.html.

333 Efron et al., "The Public Health Impacts of Gaza's Water Crisis," e-book, pp. 16–17.

334 Efron et al., "The Public Health Impacts of Gaza's Water Crisis," e-book, 48.

335 Michelle Malka Grossman, "'Gaza Sewage Crisis Is a Ticking Timebomb for Israel,'" *Jerusalem Post*, March 17, 2016, accessed August 8, 2019, https://www.jpost.com/Arab-Israeli-Conflict/Gaza-sewage-crisis-is-a-ticking-timebomb-for-Israel-448335.

336 "Gaza Ten Years Later."

337 "Gaza Ten Years Later."

338 "Gaza Ten Years Later."

339 "Gaza Strip: Early Warning Indicators—June 2019," UN Office for the Coordination of Humanitarian Affairs (OCHA): Occupied Palestinian Territory, July 17, 2019, accessed August 9, 2019, https://www.ochaopt.org/sites/default/files/early_warning_indicator_june_2019_23_07_2019.pdf.

340 "Gaza Strip Electricity Supply," UN Office for the Coordination of Humanitarian Affairs (OCHA): Occupied Palestinian Territory, accessed September 4, 2020, https://www.ochaopt.org/page/gaza-strip-electricity-supply; Rasha Abou Jalai, "Power Crisis Threatens Already Fragile Situation in Gaza," *Al-Monitor*, August 26, 2020, accessed September 4, 2020, https://www.al-monitor.com/pulse/originals/2020/08/gaza-power-plant-israel-ban-fuel-power-cuts-deteriorate.html.

341 "(IV) Geneva Convention Relative to the Protection of Civilian Persons in Time of War of 12 August 1949," Part III, "Status and Treatment of Protected Persons," Section I, "Provisions Common to the Territories of the Parties to the Conflict and to Occupied Territories," Article 33, "Individual Responsibility, Collective Penalties, Pillage, Reprisals," accessed January 15, 2021, https://www.un.org/en/genocideprevention/documents/atrocity-crimes/Doc.33_GC-IV-EN.pdf.

342 "Israel/Gaza Operation 'Cast Lead': 22 Days of Death and Destruction," Amnesty International, MDE 15/015/2009, July 2, 2009, accessed January 15, 2018, https://www.amnesty.org/en/documents/MDE15/015/2009/en/.

343 Yaniv Kubovich, Jack Khoury, Almog Ben Zikri, Nir Hasson, and, Noa Landau, "Jerusalem Embassy and Gaza Protests: 59 Palestinians Killed by Israeli Gunfire at Border," *Haaretz*, May 14, 2018, accessed September 4, 2020, https://www.haaretz.com/middle-east-news/u-s-embassy-gaza-protests-and-nakba-day-live-updates-1.6078190.

344 Arkush, "Moshe Dayan."

345 "Operation Pillar of Defense: Selected Statements," Israel Ministry of Foreign Affairs, November 10, 2012, accessed December 11, 2020, https://mfa.gov.il/MFA/PressRoom/2012/Pages/Operation_Pillar_of_Defense-Statements.aspx.

346 "'There Is No Israeli Occupation of Gaza,' Netanyahu Tells UN Chief," United with Israel, last modified October 13, 2014, accessed December 11, 2020, https://unitedwithisrael.org/there-is-no-israeli-occupation-of-gaza-netanyahu-tells-un-chief/.

347 Miriam Berger, "Israeli Spraying of Herbicide near Gaza Harming Palestinian Crops," *Guardian*, July 19, 2019, accessed August 9, 2019, https://www.theguardian.com/world/2019/jul/19/israeli-spraying-of-herbicide-near-gaza-harming-palestinian-crops.

348 Abier Almasri, "Israeli Forces Kill Gaza Fisherman at Sea: Fisherman's Family Already Lost Four Members in Israeli Attacks," Human Rights Watch, June 18, 2017, accessed August 9, 2019, https://www.hrw.org/news/2017/06/18/israeli-forces-kill-gaza-fisherman-sea.

349 Almasri, "Israeli Forces Kill Gaza Fisherman at Sea."

350 Almasri, "Israeli Forces Kill Gaza Fisherman at Sea."

351 "A Chronology: Key Moments in the Clinton-Lewinsky Saga," *All Politics CNN*, accessed October 18, 2017, http://www.cnn.com/ALLPOLITICS/1998/resources/lewinsky/timeline/; "Lewinsky Has Spoken," *All Politics CNN*, January 26, 1998, http://www.cnn.com/ALLPOLITICS/1998/01/26/clinton.main/.

352 "Gaza Ten Years Later."

353 UN General Assembly, Human Rights Council, "Report of the International Fact-Finding Mission to Investigate Violations of International Law, Including International Humanitarian and Human Rights Law, Resulting from the Israeli Attacks on the Flotilla of Ships Carrying Humanitarian Assistance," September 27, 2010, accessed August 9, 2019, https://www2.ohchr.org/english/bodies/hrcouncil/docs/15session/A.HRC.15.21_en.pdf.

354 "Situation on Registered Vessels of Comoros, Greece and Cambodia: Article 53(1) Report," Office of the Prosecutor, International Criminal Court, Introduction, item 27, November 6, 2014, accessed February 22, 2018, http://opiniojuris.org/wp-content/uploads/2014-11-03-Final-Report-on-Situation-ICC-01.13.pdf.

355 "Situation on Registered Vessels of Comoros, Greece and Cambodia: Article 53(1) Report."

356 "Situation on Registered Vessels of Comoros, Greece and Cambodia: Article 53(1) Report," Introduction, item 28, which cites UN International Criminal Tribunal for the Former Yugoslavia (ICTY), *Prosecutor v. Naletilić and Martinović*, Judgement, Case No. IT-98-34-T, 31 March 2003, para. 217 (footnotes omitted). *See also U.S. v. Wilhelm List et al.*, Nuremberg Military Tribunal, 8 Law Reports of Major War Criminal 38 (1949), pp. 55–56.

357 Henriette Chacar, "Israeli Incursions Into Gaza Are the Rule, Not the Exception," *+972 Magazine*, November 12, 2018, accessed August 9, 2019, https://972mag.com/israeli-incursions-in-gaza-are-the-rule-not-exception/138600/.

358 "Gaza Strip," B'Tselem: The Israeli Information Center for Human Rights in the Occupied Territories, last modified November 11, 2017, accessed August 9, 2019, http://www.btselem.org/gaza_strip.

359 Ban Ki-moon, "Remarks at the Cairo Conference on Palestine," United Nations Secretary-General, October 12, 2014, accessed April 27, 2020, https://www.un.org/sg/en/content/sg/speeches/2014-10-12/remarks-cairo-conference-palestine.

360 Charles Glass, "As Gaza Sinks into Desperation, a New Book Makes the Case against Israeli Brutality," *Intercept*, May 13, 2018, accessed August 9, 2019, https://theintercept.com/2018/05/13/as-gaza-sinks-into-desperation-a-new-book-makes-the-case-against-israeli-brutality/.

361 "Gaza Strip," *World Factbook*.

362 John Soos, "There Is No 'Post' Traumatic Stress in Gaza Because the Trauma Is Continuous," *Mondoweiss*, January 28, 2016, accessed August 9, 2019, https://mondoweiss.net/2016/01/there-is-no-post-traumatic-stress-in-gaza-because-the-trauma-is-continuous/.

363 "What is 'The Great Return March?'", American Friends Service Committee, April 19, 2019, accessed February 25, 2021, https://www.afsc.org/blogs/news-and-commentary/what-is-great-return-march.

364 "77th Friday of Demonstrations in Gaza: Protester Killed and 57 Wounded, including 23 Children, One Woman and One Paramedic," Al Mezan Center

For Human Rights, October 4, 2019, accessed February 25, 2021, http://www.mezan.org/en/post/23584.

365 Fares Akram, "Gaza Protests Driven by Desperation, Hamas Organization," Associated Press, April 4, 2018, accessed August 9, 2019, https://www.apnews.com/b97a7a87ad7d4a9783a6b448e0ca771d.

366 "Gilad Shalit," *Haaretz*, accessed October 10, 2017, https://www.haaretz.com/misc/tags/TAG-gilad-shalit-1.5599152.

367 "Gilad Shalit: Red Cross Demands Proof Israeli Is Alive," *BBC News*, last modified June 23, 2011, accessed August 12, 2019, https://www.bbc.com/news/world-middle-east-13888508.

368 Jack Moore, "Hamas Releases New Footage of Gilad Shalit in Captivity," *Newsweek*, last modified January 4, 2016, accessed October 12, 2017, https://www.newsweek.com/hamas-releases-new-footage-gilad-shalit-captivity-411152.

369 "Palestinian prisoners taken to Israel-Egypt border as part of Gilad Shalit exchange," *The Telegraph*, October 18, 2011, accessed August 12, 2019, https://www.telegraph.co.uk/news/newsvideo/8833227/Palestinian-prisoners-taken-to-Israel-Egypt-border-as-part-of-Gilad-Shalit-exchange.html.

370 Avi Issacharoff, "Hamas Official Denies His Group Has Upped Demands in Prison-Swap Talks," *Times of Israel*, last modified August 29, 2017, accessed October 12, 2017, https://www.timesofisrael.com/hamas-official-denies-his-group-has-upped-demands-in-prisoner-swap-talks/.

371 *Merriam-Webster Dictionary*, s.v. "impunity," accessed October 18, 2017, https://www.merriam-webster.com/dictionary/impunity.

372 "Netanyahu: There's a Limit to Price Israel Will Pay to Free Soldier," *CNN*, July 1, 2010, accessed September 28, 2019, http://www.cnn.com/2010/WORLD/meast/07/01/israel.netanyahu.shalit/index.html.

373 Gil Stern Stern Hoffman, "'If I Were Palestinian I'd Kidnap Soldiers,'" *Jerusalem Post*, March 14, 2012, accessed September 28, 2019, https://www.jpost.com/Diplomacy-and-Politics/If-I-were-Palestinian-Id-kidnap-soldiers.

374 "Peace to Prosperity: A Vision to Improve the Lives of the Palestinian and Israeli People," Whitehouse.gov., January 2020, accessed December 14, 2020, https://www.whitehouse.gov/wp-content/uploads/2020/01/Peace-to-Prosperity-0120.pdf.

375 "Trump Middle East Plan: Palestinians Reject 'Conspiracy,'" *BBC News*, January 29, 2020, accessed August 28, 2020, https://www.bbc.com/news/world-middle-east-51292865.

376 "Amira Hass 2020 3 Min Clip," Freedom Flotilla Coalition, August 23, 2020, accessed August 28, 2020, https://youtu.be/xeNBLfg_whY.

377 Alistair Dawber, "Tales from Gaza: What Is Life Really Like in 'the World's Largest Outdoor Prison'?" *The Independent*, last modified April 13, 2013, https://www.independent.co.uk/news/world/middle-east/tales-from-gaza-what-is-life-really-like-in-the-worlds-largest-outdoor-prison-8567611.html.

378 "Behind the Headlines: The Myth of an Israeli Siege on Gaza," Israel Ministry of Foreign Affairs, August 17, 2014, accessed April 27, 2020, https://www.mfa. gov.il/MFA/ForeignPolicy/Issues/Pages/The-myth-of-an-Israeli-siege-on-Gaza-17-Aug-2014.aspx.

379 "Gaza Strip," UN Office for the Coordination of Humanitarian Affairs (OCHA): Occupied Palestinian Territory, accessed October 18, 2017, https://www.ochaopt. org/location/gaza-strip.

380 Adel Hana, "UN Chief Decries 'Dramatic' Humanitarian Crisis in Gaza," Associated Press, last modified August 30, 2017, accessed October 4, 2017, https://apnews.com/bb250f481dc64b2380d5118113b84555.

381 Robert Booth, "Israeli Attack on Gaza Flotilla Sparks International Outrage," Guardian, last modified May 31, 2010, accessed October 18, 2017, https://www. theguardian.com/world/2010/may/31/israeli-attacks-gaza-flotilla-activists.

382 Asher Schechter, "The Orwellian Logic of Israel's Blockade of Gaza," Haaretz, last modified July 2, 2015, accessed April 27, 2020, https://www.haaretz.com/ opinion/.premium-the-orwellian-logic-of-israels-blockade-of-gaza-1.5374915; Asher Schechter, "The Orwellian Logic of Israel's Blockade of Gaza," Palestine Project, last modified July 2, 2015, accessed October 3, 2017, https://medium.com/@ thepalestineproject/the-orwellian-logic-of-israel-s-blockade-of-gaza-4f80fe41f101.

383 George Orwell, 1984 (New York: Alfred A. Knopf, 1949), 8.

384 Merriam-Webster Dictionary, s.v. "piracy," accessed April 3, 2019, https://www. merriam-webster.com/dictionary/piracy.

385 Isabel Kershner and Majd Al Waheidi, "Israel Halts Yacht Trying to Break Its Blockade of Gaza Strip," New York Times, last modified October 5, 2016, accessed October 3, 2017, https://www.nytimes.com/2016/10/06/world/ middleeast/gaza-israel-blockade-activists-hamas.html.

386 UN General Assembly, Human Rights Council, "Human Rights Situation in the Occupied Palestinian Territory, including East Jerusalem," A/HRC/24/30, Introduction, item 11, August 22, 2013, accessed April 27, 2020, http:// www.ohchr.org/EN/HRBodies/HRC/RegularSessions/Session24/Documents/A_ HRC_24_30_ENG.doc.

387 "Guide: Gaza under Blockade," BBC News, last modified July 6, 2010, accessed October 18, 2017, http://news.bbc.co.uk/2/hi/middle_east/7545636. stm#businesses.

388 Michael Hirst, "Mid-East Crisis: The Blockade of Gaza—in 60 Seconds," BBC News, last modified August 13, 2014, accessed April 27, 2020, https://www.bbc. com/news/av/world-middle-east-28757657/mid-east-crisis-the-blockade-of-gaza-in-60-seconds.

389 "King Bibi: A Parable of Modern Populism," Economist, March 30, 2019, accessed January 15, 2021, https://www.economist.com/leaders/2019/03/30/ binyamin-netanyahu-a-parable-of-modern-populism.

390 Sharon Weinberger, "Donkey Business: The Only Zebra in Gaza," Slate, last modified July 23, 2009, accessed September 24, 2017, https://slate.com/

news-and-politics/2009/07/the-only-zoos-in-the-world-where-the-animals-are-smuggled-through-tunnels.html; Reuters, "Rescued Gaza Zoo Animals Move to New Sanctuaries," *Guardian*, last modified August 24, 2016, accessed September 24, 2017, https://www.theguardian.com/world/2016/aug/24/rescued-gaza-zoo-animals-tiger-porcupines-move-to-new-sanctuaries.

391 "Israel: Stop Blocking School Supplies from Entering Gaza," Human Rights Watch, last modified October 11, 2009, accessed April 27, 2020, https://www.hrw.org/news/2009/10/11/israel-stop-blocking-school-supplies-entering-gaza.

392 Howard Schweber, "Israel's Blockade of Gaza: What Items Are Allowed In?" *Huffpost*, updated May 25, 2011, accessed February 1, 2021, https://www.huffpost.com/entry/israels-blockade-of-gaza_b_605780?guccounter=1.

393 Peter Hessler, "Egypt's Failed Revolution: President Abdel Fattah El-Sisi Has Unwittingly Revealed More about His Country's Political Structures Than Anybody Could Have Imagined," *New Yorker*, December 26, 2016, accessed September 15, 2019, https://www.newyorker.com/magazine/2017/01/02/egypts-failed-revolution.

394 Steve Clemons, "Sgt. Chuck Hagel Still: Talking with the Defense Secretary," *Huffpost*, October 12, 2013, updated December 6, 2017, accessed January 16, 2021, https://www.huffpost.com/entry/sgt-chuck-hagel-still-tal_b_4091407; Reid Standish, "Egypt's Sisi on to Hagel's Fractured Legacy," *Foreign Policy*, November 25, 2014, accessed January 16, 2021, https://foreignpolicy.com/2014/11/25/egypts-sisi-piles-on-to-hagels-fractured-legacy/.

395 "Egypt Crisis: Army Ousts President Mohammed Morsi," *BBC*, July 4, 2013, accessed August 16, 2019, https://www.bbc.com/news/world-middle-east-23173794.

396 Ezzedine C. Fishere, "Sissi's Constitutional Coup Threatens Egypt's Stability," *Washington Post*, February 19, 2019, accessed September 15, 2019, https://www.washingtonpost.com/opinions/2019/02/19/sisis-constitutional-coup-threatens-egypts-stability/?noredirect=on.

397 Ahmed Aboulenein, "Egyptian President Upstages World Leaders to Congratulate Trump," *Reuters*, November 9, 2016, accessed September 15, 2019, https://uk.reuters.com/article/uk-usa-election-reaction-sisi-idUKKBN13425B.

398 Nancy A. Youssef, Vivian Salama and Michael C. Bender, "Trump, Awaiting Egyptian Counterpart at Summit, Called Out for 'My Favorite Dictator," *Wall Street Journal*, September 13, 2019, accessed September 28, 2019, https://www.wsj.com/articles/trump-awaiting-egyptian-counterpart-at-summit-called-out-for-my-favorite-dictator-11568403645.

399 "Egypt and Israel," *Jerusalem Post*, last modified October 25, 2016, accessed April 3, 2019, https://www.jpost.com/Opinion/Egypt-and-Israel-470853.

400 "Agreed Documents on Movement and Access from and to Gaza," Israel Ministry of Foreign Affairs, November 15, 2005, accessed October 18, 2017, https://www.mfa.gov.il/mfa/foreignpolicy/peace/mfadocuments/pages/agreed%20documents%20on%20movement%20and%20access%20from%20and%20to%20gaza%2015-nov-2005.aspx.

401 "Agreed Documents on Movement and Access from and to Gaza."

402 Linah Alsaafin, "The Colour-Coded Israeli ID System for Palestinians," *Al Jazeera*, November 18, 2017, accessed January 16, 2021, https://www.aljazeera.com/news/2017/11/18/the-colour-coded-israeli-id-system-for-palestinians/.

403 "Agreed Documents on Movement and Access from and to Gaza."

404 "Agreed Documents on Movement and Access from and to Gaza."

405 "Agreed Documents on Movement and Access from and to Gaza."

406 "Gaza Strip: Rafah Crossing," B'Tselem: The Israeli Information Center for Human Rights in the Occupied Territories, January 1, 2015, accessed February 2, 2021, https://www.btselem.org/gaza-strip/gaza-strip-rafah-crossing.

407 Shaul Shay, "Egypt's War against the Tunnels between Sinai and Gaza Strip," IPS Publications: Interdisciplinary Center (IDC) Herzliya, Institute for Policy and Strategy (IPS), Lauder School of Government, Diplomacy and Strategy, January 2016, accessed August 16, 2019, https://www.idc.ac.il/he/research/ips/Documents/publication/5/EgyptTunnelsShaulShay01-16.pdf.

408 Shay, "Egypt's War against the Tunnels between Sinai and Gaza Strip."

409 Jeremy M. Sharp, "The Egypt-Gaza Border and Its Effect on Israeli-Egyptian Relations," *CRS Report for Congress,* order code RL34346, Congressional Research Service, February 1, 2008, accessed August 16, 2019, https://fas.org/sgp/crs/mideast/RL34346.pdf.

410 "Strengthening America's Security in the Middle East Act of 2019," S. 1, 116th Cong. (2019), accessed August 16, 2019, https://www.congress.gov/bill/116th-congress/senate-bill/1/text.

411 Peter Beaumont, "Hamas Hands Control of Gaza Crossings to Palestinian Authority," *Guardian*, last modified November 1, 2017, accessed April 3, 2019, https://www.theguardian.com/world/2017/nov/01/hamas-hand-over-control-of-crossings-to-palestinian-authority.

412 "Palestinian Authority Removes Staff from Gaza-Egypt Crossing," *BBC News*, last modified January 7, 2019, accessed April 3, 2019, https://www.bbc.com/news/world-middle-east-46782179.

413 Dictionary.com, s.v. "blockade," accessed October 18, 2017, https://www.dictionary.com/browse/blockade?s=t.

414 "The Agreement on Movement and Access One Year On," UN Office for the Coordination of Humanitarian Affairs (OCHA): Occupied Palestinian Territory, November 2006, accessed January 16, 2021, http://www.ochaopt.org/documents/ama_one_year_on_nov06_final.pdf.

415 John Crace, "Why Is Israel Picking on Ducks?" *Guardian*, March 7, 2012, accessed December 16, 2020, https://www.theguardian.com/world/shortcuts/2012/mar/07/israel-picking-on-ducks.

416 Gilbert Achcar, "US Imperial Strategy in the Middle East," *Monthly Review*, February 1, 2004, accessed August 9, 2019, https://monthlyreview.org/2004/02/01/u-s-imperial-strategy-in-the-middle-east/.

417 "White House Confirms Sharon, Abbas Visits," *CNN World*, July 17, 2003, accessed August 9, 2019, http://edition.cnn.com/2003/WORLD/meast/07/17/mideast.invites/.

418 Jill Lawless and Maria Cheng, Associated Press, "What Is Polonium, and How Deadly Is It?" *NBC News*, November 7, 2013, accessed January 16, 2021, https://www.nbcnews.com/news/world/what-polonium-how-deadly-it-flna8C11551753; "Angelique Chrisafis and Harriet Sherwood, "Yasser Arafat May Have Been Poisoned with Polonium, Tests Show," *Guardian*, November 6, 2013, accessed August 9, 2019, https://www.theguardian.com/world/2013/nov/06/yasser-arafat-poisoned-polonium-tests-scientists.

419 "Palestinian, Israeli Leaders Announce Cease-Fire," *CNN World*, February 9, 2005, accessed August 9, 2019, http://www.cnn.com/2005/WORLD/meast/02/08/mideast/.

420 Steven R. Weisman, "Sharon: Pullout Will Proceed," *Chicago Tribune*, May 25, 2005, accessed August 9, 2019, https://www.chicagotribune.com/news/ct-xpm-2005-05-25-0505250215-story.html.

421 "Israel's Disengagement from Gaza, Northern West Bank 'Watershed, Under-Secretary-General Tells Security Council," UN Security Council (Meetings Coverage and Press Releases), SC/8479, August 24, 2005, accessed August 12, 2019, https://www.un.org/press/en/2005/sc8479.doc.htm.

422 "Territorial Fragmentation of the West Bank, May 2006," UN Office for the Coordination of Humanitarian Affairs (OCHA): Occupied Palestinian Territory, accessed August 9, 2019, https://www.ochaopt.org/sites/default/files/TerritorialFrag_18May06_web.pdf.

423 Yaakov Katz, "Karni Opening Helped Gaza Economy," *Jerusalem Post*, May 13, 2007, accessed August 12, 2019, https://www.jpost.com/Middle-East/Karni-opening-helped-Gaza-economy.

424 "Gaza Strip Situation Report—The Humanitarian Impact of the Karni Crossing Closure: Bread Running Out in Gaza," UN Office for the Coordination of Humanitarian Affairs (OCHA): Occupied Palestinian Territory, March 19, 2006, accessed August 12, 2019, https://www.un.org/unispal/document/auto-insert-196729/.

425 "Israel Stops Payments to Palestinians," *CNN World*, February 20, 2006, accessed August 9, 2019, http://edition.cnn.com/2006/WORLD/meast/02/19/mideast/.

426 Peter Beaumont and Ned Temko, "Abbas Threatens to Sack Hamas-Led Government," *Guardian*, December 16, 2006, accessed August 9, 2019, https://www.theguardian.com/world/2006/dec/17/israel.

427 "Israel Arrests Top Hamas Officials," *Chicago Tribune*, last modified June 29, 2006, accessed January 17, 2018, http://articles.chicagotribune.com/2006-06-29/news/0606300358_1_hamas-leaders-gaza-israeli-tanks-and-bulldozers.

428 "Act of Vengeance: Israel's Bombing of the Gaza Power Plant and its Effects—September 2006, Status Report," B'Tselem: The Israeli Information Center for

Human Rights in the Occupied Territories, accessed August 10, 2019, https://www.btselem.org/publications/summaries/200609_act_of_vengeance.

429 "Palestinians Killed by Israeli Security Forces in the Gaza Strip, before Operation 'Cast Lead,'" B'Tselem: The Israeli Information Center for Human Rights in the Occupied Territories, accessed August 10, 2019, https://www.btselem.org/statistics/fatalities/before-cast-lead/by-date-of-event/gaza/palestinians-killed-by-israeli-security-forces; "Fatalites before Operation 'Cast Lead,'" B'Tselem: The Israeli Information Center for Human Rights in the Occupied Territories, accessed August 10, 2019, https://www.btselem.org/statistics/fatalities/before-cast-lead/by-date-of-event; Gary Fields, "Lockdown: Gaza through a Camera Lens and Historical Mirror," *Journal of Palestine Studies* 49, no. 3 (Spring 2020), 41–69, accessed January 16, 2021, https://online.ucpress.edu/jps/article/49/3/41/110802/Lockdown-Gaza-through-a-Camera-Lens-and-Historical.

430 Isabel Debre, "Gaza Timeline: Main Events in Years of Israel-Hamas Clashes," Associated Press, November 13, 2018, accessed August 12, 2019, https://apnews.com/febf01e1d4474e1cba1fa3615922f8d8; "Palestinian Territories: Timeline," *BBC News*, April 8, 2019, accessed August 12, 2019, https://www.bbc.com/news/world-middle-east-29362505.

431 "End the Blockade on Gaza," Freedom Flotilla Coalition, August 22, 2020, accessed August 24, 2020, timestamp 52:18 in https://www.youtube.com/watch?v=7i_606gqIGc&vl=en.

432 "End the Blockade on Gaza," timestamp 53:01.

433 "Speak Truth to Power: The Defenders, Bishop Desmond Tutu," Discovery Education, Robert F. Kennedy Human Rights, accessed December 17, 2020, https://www.speaktruthtopowerinschool.com/defenders-map/bishop-desmond-tutu#:~:text=%E2%80%9CIf%20you%20are%20neutral%20in,1931%20in%20Transvaal%2C%20South%20Africa.

434 "Israel Defense Forces: Ruach Tzahal—Code of Ethics," Jewish Virtual Library, American-Israeli Cooperative Enterprise (AICE), accessed November 7, 2019, https://www.jewishvirtuallibrary.org/ruach-tzahal-idf-code-of-ethics.

435 "Norman Finkelstein Quotes," AZ Quotes, accessed November 7, 2019, https://www.azquotes.com/author/22795-Norman_Finkelstein.

436 "Barack Obama Visits Sderot, Israel," BarackObamadotcom, July 23, 2008, accessed December 17, 2020, https://www.youtube.com/watch?v=PFoj-PKJhck.

437 Ann Wright, "Celebrating Our Ten Year Anniversary," Free Gaza Movement, 2018, accessed May 26, 2019, https://www.freegaza.org/Celebrating-Our-Ten-Year-Anniversary/.

438 "When Gandhi's Salt March Rattled British Colonial Rule," History.com, last modified October 2, 2019, accessed May 20, 2020, https://www.history.com/news/gandhi-salt-march-india-british-colonial-rule.

439 Shira Efron, Jordan R. Fischbach, Ilana Blum, Rouslan I. Karimov, and Melinda Moore, "The Public Health Impacts of Gaza's Water Crisis," *Rand Health*

Quarterly, PMCID: PMC6557038, May 16, 2019, accessed April 1, 2020, https://www.ncbi.nlm.nih.gov/pmc/articles/PMC6557038/.

440 "One on One: Interview with Haneen Zoabi," TRT World, April 30, 2018, accessed February 25, 2021, https://youtu.be/8E0f6iA0nbg.

441 "Gaza Strip," B'Tselem.

442 Paul Reynolds, "White Phosphorus: Weapon on the Edge," *BBC News*, November 16, 2005, accessed March 26, 2020, http://news.bbc.co.uk/2/hi/americas/4442988.stm.

443 "Chemical Weapons Convention Signatories and States-Parties," Arms Control Association, last modified June 2018, accessed March 26, 2020, https://www.armscontrol.org/factsheets/cwcsig.

444 "Israel/Gaza Operation 'Cast Lead': 22 Days of Death and Destruction," Amnesty International, MDE 15/015/2009, July 2, 2009, accessed January 17, 2018, https://www.amnesty.org/en/documents/MDE15/015/2009/en/.

445 "Israel/Gaza Operation 'Cast Lead': 22 Days of Death and Destruction."

446 "Israel/Gaza Operation 'Cast Lead': 22 Days of Death and Destruction."

447 Peter Beaumont, "Israel Admits Troops May Have Used Phosphorus Shells in Gaza," *Guardian*, last modified January 21, 2009, accessed January 17, 2018, https://www.theguardian.com/world/2009/jan/21/gaza-phosphorus-shells.

448 "Gaza Strip," B'Tselem.

449 "2014 Gaza Conflict and UNRWA Shelter Response," United Nations Relief and Works Agency for Palestine Refugees in the Near East (UNRWA), accessed November 3, 2020, https://www.unrwa.org/sites/default/files/2014_gaza_conflict_and_unrwa_shelter_response.pdf.

450 "2014 Gaza Conflict," United Nations Relief and Works Agency for Palestine Refugees in the Near East (UNRWA), accessed November 3, 2020, https://www.unrwa.org/2014-gaza-conflict; "Gaza Emergency," United Nations Relief and Works Agency for Palestine Refugees in the Near East, accessed October 10, 2017, https://www.unrwa.org/gaza-emergency.

451 "Gaza: Two Years After," United Nations, UN Country Team in the State of Palestine, August 26, 2016, accessed February 2, 2021, https://www.ochaopt.org/sites/default/files/gaza_war_2_years_after_english.pdf.

452 Chris Hedges, *War Is a Force That Gives Us Meaning* (New York: PublicAffairs, 2002), 16.

453 "2014 Gaza War Assessment: The New Face of Conflict," Jewish Institute for National Security of America (JINSA), March 1, 2015, accessed February 2, 2021, https://jinsa.org/jinsa_report/2014-gaza-war-assessment-new-face-conflict/.

454 "2014 Gaza Conflict," United Nations Relief and Works Agency for Palestine Refugees in the Near East (UNRWA).

455 "2014 Gaza War Assessment: The New Face of Conflict."

456 Orwell, *1984*, 33.

457 "Hamas Official Denies His Group Has Upped Demands in Prison-Swap Talks."

12. Terrorism

458 Jonathan Swan, "Rubio to Trump: Israeli-Palestinian Conflict Isn't a 'Real Estate Deal,'" *The Hill*, last modified February 25, 2016, accessed May 7, 2018, https://thehill.com/blogs/ballot-box/presidential-races/270866-rubio-to-trump-israel-palestinian-conflict-isnt-a-real.

459 Ahmed Shihab-Eldin, "Elect Livni, Not Netanyahu, to Keep Peace in Reach for Israel," *HuffPost*, December 6, 2017, accessed October 8, 2019, https://www.huffpost.com/entry/elect-livni-not-netanyahu_b_164937.

460 "Erdogan Calls Netanyahu 'Terrorist' As Insults Fly after Gaza Deaths," *Reuters*, last modified April 1, 2018, accessed May 7, 2018, https://www.reuters.com/article/us-israel-palestinians-erdogan-netanyahu/erdogan-calls-netanyahu-terrorist-as-insults-fly-after-gaza-deaths-idUSKCN1H81AH.

461 "Palestinian Poet Convicted of Inciting Terror in Facebook Poem," *+972 Magazine*, last modified May 3, 2018, accessed May 7, 2018, https://972mag.com/palestinian-poet-convicted-of-inciting-terror-in-facebook-poem/135087/.

462 "About," *+972 Magazine*, accessed December 18, 2020, https://www.972mag.com/about/.

463 "Dareen Tatour: Israeli Arab Poet Convicted of Incitement," *BBC News*, last modified May 3, 2018, accessed May 7, 2018, https://www.bbc.com/news/world-middle-east-43990577.

464 Max Abrahms, "The T-Word: When Is an Attack Terrorism?" *Los Angeles Times*, last modified November 8, 2017, accessed April 16, 2018, https://www.latimes.com/opinion/op-ed/la-oe-abrahms-terrorist-definition-20171108-story.html.

465 "18 US Code §2331. Definitions," Legal Information Institute, Cornell Law School, accessed May 18, 2020, https://www.law.cornell.edu/uscode/text/18/2331.

466 "What We Investigate: Terrorism," Federal Bureau of Investigation, accessed May 18, 2020, https://www.fbi.gov/investigate/terrorism.

467 "How the USA Patriot Act Redefines 'Domestic Terrorism,'" American Civil Liberties Union, accessed May 18, 2020, https://www.aclu.org/other/how-usa-patriot-act-redefines-domestic-terrorism.

468 "18 US Code §2331. Definitions."

469 "Legislative Requirements and Key Terms," US Department of State, ch. 1, accessed April 24, 2020, https://2009-2017.state.gov/documents/organization/65464.pdf.

470 Dictionary.com, s.v. "terrorism," accessed September 11, 2017, https://www.dictionary.com/browse/terrorism.

471 Free Dictionary by Farlex, s.v. "terrorism," accessed April 24, 2020, https://www.thefreedictionary.com/terrorism.

472 "Israel (02/22/12)," US Department of State, February 22, 2012, accessed June 24, 2019, https://2009-2017.state.gov/outofdate/bgn/israel/196735.htm; "Israel and the Occupied Territories," US Department of State, March 11, 2010, accessed January 18, 2021, https://2009-2017.state.gov/j/drl/rls/hrrpt/2009/nea/136070.htm.

473 "Rockets from Gaza: Harm to Civilians from Palestinian Armed Groups' Rocket Attacks," Human Rights Watch, August 6, 2009, accessed December 19, 2020, https://www.hrw.org/report/2009/08/06/rockets-gaza/harm-civilians-palestinian-armed-groups-rocket-attacks.

474 "Gaza Crisis: Toll of Operations in Gaza," *BBC News*, last modified September 1, 2014, accessed June 24, 2019, https://www.bbc.com/news/world-middle-east-28439404.

475 "'I Lost Everything': Israel's Unlawful Destruction of Property during Operation Cast Lead," Human Rights Watch, May 13, 2010, accessed June 24, 2019, https://www.hrw.org/report/2010/05/13/i-lost-everything/israels-unlawful-destruction-property-during-operation-cast-lead.

476 "Rachel Corrie," Rachel Corrie Foundation for Peace & Justice, accessed January 29, 2021, https://rachelcorriefoundation.org/rachel; "Rachel Corrie: Real Footage of Death," posted December 25, 2011, accessed January 29, 2021, https://www.youtube.com/watch?v=ZjuweNjJwrk&feature=youtu.be; Joshua Hammer, "The Death of Rachel Corrie," *Mother Jones*, September/October 2003, https://www.motherjones.com/politics/2003/09/death-rachel-corrie/.

477 "Gaza: Healthcare System Crippled by the Embargo," Doctors without Borders, USA, November 29, 2010, accessed December 19, 2020, timestamp 1:02 in https://www.youtube.com/watch?v=sBKn-VrYbP8.

478 Lawrence Bush, "July 10: A Jewish Member of the PLO," *Jewish Currents*, July 9, 2015, accessed October 21, 2019, https://jewishcurrents.org/july-10-a-jewish-member-of-the-plo/.

479 "Israel Suspends Cash to Palestinians after Hamas Deal," *BBC News*, last modified May 1, 2011, accessed January 17, 2018, https://www.bbc.com/news/world-middle-east-13254155.

480 Jeremy Bowen, "Is a Slap an Act of Terror?," *BBC News at Ten*, last modified January 31, 2018, timestamp 0:27 in https://www.bbc.co.uk/programmes/p05wqg1f.

481 Omar H. Rahman, "Co-Existence vs. Co-Resistance: A Case against Normalization," *+972 Magazine*, January 3, 2012, accessed April 24, 2020, https://www.972mag.com/co-existence-vs-co-resistance-a-case-against-normalization/. Rahman quoted Eyal Weizman, *Hollow Land: Israel's Architecture of Occupation* (London: Verso, 2007), 37.

482 "Control of Economic Activity (Occupied Territories) Bill 2018: Second Stage (Resumed)," Seanad Éireann Debate, Wednesday, July 11, 2018, accessed August 23, 2019, https://www.oireachtas.ie/en/debates/debate/seanad/2018-07-11/18/. Also of interest may be: https://www.oireachtas.ie/en/bills/bill/2018/6/; Senator

Frances Black, "July 2019 Update: Occupied Territories Bill," accessed August 23, 2019, https://www.francesblack.ie/single-post/OTBillJuly2019?fbclid=IwAR2 qWWGvbnA1wodSBJw-oNL1Y5p3woevo3RmGIIANJGT74K49OubEuCrehI.

483 "Robert Fisk on Osama bin Laden at 50, Iraqi Death Squads and Why the Middle East Is More Dangerous Now Than in Past 30 Years," *Democracy Now!* last modified March 5, 2007, accessed October 18, 2017, https://www.democracynow.org/2007/3/5/robert_fisk_on_osama_bin_laden.

484 "Hitnachlut," *Encyclopedia of the Middle East*, accessed January 18, 2021, http://mideastweb.org/Middle-East-Encyclopedia/hitnachlut.htm.

485 Robert Fisk, "Israel Is Building Another 1,000 Homes on Palestinian Land. Where's the Outrage?" *The Independent*, August 23, 2018, accessed October 21, 2019, https://www.independent.co.uk/voices/israel-settlement-expansion-1000-new-homes-palestinian-land-robert-fisk-wheres-the-outrage-a8504471.html.

486 Edward E. Baptist, "Edward E. Baptist: On Slavery and Management," *Publishers Weekly*, August 1, 2014, accessed January 3, 2019, https://www.publishersweekly.com/pw/by-topic/authors/interviews/article/63523-edward-e-baptist-on-slavery-and-management.html.

487 "Statistics on Settlements and Settler Population," B'Tselem: The Israeli Information Center for Human Rights in the Occupied Territories, January 1, 2011, updated January 16, 2019, accessed October 21, 2019, https://www.btselem.org/settlements/statistics.

488 "At 70, Israel's Population Is 8.842 Million, 43% of World Jewry," *Times of Israel*, April 16, 2018, accessed October 21, 2019, https://www.timesofisrael.com/at-70-israels-population-is-8-842-million-43-of-world-jewry/.

489 Joseph Krauss and Mohammed Daraghmeh, "New Data Shows Israeli Settlement Surge in East Jerusalem," Associated Press, September 12, 2019, accessed October 22, 2019, https://news.yahoo.com/data-shows-israeli-settlement-surge-054605902.html.

490 Phil Reeves, "Bat Mitzvah Massacre in Israel Leaves Seven Dead," *The Independent*, January 18, 2002, accessed October 8, 2019, https://www.independent.co.uk/news/world/middle-east/bat-mitzvah-massacre-in-israel-leaves-seven-dead-5362530.html.

491 Flore de Preneuf, "Palestinians Are Not Afraid of Death," *Salon*, August 11, 2001, accessed October 21, 2019, https://www.salon.com/2001/08/11/yassin/.

492 "The Life and Death of Shaikh Yasin," *Al Jazeera*, March 24, 2004, accessed October 21, 2019, https://www.aljazeera.com/archive/2004/03/200849163312822658.html.

493 Ilene R. Prusher and Ben Lynfield, "Killing of Yassin a Turning Point," *Christian Science Monitor*, March 23, 2004, accessed October 21, 2019, https://www.csmonitor.com/2004/0323/p01s04-wome.html.

494 "Erased in a Moment: Suicide Bombing Attacks against Israeli Civilians," IV. Legal Standards, Human Rights Watch, October 2002, accessed February 2, 2021, https://www.hrw.org/reports/2002/isrl-pa/ISRAELPA1002-04.htm#P564_114276.

495 "Erased in a Moment: Suicide Bombing Attacks against Israeli Civilians."

496 "Protocols Additional to the Geneva Conventions of 12 August 1949," International Committee of the Red Cross, adopted on November 30, 1993 and effective March 1, 1994, accessed October 21, 2019, https://www.icrc.org/en/doc/assets/files/other/icrc_002_0321.pdf.

497 "Protocols Additional to the Geneva Conventions of 12 August 1949."

498 Michael Parks, "Next Step: Jewish Settlers Vow to Fight for Land," *Los Angeles Times*, June 1, 1993, accessed October 21, 2019, https://www.latimes.com/archives/la-xpm-1993-06-01-wr-42048-story.html.

499 Elisha Ben Kimon, "Summer Camp in Samaria: Firearm Training for 10-Year-Olds," *Ynet News*, July 7, 2017, accessed October 8, 2019, https://www.ynetnews.com/articles/0,7340,L-4986185,00.html.

500 Avi Mor, Tal Pavel, Don Radlauer, and Yael Shahar, "Casualties in Operation Cast Lead: A Closer Look," International Institute for Counter-Terrorism, Interdisciplinary Center (IDC) Herzliya, 2009, http://www.ict.org.il/Portals/0/Articles/ICT_Cast_Lead_Casualties-A_Closer_Look.pdf.

501 United Nations Security Council, "Resolution 242 of 22 November 1967," S/RES/242 (1967), November 22, 1967, accessed September 17, 2017, https://unispal.un.org/DPA/DPR/unispal.nsf/0/7D35E1F729DF491C85256EE700686136.

502 "Treaties, States Parties and Commentaries: Convention (IV) Relative to the Protection of Civilian Persons in Time of War (Geneva, 12 August 1949), Deportations, Transfers, Evacuations," International Committee of the Red Cross, accessed December 20, 2020, https://ihl-databases.icrc.org/ihl/WebART/380-600056.

503 "Israel: New Comprehensive Counterterrorism Legislation Adopted," Library of Congress, July 15, 2016, accessed October 16, 2018, https://www.loc.gov/law/foreign-news/article/israel-new-comprehensive-counterterrorism-legislation-adopted/.

504 "'Anti-Terror' (Counter-Terrorism) Law," Adalah: Legal Center for Arab Minority Rights in Israel, 2016, accessed October 16, 2019, https://www.adalah.org/en/law/view/598.

505 "Israel's New Anti-Terror Law Violates Arab Citizens' Human Rights," Adalah: Legal Center for Arab Minority Rights in Israel, June 19, 2016, accessed October 16, 2019, https://www.adalah.org/en/content/view/8834.

506 "Declaration of the Rights of Man—1789," Yale Law School Lillian Goldman Law Library: Avalon Project, accessed October 16, 2019, https://avalon.law.yale.edu/18th_century/rightsof.asp.

507 "Universal Declaration of Human Rights," Office of the High Commissioner, Human Rights, United Nations, adopted December 10, 1948, accessed October 16, 2019, https://www.ohchr.org/EN/UDHR/Documents/UDHR_Translations/eng.pdf.

508 "Universal Declaration of Human Rights."

509 "Marian Anderson Quotes," BrainyQuote.com, BrainyMedia Inc., 2019, accessed December 20, 2020, https://www.brainyquote.com/quotes/marian_anderson_131749.

510 Katie Mettler, "After Minneapolis Officer in Police Shooting Is Named, Somali Community Braces for Backlash," *Washington Post*, last modified July 18, 2017, accessed December 21, 2020, https://www.washingtonpost.com/news/morning-mix/wp/2017/07/18/after-media-identifies-officer-in-minneapolis-shooting-somali-community-braces-for-backlash/?utm_term=.e081a310e6be.

511 Kimberly Kindy, Wesley Lowery, Steven Rich, Julie Tate, and Jennifer Jenkins, "Fatal Shootings by Police Are Up in the First Six Months of 2016, Post Analysis Finds," *Washington Post*, last modified July 7, 2016, accessed December 21, 2020, https://www.washingtonpost.com/national/fatal-shootings-by-police-surpass-2015s-rate/2016/07/07/81b708f2-3d42-11e6-84e8-1580c7db5275_story.html.

512 "Chapter 113. Texas Essential Knowledge and Skills for Social Studies, Subchapter C. High School," §113.42. World History Studies (One Credit), Adopted 2018, (c) Knowledge and skills, item 14, Texas Education Agency, adopted to be effective August 1, 2019, accessed October 9, 2020, http://ritter.tea.state.tx.us/rules/tac/chapter113/ch113c.html#113.42.

513 Robert A. Pape, *Dying to Win: The Strategic Logic of Suicide Terrorism* (New York: Random House Trade Paperbacks, 2006).

514 Dan Eggen and Scott Wilson, "Suicide Bombs Potent Tools of Terrorists," *Washington Post*, last modified July 17, 2005, accessed June 11, 2016, https://www.washingtonpost.com/archive/politics/2005/07/17/suicide-bombs-potent-tools-of-terrorists/e11ed483-9936-45c0-b6c6-2653d4519ff5/.

515 Pape, *Dying to Win*, 38.

516 Robert A. Pape, "It's the Occupation, Stupid," *Foreign Policy*, last modified October 18, 2010, accessed April 16, 2018, https://foreignpolicy.com/2010/10/18/its-the-occupation-stupid/.

517 "Israel (02/22/12)," US Department of State.

518 Isabel Kershner, "Israel Agrees to Truce with Hamas on Gaza," *New York Times*, last modified June 18, 2008, accessed March 22, 2019, http://www.nytimes.com/2008/06/18/world/middleeast/18mideast.html.

519 Rory McCarthy, "Gaza Truce Broken As Israeli Raid Kills Six Hamas Gunmen," *Guardian*, last modified November 5, 2008, accessed March 22, 2019, https://www.theguardian.com/world/2008/nov/05/israelandthepalestinians.

520 "Israel (02/22/12)," US Department of State.

521 "Israeli Army Razes Entire Village in Occupied West Bank," *Al Jazeera*, last modified November 4, 2020, accessed November 4, 2020, https://www.aljazeera.com/news/2020/11/4/israeli-troops-raze-an-entire-village-in-occupied-west-bank.

522 Ian Fisher, "Israeli Fires on Palestinian Protesters in the West Bank, Killing One," *New York Times*, last modified May 18, 2017, accessed January 5, 2018, https://www.nytimes.com/2017/05/18/world/middleeast/israeli-settler-palestinian-protesters.html.

523 Yotam Berger, Jack Khoury, and Gili Cohen, "Settler Defends Killing of Palestinian: They Almost Lynched Me," *Haaretz*, last modified May 18, 2017, accessed January 5, 2018, https://www.haaretz.com/israel-news/1.790178.

524 "The Moment the Settler Shot the Martyr Muataz Bani Shamsa," Palestine Today Channel [in Arabic], May 18, 2017, accessed July 23, 2017, https://www.youtube.com/watch?v=pa5QFib6Q0I&feature=youtu.be; "Documentation of the Attack on the Settler in Hawara," *Haaretz* [in Hebrew], May 18, 2017, accessed July 23, 2017, https://www.youtube.com/watch?v=kXehzXdq0qQ&feature=youtu.be.

525 Patrick Wintour, "Hamas Presents New Charter Accepting a Palestine Based on 1967 Borders," *Guardian*, last modified May 1, 2017, accessed December 21, 2020, https://www.theguardian.com/world/2017/may/01/hamas-new-charter-palestine-israel-1967-borders.

526 Chris McGreal, "Hamas Drops Call for Destruction of Israel from Manifesto," *Guardian*, last modified January 11, 2006, accessed January 5, 2018, https://www.theguardian.com/world/2006/jan/12/israel; "Hamas: A Document of General Principles and Policies," Hamas Islamic Resistance, May 1, 2017, accessed June 24, 2018, http://hamas.ps/en/post/678/a-document-of-general-principles-and-policies; Reuters, "Hamas Drops Call for Destruction of Israel and War against Jewish Faith," *Newsweek*, last modified May 2, 2017, accessed January 5, 2018, https://www.newsweek.com/hamas-drops-call-destruction-israel-and-war-against-jewish-faith-593266.

527 Marc Lamont Hill, "Our Solidarity Must Become a Verb," *Jacobin*, last modified December 5, 2018, accessed May 20, 2019, https://www.jacobinmag.com/2018/12/marc-lamont-hill-united-nations-palestine-speech-transcript.

528 Hussein Ibish, "How Many Times Must the Palestinians Recognize Israel?" *Haaretz*, last modified March 13, 2014, accessed September 14, 2018, https://www.haaretz.com/opinion/.premium-1.579701.

529 Wintour, "Hamas Presents New Charter Accepting a Palestine Based on 1967 Borders."

530 "Strip Maul," *The Daily Show with Jon Stewart*, Comedy Central, January 5, 2009, accessed December 22, 2020, http://www.cc.com/video-clips/0hlk16/the-daily-show-with-jon-stewart-strip-maul.

531 "(500) Crazies of Summer," *The Daily Show with Jon Stewart*, Comedy Central, July 14, 2014, accessed December 7, 2017, http://www.cc.com/video-clips/zlzdov/the-daily-show-with-jon-stewart--500--crazies-of-summer.

532 "(500) Crazies of Summer."

533 "Simmering Military Conflict between Israel and Iran Heats Up," *Morning Edition*, National Public Radio, May 10, 2018, accessed May 10, 2018, https://www.npr.org/2018/05/10/609979548/simmering-military-conflict-between-israel-and-iran-heats-up.

534 "Simmering Military Conflict between Israel and Iran Heats Up."

535 Loveday Morris and Hazem Balousha, "Israelis Kill More Than 50 Palestinians in Gaza Protests, Health Officials Say," *Washington Post*, last modified May 14, 2018, accessed May 16, 2018, https://www.washingtonpost.com/world/middle_east/gaza-protests-take-off-ahead-of-new-us-embassy-inauguration-in-jerusalem/2018/05/14/eb6396ae-56e4-11e8-9889-07bcc1327f4b_story.html?noredirect=on&utm_term=.5656ffb385de.

536 John Paul Tasker, "Trudeau Calling for Independent Probe of Reported Use of 'Excessive Force' in Gaza Shootings," *CBC News*, last modified May 16, 2018, accessed May 22, 2018, http://www.cbc.ca/news/politics/trudeau-statement-gaza-independent-investigation-1.4665858.

537 "Press Briefing by Principal Deputy Press Secretary Raj Shah," Whitehouse. gov: Press Briefings, May 14, 2018, accessed December 22, 2020, https:// www.whitehouse.gov/briefings-statements/press-briefing-principal-deputy-press-secretary-raj-shah-051418/ (backed up at https://www.presidency.ucsb.edu/ documents/press-briefing-principal-deputy-press-secretary-raj-shah-1).

13. Hamas: A Terrorist Organization

538 "Federal Judge Hands Downs Sentences in Holy Land Foundation Case," Federal Bureau of Investigation, Dallas Division, US Attorney's Office, May 27, 2009, accessed August 15, 2019, https://archives.fbi.gov/archives/dallas/press-releases/2009/dl052709.htm.

539 Michael Omer-Man, "The Accident That Sparked an Intifada," *Jerusalem Post*, December 4, 2011, accessed August 16, 2019, https://www.jpost.com/Features/ In-Thespotlight/The-accident-that-sparked-an-Intifada; Edward Said, *Intifada: The Palestinian Uprising against Israeli Occupation* (Boston: South End, 1989), 5–22.

540 "Intifada: What Is It and What Would a Third Palestinian Uprising Mean for Israel and the Middle East?" *The Independent*, December 7, 2017, accessed August 16, 2019, https://www.independent.co.uk/news/world/middle-east/ intifada-what-is-palestinian-uprising-israel-jerusalem-trump-hamas-capital-west-bank-palestine-a8097331.html.

541 "Fatalities in the First Intifada," B'Tselem: The Israeli Information Center for Human Rights in the Occupied Territories, accessed July 18, 2018, https://www. btselem.org/statistics/first_intifada_tables.

542 Wendy Pearlman, *Violence, Nonviolence, and the Palestinian National Movement* (New York: Cambridge University Press, 2011), 114, accessed August 16, 2019, https://books.google.com/books?id=5Rn3CgDAymEC&pg=PG114.

543 Pearlman, *Violence, Nonviolence, and the Palestinian National Movement*, 114–115.

544 Omer-Man, "The Accident That Sparked an Intifada."

545 Adam Taylor, "Is This How the Third Intifada Begins?" *Washington Post*, July 2, 2014, accessed August 16, 2019, https://www.washingtonpost.com/news/ worldviews/wp/2014/07/02/is-this-how-the-third-intifada-begins.

546 John Daniszewski, "Remarks on Terror Become Fighting Words in Israel," *Los Angeles Times*, March 11, 1998, accessed September 28, 2019, https://www. latimes.com/archives/la-xpm-1998-mar-11-mn-27709-story.html.

547 Lizzie Dearden, "Hamas Declared a Terrorist Organisation by the European Court of Justice," *The Independent*, July 26, 2017, accessed January 25, 2021,

https://www.independent.co.uk/news/world/europe/hamas-terrorist-organisation-ecj-european-court-justice-eu-uk-palestinian-israel-a7860301.html.

548 Kim Murphy, "Hamas Victory Is Built on Social Work," *Los Angeles Times*, March 2, 2006, accessed August 16, 2019, https://www.latimes.com/archives/la-xpm-2006-mar-02-fg-charity2-story.html.

549 Middle East Media Research Institute, "The Covenant of the Islamic Resistance Movement: Hamas" (translation of the Hamas Covenant, written in 1988), Palestine Special Dispatch 1092, February 14, 2006, accessed August 16, 2019, https://www.memri.org/reports/covenant-islamic-resistance-movement-%E2%80%93-hamas.

550 Steven Eke, "Moscow Risks Anger over Hamas Visit," *BBC News*, March 3, 2006, accessed August 13, 2019, http://news.bbc.co.uk/2/hi/middle_east/4769204.stm.

551 "Analysis: Palestinian Suicide Attacks," *BBC News*, January 29, 2007, accessed August 14, 2019, http://news.bbc.co.uk/2/hi/middle_east/3256858.stm.

552 Clyde Haberman, "Attack in Israel: 20 Killed in Terrorist Bombing of Bus in Tel Aviv; 48 Are Hurt," *New York Times*, October 20, 1994, accessed August 13, 2019, https://www.nytimes.com/1994/10/20/world/attack-israel-overview-20-killed-terrorist-bombing-bus-tel-aviv-48-are-hurt.html.

553 Serge Schmemann, "Bus Bombing Kills Five in Jerusalem; 100 Are Wounded," *New York Times*, August 22, 1995, accessed August 13, 2019, https://www.nytimes.com/1995/08/22/world/bus-bombing-kills-five-in-jerusalem-100-are-wounded.html; "Suicide and Other Bombing Attacks in Israel since the Declaration of Principles (Sept 1993)," Israel Ministry of Foreign Affairs, accessed March 2, 2020, https://mfa.gov.il/mfa/foreignpolicy/terrorism/palestinian/pages/suicide%20and%20other%20bombing%20attacks%20in%20israel%20since.aspx.

554 "Intifada Toll Sept 2000–Sept 2005," *BBC News*, September 30, 2005, accessed August 14, 2019, http://news.bbc.co.uk/2/hi/middle_east/4294502.stm.

555 "Intifada Toll Sept 2000–Sept 2005."

556 "Terrorism against Israel: Number of Fatalities (1920–Present)," Jewish Virtual Library, American-Israeli Cooperative Enterprise (AICE), accessed August 14, 2019, https://www.jewishvirtuallibrary.org/number-of-terrorism-fatalities-in-israel.

557 Mark Oliver, "Sharon and Abbas Agree Ceasefire," *Guardian*, February 8, 2005, accessed August 14, 2019, https://www.theguardian.com/world/2005/feb/08/israel4.

558 "Gaza: Palestinian Rockets Unlawfully Targeted Israeli Civilians," Human Rights Watch, December 24, 2012, accessed August 14, 2019, https://www.hrw.org/news/2012/12/24/gaza-palestinian-rockets-unlawfully-targeted-israeli-civilians.

559 "Gaza: Palestinian Rockets Unlawfully Targeted Israeli Civilians."

560 "Gaza: Palestinian Rockets Unlawfully Targeted Israeli Civilians."

561 "Q & A on Hostilities between Israel and Hamas," Human Rights Watch, November 20, 2012, accessed August 14, 2019, https://www.hrw.org/news/2012/11/20/q-hostilities-between-israel-and-hamas#3.

562 "Gaza: Palestinian Rockets Unlawfully Targeted Israeli Civilians"; "Human Rights Violations during Operation Pillar of Defense, 14–21 November 2012," B'Tselem: The Israeli Information Center for Human Rights in the Occupied Territories, May 2013, accessed August 14, 2019, https://www.btselem.org/sites/default/files2/201305_pillar_of_defense_operation_eng.pdf.

563 "Victims of Palestinian Violence and Terrorism since September 2000," Israel Ministry of Foreign Affairs, accessed August 14, 2019, https://www.mfa.gov.il/mfa/foreignpolicy/terrorism/palestinian/pages/victims%20of%20palestinian%20violence%20and%20terrorism%20sinc.aspx.

564 "Palestinian Public Opinion Poll No (54)," Palestinian Center for Policy and Survey Research (PSR), January 15, 2015, accessed August 14, 2019, http://www.pcpsr.org/sites/default/files/poll-54-Dec2014-English%20new.pdf.

565 Efraim Benmelech and Claude Berrebi, "Human Capital and the Productivity of Suicide Bombers," *Journal of Economic Perspectives* 21, no. 3 (Summer 2007), 227, archived January 27, 2013, at the Wayback Machine, accessed August 13, 2019, https://web.archive.org/web/20130127151257/http://www.economics.harvard.edu/faculty/benmelech/files/JEP_0807.pdf.

566 Dr. Ahmed Yousef, "Hamas Charter: Vision, Fact and Fiction," Islamic Resistance Movement, January 23, 2011, accessed June 23, 2018, http://hamas.ps/en/post/23/hamas-charter-vision-fact-and-fiction.

567 "Hamas: A Document of General Principles and Policies," Islamic Resistance Movement, May 1, 2017, accessed January 6, 2018, http://hamas.ps/en/post/678/a-document-of-general-principles-and-policies.

568 Yousef, "Hamas Charter: Vision, Fact and Fiction."

569 "Hamas: A Document of General Principles and Policies."

570 "Hamas: A Document of General Principles and Policies."

571 "Hamas: A Document of General Principles and Policies."

572 "Hamas: A Document of General Principles and Policies."

573 "Hamas: A Document of General Principles and Policies."

574 "Hamas: A Document of General Principles and Policies."

575 "Gaza Strip," B'Tselem: The Israeli Information Center for Human Rights in the Occupied Territories, last modified November 11, 2017, accessed August 9, 2019, http://www.btselem.org/gaza_strip; "2014 Gaza Conflict," United Nations Relief and Works Agency for Palestine Refugees in the Near East (UNRWA), accessed November 3, 2020, https://www.unrwa.org/2014-gaza-conflict; "Gaza Emergency," United Nations Relief and Works Agency for Palestine Refugees in the Near East, accessed October 10, 2017, https://www.unrwa.org/gaza-emergency.

576 "Gaza Crisis: Toll of Operations in Gaza," *BBC News*, last modified September 1, 2014, accessed August 15, 2019, https://www.bbc.com/news/world-middle-east-28439404.

577 "'Advocate': Israeli Attorney Lea Tsemel Reflects on Defending Palestinians Who Resist Occupation," *Democracy Now!* last modified June 14, 2019, accessed June 20, 2019, https://www.democracynow.org/2019/6/14/lea_tsemel_advocate_documentary_israel_palestine.

14. Christians and the Holy Land

578 Christians United for Israel, accessed November 1, 2019, https://www.cufi.org/.

579 M. J. Rosenberg, "This Is How AIPAC Really Works," *The Nation*, February 14, 2019, accessed November 1, 2019, https://www.thenation.com/article/aipac-omar-israel-congress-anti-semitism.

580 Matthew Haag, "Robert Jeffress, Pastor Who Said Jews Are Going to Hell, Led Prayer at Jerusalem Embassy," *New York Times*, May 14, 2018, accessed November 1, 2019, https://www.nytimes.com/2018/05/14/world/middleeast/robert-jeffress-embassy-jerusalem-us.html.

581 Terry Gross, "Pastor John Hagee on Christian Zionism," *Fresh Air*, National Public Radio, September 18, 2006, accessed November 1, 2019, https://www.npr.org/programs/fresh-air/2006/09/18/13077578/.

582 Gross, "Pastor John Hagee on Christian Zionism," quoting Joel 3:2.

583 Gross, "Pastor John Hagee on Christian Zionism," quoting Rev. 14 and Zech. 14.

584 Kate Ng, "Trump Hosts Pastor Who Says 'Jews Are Going to Hell' at White House Hanukkah Party," *The Independent*, December 12, 2019, accessed October 7, 2020, https://www.independent.co.uk/news/world/americas/trump-pastor-robert-jeffress-jews-white-house-hanukkah-a9243631.html.

585 Stoyan Zaimov, "Robert Jeffress: Gandhi Going to Hell; Jimmy Carter May Be Leading People to Hell," *Christian Post*, April 25, 2017, accessed November 1, 2019, https://www.christianpost.com/news/robert-jeffress-gandhi-going-to-hell-jimmy-carter-may-be-leading-people-to-hell.html.

586 Haag, "Robert Jeffress, Pastor Who Said Jews Are Going to Hell, Led Prayer at Jerusalem Embassy."

587 Ng, "Trump Hosts Pastor Who Says 'Jews Are Going to Hell' at White House Hanukkah Party."

588 Gross, "Pastor John Hagee on Christian Zionism."

589 Mark Silk, "The Protestant Problem(s) of American Jewry," in *The Protestant-Jewish Conundrum: Studies in Contemporary Jewry*, vol. 24, Institute of Contemporary Jewry, Hebrew University of Jerusalem, ed. Jonathan Frankel and Ezra Mendelsohn (New York: Oxford University Press, 2010), 126.

590 "Pastor John C. Hagee," Christians United for Israel, accessed November 2, 2019, https://cufi.org/about/leadership/ (*then click on Hagee's picture or name*).

591 "Response to Christian Zionism," National Council of the Churches of Christ in the USA, accessed November 1, 2019, http://nationalcouncilofchurches.us/common-witness/2007/christian-zionism.php.

592 Zaimov, "Robert Jeffress: Gandhi Going to Hell; Jimmy Carter May Be Leading People to Hell," quoting John 14:6 (NIV).

593 L. Michael White, "Understanding the Book of Revelation," *Frontline*, PBS, accessed March 25, 2020, https://www.pbs.org/wgbh/pages/frontline/shows/apocalypse/revelation/white.html.

594 Bob Simon, "Christians of the Holy Land," *CBS News, 60 Minutes*, last modified April 22, 2012, accessed September 18, 2017, https://www.cbsnews.com/news/christsians-of-the-holy-land/.

595 Ian Lee, "From Pilgrimage to Exodus: Is the End Nigh for Palestinian Christians?" *CNN World*, last modified January 22, 2018, accessed May 1, 2018, https://www.cnn.com/2018/01/22/middleeast/bethlehem-christians-israel-palestinians-intl/index.html.

596 "Kairos Document," Kairos Palestine, accessed February 9, 2021, https://www.kairospalestine.ps/index.php/about-kairos/kairos-palestine-document.

597 "Kairos Document," Kairos Palestine.

598 "Kairos Document," Kairos Palestine.

599 "WCC General Secretary Meets with Palestinian President Mahmoud Abbas," World Council of Churches, last modified February 26, 2017, accessed June 21, 2019, https://www.oikoumene.org/en/press-centre/news/wcc-general-secretary-meets-with-palestinian-president-mahmoud-abbas.

600 "Israel Starts Building New Part of Controversial West Bank Wall," *Daily Mail*, last modified April 7, 2016, accessed October 3, 2017, https://www.dailymail.co.uk/wires/afp/article-3528547/Israel-starts-building-new-controversial-West-Bank-wall.html.

601 Yolande Knell, "Palestinian Christians Urge Help against West Bank Barrier," *BBC News*, last modified August 21, 2015, accessed June 7, 2019, https://www.bbc.com/news/world-middle-east-34020724.

602 Knell, "Palestinian Christians Urge Help against West Bank Barrier."

15. "America's Greatest Ally"

603 US Congressman John Culberson, TX-7, "Supporting Our Greatest Ally," April 13, 2017, accessed September 12, 2018, https://culberson.house.gov/news/email/show.aspx?ID=QO5DNTXT2O7AE72B3QWV3O6XHQ.

604 US Congressman Lee Zeldin, NY-1, "Standing with Our Greatest Ally Israel," Press Release, October 17, 2016, accessed September 12, 2018, https://zeldin.house.gov/media-center/press-releases/standing-our-greatest-ally-israel.

605 "113th Congress Congressional Member Organizations (CMOs)," Committee on House Administration, May 6, 2014, accessed February 9, 2021, https://

www.yumpu.com/en/document/view/34717924/113th-congress-congressional-member-organizations-updated-5-6-14/20.

606 "USS *Liberty* Veterans Association," USS *Liberty* Veterans Association, accessed May 13, 2019, https://usslibertyveterans.org.

607 Amy Tikkanen, ed., "Jonathan Pollard: American Civilian Defense Analyst and Spy," *Encyclopædia Britannica*, August 3, 2019, accessed November 25, 2019, https://www.britannica.com/biography/Jonathan-Pollard.

608 "Jerusalem Square to Be 'Named' after Pollard," *Jerusalem Post*, January 1, 2008, accessed August 18, 2019, https://www.jpost.com/Israel/Jerusalem-square-to-be-named-after-Pollard.

609 "Jonathan Pollard, Who Spent 30 Years in U.S. Prison for Spying, Arrives in Israel," *CBS News*, December 30, 2020, accessed January 26, 2021, https://www.cbsnews.com/news/jonathan-pollard-released-free-landed-israel-spy-with-wife/.

610 Jeff Stein, "Israel Won't Stop Spying on the U.S.," *Newsweek*, May 6, 2014, accessed September 12, 2018, https://www.newsweek.com/2014/05/16/israel-wont-stop-spying-us-249757.html.

611 Stein, "Israel Won't Stop Spying on the US."

612 John Cornyn to Alex McDonald, July 31, 2019.

613 Caroline Linton, "'More Than Anything, I'm a Granddaughter': Tlaib Addresses Supporters," *CBS News*, August 17, 2019, accessed August 18, 2019, https://www.cbsnews.com/news/rashida-tlaib-addresses-supporters-grandmother-reacts-angrily-to-trump-tweets-2019-08-17.Also see the tweet: Donald J. Trump, @realDonaldTrump, Twitter, August 15, 2019, 6:57 a.m. [CDT], https://twitter.com/realDonaldTrump/status/1162000480681287683.

614 Donald J. Trump, @realDonaldTrump, Twitter, August 16, 2019, 5:37 p.m. [CDT], accessed October 8, 2020, https://twitter.com/realDonaldTrump/status/1162493654432460801.

615 "Israel-Palestine Timeline: The Human Cost of the Conflict," If Americans Knew: What Every American Needs to Know about Israel-Palestine, accessed December 25, 2020, https://israelpalestinetimeline.org/.

616 *Merriam-Webster Dictionary*, s.v. "treachery," accessed December 25, 2020, https://www.merriam-webster.com/dictionary/treachery.

617 Justin Elliott, "Trump's Patron-in-Chief," ProPublica, October 10, 2018, accessed January 27, 2021, https://features.propublica.org/trump-inc-podcast/sheldon-adelson-casino-magnate-trump-macau-and-japan/.

618 "Sheldon Adelson in Israel Regrets Having Worn the Uniform of the United States," YouTube, July 7, 2012, accessed January 27, 2021, https://www.youtube.com/watch?v=d9jX7a9DFJE&feature=youtu.be; Alex Kane, "Sheldon Adelson's Fortune Helped Turn the GOP into the Party of Israeli Apartheid," *Intercept*, January 12, 2021, accessed January 27, 2021, https://theintercept.com/2021/01/12/sheldon-adelson-trump-israel-republican-party/.

619 Eric Alterman, "The Fraying Ties between Liberal American Jews and Israel," *The Nation*, last modified May 23, 2018, accessed May 27, 2018, https://www. thenation.com/article/the-fraying-ties-between-liberal-american-jews-and-israel/.

620 Ivona Iacob, "The Top Donors Backing Hillary Clinton's Super PAC," *Forbes*, last modified May 27, 2016, accessed September 12, 2018, https://www.forbes. com/sites/ivonaiacob/2016/05/27/top-donors-hillary-clinton-superpac.

621 Federal Election Commission, Federal Election Commission Clinton Priorities USA Action PAC contributions schedule_a-2018-09-12T17_09_56.csv, accessed September 12, 2018, https://www.fec.gov/data/receipts/?two_year_ transaction_period=2016&cycle=2016&data_type=processed&committee_ id=C00495861&committee_id=C0059; "Priorities USA Action," OpenSecrets. org, Center for Responsive Politics, accessed May 5, 2020: https://www. opensecrets.org/pacs/pacgave2.php?cmte=C00495861&cycle=2016.

622 Hillary Clinton to Haim Saban, July 2, 2015, accessed September 12, 2018, https://www.documentcloud.org/documents/2158218-hillary-clintons-letter-to- haim-saban-against-bds.html.

623 Clinton to Saban, July 2, 2015.

624 UN General Assembly, Human Rights Council, "Human Rights in Palestine and Other Occupied Arab Territories: Report of the United Nations Fact- Finding Mission on the Gaza Conflict," A/HRC/12/48, September 25, 2009, accessed December 25, 2020, https://www2.ohchr.org/english/bodies/hrcouncil/ docs/12session/A-HRC-12-48.pdf.

625 Conal Urquhart, "The Goldstone Report: A History," *Guardian*, April 14, 2011, accessed August 19, 2019, https://www.theguardian.com/world/2011/apr/14/ goldstone-report-history.

626 Yitzhak Benhorin, "Clinton: Goldstone Problematic for Other Countries," *Ynet News*, February 26, 2010, accessed May 21, 2020, https://www.ynetnews.com/ articles/0,7340,L-3854841,00.html.

627 United Nations, "Charter of the United Nations," Chapter I, June 26, 1945, accessed September 12, 2018, https://www.un.org/en/sections/un-charter/ chapter-i/index.html.

628 Clinton to Saban, July 2, 2015.

629 "High School Textbooks in Texas Blame Arab World for Conflict with Israel," *Haaretz*, September 9, 2018, accessed September 24, 2018, https://www.haaretz. com/us-news/high-school-textbooks-in-texas-blame-arab-world-for-conflict-with- israel-1.6494168.

630 Jeffrey Goldberg, "Is Israel America's Ultimate Ally?" *The Atlantic*, April 26, 2011, accessed September 12, 2018, https://www.theatlantic.com/international/ archive/2011/04/is-israel-americas-ultimate-ally/237864/.

16. A Call to Action

631 "Barry Goldwater Quotes," BrainyQuote.com, BrainyMedia Inc., 2019, accessed May 5, 2020, https://www.brainyquote.com/quotes/barry_goldwater_145889.

632 "Marc Morial Quotes," BrainyQuote.com, BrainyMedia Inc, 2019, accessed May 5, 2020, https://www.brainyquote.com/quotes/marc_morial_375058.

633 Dietrich Bonhoeffer, Goodreads, accessed October 19, 2019, https://www. goodreads.com/quotes/601807-silence-in-the-face-of-evil-is-itself-evil-god.(Note: *The quote is often attributed to Bonhoeffer, but it appears in none of his writings or recorded speeches. See https://www.wthrockmorton.com/2016/08/25/the-popular-bonhoeffer-quote-that-isnt-in-bonhoeffers-works/.)*

634 Dargan Thompson, "11 Essential Bonhoeffer Quotes," *Relevant*, April 8, 2016, accessed October 19, 2019, https://relevantmagazine.com/culture/12-essential-bonhoeffer-quotes/.

635 Nur Masalha, Palestine – A Four Thousand Year History (London: Zed Books, 2020), 33.

636 Henry Curtis Pelgrift, "Tel Kabri," *Ancient History Encyclopedia*, November 1, 2015, accessed January 2, 2021, https://www.ancient.eu/Tel_Kabri/; André Parrot, "Abraham: Hebrew Patriarch," *Encyclopædia Britannica*, n.d., accessed January 2, 2021, https://www.britannica.com/biography/Abraham.

637 Masalha, 17.

638 Thinley Kalsang Bhutia, "Israel: Old Testament Kingdom," *Encyclopædia Britannica*, accessed August 8, 2020, https://www.britannica.com/topic/ Israel-Old-Testament-kingdom; Noah Tesch, "Israelite: People," *Encyclopædia Britannica*, accessed August 8, 2020, https://www.britannica.com/topic/Israelite.

639 Syed Muhammad Khan, "Saladin's Conquest of Jerusalem (1187 CE)," *Ancient History Encyclopedia*, last modified May 18, 2020, accessed January 29, 2021, https://www.ancient.eu/article/1553/saladins-conquest-of-jerusalem-1187-ce/.

640 Nina Paley, "This Land Is Mine," Vimeo, https://vimeo.com/50531435.

641 Benny Morris, *The Birth of the Palestinian Refugee Problem Revisited* (Cambridge, UK: Cambridge University Press, 2004), 589.

642 "The Nakba Did Not Start or End in 1948: Key Facts and Figures on the Ethnic Cleansing of Palestine," *Al Jazeera*, last modified May 23, 2017, accessed December 4, 2017, https://www.aljazeera.com/indepth/features/2017/05/nakba-start-1948-170522073908625.html.

643 "The Right of Return of the Palestinian People," Committee on the Exercise of the Inalienable Rights of the Palestinian People, United Nations, November 1, 1978, accessed December 20, 2020, https://unispal.un.org/UNISPAL. NSF/0/805C731452035912852569D1005C1201.

644 United Nations Security Council, "Resolution 242 of 22 November 1967," S/ RES/242 (1967), November 22, 1967, accessed September 17, 2017, https://unispal. un.org/DPA/DPR/unispal.nsf/0/7D35E1F729DF491C85256EE700686136.

645 "Amira Hass 2020 3 Min Clip," Freedom Flotilla Coalition, August 23, 2020, accessed August 24, 2020, https://youtu.be/xeNBLfg_whY.

646 Caleb Parke, "Largest Pro-Israel Group Grows to 7M Members, Lauded by Netanyahu, Trump Administration," *Fox News*, July 9, 2019, accessed September 21, 2019, https://www.foxnews.com/faith-values/largest-israel-trump-netanyahu-christians-united.

647 Carolyn L. Karcher, ed., *Reclaiming Judaism from Zionism: Stories of Personal Transformation* (Northampton, MA: Olive Branch Press, 2019), 70.

Appendix: "The Promised Land"

648 Serge Schmemann, "In Parliament and on the Streets, Israelis Debate the P.L.O. Accord," *New York Times*, last modified October 6, 1995, accessed May 2, 2018, https://www.nytimes.com/1995/10/06/world/in-parliament-and-on-the-streets-israelis-debate-the-plo-accord.html.

649 "Remarks by Vice President Mike Pence in Special Session of the Knesset," US Embassy in Israel, January 22, 2018, accessed May 1, 2018, https://il.usembassy.gov/remarks-vice-president-mike-pence-special-session-knesset/.

650 "Why Orthodox Jews Are Opposed to a Zionist State," Neturei Karta International, accessed December 22, 2017, http://www.nkusa.org/AboutUs/Zionism/opposition.cfm.

651 "Why Orthodox Jews Are Opposed to a Zionist State."

652 "Who Was Hillel?" My Jewish Learning, https://www.myjewishlearning.com/article/hillel/.

653 "Lebanon," World Factbook, Central Intelligence Agency, accessed November 5, 2019, https://www.cia.gov/library/publications/the-world-factbook/geos/le.html; "Jordan," World Factbook, Central Intelligence Agency, accessed November 5, 2019, https://www.cia.gov/library/publications/the-world-factbook/geos/jo.html; "Syria," World Factbook, Central Intelligence Agency, accessed November 5, 2019, https://www.cia.gov/library/publications/the-world-factbook/geos/sy.html; "Egypt," World Factbook, Central Intelligence Agency, accessed November 5, 2019, https://www.cia.gov/library/publications/the-world-factbook/geos/eg.html; "Iraq," World Factbook, Central Intelligence Agency, accessed November 5, 2019, https://www.cia.gov/library/publications/the-world-factbook/geos/iz.html.

654 "Lebanon," World Factbook; "Egypt," World Factbook.

655 Lisa Palmieri-Billig, "Vatican Synod Calls for End to Israel's 'Occupation,'" *Jerusalem Post*, last modified October 23, 2010, accessed December 23, 2017, https://www.jpost.com/International/Vatican-synod-calls-for-end-to-Israels-occupation.

656 Sewell Chan, "Hilarion Capucci, Archbishop Jailed for Aiding Palestinian Militants, Dies at 94," *New York Times*, January 2, 2017, accessed December 27, 2020, https://www.nytimes.com/2017/01/02/world/middleeast/hilarion-capucci-

archbishop-jailed-for-aiding-palestinian-militants-dies-at-94.html; Robert Booth, "Israeli Attack on Gaza Flotilla Sparks International Outrage," *Guardian*, last modified May 31, 2010, accessed October 18, 2017, https://www.theguardian.com/world/2010/may/31/israeli-attacks-gaza-flotilla-activists; "Archbishop Capucci Sends Message of Solidarity to Palestinian Hunger Strikers," *Middle East Monitor*, June 18, 2015, accessed April 7, 2020, https://www.middleeastmonitor.com/20150618-archbishop-capucci-sends-message-of-solidarity-to-palestinian-hunger-strikers/; "Controversial Catholic Priest Who Supplied Arms to Palestinian Militants Dies Age 94 in Rome," *The Independent*, January 4, 2017, accessed April 7, 2020, https://www.independent.co.uk/news/catholic-priest-archbishop-hilarion-capucci-dead-palestinian-militants-supply-arms-rome-dies-94-died-a7509216.html; "Hilarion Capucci, Archbishop Convicted of Smuggling Arms to Palestinian Militants, Dies at 94," *Washington Post*, January 3, 2017, accessed April 7, 2020, https://www.washingtonpost.com/world/hilarion-capucci-archbishop-convicted-of-smuggling-arms-to-palestinian-militants-dies-at-94/2017/01/03/8f62ed24-d1ce-11e6-945a-76f69a399dd5_story.html.

657 "*Mavi Marmara* Death Toll Rises to 10," Al Jazeera, May 25, 2014, accessed December 27, 2020, https://www.aljazeera.com/news/2014/5/25/mavi-marmara-death-toll-rises-to-10.

658 Elisabetta Povoledo, "Vatican Formally Recognizes Palestinian State by Signing Treaty," *New York Times*, last modified June 26, 2015, accessed December 23, 2017, https://www.nytimes.com/2015/06/27/world/middleeast/vatican-palestinian-state.html.

659 Desmond Tutu, "My Plea to the People of Israel: Liberate Yourselves by Liberating Palestine," *Haaretz*, August 14, 2014, accessed April 7, 2020, https://www.haaretz.com/opinion/my-plea-to-the-people-of-israel-1.5259517.

660 "Major Churches Divest," BDS National Committee (BNC), accessed December 23, 2017, https://bdsmovement.net/impact/major-churches-divest.

661 "Fayad Says He Won't Tolerate Incitement," *Jerusalem Post*, last modified June 28, 2007, accessed May 24, 2019, https://www.jpost.com/Middle-East/Fayad-says-he-wont-tolerate-incitement.

Glossary

662 "America's Pro-Israel Lobby," The American Israel Public Affairs Committee (AIPAC), accessed February 16, 2021, https://www.aipac.org/.

663 "Who We Are," Anti-Defamation League, accessed April 15, 2019, https://www.adl.org/who-we-are.

664 *Merriam-Webster Dictionary*, s.v. "anti-Semitism," accessed October 25, 2017, https://www.merriam-webster.com/dictionary/anti-Semitism.

665 UN General Assembly, Resolution 3068 (XXVIII), International Convention on the Suppression and Punishment of the Crime of *Apartheid* (in force July 18, 1976), II, accessed November 18, 2020, https://www.un.org/en/genocideprevention/documents/atrocity-crimes/Doc.10_International%20

Convention%20on%20the%20Suppression%20and%20Punishment%20of%20
the%20Crime%20of%20Apartheid.pdf.

666 UN General Assembly, Resolution 3068 (XXVIII), II (c).

667 *BDS*, Palestinian BDS National Committee (BNC) and Palestinian Campaign for the Academic and Cultural Boycott of Israel (PACBI), accessed July 25, 2018, https://bdsmovement.net.

668 B'Tselem: The Israeli Information Center for Human Rights in the Occupied Territories, https://www.btselem.org/.

669 *Merriam-Webster Dictionary*, s.v. "democracy," accessed January 12, 2018, https://www.merriam-webster.com/dictionary/democracy.

670 Robert Green McCloskey, ed., *The Works of James Wilson*, vol. 1, chap. 15 ("Equality"), doc. 48 ("Of Man, as a Member of Society, Lectures on Law," *Works* 1:240–241 [1791]) (Cambridge, MA: Belknap Press of Harvard University Press, 1967), accessed November 18, 2020, https://press-pubs.uchicago.edu/founders/documents/v1ch15s48.html.

671 *Dictionary.com*, s.v. "ethnic cleansing," accessed February 16, 2021, https://www.dictionary.com/browse/ethnic-cleansing.

672 *Merriam-Webster Dictionary*, s.v. "impunity," accessed October 18, 2017, https://www.merriam-webster.com/dictionary/impunity.

673 "The Court," International Court of Justice, accessed February 16, 2021, https://www.icj-cij.org/en/court.

674 "Our Mission," Jewish Institute for National Security of America, accessed April 8, 2019, https://jinsa.org/about/.

675 "We Are JNF," Jewish National Fund, accessed February 16, 2021, https://www.jnf.org/menu-3/about-jnf.

676 *Merriam-Webster Dictionary*, s.v. "massacre," accessed December 18, 2020, https://www.merriam-webster.com/dictionary/massacre.

677 George Orwell, *1984* (New York: Alfred A. Knopf, 1949), 300.

678 Orwell, *1984*, 199.

679 *Merriam-Webster Dictionary*, s.v. "piracy," accessed December 18, 2020, https://www.merriam-webster.com/dictionary/piracy.

680 "International Convention on the Elimination of All Forms of Racial Discrimination," Office of the High Commissioner, Human Rights, United Nations, I.1.1, adopted per General Assembly Resolution 2106 (XX) December 21, 1965, into force January 4, 1969, accessed October 25, 2017, https://www.ohchr.org/en/professionalinterest/pages/cerd.aspx.

681 Tjasa Leskovic Vendramin, "The Right of Return of Refugees in International Law: The Case Study of Bosnia and Herzegovina" (master's thesis, International University Institute for European Studies, 2006–2008).

682 "Universal Declaration of Human Rights," Office of the High Commissioner, Human Rights, United Nations, 13, adopted December 10, 1948, accessed

October 16, 2019, https://www.ohchr.org/EN/UDHR/Documents/UDHR_Translations/eng.pdf.

683 *Merriam-Webster Dictionary*, s.v. "steal," accessed December 18, 2020, https://www.merriam-webster.com/dictionary/steal.

684 *Merriam-Webster Dictionary*, s.v. "treachery," accessed December 18, 2020, https://www.merriam-webster.com/dictionary/treachery.

685 United Nations, Economic and Social Commission for Western Asia (ESCWA), accessed December 28, 2020, https://www.unescwa.org/about-escwa.

686 "UNESCO in Brief: Mission and Mandate," United Nations Educational, Scientific and Cultural Organization (UNESCO), accessed December 28, 2020, https://en.unesco.org/about-us/introducing-unesco.

687 "History of OCHA," UN Office for the Coordination of Humanitarian Affairs (OCHA), accessed December 29, 2020, https://www.unocha.org/about-ocha/history-ocha.

688 "OCHA in the Occupied Palestinian Territory," UN Office for the Coordination of Humanitarian Affairs (OCHA): Occupied Palestinian Territory, accessed December 29, 2020, https://www.ochaopt.org/page/about-us.

689 "Who We Are," United Nations Relief and Works Agency for Palestine Refugees in the Near East (UNRWA), accessed December 29, 2020, https://www.unrwa.org/who-we-are.

690 UN General Assembly, Resolution 194 (III), The Right of Return of the Palestinian People (December 11, 1948), Annex II, par. 11, accessed July 12, 2018, https://unispal.un.org/DPA/DPR/unispal.nsf/0/C758572B78D1CD0085256BCF0077E51A.

691 United Nations Security Council, "Resolution 242 of 22 November 1967," S/RES/242 (1967), November 22, 1967, accessed September 17, 2017, https://unispal.un.org/DPA/DPR/unispal.nsf/0/7D35E1F729DF491C85256EE700686136.

692 *Merriam-Webster Dictionary*, s.v. "Zionism," accessed December 18, 2020, https://www.merriam-webster.com/dictionary/Zionism.

CPSIA information can be obtained
at www.ICGtesting.com
Printed in the USA
LVHW111317170621
690490LV00003B/23